The Great "What Ifs" of the American Civil War

of the

American Civil War

Historians Tackle the Conflict's
Most Intriguing Possibilities

Edited by
Chris Mackowski & Brian Matthew Jordan

The Great "What Ifs"
of the
American Civil War

Historians Tackle the Conflict's
Most Intriguing Possibilities

Edited by
Chris Mackowski & Brian Matthew Jordan

Savas Beatie
California

First edition, first printing

ISBN 9781611215731 (hardcover)
ISBN 9781954547063 (ebook)

Library of Congress Cataloging-in-Publication Data

Names: Mackowski, Chris, editor. | Jordan, Brian Matthew, 1986- editor.
Title: The great "what ifs" of the American Civil War : historians tackle
   the conflict's most intriguing possibilities / edited by Chris
   Mackowski, and Brian Matthew Jordan.
Other titles: Emerging Civil War (Website)
Description: El Dorado Hills, CA : Savas Beatie LLC, [2021] | Includes
   bibliographical references and index. | Summary: ""What If . . . ?"
   Every Civil War armchair general asks the question. A serious inquiry
   sparks rigorous exploration, demands critical thinking, and unlocks
   important insights. This is a collection of thirteen essays by the
   historians at Emerging Civil War which focus on one of the most
   important events of the war and unpacks the options of the moment. It is
   an invitation to ask, to learn, and to wonder, "What if . . . ?""--
   Provided by publisher.
Identifiers: LCCN 2021007879 | ISBN 9781611215731 (hardcover) | ISBN
   9781954547063 (ebook)
Subjects: LCSH: United States--History--Civil War, 1861-1865--Campaigns. |
   Imaginary histories.
Classification: LCC E470 .G814 2021 | DDC 973.7/3--dc23
LC record available at https://lccn.loc.gov/2021007879

Savas Beatie
989 Governor Drive, Suite 102
El Dorado Hills, CA 95762
916-941-6896 / sales@savasbeatie.com / www.savasbeatie.com

MIX
Paper from
responsible sources
FSC
www.fsc.org   FSC® C011935

All of our titles are available at special discount rates for bulk purchases in the United States. Contact us for information.

Proudly published, printed, and warehoused in the United States of America.

To all of those who taught, mentored, encouraged,
and supported us along the way—
to those who never doubted and dared to ask, "What if?"

Table of Contents

List of Maps
VIII

Acknowledgments
IX

Foreword
"Paths Not Taken": Thoughts of an Alternate Historian
Peter G. Tsouras
XII

Introduction
Chris Mackowski
XXV

Chapter One
"Persistently Misunderstood": The What Ifs of Shiloh
Timothy B. Smith
1

Chapter Two
What Ifs of the Maryland Campaign
Kevin Pawlak
19

Chapter Three
What If Great Britain Had Intervened
in the American Civil War?
Dwight Hughes
46

Chapter Four
What If Someone Else Had Been Offered Command
of the Army of the Potomac?
Frank Jastrzembski
64

Chapter Five
What If Stonewall Jackson Had Not Been Shot?
Kristopher D. White
93

Chapter Six
"To Go Around to the Right?"
Longstreet's Great What If at Gettysburg
Dan Welch
113

Chapter Seven
What If Jefferson Davis Had Not Been So Loyal to Braxton Bragg?
Cecily N. Zander
130

Chapter Eight
What If Robert E. Lee had Struck a Blow at the North Anna River?
Chris Mackowski
147

Chapter Nine
"Rally the Loyal Men of Missouri"
What If Sterling Price's 1864 Missouri Expedition
Had Been Successful?
Kristen M. Trout
173

Chapter Ten
"A New Endorsement of Abraham Lincoln": Could Lincoln Have Won
Reelection without Sherman's and Sheridan's Successes?
Jonathan A. Noyalas
191

Chapter Eleven
What If Robert E. Lee Had Waged a Guerrilla War
with His Army of Northern Virginia in April 1865?
Barton A. Myers
209

Chapter Twelve
"What If Lincoln Lived?"
The Civil War's Perennial Counterfactual
Brian Matthew Jordan and Evan C. Rothera
230

Suggested Reading
250

Contributor Notes
264

Postscript
268

Index
273

List of Maps

Maps by Edward Alexander

Shiloh—April 6, 1862
7

Antietam—September 17, 1862
30

Chancellorsville—May 2, 1863, 9 p.m.
100

Gettysburg—July 2, 1863
119

North Anna—May 21-22, 1864
154

Price's Expedition—Aug.-Dec. 1864
180

www.emergingcivilwar.com

Acknowledgments

This book had an interesting road to publication. Ted Savas eagerly snatched it up when we presented it to him, and he made a significant effort to get it to press quickly and cleanly. We're indebted to him for his enthusiastic embrace of the project, and we thank his entire team at SB for their work on its behalf. Thanks particularly to Wayne Wolfe and Patrick McCormack for their copyediting—always a challenge (and usually a thankless one). Thanks also to Chris Heisey for his cover photo.

Along the way, we were fortunate to work with Sylvia Frank Rodrigue, who also showed enthusiasm for the project. Sylvia is always a joy to work with, combining professionalism and good cheer in equally large doses. We thank, too, all her colleagues at Southern Illinois University Press.

We have also been fortunate along the way to work with a diverse array of colleagues who posed some fascinating "What If" scenarios to us. We wish we could have fit more of them into this volume (more on that to come. . . .) We are grateful to the Emerging Civil War community for providing an intellectual and digital space where we can all bounce ideas around.

The historians whose work we are privileged to include in this first collection make up an extraordinary who's-who of emerging and established talent in the Civil War field: Dwight Hughes, Frank Jastrzembski, Barton Myers, Kevin Pawlak, Evan Rothera, Timothy B. Smith, Kristen Trout, Peter Tsouras, Dan Welch, Kristopher D. White, Cecily Nelson Zander, and cartographer Edward Alexander. We are grateful for not only their excellent contributions but also for giving us a lot of thought-provoking material along the way.

Finally, we'd like to thank all those with whom we've engaged in lively conversation over the years regarding this or that counterfactual question. No battle is quite so fascinating as the one we can armchair-general our way through with good friends and sharp colleagues.

From Chris: Brian and I first met on July 1 of the Gettysburg Sesquicentennial. He and I and Kris White were being interviewed in a pop-up tent by the Pennsylvania Cable Network as part of PCN's live coverage of the anniversary. I was the monkey between two 800-pound gorillas! I've been sharply impressed by Brian ever since, and I always leap at an opportunity to collaborate with him beause I know I'll always get a lot out of the experience. This was our first chance to co-edit a book, and I'm grateful for the opportunity. He's a brilliant mind, an insightful historian, and an exacting editor—and, man, can that guy write!

My thanks, too, to Dean Aaron Chimbel of St. Bonaventure University's Jandoli School of Communication for his ongoing support of my scholarship.

And most of all, thanks to my family: my daughter, Stephanie; her husband, Thomas; their daughter, Sophie (my first grandchild!); my sons, Jackson and Maxwell; and my wife, Jennifer. I cannot imagine life without them.

From Brian: This book was the brainchild of my co-editor, Chris Mackowski, with whom it has been a genuine pleasure to work. I hope this is just the first of many fruitful collaborations. I thank my friend for his patience, sharp insight, and collaborative spirit; it is an honor to share a title page with him. Legions of young scholars—including many whose work appears here—have been the beneficiaries of his generosity and vision.

Thanks to my hard-working colleagues in the Department of History at Sam Houston State University, and to Chien-pin Li, Dean of the College of Humanities and Social Sciences, for his always cheerful support of my scholarly endeavors.

A book about counterfactual questions necessarily invites some personal reflection. I have been unusually fortunate to work with teachers and scholars at every level who sharpened my thinking, improved my prose, and otherwise took a chance on a kid from Akron, Ohio. Lorraine Caswell and Nancy Drugan taught me how to write. Gabor S. Boritt, Allen C. Guelzo, Matthew D. Norman, David W. Blight, Bruno Cabanes, and John Demos taught me the historian's craft. My family made it all possible; they continue to make it all worthwhile.

"Wars tend to be iffy. And there were undoubtedly ifs in the Civil War—historians are still engaged with them."

— Robert Penn Warren,
Jefferson Davis Gets His Citizenship Back

"Might-have-beens was a stupid game, when you got right down to it. Look back on things, and you couldn't help but see they'd come out the way they had to come out."

— Harry Turtledove,
The Great War: Breakthroughs

Paths Not Taken
Thougths of an Alternate Historian

Foreword by Peter G. Tsouras

I've followed these paths for twenty-eight years now, with four battle alternate histories and seven anthologies (that paid for a few college semesters for three children). I took my first step when approached by Lionel Leventhal, the grand old man of British military history publishing, with an intriguing idea. It was 1992, and he reminded me the fiftieth anniversary of D-Day would be coming in two years. There would be any number of histories written for the anniversary. Then, he said, therein lay a niche: "Let's have the Germans win."

Until that time, alternate history was not a thickly populated genre. The number of serious alternate history books could be numbered on the fingers of one hand, if you had had a chainsaw accident. The author of one of those few books, Ken Macksey (*Invasion 1940*, the German invasion of Britain in Operation Sea Lion), was a retired British colonel, one of the most distinguished British military historians, and an actual veteran of D-Day. He recounted to me that he had been signing his book in Dover when a middle-aged woman remarked that she had lived there all her life and had never known there had been a battle!

Lionel and I leapt into the project, and *Disaster at D-Day: The Germans Defeat the Allies, June 1944* came out just in time for the anniversary.

I had to understand the battle that actually happened and its strategic, operational, and tactical dynamics. Only then would the critical decision nodes that could plausibly be altered by the stream of chance become apparent. I chose to write it in the style of an actual history, complete with endnotes. Lionel suggested fake footnotes to reference the new realities of this alternate outcome. The idea of fake endnotes adds a great deal to the alternate world that the book describes and offers the chance to add tantalizing hints of the nature of that future. I have used them in all my alternate history writing since then. To prevent the reader from fruitlessly chasing after a fictitious title, each alternate history footnote is preceded by an asterisk.

In the end, the book had to stand on its own as an entirely plausible alternate reality. There would be no *Deus ex machina*, the bane of alternate history. A note on this term is important to illustrate its meaning. In ancient Greek theater, a tangled plot would often be

Peter G. Tsouras: for alternative history to be truly effective, "the arts of the historian and storyteller must be given full play." *Peter G. Tsouras*

resolved by the appearance of a god lowered onto the stage by an intricate piece of stage machinery to announce how he has resolved the story with one stroke of divine intervention. The Romans defined this as *Deus ex machine*, god out of the machine. An example of this would be the appearance of Stonewall Jackson at Gettysburg, which would not take into account all the changes his survival would have entailed in the events leading up to Gettysburg, probably ensuring that there never would have been a battle of Gettysburg at all.

All the realities of wind and wave, march rates, the physical characteristics of weapons, etc., all had to be strictly within the realm of reality. Historical figures had to act within their own characters. You gain a truer appreciation of the dynamics of an actual battle by finding those decision nodes, understanding how contingent they were, and realizing how many different roads beckoned. You realize there was nothing inevitable about any particular outcome. History does not roll down a smooth groove but bounces all over the place. Alter one critical thing and the emerging changes are geometrical. A different rock thrown in a pond at different time makes different ripples that rush out, pushing everything into different paths.

I approached the book from the point of view of a historian. This would not be a novel although it would not be shorn of character development. My emphasis in writing alternate history is the word "history." It would not be a dry history full of mummy dust. No, there must be the drama inherent in such desperate affairs. Alternate history, like all good history, is at its core story telling. A note here for those who quibble that the proper word should be "alternative" rather than "alternate" history. True—but even by the time this book was written, the use of "alternate" had become fixed.

Lionel told me that three experts who had reviewed the manuscript insisted it not be published because it was too real and might confuse the general public. One of them made a special trip into London to urge Lionel not to publish it. All three reviewers insisted that book was so real it would confuse readers. Lionel instead thought experts' criticism was an enormous selling point in favor of the book. The book was grandly reviewed as mind candy by the *New York Review of Books* while we were at the American Booksellers annual fair in 1994, a fact Lionel was able to take immediate advantage of.

D-Day was a thoroughly and cleverly planned operation, for which Field Marshal Montgomery has not been given just credit. But as the great Prussian chief of staff, Field Marshall Prince Helmuth von Moltke, had said, "Plans are nothing; planning is everything." Something must be left to chance as in all human affairs and most powerfully in war. The effort in planning provides the flexibility to meet unexpected events. Montgomery and his planners realized that all the landing beaches must be both secured and united to create sufficiently large enough lodgment to allow the large-scale build up of forces for a decisive breakout and exploitation. The American Omaha Beach was the hinge of that strategy for it connected the British-Canadian beaches on the east with the American Utah beach on the west. If Omaha failed, neither of the eastern or western beaches could have sustained the vital buildup. As it was, Omaha came within a hair of disaster. In an excusable intelligence failure, the Allies failed to detect the replacement of a weak coastal defense division with the tough, veteran 352nd Infantry Division. These Germans made the Americans of the 1st and 29th Infantry Divisions pay an enormous price in blood.

Two men, Brig. Gen. Norman "Dutch" Cota, assistant division commander of the 29th Infantry Division, and Col. George A. Taylor, commander of the 16th Infantry Regiment, 1st Infantry Division, were responsible for preventing the hinge from snapping. The fate of the entire invasion then fell upon these two men as they rallied their bloodied and stunned men off the beaches to break through the Germans. A third decisive man was the one who was not there on Omaha Beach—Field Marshall Erwin Rommel. The Allies could not have wished for a greater gift than his absence on leave in Germany as the invasion unfolded. Such a man would have been immediately at the point of action to organize the Germans for maximum effort. Rommel had an amazing sixth sense for the *Schwerpunkt*, the decisive place and time of any battle. Without him confusion reigned, into which the heroic initiative and courage of Cota and Taylor was the sword throne on the scales of the battle. Imagine, though, Rommel's presence at Omaha. Any number of events could have postponed his departure for leave in Germany the day before the invasion.

At the time, I was a military intelligence analyst working for the U.S. Army's National Ground Intelligence Center (NGIC) of blessed memory. The skills of military intelligence analysis were well-suited to this project, in particular of the subset of order-of-battle analysis that addresses the organization and strength of military organizations. It is important to know whether a regiment had three or four battalions, what its actual strength was, its recent battle-worthiness, and combat record. All counters on the board are not the same. A story in point. In the Boer War, a British train was ambushed by the Boers. The surviving train guards did not surrender until all the survivors were wounded. Asked why they did not give up sooner, one replied, "But we are the Gordon Highlanders!" Or the bitter fruit of two world wars—Churchill's comment that one does not know war unless one had fought the Germans, "a valiant and disciplined" enemy. Still, such things have a shelf life. In Afghanistan, the modern Bundeswehr instead of an Iron Cross for heroism gives a soldier a day off. *Sic transit gloria mundi.*

*   *   *

My next book for Lionel was *Gettysburg: An Alternate History,* which came out in 1997. This book was banned from the Gettysburg Military Park bookstore by the park historian because, as he said, it was too real. He even had to look some things up because he said fact blended into fiction too well to be easily detected. The objection to its sale was that it would surely confuse the peasantry that shopped at the bookstore, a policy that persists to this day. Despite that, the book was nominated for the Lincoln Prize, the most distinguished Civil War literary prize. So, there!

Again, I wrote this book as history, exploring the roads not taken in the three great controversies that continue to haunt the study of this greatest battle ever fought in North America: (1) Stuart's arrival late on 2 July; (2) Lee's refusal to let Longstreet maneuver around the Union flank on 2 July; and, (3) Lee's failure to properly organize the attacks on 3 July. I must have walked almost every foot of the battlefield, getting a feel for the ground and the alternate possibilities inherent in it. In one trip with my good friend Jay Zollitsch, we walked through the marsh on the other side of Big Round Top to see if troops could move through it. Checking each other for ticks was male bonding at its most noble. My wife even volunteered to go to Gettysburg for our anniversary because she knew I needed one more trip there. She is the most unselfish person I know. God bless her.

It became apparent in studying the battle that the balance of the armies was highly unstable. Riding a floodtide of victories, Lee thought his Army of Northern Virginia was invincible.

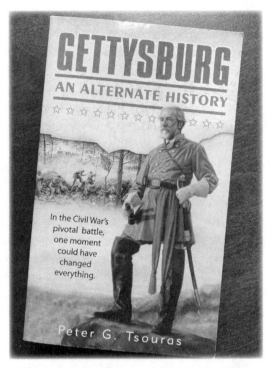

The battle of Gettysburg spawned so many "What Ifs" they could fill a book of their own—and they have. Peter G. Tsouras's novel-length alternate history explores them. *book cover courtesy Presidio Press*

Most contemporaries would have agreed. Yet, this was seed of Lee's undoing. In expanding his army, he found it necessary to split it into three instead of two already existing corps, requiring two new corps commanders, Gens. Richard Ewell and A.P. Hill, who would prove to be bruised reeds. Too high a proportion of division and brigade commanders were also new to their commands. A professional staff would have done much to help the new command arrangements sort themselves out, but such Lee did not have. This resulted in a lamentable failure of coordination and initiative at all levels. Lee had been fortunate in that, previously, he had had in Stonewall Jackson and James Longstreet two subordinates with whom he worked brilliantly at an intuitive level. He fatally assumed that he could do so with Ewell and Hill. Lee also had suffered a heart attack in March and said thereafter he had never been as mentally or physically fit as before. Fate must have licked its lips at the opportunity to punish hubris. The alternate history does not have to look forward to find in this numerous pivot points.

Compared to the new brittleness of the Army of Northern Virginia, the Army of the Potomac was far more tempered, something that escaped most observers. Finally, the army had a sound and competent commander in George G. Meade. The man knew his job, as did his experienced corps commanders. They did something their Confederate counterparts did not do: they cooperated and showed initiative to do as the situation demanded. Reinforcing this was a highly professional staff that served Meade well. The Army of the Potomac's artillery was also vastly superior. The chief of artillery, Brig. Gen. Henry Hunt, had had the gutsy initiative to acquire, outside of regulations, a second artillery train that proved decisive in breaking Pickett's charge. The Confederate artillery, on the other hand, had been threatened by the infantry never to fire over them in support because so many badly manufactured rounds fell short into their ranks—the very reason the artillery support for Pickett's charge lifted before the attack. Into this mix of the brittle and tempered waited immense opportunity for history to leap onto a new path.

Finally, what saved Lee from a crushing counterattack after the collapse of Pickett's Charge ironically was his own failure to properly coordinate the attacks of 3 July. Meade observed that morning that Lee had struck his right and his left and would surely now strike his center, a prescient analysis. He said that he would then have a golden opportunity to counterpunch. He had more than twenty thousand men in reserve, including most of the yet-uncommitted tough 6th Corps. Yet when Ewell's attack went in on time and Longstreet's did not, Meade concluded he had been wrong and concentrated on the attack on Culp's Hill. Thus, when Longstreet's attack struck and failed, Meade had not been able to assemble his counterattack force which could well have smashed through a disorganized and demoralized Confederate center, fatally shattering the Army of Northern Virginia.

*   *   *

Stalingrad was the subject of the third of my alternate histories. In July 1992, I attended a military history seminar at the Russian Military History Institute in Moscow. The Russian military historians stated how vital Lend-Lease was even before Stalingrad, contrary to Western historians who said it was too early to have been decisive. They stated that British and American aid in October of 1941 already exceeded their own production. Lend-Lease supplied half of the magnesium, aluminum, and copper the Soviets used to build their vast fleets of tanks and airplanes. The British transferred their entire clothing allotment for 1942 over to the Soviets. General Chuikov, who commanded at Stalingrad, was almost shot by a sentry who did not recognize the British raincoat he was wearing. Outside of Stalingrad, the Germans captured a train carrying a vast amount of American engineering equipment.

The fate of the battle ran then not between the Don and the Volga but across the North Atlantic to Murmansk. Crimp it to cut off the metals for building tank and aircraft engines, and far fewer would be built, altering the correlation of forces. The battle of Stalingrad would then logically be decided in the cold waters between Iceland and Norway, entailing a major fleet action.

*   *   *

Waterloo was retold in *Napoleon Victorious*. It was clear, in examining the battle, that Napoleon caught very few of the breaks. Yet his organization for the battle was superb. He concentrated his Grande Armee in complete security undetected by Wellington and Blücher. His opening moves were such a surprise and so adroit in breaking the ability of the enemy to unite against him that Wellington said of him, "He does war honor." Things should have gone well for Napoleon from there. Wellington's army was especially vulnerable—three nationalities speaking four languages, more of whom were Germans than Britons. Not enough were his old tough-as-nails Peninsular veterans, too many of whose lives had been thrown away at the battle of New Orleans. Too many senior commanders he did not trust, especially on the Dutch side, had been forced on him. There was no love lost in the British-Prussian alliance either. Blücher's chief of staff, von Gneisenau, detested the British, who saw treachery in their every move. By inclination he was all too happy to fall back on his main supply route than risk his army in coming to Wellington's aid. The Prussian Army of the Rhine was not the best of the Prussian service, either, consisting of far too many inexperienced *Landwher* regiments and, until recently, thousands of unreliable Saxon troops.

Napoleon should have shattered them. Yet most of the bad breaks fell to him, some through his own fault—mostly faulty command choices who let him down—and others by chance. The rain on the night of 17 June left the battlefield so soaked that it delayed the battle by hours and even then reduced the power of his artillery by smothering its shot in mud. Even so, Napoleon handled Wellington so hard that he prayed for the Prussians or night in what he would later write, "It has been a damned nice thing—the nearest run thing you ever saw in your life." Rarely has a battle trembled on such a knife-edge. The weather can't be changed but events can lead to the battle on the day, as Napoleon probably planned, before it actually happened, when the ground was rock hard, ideal for the bloody work of ricochetting shot, an important contemporary gunnery technique.

Wellington put a lot of pressure on the "nearest run thing." A glaring example was how close Blücher came to getting killed. At the close of the battle of Ligny, leading a last forlorn charge, his charger had been killed falling on him, pinning him to the ground as French lancers leaped over him. He only survived when his aide stopped a few uhlans to rescue him. If he had perished or been captured, von Gneisenau would have been reluctant at best to come to Wellington's rescue, and far more likely to gather up the shattered army and retreat upon his communications. Then it would have been only night upon which Wellington could have prayed. Such are the contingencies upon which history is built.

*   *   *

My most ambitious alternate history project was a Civil War trilogy with the point of departure being Britain stumbling into war with the Union in late 1863, triggering a world war, in this new reality, the Great War or the First World War. The books of the trilogy *were Britannia's Fist: From Civil War to World War* (2008); *A Rainbow of Blood: The Union in Peril* (2010); and *Bayonets, Balloons, and Ironclads: Britain and France Take Sides with the South* (2015).

Ever since I had written the paper, "God Bless the Russians," based on the visit of the Russian Baltic Squadron to New York and the Pacific Squadron to San Francisco in October 1863, for that same seminar at the Russian Military History Institute in Moscow, I had been intrigued by the Russian influence on events in our Civil War. Russia at that time was our only serious friend in Europe, offering us invaluable diplomatic advice and frustrating every British or French attempt to force a mediation that would have resulted in the independence of the South, an outcome eagerly sought by both powers. That friendship was based on the fact that we had no strategic conflicts and Russia's fear of British world hegemony, rubbed in their face by their defeat in the Crimean War. Russia saw the United States as the only counterbalance to British world hegemony.

A world war with Russia and the United States allied against Britain, France, and the Confederacy was a real possibility, especially since the reckless building of commerce raiders for the Confederacy in British shipyards forced Lincoln to draw a line in the sand and threaten the British with war in September 1863. Luckily for everyone, the British finally saw the danger and seized the warships in question. But what if they had miscalculated? And those last moments were filled with dangerous miscalculations. That was a very real possibility since their margin of error in actual events was so very thin. Upon this flimsy margin, the pivot of history turned in this trilogy.

Unable to subdue the Confederacy, the Union now finds itself at war with the two greatest powers in Europe, whose industrial and manpower resources far outweigh the Union's. How does Lincoln narrow the odds? Firstly, Russia has now entered the war on the side of the Union, forcing the British and French to fight on two widely separated fronts and fear that the rest of Europe would be dragged into war on either side.

Secondly, there were also two wasted opportunities in the Civil War to create combat multipliers that screamed out to be explored: (1) the failure to create a national

What if someone with more vision than Brig. Gen. James Ripley had been in charge of the U. S. Army's Bureau of Ordnance? Ripley, "a crabbed and visionless old cog," stayed married to old technology in a way that single-handedly dragged out the war effort. *Library of Congress*

intelligence service, and, (2) the failure to properly exploit the Union's long lead in military technology, especially in repeating weapons, balloons, and the revolutionary monitor warship wedded to superlative Dahlgren guns. The heavy Dahlgrens were deadly ship busters, far more destructive than anything the British or French had. They were the apogee of the muzzle-loading gun. The British had been so impressed that they had tried unsuccessfully to buy them before the war. A pair of heavy Dahlgrens in a monitor turret were more effective than a broadside of contemporary British guns, even those on their broadside ironclads whose armor was not resistant to the American guns.

American technological superiority in repeating weapons was single-handedly sabotaged by the Army's Ordnance Bureau chief, Brig. Gen. James Ripley. He even disobeyed Lincoln's direct order to produce such weapons by putting poison pills in the contracts. He was conservative in the most negative connotation, considering technological innovation as "newfangled gimcracks." He was blind to the possibility that early mass production of the several effective repeating weapons would have

George Sharpe modernized the Army of the Potomac's intelligence-gathering capabilities, creating remarkably accurate reports that first came into play under Maj. Gen. Joe Hooker. In contrast, detective Allan Pinkerton had provided intelligence reports for former army commander Maj. Gen. George B. McClellan—reports that proved wildly inaccurate and inspired McClellan to inflate Confederate numbers by twofold or more. What if McClellan had been given the kind of reliable intelligence information Sharpe later produced? *Library of Congress*

achieved such firepower dominance on the battlefield that no Confederate army could have even come close to matching. Those few Union units that were actually so equipped crippled their opponents. It would not have taken more than a few battles to melt away the armies of the Confederacy as well any British or French that opposed them. The vastly greater military production of the British and French would have been useless for it would have been producing out-of-date technology.

Ripley would stipulate that if the contractor was one day late, the contract was cancelled. When Maj. Gen. Rosecrans inquired of the proto-machine guns that Lincoln had given Ripley a direct order to buy, he lied and said he knew nothing about them. He then ordered the 50 guns already purchased to be withdrawn and put into storage despite the gun's only successful use at Chantilly, Virginia, where it cut a Confederate cavalry unit to pieces. Ripley was viscerally opposed to modern innovations.

The opportunity to create a national intelligence service lay unused, though the first professional all-source military intelligence organization in history was in existence. The Bureau of Military Intelligence (BMI) had been created in the Army of the Potomac by Col. George H. Sharpe. This brilliant man had built his fully functioning organization from the ground up between February and April in 1863. He was able to hand Robert E. Lee's head on a silver platter to the commander of the Army of the Potomac, Maj. Gen. Joseph Hooker, before the Chancellorsville Campaign. He was able to report Lee's ration strength within 1.5 percent. It was not Sharpe's fault that Hooker bungled the battle. As it was, Sharpe's subsequent provision of timely actionable intelligence was crucial to Meade's victory at Gettysburg. Grant would make him one of his trusted family of generals, promoting him to brevet brigadier. Sharpe and his staff were, I maintain, crucial to the victory of the Union.[1] Tasking Sharpe with replicating his achievement at the national level would indeed have extended this combat-multiplication to the entire war effort against both the Confederacy and Britain and France.

*   *   *

For many historians their field of study moves under the pressure of great causes and inexorable tides of human development. That approach betrays the taint of too close an affection for the idiocies of Marx and his disciples. History, all too often, pivots on great or petty men, mixed signals, lost letters, spite, nobility, greed, sacrifice, and the like as much as it does on the great transformations produced by sharp bronze, the industrial age, democracy, and the sublime message of a Galilean rabbi. Two centuries ago, Samuel Johnson had already put his finger on it.

> It seems to be almost the universal error of historians to suppose it politically, as it is physically true, that every effort has proportionate cause. In the inanimate action of matter upon matter, the motion produced can be but equal to the force of the moving power; but the operations of life, whether private or public, admit no such laws. The caprices of voluntary agents laugh at calculations. It is not always that there is a strong reason for a great event. Obstinacy and flexibility, malignity and kindness, give place alternately to each other, and the reason of these vicissitudes, however important may be the consequences, often escapes the mind in which the changes are made.[2]

Johnson's observation reaches deep into the past. The great Theban general Epaminondas (418-363 BC) called the great plain of Boeotia "the dancing floor

---

1   For a biography of Sharpe and his BMI, see Peter G. Tsouras, *Maj. Gen. George H. Sharpe and the Creation of American Military All-Source Intelligence* (Mechanicsburg, PA: Stackpole Books, 2018).

2   Samuel Johnson, "Thoughts on the late transactions respecting Falkland islands" (1771), *Political Writings*, Vol. X, 365-66, cited in Geoffrey Parker, *The Grand Strategy of Phillip II* (New Haven: Yale University Press, 1998), 293.

of war," a primal description of that blood-soaked ground of battle. There have been many, many more. The task of alternate history is to change the tune on those dancing floors, to see what unexpected fate the new beat and step will bring forth.

To describe these new beats, the arts of the historian and storyteller must be given full play. Writing alternate history must follow rigorous rules to create plausible scenarios. Author, historian, strategist and soldier Ralph Peters has described the 'Five Pillars of alternative history,' in Frontline's recent *Disaster at Stalingrad: An Alternate History*. They are worth summarizing here for there is no more perceptive analysis in the requirements of writing for this new genre. Good alternate history must have:

The Five Pillars of "Alternative" History

1. *A compelling, convincing vision.* "If the alternative-history does not grip us with logic—the recognition that this could have happened—the entire structure falls flat. . . . We have to be captured by the recognition that, yes, but for a few matters of happenstance, the author's vision might have come to pass, changing history."

2. *Historical and technical knowledge.* The writer must know "what has happened" down to the "sub-atomic" details. He must also grasp "why things happened" and how slight alterations in events or personal relations might have led to very different outcomes. He must also "know what soldiers can do and won't do" and know "not only what political leaders are supposed to do, but what they actually end up doing."

3. *Grasp of character.* "Alternative history doesn't work if the author doesn't understand the actual personalities of the figures he enlivens on the page—or human complexity in general. . . . [T]he actions men make and the actions they take must be grounded in their actual psychology and mundane circumstances." Characters must "make credible decisions based on the different developments confronting them."

4. *Writing ability.* "In alternative history, the focus should be on events and characters presented in transparent prose that never calls attention to itself. The writing should be so clean and clear that it disappears leaving only the author's vision. . . ." Even when addressing "infernally complex situations

or arcane technical details, the writing is a spotless window that lures the reader to look deeper inside."

5. *Storytelling ability.* "Writing ability and storytelling are often confused with one another, but while related involve separate talents and skill-sets. . . . The novelist/storyteller . . . is a literary Dr. Frankenstein, struggling bravely to create not only a living being, but an entire living world . . ." choosing "from an infinite number of possibilities, the unique combination of body parts that will spring to life for the reader. The non-fiction writer declares, 'It's a fact.' The novelist cries 'It's alive!'"[3]

One last thought: no greater example of how history all too often pivots on the oddest things is that of the already-mention Brig. Gen. Ripley, a crabbed and visionless old cog who single-handedly saw that our Civil War went on and on, ever increasing its butcher's bill. History is replete with such cogs and nonentities and all too often they have a greater effect on events than the great captains of mighty hosts. We remember U.S. Grant and Robert E. Lee as titans of the battlefield, yet both danced to Ripley's tune on the American dancing floor of war, Shakepeare's "harsh discords and unpleasing sharps."[4]

Peter G. Tsouras
Lieut. Col., USAR (ret)

---

3   Ralph Peters, "A Matter of Mastery," introduction to Peter G. Tsouras, *Disaster at Stalingrad: An Alternate History* (London: Frontline Books, 2013), xi-xv.

4   William Shakespeare, *Romeo and Juliet*, Act 3, Scene 5.

Introduction

Chris Mackowski

Two of the most underrated tools of the historian's trade are beer and cigars. Their potent value comes from their ability to stimulate lively discussion in a relaxed environment, promoting the free exchange and exploration of ideas—sometimes crazy ideas. The Civil War has been refought many a time over many a pint. If the cigar smoke is a poor imitation of the smoke of gunfire, it emulates the scale of battle encapsulated in these conversations, where everyone becomes their own armchair general.

"That was a bad decision because. . . ."

"That wouldn't have happened if. . . ."

"What if such-and-such happened instead. . . ?"

In 2018, Emerging Civil War published the first book in the Engaging the Civil War Series, *Turning Points of the American Civil War*, which examined key shifts during the war and the context surrounding them to show that a chain of many events caused the course of the war to turn and turn again. In its way, this book is the beers-and-cigars version of *Turning Points*. It similarly looks at pivotal moments of the war and wonders aloud about the inevitable question that arises each time: "What if a turning point had turned in a different direction?"

The pasttime of asking "What if" about the Civil War dates back as far as the veterans themselves with their own home-brewed or home-distilled libations and rolls of tobacco. Civil War buffs have carried on the tradition; novelists have joined in, too, as have, more recently, some historians. It's a huge question, really, and one endlessly fun to ponder even if ultimately impossible to answer.

Cigar in hand, Ulysses S. Grant seems primed for a good "What if" discussion. His memoirs have provided excellent fodder for armchair generals, but consider all the things he did not have the chance to write about because he suffered from terminal throat cancer as he wrote. What if, for instance, he had written about his presidency? Or his post-presidency round-the-world trip? Or more about controversial battles like North Anna or Cold Harbor? *Library of Congress*

Perhaps for that reason, "What If" is not respectable conversation in professional history circles. Sure, it's fine for the pub, but "What If" is not ready for prime time. It doesn't show up in conference presentations or on panel discussions. Historian Robert Cowley describes "What If" as "the historian's favorite secret question" because no one likes to ask it aloud.[1] In that way, at least, the beer and cigars provide a smokescreen.

Writers who tackle "What If" questions typically follow one of two traditions. The first is called "alternate history" or "alternative historical fiction," an approach that employs the techniques of creative writing. The second is called "counterfactual history," a nonfiction approach that employs the same methodologies and analysis used in traditional history writing.

Alternate histories are typically shelved at the local bookstore under "science fiction." "Both seek to extrapolate logically from a change in the world as we know it," explains novelist Harry Turtledove, dubbed by *Publisher's Weekly* as "the master of alternate history."[2] Says Turtledove:

---

1   Cowley, What If?, quoted in Roger L. Ransom, *The Confederate States of America* (New York, W. W. Norton & Company, 2005), 4.

2   Mellissa Mia Hall, "Master of Alternate History," *Publishers Weekly*, 7 April 2008. https://www.publishersweekly.com/pw/by-topic/authors/interviews/article/6996-master-of-alternate-history.html.

> Most forms of science fiction posit a change in the present or nearer future and imagine its effect on the more distant future. Alternate history, on the other hand, imagines a change in the more distant past and examines its consequences for the nearer past and the present. The technique is the same in both cases; the difference lies in where in time it is applied.[3]

The results can fall anywhere on a spectrum that novelists Newt Gingrich and William Forstchen define as "a rigid adherence to reality" to "an exercise in fantasy."[4] Books like Ward Moore's 1953 *Bring the Jubilee* fall into this latter category. In *Jubilee*, a time-traveler from a future where the United States lost the "War of Southron Independence" travels back to see the moment the South won the battle of Gettysburg—but in doing so inadvertently changes the course of events, leading to a northern victory. Turtledove's 1992 *The Guns of the South*, where time travelers from Apartheid-era South Africa show up to give AK-47s to Robert E. Lee, is another example—great brain candy but of little historical value.

However, Turtledove's 1997 *How Few Remain: A Novel of the Second War Between the States*—which kicks off a mammoth eleven-part series that runs through World War II—is predicated on a much more realistic premise: "What If George McClellan had never found Lee's 'Lost Order'?" Similarly, Terry Bisson's 1988 *Fire on the Mountain* is predicated on the question, "What If John Brown's raid on Harpers Ferry had been successful?" Kevin Willmott's 2004 "mockumentary" *C.S.A.: The Confederate States of America* is predicated on the question, "What If Lincoln's Emancipation Proclamation failed, and Europe intervened in the war?" Similarly, Robert Conroy's 2006 novel *1862* asks "What if Great Britain intervened in the war as a result of the 1861 Trent Affair?" Such stories—with their "rigid adherence to reality"—spring from tantalizing questions arising at key turning points. Peter Tsouras's trilogy beginning with *Britannica's Fist*, tackles a similar scenario but with Great Britain and France entering the war in 1863 and triggering a First World War.

---

3 Harry Turtledove, "Introduction," in *If the South Had Won the Civil War* by MacKinlay Kantor (New York: Forge, 2001), vii-viii.

4 Newt Gingrich and William R. Forstchen, "Introduction," *Gettysburg: A Novel of the Civil War*, audiobook edition (New York: Recorded Books, 2003).

Such stories—with their "rigid adherence to reality"—spring from tantalizing questions arising at key turning points.

Good alternate history doesn't just explore the historical questions, either. They have a richness of vision, as one of Turtledove's editors, Betsy Mitchell, once explained. "His novels illustrate the differences radiating from his 'what ifs,'" she said of Turtledove, but could have been referring to any well-written novel of the genre, "not just through what happens to history's famous names but by showing us changes in the lives of everyday workers as well: secretaries, truck drivers, soldiers in the trenches."[5]

Other alternate histories weave their stories from a "magic bullet or acts of God," as Gingrich and Forstchen call them.[6] As an example, MacKinlay Kantor's *If The South Had Won the Civil War* begins with Ulysses S. Grant— renowned as an excellent equestrian—getting pitched from a spooked horse following the May 12, 1863, battle of Raymond, Mississippi. Grant hits his head on a rock in the road and dies, and thus the Federals never take Vicksburg and end up losing the war. Kantor throws in a Confederate victory at Gettysburg for good measure. "The Past is immutable as such," Kantor waxes poetically. "Yet, in Present and in Future, its accumulated works can be altered by the whim of Time. . . . "[7] Or, as it happens, by the whim of a fiction writer.

Gingrich and Forstchen describe their own approach as "active history," which requires thinking about alternate history that would have been "within the limitations of the circumstances."[8] Such novels are "based on solid historical facts combined with a clear understanding of the nature of the leaders who ultimately made the decisions, their leadership style, their ability to react, and their historical behavior," Gingrich and Forstchen say. The goal of such an approach, they argue, is "to grasp the reality of the moment when critical decisions were made and consider the alternatives of decisions *not* made."[9] Their Gettysburg-based trilogy—*Gettysburg*

---

5   Quoted in Hall, "Master of Alternate History."

6   Ibid.

7   Kantor, 1.

8   Ibid.

9   Gingrich and Forstchen, "Introduction."

(2003), *Grant Comes East* (2004), and *Never Call Retreat* (2005)—falls into this category. They maintain Lee worked best on the operational level, basing their argument on his plans and performance at Second Manassas, Chancellorsville, and even Antietam. What if he maintained that same level of perspective at Gettysburg rather than getting sucked into a poor tactical situation because his blood was up?

Gingrich and Forstchen hope their approach can "show how much can be learned by thinking about history in an active rather than passive sense and then exploring in a disciplined manner the options that were not taken," including an examination "of the principles and systems which shape and enable events" and an "understanding of the subtleties and shadings that are at the heart of decision-making."[10]

This has particular applications for understanding leadership decisions and crisis response. "This is precisely what professional soldiers are taught to do," the authors say, pointing to the modern staff ride, where officers learn about decision-making by examining options on a battlefield. It's why the army conducts wargames and maneuvers and, they add, "why Napoleon said officers should immerse themselves in history."[11]

Despite the intellectual underpinning of "active histories," some historians dismiss fiction as a useful tool for understanding history. "[T]he novelists writing alternative historical fiction avoid dealing with the myriad of historical details that arise from their choices of counterfactual worlds," argues historian Roger L. Ransom in the preface of his 2005 *The Confederate States of America*. "They simply present the counterfactual events as backgrounds to the plots rather than the focus of historical inquiry."[12] It's a mistake, however, to dismiss fiction's incredible power to get at truths that traditional fact-bound histories cannot. For instance, Turtledove's eleven-book series, Bisson's *Fire on the Mountain,* and Willmott's *C.S.A.*, among others, probe vital questions about race relations, class struggle, politics, and more, making their alternate histories worthwhile explorations of universal human conditions.

The second writing tradition that explores "What If" questions embraces

10 Ibid.

11 Ibid.

12 Ransom, 12.

The bronze figure of "Fame" on the Iowa state monument at Shiloh "with immortal pen/Inscribes their names on the enduring rock." Is history quite so set in stone, or does it become mutable as new information emerges and our understanding of events changes? What if. . . ? *Chris Mackowski*

a more fact-bound approach: counterfactual history. Counterfactual history seeks to better understand what actually happened by understanding what *might have* happened. How can we know the true importance of an outcome, for instance, unless we understand what other possible outcomes existed in a given moment? "History is not merely what happened: it is what happened in the context of what might have happened," historian Hugh Trevor-Roper has pointed out.[13] As Roger Ransom goes on to add, "[W]hat historians looking at the problem years later treat as 'counterfactual' possibilities that did *not* happen, contemporaries at the time viewed as possibilities of the future that *might* happen."[14] Taking that a step further, Cowley asks, "At what point did possibilities become impossibilities?"[15]

13   Hugh Trevor-Roper, quoted in Ransom, 4.

14   Ransom, 14.

The greatest value of asking "What if" is that it embodies an inherent invitation to stretch one's critical thinking skills. "Counterfactual questions, if kept more or less within the parameters of what was possible at the time and place, can often help us better understand events of the past . . ." argues historian Richard M. McMurry in the prologue of his 2002 counterfactual book *The Fourth Battle of Winchester.* "To the extent that such inquiries fulfill that purpose and lead us to a fuller appreciation of history, they can be legitimate and useful devices for the study of the past."[16] They have a unique way of illuminating facts, says Cowley. "Counterfactual history may be the history of what didn't happen, a shadow universe," he admits, "but it casts a reflective light on what did."[17]

Counterfactual history requires an explicitly analytical approach, although a dose of creativity also helps. Ironically, opening the door for imagination makes some professional historians uncomfortable or even dismissive. Ransom describes a "general aversion of historians to counterfactual history" because it deals with "unprovable might-have-beens, requiring powers of imagination that belong more to novelists than historians."[18] However, this very same combination of analytic and creative thought, deeply rooted in the liberal arts tradition, has become prized in the Information Age workplace.

In this book, we're coming at the question "What If" a little sideways. We're not just asking the question, we're trying to subvert it. When someone asks "What If," we want to challenge them to really examine the question and all the assumptions that might surround it. We want to, in the words of Gingrich and Forstchen, pay special attention to the "limitations of the circumstances." When people ask "What If," they tend to forget about those limitations.

Take, for instance, the wounding of Stonewall Jackson, which historian William C. Davis has called, "The oldest and most often asked 'What if' question of the Civil War."[19] If Stonewall Jackson doesn't get shot, he's of

---

15   Robert Cowley, editor, "Introduction," *What Ifs? Of American History* (New York: G.P. Putman's Sons, 2003), xiii.

16   Richard M. McMurry, *The Fourth Battle of Winchester: Toward a New Civil War Paradigm* (Kent, OH: Kent State University Press, 1998), xvi.

17   Cowley, xiii.

18   Ransom, 2.

course rolling up over the top of Cemetery Hill in Gettysburg two months later. And if he does that? Well, Confederates win the battle of Gettysburg and probably the Civil War, too!

Um, no. And it doesn't matter how many beers or cigars you have, that answer won't change. See Kris White's essay in this volume, "What if Stonewall Jackson had not been shot," to find out why.

Stonewall Jackson's death became one of the fundamental pillars of the nascent Lost Cause mythology, which elevated Jackson to martyrdom. So, too, did Albert Sidney Johnston's accidental death along the banks of the Tennessee River. That's one of several topics Timothy B. Smith addresses in his essay, "The What Ifs of Shiloh." Smith's conclusions about the many possibilities raised in that battle might surprise you.

Kevin Pawlak takes a similar approach in his essay, "What Ifs of Antietam." Among them are another of the most popular what-if questions of the war: What if George McClellan hadn't found Lee's "Lost Order"?

Dwight Hughes touches on a political topic in his essay, "What if Great Britain and other foreign powers had intervened in the war?" Dwight parses the complicated international dynamics at play in 1862.

Gettysburg could merit a "What If" volume all its own, but Dan Welch tackles one of the most popular questions from the battle, "What If Longstreet had moved around to the right at Gettysburg?" Other military topics include Chris Mackowski's "What if Lee had struck a blow at the North Anna River?" and Kristen Pawlak's "What if Sterling Price had secured Missouri during his 1864 campaign?"

Another key theme that weaves through several essays is leadership. Cecily Nelson Zander looks at the seemingly baffling loyalty Jefferson Davis showed toward Army of Tennessee commander Braxton Bragg. Barton Myers considers the character of Robert E. Lee when Lee is faced, near war's end, with the choice of embracing an irregular strategy. Most tantalizingly, Brian Matthew Jordan asks, "What if Lincoln had not been assassinated?"

Unfortunately—but understandably—when people ask these and

---

19   Davis's comment comes from the book blurb for Douglas Lee Gibboney's *Stonewall Jackson at Gettysburg* (Sgt. Kirkland's Press, 1996), which gives the scenario book-length treatment. See also R. E. Thomas's *Stonewall Goes West* trilogy (Black Gold Media, 2013).

other "What Ifs," they often jump to the conclusions they prefer without really thinking through the facts of the moment. "Wishful thinking is an unhistorical trap," Cowley cautions, "and one we can do without."[20]

Each of the questions we present in this collection represents a potential turning point in the war.[21] Each turning point, in turn, spawned one or more "What Ifs," with one or more potential outcomes. We invite you, before jumping to your preferred pre-ordained outcome, to consider the situation on the ground, understand the context, look at the potential courses of action as confined by the limitations of the circumstances. Use the lens offered by Peter G. Tsouras in the foreword to this book. Be creative, but be critical.

Of course, we can't fit all of even the most popular "What Ifs" into this single volume. In order to provoke more thinking for our readers, though, we've tried to raise as many questions as a single book will let us. To that end, we hope our photos captions will pose more interesting topics of speculation for you to mull over. Look for more "What Ifs" from us down the road, particularly on our blog, www.emergingcivilwar.com.

---

20 Cowley, xvi.

21 In that vein, you can look at ECW's essay collection *Turning Points of the American Civil War* (SIUP, 2017) as a companion volume to this collection. Each "turning point" represents a variety of potential outcomes, inviting good "What If" fodder.

What if Death and Night had not conspired to snatch victory from the Confederates at Shiloh on April 6, 1862? So asks the Confederate memorial on the Shiloh battlefield. *Chris Mackowski*

CHAPTER ONE

Persistently Misunderstood

The What Ifs of Shiloh

Timothy B. Smith

In the center of Shiloh National Military Park stands one of the most impressive monuments on the battlefield. The United Daughters of the Confederacy (UDC) monument, erected in 1917 at a cost of $50,000 and dedicated in front of a crowd of fifteen thousand, is very impressive in its elegant lines, moving statuary, and symbolism. Erected with money raised by school children and the ladies of the South to mark a battlefield at that time (and still today) sharply tilted toward Union memorialization, the UDC monument loudly proclaims the honor and duty of Confederate soldiers at Shiloh.[1]

Besides the beauty, elegance, and size of the monument, the symbolism it portrays is perhaps most important. Placed on the battlefield in the heyday of the Lost Cause movement wherein proud Southerners sought to explain their defeat in the Civil War, the symbolism of the monument is classic Lost Cause. The bronze figures adorning each flank represent the four branches of the Confederate army (infantry, artillery, cavalry, and officer corps), with each providing their own view of the fighting. For instance, the infantry and artillery proudly look to the field while the cavalryman, little used in

---

1 "The Confederate Monument" Series 1, Box 26, Folder 373, Shiloh National Military Park.

the heavily wooded terrain, spreads his hands in frustration and the officer bows his head in defeat. The heads on each side represent the two days of battle, with eleven (for the number of Confederate states) on the right denoting the first day's fighting and lifted up in victory and the ten (fewer because of casualties) on the left bowed in defeat on the second day. Even the placement of the monument, at the high water mark of the Confederate struggle on the first day where the Hornet's Nest defenders surrendered, speaks volumes.[2]

The most symbolism resides, as would be expected, in the center of the monument. There, three bronze figures are caught in a seeming dance of defeat. Two veiled figures are taking from a front feminine figure a laurel wreath. The two veiled figures represent death and night, and they are symbolically taking the laurel wreath of victory from the figure in front, who represents the South. In effect, the Lost Cause argument is that death and night stole victory from the Confederates at Shiloh, the night of April 6, 1862, coming too quickly and many Confederates later arguing that if they just had a few more hours of daylight the victory would have been complete. Similarly, death stole victory from the Confederacy in the form of Albert Sidney Johnston, whose bust profile can be seen directly below the three central bronze figures. Many Southerners argued that had Johnston not perished on the battlefield, he would have continued the victory on to fulfillment while his successor threw away the triumph. As a result, the what-if questions have long raged over what would have happened if Johnston had not died or if his successor had not thrown away the victory by calling off the assaults because of looming darkness.[3]

These questions are central to understanding Shiloh as a whole, and they are certainly not new, and they were not in 1917 when the two foremost what ifs were put on such beautiful display. The question of what would have happened had Johnston not perished or if P. G. T. Beauregard had not called off the final attacks of the day due to the lateness of the hour have

---

2 Timothy B. Smith, *This Great Battlefield of Shiloh: History, Memory, and the Establishment of a Civil War National Military Park* (Knoxville: The University of Tennessee Press, 2004), 89-90. For the Lost Cause, see Gaines M. Foster, *Ghosts of the Confederacy: Defeat, The Lost Cause, and the Emergence of the New South* (New York: Oxford University Press, 1987).

3 William Preston Johnston, "Albert Sidney Johnston at Shiloh," *Battles and Leaders of the Civil War*, 4 vols. (New York, 1884-1887), 1: 540-568; P. G. T. Beauregard, "The Campaign of Shiloh," *Battles and Leaders*, 1: 569-593.

been debated since the battle ended and well before their Lost Cause personification in 1917 in the UDC monument. No less an authority than Ulysses S. Grant himself wrote in 1885 that Shiloh "has been perhaps less understood, or, to state the case more accurately, more persistently misunderstood, than any other engagement . . . during the entire rebellion." Similarly, the first park historian David W. Reed wrote in 1912 that "occasionally . . . some one thinks that his unaided memory of the events of 50 years ago is superior to the official reports of officers which were made at [the] time of the battle. It seems hard for them to realize that oft-repeated campfire stories, added to and enlarged, become impressed on the memory as real facts."[4]

Lew Wallace, ordered to join the rest of the Federal army at Shiloh, took an alternate road—one that ultimately would have led him onto the battlefield on the left flank of an unsuspecting Confederate army. Instead, he doubled back to take the main road and got to the battle late. What if he had continued on his original path instead? *Library of Congress*

Certainly, many other what if scenarios abound at Shiloh as well, including questions such as what would have happened if the Confederates had managed to attack on April 5 instead of the next day? What would have happened if Buell had not arrived at the end of the first day? What would have happened if Lew Wallace had not been delayed in arriving on the field? What would have happened if Benjamin Prentiss and W. H. L. Wallace had not held the Hornet's Nest to the point of sacrifice? The evidence indicates that few if any would have made much of a difference if the "what if" had been true. The record is clear that the paltry number of troops Buell managed to put into line on the evening of the first day made little difference in blunting the Confederate attack. Consequently, had the Confederates attacked as intended on April 5

4 Ulysses S. Grant, "The Battle of Shiloh," *Battles and Leaders*, 1: 465; *Annual Report of the Secretary of War – 1912* (Washington: Government Printing Office, 1913), 195-196.

or even April 4, as some historians claim but the evidence does not back up, the same problems would have appeared to stymie the Confederate advance short of Buell's arrival, which made little actual difference in reality. So his absence would not have made much difference a day or two earlier. As Grant was able to hold his final line at Pittsburg Landing without Lew Wallace's arrival, he certainly could have done so if he had shown up on the battlefield hours earlier, making the Confederate advance only that much more difficult. And finally, would a lesser defense of the Hornet's Nest have given the Confederates a victory? Modern research and a growing school of thought is that Grant's final line was so strong and was developed so early in the day (started around 2:30 p.m.) that Wallace and Prentiss holding out until nearly dark provided little additional benefit. Certainly, Ulysses S. Grant did not single the Hornet's Nest defense out as the key to victory.[5]

Despite these what ifs potentially making little difference in the result of the battle, what about death and night stealing victory from the Confederates? Of all the questions that the soldiers of the battle as well as historians and buffs ever since have debated, Johnston's death and the stoppage of the Confederate advance at night have emerged as the key explanations causing defeat for the Confederates at Shiloh. But did they?[6]

The effect of Albert Sidney Johnston's death has long been a source of debate. Participants in the battle itself first made claims as to whether his death affected the outcome, and the major actors in the debate, or in the deceased Johnston's case his son, succinctly analyzed both arguments in major articles that appeared primarily and most concisely in the famed *Century* (*Battles and Leaders*) series of publications in the 1880s.[7]

---

5   Timothy B. Smith, *Shiloh: Conquer or Perish* (Lawrence: University Press of Kansas, 2014); Larry J. Daniel, *Shiloh: The Battle That Changed the Civil War* (New York: Simon and Shuster, 1997); Edward Cunningham, *Shiloh and the Western Campaign of 1862*, Gary D. Joiner and Timothy B. Smith, eds. (New York: Savas Beatie, 2007); Timothy B. Smith, "Myths of Shiloh," *America's Civil War* (May 2006): 30-36, 71.

6   Grant, "The Battle of Shiloh," 465-486; Don Carlos Buell, "Shiloh Reviewed," *Battles and Leaders*), 1: 487-536; Timothy B. Smith, "Historians and the Battle of Shiloh: One Hundred and Forty Years of Controversy," *Tennessee Historical Quarterly*, vol. 62, no. 4 (2003): 332-353.

7   Robert Underwood Johnson and Clarence Clough Buel, eds., *Battles and Leaders of the Civil War, Being For the Most Part Contributions By Union and Confederate Officers: Based upon "The Century" War Series*, 4 vols. (New York, 1884-1887).

The arguments are plain on the surface. Johnston's son, William Preston Johnston who was later an aide to Jefferson Davis in Richmond, argued that his father was on the verge of victory at 2:30 p.m. when he bled to death. Johnston had moved to the right of the Confederate line, where the all-important turning movement around the Union left flank was to occur. Because the right flank was stalled, Johnston determined he had to put his substantial leadership abilities in the fight and lead from the front. It worked, at least on the isolated tactical level at the time, and the charge Johnston led in part moved the Union line rearward through the Peach Orchard area.[8]

After Shiloh, the Confederacy suffered from command problems in the western theater for the rest of the war, from incompetent leadership to infighting. Win or lose, what if Albert Sidney Johnston had lived beyond the battle of Shiloh? *Chris Mackowski*

Unfortunately, during the advance Johnston took a bullet in the right leg just behind the knee and in the course of thirty minutes or so bled to death right on the battlefield. A simple tourniquet could potentially have saved his life, but Johnston probably did not even know he was wounded until far too late. And, his staff surgeon, D. W. Yandell, had been left in the rear to care for wounded in some of the Union camps. The result was that Johnston perished in a ravine behind the lines, his call to conquer or perish

---

8 Timothy B. Smith, "To Conquer or Perish: The Last Hours of Albert Sidney Johnston," in *Confederate Generals in the Western Theater: An Anthology*, Volume 3, edited by Larry Hewitt and Art Bergeron (Knoxville: University of Tennessee Press, 2011), 21-37.

Shiloh Argument over what would have happened if Albert Sidney Johnston had lived at Shiloh has raged since the afternoon he died. Having put the Confederate army in motion and attacking on the morning of April 6, 1862, Johnston perished in the early afternoon, a result of bleeding to death because an artery in his leg had been hit. Many historians have argued that Johnston was in the process of winning the victory at the time of his death but that his successor, P. G. T. Beauregard, threw away Johnston's victory when he called off the final assaults on the Union last line of defense nearer to Pittsburg Landing. In reality, Beauregard continued Johnston's push forward after the army commander's death—even faster that Johnston had been pushing, in fact— and managed to neutralize the famed Hornet's Nest, something Johnston had failed to do throughout the day. And Beauregard's final recall order stopping the attack came when Confederates at the front, on the ground itself, had already come to the same conclusion and were themselves stopping the attacks on their own. Beauregard did not throw away Johnston's victory, which Johnston was not actually winning when he died. As a result, the "what if" of Johnston living would have made no appreciable difference in the outcome of the Battle of Shiloh.

---

having become partly true as Johnston perished in the attempt. Whether the conquer part would fade would be up to his successor in command of the army, General P. G. T. Beauregard.[9]

William Preston Johnston argued that his father was on the verge of victory, the successful charge he had just led a case in point. He made elaborate arguments in both his article for *Battle and Leaders* as well as a lengthy biography of his father published in 1879. It was there that he argued that his father died at the height of victory but that Beauregard took the reins of command and promptly threw away the hard earned success. He wrote that up until his father's death there was "the predominance of intelligent design; a master mind, keeping in clear view its purpose." This argument, of course, made its way into the UDC monument at Shiloh, where Johnston's bust figured prominently on the center front and where the veiled figure of death (Johnston's) snatched the laurel wreath of victory from the South. Illustrating the importance of Johnston to the Confederate effort at Shiloh, the UDC placed a lock of the general's hair in the cornerstone of the monument.[10]

Others elaborated on the effect of Johnston's death as well, the major theory being that a supposed lull took place after Johnston's death, some

---

9   Charles P. Roland, *Albert Sidney Johnston: Soldier of Three Republics* (Austin: University of Texas Press, 1964), 336-338.

10   William Preston Johnston, *The Life of Gen. Albert Sidney Johnston: His Service in the Armies of the United States, The Republic of Texas, and the Confederate States* (New York: D. Appleton and Co., 1879); Johnston, "Albert Sidney Johnston at Shiloh," 1: 565, 568.

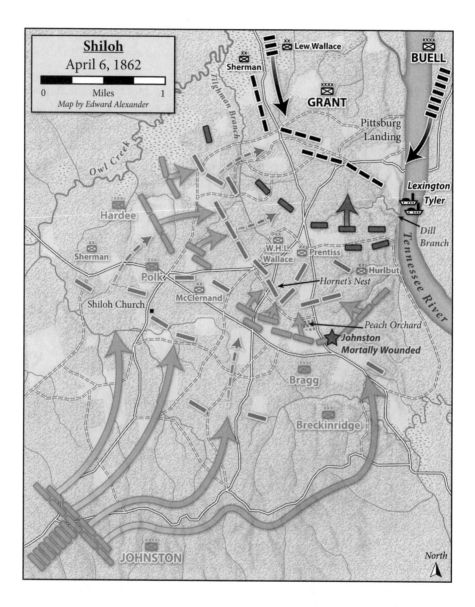

Shiloh
April 6, 1862

0   Miles   1
Map by Edward Alexander

said for many hours' duration. In that time, Johnston's supporters argued, the Federals were able to reform their lines with little to no pressure on the Union left, where the Confederate push had to succeed if they were to have any chance of victory. In particular, William T. Sherman described a pause, as did William J. Hardee, who spoke of "a lull in the attack on the right and precious hours were wasted." He went on to say, "It is, in my opinion, the candid belief of intelligent men that, but for this calamity, we would have achieved before sunset a triumph signal not only in the annals of this war, but memorable in future history."[11]

Others involved in the war also agreed, none more influential than Confederate President Jefferson Davis himself. Johnston's close friend and significantly a bitter enemy of Beauregard, Davis argued in his mammoth *The Rise and Fall of the Confederate Government* that the fault for defeat lay squarely on Beauregard's shoulders. And in some cases, the effect was larger than just at Shiloh; the younger Johnston used one Confederate officer's quote that "the West perished with Albert Sidney Johnston, and the Southern country followed."[12]

Modern historians have taken this debate to new levels, with many of the stalwart historians siding with the younger Johnston that the elder's death made a huge difference. Most notably, Johnston's biographer Charles P. Roland argued in his major work in the 1960s, and then in a smaller volume since, that Johnston's death was the key factor in defeat. He asserted that the "Confederate drive lost momentum when Johnston fell" and that "the fury of the Confederate assault waned." Most significantly, he added that Beauregard threw away the victory, and had Johnston lived "he might well have achieved it."[13]

Wiley Sword in *Shiloh: Bloody April* continued the emphasis on Johnston's death, stating that "no one now seemed to be in control of the situation on the extreme Confederate right." Sword went so far as to begin a single handed process to locate what he viewed as the correct death spot on the battlefield and in doing so labeled it "as perhaps an ultimate Confederate shrine; it is the spot where the South may have lost the war." More recently, Larry J. Daniel in *Shiloh: The Battle that Changed the Civil War* also argued that there was a lull.[14]

---

11   William T. Sherman, *Memoirs of General William T. Sherman: Written by Himself.* 2 vols. (New York: D. Appleton and Co., 1875), 1:247; OR, 1, 10(1): 569.

12   Jefferson Davis, *The Rise and Fall of the Confederate Government*, 2 vols. (New York: D. Appleton and Co., 1881), 2: 60-61, 66; Johnston, "Albert Sidney Johnston at Shiloh," 565, 568.

13   Roland, *Albert Sidney Johnston*, 341-342; Charles P. Roland, *Jefferson Davis's Greatest General: Albert Sidney Johnston* (Abilene: McWhiney Foundation Press, Texas, 2000), 82.

14   Wiley Sword, *Shiloh: Bloody April* (New York: William Morrow and Co., 1974), 274, 320, 310, 447; Larry J. Daniel, *Shiloh: The Battle That Changed the Civil War* (New York: Simon and Shuster, 1997), 228.

Of course, there were detractors as well, most notably Beauregard himself. In his own *Battles and Leaders* article and then in a ghost-written biography by Alfred Roman, Beauregard insisted there was no victory to throw away. He particularly railed against the idea of a lull on the Confederate right, arguing that if there was one it was no more than fifteen minutes. Major historians have also ascribed to this view, including James Lee McDonough in *Shiloh: In Hell Before Night* who argued there was no lull after Johnston's death. Edward Cunningham similarly argued that although a lull did develop on the field after Johnston's death, it was no more so on the right than anywhere else.[15]

In actuality, Johnston's death made little difference in the fighting. He had long by this point in the battle given up any role as army commander, and was acting at the time of his death as a brigade commander would, leading troops in an assault. In a larger context, the Confederate army had by this point spent much of its force, and while Johnston's attack drove the Federals back momentarily, there was still no clear path to turning the Union left. As for the lull, there is no clear consensus if there was even one, and certainly none on how long it was. And while the participants who were there certainly deserve our respect and ear, it is important to note that the two main sources of the lull thesis, Sherman and Hardee, were significantly on the other side of the battlefield at the time of the described lull, nearly two miles away. Clearly, there were lulls during all battles, Shiloh included. Braxton Bragg described as much: "all parts of our line were not constantly engaged, but there was no time without heavy firing in some portion of it." Grant similarly wrote, "there was no hour during the day when there was not heavy firing and generally hard fighting at some point on the line, but seldom at all points at the same time." Thus, any lull was due more to the natural flow of battle than because of Johnston's death. If there was a critical lull, it actually took place during the hours of little movement before his death. That lull in forward movement

---

15   Alfred Roman, *The Military Operations of General Beauregard in the War Between the States, 1861 to 1865: Including a Brief Personal Sketch of His Services in the War with Mexico, 1846-8*, 2 vols. (New York: Harper and Brothers, 1883); Beauregard, "The Campaign of Shiloh," 1: 589-590; Cunningham, *Shiloh and the Western Campaign of 1862*, 278, James L. McDonough, *Shiloh: In Hell before Night* (Knoxville: University of Tennessee Press, 1977), 153-155.

cost the Confederates more in time and space than that which occurred after Johnston's death, when the Confederates followed up the Union line more quickly.[16]

If the UDC monument at Shiloh made grand claims that Albert Sidney Johnston's death helped cause the Confederate defeat at Shiloh, the parallel argument, as encapsulated in the other veiled figure (night stealing victory from the South), also hinged somewhat on Johnston's death. When the army commander perished, that left command in the hands of Beauregard, who had actually wielded more control of the army throughout the battle than Johnston had anyway. Beauregard had been on the front lines at Manassas while Joseph E. Johnston oversaw the entire operation from the rear. This time the tables were turned and Beauregard remained more in the rear conducting the battle while another Johnston went to the front and died as a result. Accordingly, little changed in terms of the Confederate high command and the direction of the overall battle when Johnston died, adding further fuel to the idea that Johnston's death did not cause defeat.[17]

In fact, Beauregard continued the attack across the board, and contrary to those who argue that he squandered Johnston's offensive success, he actually pushed the majority of the Federal army back. It was on Beauregard's watch from around 2:30 p.m. to 6:00 p.m. that both flanks of the Union army were driven back into a final line of defense nearer the landing, a seismic shift in the fighting wherein the Federals abandoned the major line from the Peach Orchard to the Hornet's Nest and on to the Crossroads that they had held since mid morning. Johnston's isolated attack around 2:00 p.m. did not accomplish that, but rather drove back a portion of one wing into a new line a few hundred feet in the rear. Additionally, it was on Beauregard's watch after Johnston's death that the Confederates captured and neutralized the Hornet's Nest, again something Johnston had been unable to do while he lived. The result is that contrary to anti-Beauregard partisans, Beauregard continued the advance after he took command, all the way nearly to Pittsburg Landing.

---

16 Smith, *Shiloh*, 193; OR, 1, 10(1): 465, 469-470, 569; Grant, "The Battle of Shiloh," 1:473; Sherman, *Memoirs of General William T. Sherman*, 1:247; Johnston, "Albert Sidney Johnston at Shiloh," 1:565; Beauregard, "The Campaign of Shiloh," 589; Alexander R. Chisolm, "The Shiloh Battle-Order and the Withdrawal Sunday Evening," *Battles and Leaders*, 1:606; Roman, *The Military Operations of General Beauregard*, 1:551; McDonough, 154.

17 For Beauregard, see T. Harry Williams, *P. G. T. Beauregard: Napoleon in Gray* (Baton Rouge: Louisiana State University Press, 1954).

If anything, Beauregard continued the victory Johnston was winning, if he was indeed winning at all at that point, which is doubtful.[18]

The major argument concerning Beauregard throwing away the victory, however, comes in regard to his final actions of the day. Once the Confederate army drove back the flanks and captured the Hornet's Nest defenders, they reorganized and portions of the army attempted to storm Grant's last line. One Louisiana brigade assaulted the right center of the line by crossing Tilghman Branch and making a bloody attack that the Federals easily repulsed. The more famous attempts came on the far Confederate right where portions of four brigades crossed the massive Dill Branch ravine and tried to attack the heart of Grant's defenses near the landing. But before night fell, Beauregard's orders arrived to stop the advance. Thus was born the idea that had Beauregard continued the attack, he could have broken the Federal lines, perhaps driven the enemy into the river, and won the battle.[19]

Obviously, the major proponents of this theory were Johnston's backers, namely his son who wrote in his biography as well as his *Battles and Leaders* article how Beauregard failed to push his army and thus negated his father's success. Beauregard literally snatched defeat out of the jaws of victory, so the younger Johnston thought, and willingly squandered the victory his father had so sacrificially won. In the younger Johnston's words, "complete victory was in his grasp, and he threw it away."[20]

Many have disagreed over the years, and in fact the major historians of the battle have come to a rather firm consensus that Beauregard did not throw away a victory. James Lee McDonough argued that there was no lost opportunity and that the correct decision was to call off the attacks. Edward Cunningham stated that the Confederates could not have taken Grant's last line. Wiley Sword agreed, and Larry Daniel argued that the Confederates had no chance to break Grant's last line, although it should have been tried more forcefully than it was.[21]

Many factors abound that illustrate just why Beauregard did not throw

18   Smith, *Shiloh*, 217-218.

19   Ibid. 217-232.

20   Johnston, "Albert Sidney Johnston at Shiloh," 1:568.

21   McDonough, *Shiloh*, 181; Cunningham, *Shiloh and the Western Campaign of 1862*, 324-325; Sword, *Shiloh*, 450-452; Daniel, *Shiloh*, 255-256.

away Johnston's victory. One was indeed the coming of night, although Beauregard's stoppage order arrived well before it was too late to see or fight anymore. By the time the encircling Confederates rounded up the last defenders of the Hornet's Nest around 6:00 p.m., that left only about one hour of daylight to reorganize, reposition, and continue the attack. Several brigades were able to do so and actually crossed the ravine only to meet a massive barrage of Federal fire.[22]

Beauregard himself was not on the front line but back nearer to Shiloh Church, nearly a couple of miles away, when he made the fateful decision that would haunt him in Lost Cause mentality. Examining what he knew at the time so close to dark, however, paints a picture wherein Beauregard thought the heavy lifting had already been done and that the rest would be a

Following the defeat at Shiloh and subsequent siege and abandonment of Corinth, Mississippi, Gen. P. G. T. Beauregard took medical leave in June 1862— without permission from his superiors in Richmond. Events of the spring had stained the reputation of the "Hero of Ft. Sumter," so President Jefferson Davis used the opportunity as an excuse to eventually transfer Beauregard back to Charleston. The relationship between the two would continue to worsen thereafter to the detriment of the overall Confederate war effort. What if Beauregard and Davis had found a way to work past their differences? *National Archives*

mopping up action. He had continued Johnston's attacks and broken the major Federal defensive line of the day along the Peach Orchard-Hornet's

22   Smith, *Shiloh*, 223-229.

Nest-Crossroads axis, the one that had held out for many hours from mid morning to early evening. Now, the beaten Federals were in retreat and huddled near the landing, probably ready to give in.[23]

Similarly, Beauregard thought there would be no help for these defeated Federals. He had gotten word from north Alabama that Don Carlos Buell's Army of the Ohio was spotted there and thus would be of no aid to Grant at Pittsburg Landing. While in reality one division was indeed in north Alabama, five more were being even then funneled to the battlefield, the advance of one already coming ashore on the western bank of the river and going into line. Beauregard clearly thought he had the Federals right where he wanted them and saw no need to push further this late in the day when it could be done easily the next morning.[24]

The exhaustion of the Confederate army was also a factor. The battle had begun at daylight, now some thirteen hours earlier, so the army had been in action a long time and was tired, bloody, and hungry. Moreover, the three or four days previous had been anything but easy as well, with long marches, harsh weather, and much chaos. Beauregard simply thought that instead of making his famished troops do any more today, he could let them rest during the night and mop up the next morning.[25]

Accordingly, Beauregard sent the fateful message to end the action late in the evening. It was certainly the right choice, given all the contributing factors, but perhaps Beauregard can be faulted for making this right decision for all the wrong reasons. For whatever reason, however, the choice was correct, although the crux of the debate is whether a continued assault, had Johnston been around to push it, would have won the victory. Much evidence says it would not have.[26]

The Federal defense at the last line was enormously strong. Grant's chief of staff Joseph D. Webster had begun forming this line as early as 2:30 that afternoon, studding it with assorted artillery that had not yet gotten into the fight, including huge siege guns intended for use at Corinth,

23 Williams, *P. G. T. Beauregard*, 140-142.

24 Ibid.

25 Smith, *Shiloh*, 230.

26 Ibid., 232.

Mississippi, when the army advanced on that defended bastion. Other artillery batteries also went into the line (ultimately making around fifty guns in a short span of ground near the landing), as did those coming in from the field itself in retreat. Masses of retreating infantry also followed northward (as well as the first companies of Buell's army arriving via Pittsburg Landing), and they all, with the exception of those captured in the Hornet's Nest, went into line and solidified it even more. That the battlefield continually narrowed the farther northward the fighting moved also aided the Federals as their required lines of defense were much shorter and thereby much stronger. Adding more defensibility to this last line were the huge ravines that fronted most of it, Dill Branch on the east and Tilghman Branch on the western side. Just getting across them without any defense is difficult even today, but was significantly more so under fire then. And then, of course, the naval gunboats *Tyler* and *Lexington* in the river firing up Dill Branch ravine also aided the defense and shocked Confederate morale. While their role in the battle and contribution to Union victory, like Buell's arrival, has been debated just about as much as any of the other questions of Shiloh, it is no doubt that the gunboats were an important part of the last Union defense.[27]

Making a successful assault across this harsh terrain against so much defensibility was a recipe for disaster. But Beauregard was not on site and knew little if any of the details facing the Confederate brigades that managed to cross Dill and Tilghman branches. For that reason, Beauregard made the right decision but for a completely different set of reasons. It is the remarkable consensus that the Confederate assaults would not have succeeded had they been fully launched, but in part because of Beauregard's order, they were not pushed forward with any gusto at all. Thus emerged the argument that Beauregard threw away the victory Johnston had won.[28]

There is yet another factor in the wilting Confederate advance at dark on April 6, however, and that regards who actually made the decision to call off the assaults. While Beauregard received the blame in Lost Cause mythology as Confederates were casting about looking

---

27 Ibid., 217-235.

28 Johnston, "Albert Sidney Johnston at Shiloh," 1: 567-568.

for those to fault, there is much evidence that the actual decision to stop the assaults was made not by Beauregard but by those lower-ranking officers physically on the ground who saw the enormous factors against them and the seeming impossibility of succeeding, and that was before Beauregard's order arrived. Colonel Robert A. Smith of the 10th Mississippi in James Chalmers's brigade, the only one who actually even attempted an advance, explained that "several ineffectual attempts were made to induce a charge but the exhaustion of the troops was so great that . . . our weakened line could not attempt it and a retreat to the ravine back out of range was ordered." Chalmers described how his men were "attempting to mount the last ridge" and were "met by a fire from the whole line of batteries protected by infantry and assisted by shells from the gunboats." In fact, Chalmers declared that he never got an order to fall back but did so on his own. Similarly, John K. Jackson commanding another ammunitionless brigade that crossed the ravine under fire wrote, "Finding an advance without support impracticable, remaining there under fire useless, and believing any forward movement should be made simultaneously along our whole line, I proceeded to obtain orders from General Withers."[29]

Even more telling, there was at the time little if any remonstration against Beauregard's order when it did come, it merely stamping official approval on what had already been decided on the ground. Some Confederates stated years later that they had objected, but no contemporary evidence shows any argument against Beauregard's order that evening. An officer on Braxton Bragg's staff (Bragg having come to the right to oversee operations there after Johnston's death) wrote, "At the time the order was given, the plain truth must be told, that our troops at the front were a thin line of exhausted men, who were making no further headway, and were glad to receive orders to fall back," adding that the recall order was "most timely." Another Bragg staff officer explained, "My impression was (this was also the conclusion of General Bragg), that our troops had done all that they would do and had better

---

29   Robert A. Smith Report, April 9, 1862, Robert A. Smith Papers, MDAH; OR, 1, 10(1): 134, 386-387, 410, 534, 550-551, 555, 616-617.

be withdrawn." He also related, "If he had received and disproved such an order, it is probable that something would have been said about it."[30]

Consequently, Beauregard has been faulted for calling off attacks that would almost certainly have failed and for that reason were abandoned on the spot even before Beauregard's formal orders arrived. Thus, the idea that night came on too soon and stole victory from the Confederates is a what if of mammoth proportions that has no base in reality. The Confederate army by 6:30 p.m. on April 6 was so tired and disorganized and facing such a strong line of defense behind almost impossible terrain to surmount that even several more hours of daylight, or Johnston's presence pushing his men onward, would likely have made little difference.

As the congress debated creating the Shiloh National Military Park in 1894, Representative Joseph H. Outhwaite of Ohio argued that establishing the park would "put at rest once and for all time to come the uncertainties and misrepresentations surrounding the battle." Such has obviously not been the case as historians and buffs have debated the battle of Shiloh ever since, perhaps even more so since the park's establishment and the erection of its attending monuments such as the UDC memorial with all its symbolism.[31]

Yet those debates are central to the history of the battle and cannot be delineated specifically in facts, but are more akin to how to interpret the facts. And those debates rightly include some of the major what ifs of Shiloh, although it is prudent to remember that what ifs are just that, possibilities. One can ponder what would have happened if Lew Wallace had arrived on the field earlier, or if the Confederates had attacked a day or two earlier, or if Buell's army had not arrived when it did, or if the Federals had not sacrificed themselves at the Hornet's Nest. In each case, the evidence points to the fact that none of these what-if scenarios would have made any difference at Shiloh.

Certainly, the two main debated points concerning Johnston's death and Beauregard's calling off the final attack at nightfall seem equally as evident. Although some claimed a lull occurred or that there was no direction on

---

30 OR, 1, 10(1): 410, 467; Roman, *The Military Operations of General Beauregard*, 1:535-536, 551; "The Battle of Shiloh: The Second Day's Fight," *Southern Watchman*, April 30, 1862 (copy in E. Merton Coulter Collection, UGA); David Urquhart to Thomas Jordan, August 25, 1880, David Urquhart Letter Book, UNC.

31 House Reports, 53rd Congress, 2nd Session, Report No. 1139, 1-5.

the Confederate right after Johnston's death, it is clear that Beauregard continued the advance and actually gained more ground under his watch than Johnston had done for hours. Similarly, the idea that Beauregard called off the attack at the end of the day because of the coming night is equally odious, the commanders on the ground themselves calling it quits with no correlation with Beauregard's order.

Thus, had Johnston lived, it is hard to believe he could have done any more than Beauregard did in reality, when he would have faced the same daunting defense and terrain Beauregard did. And had Beauregard not called off the attacks at the end of the day, it is equally evident that they would not have succeeded, those tasked with making the assaults having already decided among themselves to stop for the day. Accordingly, Beauregard did not throw away Johnston's victory. In fact, there was no victory to throw away. Thus, there is no basis for the Lost Cause argument that death and night stole victory from the Confederates at Shiloh, although it does make for a provocative and beautiful monument.

While many cannot even concur on what did happen at Shiloh, agreement over what might have happened, while certainly in the realm of debate, is extremely elusive. Yet the most likely outcome for all is that none of the what ifs would have made much difference. Shiloh, a gamble as described by Albert Sidney Johnston himself, was from the beginning an extremely long shot for the Confederates, even if everything had gone perfectly for them.[32]

---

32 Timothy B. Smith, *Rethinking Shiloh: Myth and Memory* (Knoxville: University of Tennessee Press, 2013), 28.

Lincoln restored George B. McClellan to command in September 1862 because he said he had to work with the tools he had available. What if Lincoln had more tools to choose from?
photo illustration by Chris Mackowski from photos at the Library of Congress

CHAPTER TWO

What Ifs

of the Maryland Campaign

Kevin Pawlak

On September 13, 1862, the Army of the Potomac trudged toward Frederick, Maryland, a steepled crossroads in the shadow of the Catoctin Mountains. Outside of town, Sgt. John Bloss and Cpl. Barton W. Mitchell of the 27th Indiana Infantry found a soft bed of wheat in a farm field—a place to rest their legs after a hard morning's march. Mitchell stretched out in the wheat but quickly noticed an envelope resting nearby. Curious, the Hoosier soldier rose from his slumber to grab it. The private opened the package and discovered paper wrapped around two cigars. Mitchell browsed the letter's contents before he passed it to Sergeant Bloss. The non-commissioned officer read through the document and was astounded to learn that it outlined the campaign plans of Robert E. Lee and the Confederate Army of Northern Virginia! Recognizing Mitchell's critical discovery, Bloss forwarded this lost copy of Confederate Special Orders No. 191 up the chain of command until it found its way to army headquarters.[1]

When the document reached Maj. Gen. George B. McClellan's hands, he speedily reviewed it. The document called for the splintering of Lee's army into multiple columns. In a fit of excitement, McClellan reportedly claimed, "Now I know what to do!"

Ever since then—September 13, 1862—the question has been asked:

---

1 John McKnight Bloss, "Letter written from the barn hospital at Antietam," in Bloss Family Papers, September 25, 1862. Copy of letter provided by Monocacy National Battlefield.

could he have done what he actually did differently? And what if he did?[2]

Admittedly, posing counterfactual questions can be a dangerous road to travel. But the allure of "what ifs" is fixating enough that even the most professional historians sometimes cannot avoid playing the game. In his book on the Maryland Campaign, *Crossroads*

Robert E. Lee's "Lost Order" has been a favorite source of "What if" speculation. A historical marker across from the Monocacy National Battlefield visitor center commemorates the order's place in Civil War lore. What if the "Lost Order" had never been found? *Chris Mackowski*

of Freedom, James M. McPherson used counterfactual thinking to bludgeon McClellan. "One can readily imagine," the historian wrote, "what would have happened if the situation had been reversed and Lee had discovered that McClellan's army was split into four parts too distant from each other for mutual support. He would have had Jackson on the march within the hour, with Longstreet right behind." Inevitably, such a gifted find for McClellan could only lead to the destruction of the enemy army.[3]

This "what if," among several others, are often tossed around regarding the Maryland Campaign. In fact, they seem to be asked and answered with such regularity and unanimity that the hypothetical outcome becomes cemented as the certain outcome if events had transpired the way of the theoretical rather than the actual. However, a closer look at the facts often renders these discussions doubtful and illegitimate.

For a campaign that holds such importance in the course of the Civil War, the Maryland Campaign is open to multiple "what if" questions beyond the finding of a lost copy of Special Orders No. 191. Other hypothetical

2 Sears, *The Young Napoleon*, 281.

3 McPherson, *Crossroads of Freedom*, 109.

questions with answers commonly accepted as if they were fact include the use of the Army of the Potomac's reserves at the battle of Antietam and McClellan's subsequent pursuit of the withdrawing Confederate army from the banks of the Antietam Creek to the banks of the Potomac River.

What If McClellan Acted Quickly Upon Finding the Lost Orders?

Covering and attempting to answer all of the uncertainties still surrounding the lost copy of Special Orders No. 191 goes beyond the scope of this piece. More than enough ink—well more than what is contained in the Lost Order—has been spilled in attempts to solve all of the uncertainties. Instead, this essay aims to strip away the veneer painted over the Lost Order over the course of more than a century and a half, forego the art of repeating historian after historian, and return to the written record of September 1862 to answer the question, how much of a turning point was the discovery of the Lost Order?[4]

Early September 1862 generated rumors in epidemic proportions in Washington City and amongst the Federal high command. "Rumors of all kinds, defeats, victories," one Union soldier jotted in his diary.[5] As the Army of the Potomac began its advance northwest from Washington, it might as well have marched with a blindfold over one eye. Information from multiple sources flooded McClellan's mind, much of it coming from "unreliable sources & is vague & conflicting."[6]

For McClellan's superior, Henry W. Halleck, Lee's move into Maryland was nothing more than a ruse to draw much of the Union army away from Washington, thus draining the city's defenses. Once Lee felt the Federal forces pursuing him were far enough away from the nation's capital, he would turn his columns south, re-cross the Potomac River back into Virginia,

---

4 For an excellent and recent treatment of this debate, see Steven R. Stotelmyer, *Too Useful to Sacrifice: Reconsidering George B. McClellan's Generalship in the Maryland Campaign from South Mountain to Antietam* (El Dorado Hills, CA: Savas Beatie, 2019), 1-45.

5 John S. Ellen Journal, September 2, 1862, Western Reserve Historical Society.

6 George B. McClellan to Andrew G. Curtin, September 8, 1862, 9:00 pm, *The Civil War Papers of George B. McClellan: Selected Correspondence, 1860-1865* (hereafter cited as *GBM Papers*), ed. Stephen W. Sears (New York: Houghton Mifflin Harcourt, 1989), 439.

Three Federal infantrymen found Special Order 191 wrapped around two cigars and passed the bundle up the chain of command (this Civil War Trails sign at the Best farm on the Monocacy battlefield tells the story, although research suggests the site of the discovery was a bit closer to Frederick). The Federal high command could confirm the veracity of the orders because, along the way, an aide to Brig. Gen. Alpheus Williams, Col. Samuel Pittman, recognized the signature of Lee's assistant adjutant, Brig. Gen. Robert H. Chilton, on the bottom of the order. What if the "Lost Order" had made its way up the chain of command through different hands? *Chris Mackowski*

and hit the weakened underbelly of Washington.[7] George B. McClellan did not—nor could he—dismiss these claims originally. "It is hard to get accurate news from the front," he wrote on September 9.[8]

But by September 11, the enemy's intentions became clearer to him. "All the evidence that has been accumulated from various sources since we left Washington goes to prove most conclusively that almost the entire rebel army in Virginia, amounting to not less than 120,000 men, is in the vicinity

7   Henry Halleck to George B. McClellan, September 13, 1862, 10:45 am, *OR*, vol. 19, pt. 2, 280-81. This belief continued to control Halleck's views of the campaign even after the Battle of Antietam concluded. See Henry Halleck to George B. McClellan, September 19, 1862, 12:30 pm, *OR*, vol. 19, pt. 2, 330.

8   George B. McClellan to Mary Ellen McClellan, September 9, 1862, 5:00 pm, *GBM Papers*, 442.

of Frederick City."[9] McClellan had cracked the first code of the Confederate invasion of Maryland. From numerous sources, he culled together the facts that the enemy meant to be—and stay—in Maryland, not move south and hit the nation's capital. Even by that same night, more information began making its way to army headquarters.

On September 10, 1862, as he advanced deeper into Maryland, Robert E. Lee began splintering his forces, as outlined in Special Orders No. 191. That day, all of his forces, mustered into five separate columns, started their movements to carry out the investment of the Federal garrisons in the Shenandoah Valley. Three of Lee's columns marched towards Harpers Ferry ("Stonewall" Jackson's column headed in that direction via a roundabout march through Williamsport, Maryland, and Martinsburg, Virginia). The two other columns—under James Longstreet and D.H. Hill—followed in Jackson's footsteps, taking the National Road out of Frederick in the direction of Hagerstown.

However, contrary to what was *written* in Special Orders No. 191, only Hill stopped at the two columns' appointed destination—Boonsboro.[10] Rumors of Federals approaching Hagerstown from Pennsylvania compelled Lee to further divide his forces by continuing Longstreet's march until they reached Hagerstown, near the Mason-Dixon Line.[11]

Despite McClellan's certainty about the enemy's abandonment of Frederick, the fog of war still enveloped the enemy's movements as a new fold entered the intelligence sphere arriving at Union army headquarters. At 10 a.m. the next morning, September 12, McClellan reiterated to Halleck his belief in the enemy's abandonment of Frederick. This time, though, McClellan revealed that the route of the enemy's movement stretched in two very different directions—one on the road running practically north towards Hagerstown and the other headed south in the direction of Harpers Ferry.[12]

An enemy army in foreign territory moving two separate ways puzzled McClellan. Ambrose Burnside, in the van of the Army of the Potomac, was likewise perplexed: "I can hardly understand how they can be moving on

---

9   George B. McClellan to Henry Halleck, September 11, 1862, *OR*, vol. 19, pt. 2, 254.

10 The full text of Special Orders No. 191, *not* the Lost Order, is found in *OR*, vol. 19, pt. 2, 603.

11 Report of Robert E. Lee, *OR*, vol. 19, pt. 1, 145.

12 George B. McClellan to Henry Halleck, September 12, 1862, 10:00 am, *GBM Papers*, 448.

these two latter roads at the same time," he wondered. "If they are going into Pennsylvania they would hardly be moving upon the Harper's Ferry road, and if they are going to recross [the Potomac into Virginia], how could they be moving upon Gettysburg?"[13] Regardless of the confusion, the head of Burnside's column and portions of Alfred Pleasonton's cavalry command occupied Frederick by the evening of September 12.

The picture of Confederate dispositions percolating in McClellan's mind did become clearer to the commanding general on September 12. His afternoon dispatches show he favored the idea that Lee's main column was marching towards Williamsport, Maryland, to return to Virginia.[14] Even in a nighttime note, McClellan told President Lincoln, "The main body of my cavalry & horse artillery are ordered after the enemy's main column," using the National Road out of Frederick.[15]

However, hunches or estimations could not be solely relied upon in a campaign fraught with so many consequences should the United States Army fail. Thus, McClellan ultimately had to admit, "My movements to-morrow will be dependent upon information to be received during the night." But he told Burnside to bring his command to Frederick, prepared "to move in any direction that may be required."[16] The bloodhound caught the scent but did not yet know which path to follow. Above all of this, the question still hovered: What were the enemy's intentions by moving on two roads in opposite directions?

By September 12, the momentum of the campaign had begun to shift from Lee towards McClellan. Now in a position of relative strength, with the Army of the Potomac beginning to mass around Frederick, no longer was the talk in McClellan's dispatches of gathering reliable information. Rather, indications of striking at the enemy's main column and having his

13   Ambrose Burnside to Henry Halleck and George B. McClellan, September 12, 1862, 5:30 am, *OR*, vol. 19, pt. 2, 272-73.

14   See George B. McClellan to Mary Ellen McClellan, September 12, 1862, 3:00 pm, *GBM Papers*, 449.

15   George B. McClellan to Abraham Lincoln, September 12, 1862, 9:00 pm, *GBM Papers*, 452; Randolph B. Marcy to Ambrose Burnside, September 12, 1862, 11:00 pm, *OR*, vol. 51, pt. 1, 823.

16   George B. McClellan to Henry Halleck, September 12, 1862, 5:30 pm, *OR*, vol. 19, pt. 2, 271; Randolph B. Marcy to Ambrose Burnside, September 12, 1862, 6:15 pm, *OR*, vol. 51, pt. 1, 823; Randolph B. Marcy to Ambrose Burnside, September 12, 1862, 8:30 pm, ibid.

commands ready to move at a moment's notice dominate the correspondence of September 12. George McClellan was prepared to leap at the enemy, if only he could decipher exactly what that enemy was doing.

Saturday, September 13 began with Pleasonton's cavalrymen saddling their horses and organizing for action. By daybreak, the blue horsemen trotted out of their Frederick camps in all directions ready for another day's hard work. The weight of Pleasonton's command pushed west on the road to Williamsport and Hagerstown.[17] Alfred Pleasonton set a lofty bar for his command to meet that Saturday: "If possible I shall go to Hagerstown tomorrow," he reported on September 12.[18]

Only a few miles west of Frederick, the Union horsemen stumbled into J. E. B. Stuart's line of defense atop Catoctin Mountain. A battle ensued there for much of the morning and, with the help of Burnside's infantry, did not conclude until the early afternoon.[19] "A rapid pursuit was made," recounted Pleasonton and, following several other skirmishes around Middletown, the Army of the Potomac's cavalry ended the day at "the foot of [South] mountain."[20] The Confederate roadblock at Turner's Gap in South Mountain proved "to be too strong a position to be carried by my force," Pleasonton admitted, but help was on the way.[21]

In the time Pleasonton's soldiers further developed the enemy and its whereabouts all day on September 13, developments behind them carried the Maryland Campaign into its next stage. Sometime after noon on September 13, a lost copy of Lee's Special Orders No. 191 came into McClellan's hands.[22] What exactly the Lost Order told McClellan has been the subject of much heated debate and controversy almost from the moment he glanced at its contents.

---

17 Report of Alfred Pleasonton, *OR*, vol. 19, pt. 1, 209.

18   Alfred Pleasonton to Randolph B. Marcy, September 12, 1862, 9:15 pm, George B. McClellan Papers, Library of Congress (hereafter cited as GBM Papers, LOC) reel 31.

19 Alfred Pleasonton to Randolph B. Marcy, September 13, 1862, 1:00 pm, ibid.

20 Report of Alfred Pleasonton, *OR*, vol. 19, pt. 1, 209.

21 Ibid.

22   The timing of this being in the "evening" as compared to sometime before noon is clearly established in George B. McClellan to Henry W. Halleck, September 13, 1862, 11:00 pm, *OR*, vol. 19, pt. 2, 281.

From an intelligence standpoint, the Lost Order was important to McClellan, but not as important as has often been portrayed. It solidified in McClellan's mind exactly what Lee's odd movements were all about. "I obtained reliable information of the movements and intentions of the enemy, which made it clear that it was necessary to force the passage of the South Mountain range and gain possession of Boonsborough and Rohrersville before any relief could be afforded to Harper's Ferry."[23]

However, the Lost Order was four days old when McClellan read it, and the wording called for the various parts of Lee's plan to be achieved by Friday, September 12—the day before Union soldiers found the order.

Naturally, the first thing to be done was to get his cavalry chief Pleasonton to verify the days-old order. At 3:00 p.m., Chief of Staff Randolph B. Marcy updated Pleasonton's mission.[24] While Pleasonton's horsemen went about their business determining the veracity of the order, McClellan, now very aware of the possibility that Lee's army may be divided in his front, pushed more of his army in that direction almost instantaneously.[25]

McClellan set the van of his army in motion and continued to comb through the order. It did seem that the discovery was a great find, but for as much as it told McClellan of Lee's thus-far undetermined intentions, the fog of war did not dissipate like an early morning's blanket of haze.

First, the order—which had been addressed to Gen. D. H. Hill, dropped by someone in the Confederate army, and then scooped up by two Indiana soldiers—began with Paragraph III. Either the Confederate high command proved unable to count, or there was more to the order than what McClellan held in his hands. What did the first two paragraphs say further about Lee's intentions? A simple glance in the *Official Records* reveals that Paragraphs I and II state nothing about Confederate plans in Maryland. For McClellan to have known that, though, was an utter impossibility. Certainly, the unanswerable question hung over his head throughout all of this: What was missing from the Lost Order?[26]

---

23 Report of George B. McClellan, *OR*, vol. 19, pt. 1, 26.

24 Randolph B. Marcy to Alfred Pleasonton, September 13, 1862, 3:00 pm, *OR*, vol. 51, pt. 1, 829.

25 Randolph B. Marcy to Jacob D. Cox, September 13, 1862, 3:35 p.m., ibid., 827; Edward M. Neill to Orlando B. Willcox, September 13, 1862, ibid., 827-28.

The wayward copy of Special Orders No. 191 also did McClellan no favors in the numbers department. Earlier reports told McClellan of an enemy force numbering as high as 200,000 strong.[27] By the end of September 13, McClellan lowered this estimate not quite by half, concluding the enemy in his front "amounts to 120,000 men or more."[28] The Lost Order did not mention anything of troop strength, but clearly designates five separate enemy columns before dropping in two vague references to the main body. Was the main body another column or one of the columns already mentioned, just by a different name? In addition, the very essence of Lee's plan outlined in Special Orders No. 191 suggested a large number of Confederate soldiers in Maryland. Would the enemy divide itself into such disparate columns in a foreign land if it was such a small force? The Lost Order could not answer that question, either.

Despite all of this, McClellan did plan an attack for September 14, armed with the solid information he gleaned from Lee's campaign plan. He began moving his forces into position on September 13 to carry the next series of ridges cutting north-south across the landscape of western Maryland.[29]

So, if the Lost Order did not provide McClellan with all of the information that he might have sought from such a fortuitous find, then what did it do?

On the night of September 12, the Army of the Potomac's goal was to push west from Frederick and gain possession of Catoctin Mountain, a natural defensive barrier buttressed even more by Confederate cavalry guarding the mountain passes. McClellan hoped to carry this mountain and put Pleasonton's cavalry in position the next day to go up and over the next barrier facing him—South Mountain.

---

26   The full text of Special Orders No. 191 is found in *OR*, vol. 19, pt. 2, 603. The text of the Lost Order can be found in McClellan's Report, *OR*, vol. 19, pt. 1, 42-43. The Lost Order reproduced in McClellan's report omits the paragraph numbers, but the original copy of the Lost Order found in McClellan's papers in the Library of Congress show the oddly numbered order, GBM Papers, LOC, reel 31.

27   Andrew G. Curtin to George B. McClellan, September 10, 1862, 10:00 am, *OR*, vol. 19, pt. 2, 248.

28   McClellan to Halleck, September 13, 1862, 11:00 pm, ibid., 281.

29   In addition to the references previously cited in this work, George B. McClellan to William B. Franklin, September 13, 1862, 6:20 pm, *OR*, vol. 19, pt. 1, 45-46, also provides information about the Army of the Potomac moving into positions to strike at South Mountain and relieve Harpers Ferry on September 13.

The battle of South Mountain occurred on Sunday, September 14. Whether the Lost Order was discovered or not, the battle probably would have happened as a natural extension of the Federals' westward movement from Frederick. In McClellan's first written report of the campaign, dated October 15, 1862, he recalled that the first place he received "reliable information that the enemy's object was to move upon Harper's Ferry and the Cumberland Valley, and not upon Baltimore, Washington, or Gettysburg" was while in Urbana on September 12.[30]

This is not to declare that the Lost Order had no significance whatsoever. Until that document came into McClellan's hands, he was peering through a smoke screen, attempting to derive the intentions of his opponent mostly unsuccessfully. Where the Lost Order proved crucial to McClellan's intelligence reports was in its clear indication of what Confederate movements towards Harpers Ferry and the Maryland-Pennsylvania line meant.

The discovery of the Lost Order truly is an incredible tale. Who could not indulge in such a story? Its mysterious loss, its seemingly improbable find in an ordinary field, and its path up the chain of command into McClellan's grasp accord the story a status that few novelists could have better framed. Unfortunately, its significance to the outcome of the campaign—and the war, say some—has been too fancifully embroidered into the legend of the Civil War.

To say that the Lost Order's odyssey is insignificant misses the point. To say that everything that subsequently happened in the Maryland Campaign hinged on this amazing story likewise does not track the historical record. It is a story worthy of the ink spilled over its discovery, but the opposing armies still would have come to grips regardless of its loss and discovery.

What If McClellan Utilized His Reserves during the Battle of Antietam?

After the sun had set on the Antietam battlefield on September 17, 1862— the bloodiest day in U.S. military history—McClellan staffer David Hunter Strother settled in at army headquarters. After enjoying "a good supper," Strother began jotting his memories from the day in his diary. Reflecting on the day's action by candlelight, he concluded, "The Rebels chose their

---

30 McClellan's Report, ibid., 26-27.

position and we attacked. McClellan and Lee met face to face in a grand pitched battle on a fair field. Neither side can make excuses or complain of disadvantages. As far as the day went, we beat them with great slaughter and heavy loss to ourselves. How decisive the results of the action, time can only show when the smoke and dust shall have been blown away."[31] It has been more than one and a half centuries since the smoke and dust blew away from the Antietam Creek Valley, but the decisiveness of the battle's results are still debated today.

Historians generally accept the battle of Antietam as a tactical draw but a strategic Union victory.[32] Yet, in the earnest desire to better understand the American Civil War, students of the conflict have pondered how the Battle of Antietam might have been a truly decisive battlefield victory for the Army of the Potomac. When seeking to determine how that outcome might have happened, the Federal reserves at the battle are viewed as the hand McClellan could have used to sweep his adversaries from the field, into the Potomac River and oblivion. How many soldiers did the Army of the Potomac not utilize on September 17? And how much of a difference might they have made in the course of the war, and of American history?

As first light illuminated the fields and woodlots around Sharpsburg on September 17, 1862, two great armies awoke and prepared for their deadly task. That morning, McClellan stirred from his slumber at the Philip Pry house overlooking Antietam Creek.[33] While he pulled on his boots and buttoned his coat, the commanding general reviewed the forces at his disposal. Present with him on the field and in line were the entirety of the I, II, IX, and XII corps, plus George Sykes's V Corps division and Alfred Pleasonton's cavalry force, a total of approximately 54,300 soldiers ready for action.[34] Not on line but within a day's march of the Antietam battlefield

---

31   Cecil D. Eby Jr., ed., *A Virginia Yankee in the Civil War: The Diaries of David Hunter Strother* (Chapel Hill, NC: The University of North Carolina Press, 1989), 112.

32   The author personally believes the Army of the Potomac won a slight tactical victory on September 17.

33   Thomas G. Clemens, ed., *The Maryland Campaign of September 1862*, vol. 2, *Antietam* (El Dorado Hills, CA: Savas Beatie, 2012), 171.

34   Ibid., 569-84. The daybreak strength of Sykes' Division is not known with certainty. The figure used in this calculation, 3,900 strong, is derived from an average of the division strength figures recorded on September 10 and 20, 1862, as found in Daniel J. Vermilya, *"Perceptions,*

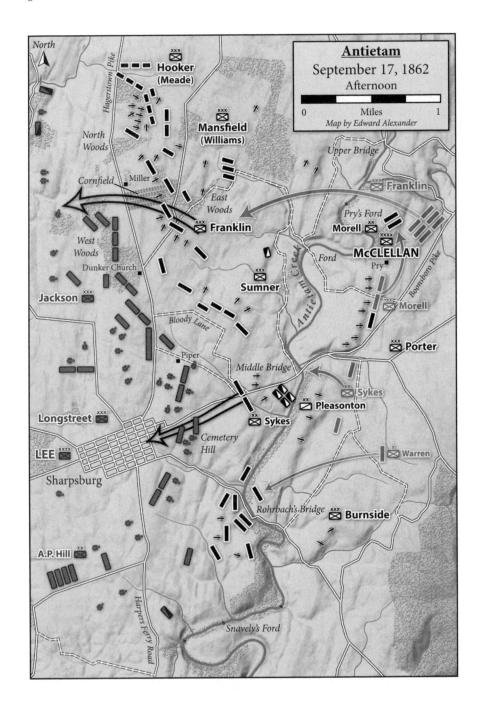

North

Antietam
September 17, 1862
Afternoon

0   Miles   1
Map by Edward Alexander

Hagerstown Pike

Hooker
(Meade)

Mansfield
(Williams)

North
Woods

Upper Bridge

Franklin

Cornfield   Miller

East
Woods

Pry's Ford
Morell

Franklin

McCLELLAN
Pry

West
Woods

Dunker Church

Ford

Boonsboro Pike

Jackson

Sumner

Antietam Creek

Morell

Bloody Lane

Piper

Porter

Middle Bridge

Longstreet

Sykes

Pleasonton

Sykes

Cemetery
Hill

Warren

LEE

Sharpsburg

Rohrbach's Bridge   Burnside

A.P. Hill

Harpers Ferry Road

Snavely's Ford

Antietam Initial success on the Federal right on the morning of September 17, 1862, preceded stalemate and repulse at the Sunken Road and West Woods, respectively. McClellan dispatched William Franklin's VI Corps to the East Woods to shore up the Federal right. Franklin sensed an opportunity to take the offensive, but II Corps commander Edwin Sumner swayed McClellan from ordering the attack. In the center of the line, roughly 2,000 Union soldiers pressed the Confederate center while the Army of the Potomac's reserves east of Antietam Creek dispersed and moved to both ends of the battlefield to support the army's flanks.

---

were George Morell's and Andrew Humphreys's V Corps divisions, Darius Couch's IV Corps troops, William Franklin's VI Corps, and 4,000 of the recently raised Pennsylvania Militia led by John Reynolds. These forces in the neighborhood of the battlefield (but not readily available at daybreak on September 17) totaled about 36,400 men.[35]

The previous evening, McClellan set his plan in motion to begin his attack against the Confederate left flank north of Sharpsburg. While this was the main effort, the commanding general built flexibility into the rest of his plan to exploit advantages as the battle developed. Ambrose Burnside commanded the assault on the Confederate right, which began several hours after the attack on the opposite end of the enemy line. For the center of his line, McClellan planned that when either of his offensives against both flanks of the enemy position "were fully successful, to attack their center with any reserve I might then have on hand."[36] However, McClellan's plan became fluid as events elsewhere on the battlefield affected the size of his reserves.

Initially, McClellan dispatched two corps under Joseph Hooker to strike the enemy's left. Thus, the entire II Corps and Sykes's division of the V Corps occupied the center of the Federal line and constituted McClellan's flexible reserve force. Once the general finished his personal preparations for the battle, he left the Pry House and moved to a commanding hill nearby

---

not Realities...": The Army of the Potomac in the Maryland Campaign (Sharpsburg, MD: Save Historic Antietam Foundation, 2012), 21.

35 The strengths for each force were drawn respectively from Vermilya, *"Perceptions,"* 21; Andrew Humphreys to Fitz John Porter, September 17, 1862, Box A80, Reel 32, George Brinton McClellan Papers, Library of Congress; A. M. Gambone, *Major-General Darius Couch: Enigmatic Valor* (Baltimore, MD: Butternut & Blue, 2000), 101; Vermilya, *"Perceptions,"* 21; John F. Reynolds to Henry Halleck, September 19, 1862, *OR*, vol. 19, pt. 2, 332.

36 *OR*, vol. 19, pt. 1, 30.

from where he could monitor the battle against the Confederate left. Here, McClellan "had a splendid view of Hooker's advance driving the enemy before them in rapid and disordered flight."[37] At this moment, buoyed by the early success, McClellan demonstrated the flexibility of his fluid reserve. At 7:20 a.m., he dispatched two-thirds of the II Corps across the Antietam Creek to support Hooker's attack.[38] In order to keep his reserve strong and ready for offensive action, McClellan offset the displacement of the II Corps with George Morell's V Corps division.[39]

Throughout September 17, the numbers at McClellan's disposal varied. Union casualties mounted, but additional troops arrived on the battlefield. The largest force to join the Army of the Potomac was William Franklin's VI Corps, which reached the rear of the army about 10 a.m.[40] When the head of the VI Corps' column reached McClellan, he remained steadfast to his philosophy of the fluid reserve and planned to mix the newly arrived soldiers into it. McClellan told one division commander of the corps "to remain with my command to be transferred to the right or left as circumstances might require."[41] Soon, circumstances out of anyone's control began to dictate the size and punch of any reserve McClellan intended to keep and use in the center of the battlefield.

On the west side of Antietam Creek, any jubilation McClellan felt over Hooker's early success had vanished by the time the VI Corps arrived. John Sedgwick's II Corps division was roughly handled by a Confederate counterattack in the West Woods that shredded it. The Federals streamed from the woodlot and left behind forty percent casualties, all in a matter of less than thirty minutes.[42] "Re-enforcements [sic] are badly wanted,"

---

37 David Hunter Strother, "Personal Recollections of the War by a Virginian," *Harper's New Monthly Magazine*, February 1868, 281.

38 Marion V. Armstrong Jr., *Unfurl Those Colors! McClellan, Sumner,* (Tuscaloosa, AL: The University of Alabama Press, 2008), 167. The last division of the II Corps later joined the two preceding divisions.

39 Clemens, ed., *The Maryland Campaign*, vol. 2, *Antietam*, 263.

40 Ibid., 304.

41 Herbert M. Schiller, ed., *Autobiography of Major General William F. Smith 1861-1864* (Dayton, OH: Morningside House, Inc., 1990), 53.

42 Clemens, ed., *The Maryland Campaign*, vol. 2, *Antietam*, 575; *OR*, vol. 19, pt. 1, 193.

Sumner wigwagged to McClellan. "Our troops are giving way."[43] Desperate messages like this forced McClellan's hand. He had to support his faltering right wing and the VI Corps provided the ideal stop gap.[44]

Franklin's men marched to bolster the beleaguered Federal right, but their transfer to this endangered sector was not instantaneous. In the interim, Sumner and his chief of artillery, Francis Clarke, wheeled together a line of guns that stretched nearly one mile and contained sixty-eight artillery pieces, roughly one gun every 26 yards. This would stabilize the army's right flank and serve as a useful support for any future infantry assaults. Buoyed by this array of artillery, Sumner went about preparing his soldiers for a renewal of the assault.[45]

Simultaneous to Sumner's strengthening of the Federal right and Franklin's march to that end of the field, McClellan's reserve in the center of the field began to stir. First, elements of Pleasonton's cavalry force streamed across the Middle Bridge. Several batteries of horse artillery trundled behind the cavalrymen, dropped trail, and began engaging the Confederate center. The Union gunners "opened such a spirited and accurate fire" against the enemy to their front and continually drove Confederate batteries to the reverse slope of the ridge they stood on.[46]

Hunkered underneath the sailing Federal shells were Confederate skirmishers posted in front of their main line. These prepared marksmen peppered the Union artillerymen with an effective fire. Pleasonton's cavalry vainly tried to give their own artillerymen breathing room, but the Confederate skirmishers could not be driven from their positions. Pleasonton needed help.

He called upon the nearest infantrymen to sweep the enemy skirmishers away. Brigadier General George Sykes's Regular infantry division stood closest. Sykes incrementally released his regiments to the ground west of Antietam Creek. By 3 p.m., 1,640 United States Regular infantrymen stood among the Federal horse artillery batteries. Before crossing the creek, their commander, Capt. Hiram Dryer, received his orders from Sykes: "support

---

43 Edwin Sumner to George McClellan, September 17, 1862, *OR*, vol. 19, pt. 1, 134.

44 Ibid., 61.

45 Armstrong, *Unfurl Those Colors!*, 268.

46 Clemens, ed., *The Maryland Campaign*, vol. 2, *Antietam*, 359-64.

the batteries and to dislodge the enemy from certain haystacks" to give the artillerymen a reprieve from the annoying rifle fire.[47]

It was about this point in the battle where McClellan's plan for his reserves changed from an offensive to a defensive strategy. McClellan telegraphed Henry Halleck in the midst of the battle at 1:20 p.m. that the result "of the most terrible battle of the war" favored his army. McClellan told Halleck that his army attacked both flanks of the Confederate line "and I hold my small reserve, consisting of Porter's (Fifth) corps, ready to attack the center as soon as the flank movements are developed."[48] His reserve was small because he stripped it of the II and VI Corps to follow up the early morning's success and to buttress the faltering situation on the army's right, respectively. All he had left in the center were the two divisions of Porter's Corps, about 8,000 men.[49]

Shortly after sending the above dispatch to Halleck, a dispute between two of his subordinates on the army's right flank compelled McClellan to travel to that sector of his line. Sumner had originally hoped to renew the Federal offensive north of Sharpsburg as did the newly arrived William Franklin.[50] However, Sumner's early enthusiasm for the offensive waned slightly, and he postponed any attack by Franklin's troops, claiming, "If it failed the right would be entirely destroyed, as there were no troops there that could be depended upon." Franklin argued the attack must be made, but Sumner won out.[51] Still believing he was right, Franklin enlisted one of McClellan's staff officers to ride to the commanding general and inform him of the dispute.

During his ride to the army's right, McClellan witnessed the destruction that siphoned multiple corps from the center of his line into the maelstrom on the field's northern end. But he initially remained committed to renewing the

---

47 Ibid., 366-69.

48 George B. McClellan to Henry Halleck, September 17, 1862, 1:20 p.m., *OR*, vol. 19, pt. 2, 312.

49 Daniel J. Vermilya, *"Perceptions, not Realities...": The Army of the Potomac in the Maryland Campaign* (Sharpsburg, MD: Save Historic Antietam Foundation, 2012), 23.

50 *OR*, vol. 19, pt. 1, 377.

51 Testimony of William B. Franklin, *Report of the Joint Committee on the Conduct of the War*, vol. 1 (Wilmington, NC: Broadfoot Publishing Company, 1998), 626.

assault here. "We must fight tonight
and to-morrow. If we cannot whip
the enemy now, we may as well die
upon the field. If we succeed we
end the war," he told one brigade
commander. However, the sights of
the battlefield dimmed McClellan's
optimism. The army's right was a
glass wall—sturdy for now, but
easily shattered if Franklin's attack
failed. Burnside's assault south of
Sharpsburg was about to begin,
and Sykes's division was across
the Middle Bridge. The risk-averse
McClellan decided that to renew
the offensive on his right with
a grim chance of success might
negate the army's accomplishments
elsewhere. No, he told Franklin.[52]
To ensure his right was secure,
the commanding general stripped
his center even further, taking two

Maj. Gen. William B. Franklin argued for a
vigorous attack north of Sharpsburg on the
afternoon of September 17, which would
have gone forward in concert with Burnside's
assault. What if McClellan had given him the
green light? *Library of Congress*

infantry brigades from Porter to shore up Sumner's line. McClellan later
countermanded the order, but by the time those brigades arrived back in the
V Corps sector, the sunlight gave way to darkness.[53]

When McClellan returned to the center of his line, Burnside's assault
was underway. Hiram Dryer's Federals had become equally engaged with
the enemy in their front and successfully drove them over Cemetery Hill
into Sharpsburg.[54] McClellan's decision not to renew attacks north of
Sharpsburg so as not to endanger the offensive operations of his center and
left seemed to be paying off. However, as Dryer prepared his men for one

---

52 Armstrong, *Unfurl Those Colors!*, 272-73.

53 *OR*, vol. 19, pt. 1, 349.

54 The most advanced position of Dryer's skirmishers is where the Antietam National
Cemetery parking lot sits today.

more push through the enemy's center, a courier arrived ordering him to halt his movements and withdraw to a ridge in their rear "and maintain a defensive position."[55]

Sykes's men initially crossed to the west side of Antietam Creek "to support the horse batteries and cavalry immediately in front of Sharpsburg," reported V Corps commander Fitz John Porter. Dryer's men were "diverted from that service, and employed to drive the enemy's skirmishers to their reserves," which resulted in their lodgment near the crest of Cemetery Hill.[56] Dryer's pushing of his men beyond to Cemetery Hill exceeded his orders. Thus, Sykes ordered the suspension of the movement altogether.[57]

While Sykes's thoughts turned to the defensive by mid-afternoon of September 17, Alfred Pleasonton, commanding the cavalry Sykes was supporting, believed otherwise. Around 3 p.m., Pleasonton sent a dispatch to army headquarters for more infantry to support his guns. "General McClellan directs me to say he has no infantry to spare," headquarters replied 30 minutes later. "Confer with Major-General Porter," the note continued.[58] Dodged by headquarters, Pleasonton followed up with Porter. All signs from his left—Burnside's sector—indicated success. Porter told Sykes, "Burnside is driving the enemy. Please send word to the command you sent to Pleasonton, to support his batteries, and let him drive them."[59] Just minutes after that dispatch left Porter's hand, the tide of Burnside's battle changed. Confederate reserves and difficult terrain spent Burnside's attack and sent it reeling back to its starting point. The withdrawal of Burnside's command left the V Corps' adjacent line exposed. With no infantry left to spare, Sykes and Porter pulled their men back from the Confederate center.

It is at this point that historians have stepped into their subjects and played the role of armchair generals. Armed with hindsight, their arsenal

---

55 Clemens, ed., *The Maryland Campaign*, vol. 2, *Antietam*, 384-85.

56 *OR*, vol. 19, pt. 1, 339.

57 Clemens, ed., *The Maryland Campaign*, vol. 2, *Antietam*, 384-85.

58 Randolph B. Marcy to Alfred Pleasonton, *OR*, vol. 51, pt. 1, 845.

59 Fitz John Porter to George Sykes, *OR*, vol. 19, pt. 2, 316.

of facts unknown to the participants have cemented in our minds without a doubt what would have happened if certain events had transpired in any other way than they actually did. However, rather than dealing in the hypothetical, it is more useful as historians to take what we know happened—to examine why those known events occurred the way they did. Dwelling on what could have been is a fruitless venture for historians.

Perhaps the largest "what if" of Antietam—maybe of McClellan's entire life—is what might have happened had McClellan determined to better utilize his reserves, Porter's V and Franklin's VI corps, to achieve an overwhelming victory.

Franklin's troops are often considered reserves on the battlefield, but the VI Corps held a

What if Maj. Gen. Fitz John Porter, arguably the most competent and hard-fighting corps commander in the Army of the Potomac, had gone in with his reserves at Antietam? Would one more strong battlefield performance have been enough to protect him from being scapegoated for Union failures at Second Manassas? His subsequent court-martial served as a proxy for his close friend, George McClellan. *Library of Congress*

position on the army's front lines to bolster the three corps of Hooker, Sumner, and Mansfield, each of which took heavy casualties in the morning's action.[60]

What then did Fitz John Porter's V Corps have available to bring to the fight in the center of the battlefield at the time of Dryer's advance? Like the rest of the army's central reserve throughout the day, Porter's corps had been cannibalized and dispersed across the fields east of the Antietam. Two brigades briefly marched north to Sumner's aid while Gouverneur Warren's small brigade went south to back Burnside. Thus, when he was asked to push more troops toward Cemetery Hill, Porter could only write, "I had not

---

60 Clemens, ed., *The Maryland Campaign*, vol. 2, *Antietam*, 584, 601. Proportionately, those three corps suffered the following casualties of their total strength: I Corps (27.4% casualties), II Corps (32.0% casualties), XII Corps (22.9% casualties).

the force asked for." Furthermore, "my small command [was] then 4,000 strong—then in the front line and unsupported," confessed Porter.[61]

George Sykes equally dimmed the strength in the Federal center. In an oft-quoted passage from Sykes's after-action report, the general wrote of Dryer's effort, "There is no doubt he could have crowned the Sharpsburg heights." But the preface to this line is sometimes omitted. Sykes wrote on September 30, 1862, "Had there been an available force for their support, there is no doubt he could have crowned the Sharpsburg heights."[62]

When the Battle of Antietam began at dawn on September 17, the forces McClellan relied upon to be in his reserve were many. Circumstances on the battlefield rushed his reserves to other sectors of the field. When the time came to throw the center of his line into action, McClellan felt it was not strong enough to risk its repulse. What that force might have accomplished if it had been used is impossible to determine.

What If McClellan Pursued the Army of Northern Virginia Immediately After the Battle of Antietam?

If McClellan's failure to use his few reserves is counted against him on the historiographical scoreboard, then the general's supposed lack of a pursuit to the Potomac River has buried him just as deeply. Unfortunately, the operations along the river in the immediate aftermath of the battle of Antietam have received little attention when compared to the rest of the campaign.[63] In fact, though the Army of the Potomac did pursue the Army

---

61   *OR*, vol. 19, pt. 1, 338-39.

62   Ibid., 351. See Timothy J. Reese, *Sykes' Regular Infantry Division, 1861-1864: A History of United States Infantry Operations in the Civil War's Eastern Theater* (Jefferson, NC: McFarland & Company, Inc., 1990), 146, for an example of Sykes' quote being cherry-picked.

63   Four of the most-read studies of the Maryland Campaign hardly pay attention to the actions along the Potomac River that occurred on September 19 and 20. James McPherson, *Battle Cry of Freedom: The Civil War Era* (New York, NY: Oxford University Press, 1988), 544, covers the actions in one sentence. McPherson, *Crossroads of Freedom*, 130-31, summarizes this period of the campaign in one paragraph, as does Stephen W. Sears, *Landscape Turned Red: The Battle of Antietam* (New York, NY: Book-of-the-Month Club, Inc., 1994), 307. James V. Murfin, *The Gleam of Bayonets: The Battle of Antietam and the Maryland Campaign of 1862* (New York, NY: Thomas Yoseloff, 1965), 304-06, dedicates the most space to these actions. It was not until 2008 when a book length study of the Battle of Shepherdstown was published. See Thomas A. McGrath, *Shepherdstown: Last Clash of the Antietam Campaign, September 19-20, 1862* (Lynchburg, VA: Schroeder Publications, 2008).

of Northern Virginia to the Potomac River and engage it in the concluding days of the Maryland Campaign, this question, or some variation of it, is still asked by visitors to Antietam National Battlefield today.[64]

With all of his options in Maryland exhausted after the battle of Antietam, Robert E. Lee determined to withdraw his army across the Potomac River into Virginia under the cover of night on September 18. But this retrograde movement was not a permanent retreat into Virginia and an abandonment of his campaign. Rather, Lee intended to bring his army into Virginia, put the Potomac River between his army and the enemy, and, stealing a march on the Army of the Potomac, reenter Maryland via Williamsport and resume the campaign.[65]

While Lee did not believe his operations in Maryland were over when he joined his soldiers in their withdrawal from Sharpsburg on the evening of September 18, he did believe the enemy was powerless to disrupt his plan. "I believed Genl. McClellan had been so crippled at Sharpsburg, that he could not follow the Confederate army into Virginia," the general recalled in 1866.[66] His dispositions at the crossing point of the river support Lee's postwar statement. At Boteler's Ford one mile downstream from Shepherdstown, Lee left a scanty rearguard to shoo any Federal pursuit. Lee's artillery chief, William Nelson Pendleton, guarded the crossing point with 44 guns, 600 infantry, and no more than 200 horsemen.[67] While Pendleton held the ford, the rest of the Confederate army trekked upriver towards Williamsport.

Lee's withdrawal began "about sundown" to cover his army's movements. Darkness dampened enemy pursuit prospects. But the darkness that obscured what the eye could see did not hide what Federal ears heard. Reports flowed into McClellan's headquarters almost immediately that movement was detected within the enemy's lines. Edwin Sumner, commanding the Union II Corps, wrote a dispatch at 11:30 p.m. on the night

64   The author has been asked a question like this multiple while giving tours of the Maryland Campaign. He is currently at work on a study of the last three days of the campaign, September 18-20, 1862.

65   Harsh, *Taken at the Flood*, 444-45.

66   Robert E. Lee to Mary Anna Jackson, January 25, 1866, Lee Family Papers, Virginia Museum of History and Culture.

67   Harsh, *Taken at the Flood*, 458.

of September 18 believing the enemy was retiring from his front.[68] Sumner, as well as other officers, reported the sounds of artillery and "chopping as of felling trees," an indicator of a retreat.[69] In response to these and other reports, McClellan instructed each of his corps commanders to advance their pickets and, if the Confederates had retreated, "to mass your troops in readiness to move in any direction." Alfred Pleasonton's cavalry forces would lead the way, follow the enemy, and determine if there were any obstructions to a pursuit.[70] Before Pleasonton's advance began however, Fitz John Porter sent six men and one officer into Sharpsburg "with orders to go as far as they could." This detachment passed through Sharpsburg and still had not encountered the enemy before they returned to their starting point, leaving Porter baffled as to the enemy's whereabouts.[71]

McClellan dispatched Pleasonton's cavalry at 8:00 a.m. to pass beyond Sharpsburg and locate the enemy. Upon reaching the banks of the Potomac River, the cavalrymen were greeted by shrieking artillery shells that cut the ground at their horses' feet.[72] Notes from the front and the boom of distant cannon told McClellan the enemy was found. "We are again in pursuit," the general told his superiors in Washington.[73]

Now that the enemy's location was discovered and the immediate pursuit over, McClellan had to determine his next step. When he entered the campaign, he embarked from Washington with the understanding that

---

68   Randolph Marcy to Edwin Sumner, September 19, 1862, 4 am, *OR* 51, 1:849-50. Sumner's dispatch of September 18, 11:30 am appears to not have survived but its content and time can be inferred from Marcy to Sumner, September 19, 1862, 4 am, *OR* 51, 1:849-50.

69   Ibid.; John W. Williams to "General," September 19, 1862, 2:45 am, GBM Papers.

70   Randolph Marcy to Fitz John Porter, September 19, 1862, *OR* 19, 2:331.

71   Fitz John Porter to George B. McClellan, September 20, 1862, GBM Papers. This dispatch is dated September 20, 1862 but that surely must be wrong, as movements described therein would only make sense when examining September 19. See also William H. Powell, *The Fifth Army Corps (Army of the Potomac)* (New York: G.P. Putnam›s Sons, 1896), 293 for a reconnaissance conducted by the Second Maine Infantry on the morning of September 19, which states that they made it all the way to the Potomac River. However, this seems unlikely based on the apparent lack of knowledge of the enemy's positions until Pleasonton's cavalry reached the river (see George McClellan to Henry Halleck, September 19, 1862, 8:30 am, *OR* 19, 2:330).

72   Abner Hard, *History of the Eighth Cavalry Regiment Illinois Volunteers, During the Great Rebellion* (Aurora, IL: n.p., 1868), 187-88.

73   George B. McClellan to Henry W. Halleck, September 19, 1862, 8:30 am, *OR* 19, 2:330.

his objectives were "to cover Baltimore, prevent the invasion of Pennsylvania, and drive [the enemy] out of Maryland." Thus far, McClellan had achieved each of those aims.[74]

The static situation along the Potomac River was changing by mid-morning of September 19. Pendleton's thin rearguard was holding its own against Pleasonton's cavalry and horse artillery. Pleasonton requested help, and McClellan forwarded Franklin's VI Corps for support. However, aware that his objectives were accomplished, that his army and its high command suffered heavily in the previous battles in Maryland, and that his forces were in need of rest, McClellan gave Franklin limited goals. He ordered his corps commander to unlimber his batteries and counter the enemy's fire but not expose his own men or "cross

What if Army of the Potomac commander George McClellan pursued the Army of Northern Virginia more aggressively in the weeks after Robert E. Lee finally gave up his invasion plans and retreated back into Virginia? Federals faced significant supply shortages and other logistics issues that no amount of political pressure could have erased. *Library of Congress*

the river without further orders."[75] McClellan pursued his enemy to the river; now, he had to ensure they remained on the south side of it.

Hours after the soldiers of the VI Corps began marching towards Shepherdstown, events elsewhere along the river altered their destination. A report from upriver reached McClellan claiming that J.E.B. Stuart "with 4,000 cavalry and six pieces of artillery" was moving in the direction of

74 *OR*, vol. 19, pt. 1, 25.

75 Randolph Marcy to William Franklin, September 19, 1862, 11:45 am, *OR* 51, 1:851.

Williamsport beyond McClellan's right flank. Behind Stuart's strike force was a column of infantry, said the rumor. To counter this threat, McClellan halted the VI Corps and ordered a division of infantry to make haste to Williamsport.[76]

Additionally, the potential for another danger existed downriver from Shepherdstown and Boteler's Ford. There, Harpers Ferry was unoccupied. As long as it remained so, Confederates could cross the Potomac River there to menace the Federals' left flank or maneuver in the direction of Washington. To seal this crossing, McClellan ordered one corps to occupy the riverine town.[77]

Meanwhile, back on the Maryland bluffs overlooking Boteler's Ford, Porter's V Corps stepped into line and replaced the VI Corps, which might be needed in the Williamsport sector. Porter's instructions from headquarters remained essentially the same: not to cross the river "unless you see a splendid opportunity to inflict great damage upon the enemy without much loss to yourself."[78] Around dusk, Porter saw his opportunity.

When the V Corps reached the Boteler's Ford sector, its commander sent infantry skirmishers to the riverbank to apply additional pressure on the Confederate rearguard. These infantrymen opened fire on the Confederate cannoneers.[79] "This proved to us an evil not slightly trying," reported Pendleton.[80] The subsequent slackening of Confederate fire drew Federal infantry across the river like a magnet. As the sun neared the horizon, 400 infantry stormed across the ford and scattered Pendleton's force. The Federals, still wringing water from their socks, counted "5 artillery pieces, 2 caissons, 2 caisson bodies, 2 forges, and some 400 stand of arms; also 1 battle-flag" as their booty.[81] Before the affair was decided,

---

76 Randolph Marcy to Darius N. Couch, September 19, 1862, *OR* 51, 1:852.

77 Randolph Marcy to Edwin Sumner, September 19, 1862, 12:15 p.m., ibid., 850.

78   Randolph Marcy to Alfred Pleasonton, September 19, 1862, 1:15 pm, *OR* 51, 1:853. While these are headquarters' instructions to Pleasonton, Porter's actions indicate that these same orders applied to his command.

79 *OR*, vol. 19, pt. 1, 340.

80 Ibid., 832.

81 Ibid., 340.

Pendleton headed for the rear to inform his commanding general of the dire situation at the river.

In the darkness, Pendleton traveled from command to command soliciting help and the whereabouts of the army commander. Finally, early the next morning, he arrived at the tent of the only man in whose power rested the ability to do anything about Pendleton's predicament at the ford. As far as the artillery officer knew, those Federals that crossed the Potomac carried away all of his artillery—44 guns! "All?" Lee asked in disbelief. "Yes, General, I fear, all," Pendleton replied sheepishly.[82] Quickly, Lee's intentions for Williamsport came unhinged. An unknown but likely sizable Federal force now stood in his rear, poised to strike the Army of Northern Virginia while in motion to Williamsport. This could not be ignored. Lee called on one of his staff officers to draw up orders to send Stonewall Jackson's command and parts of James Longstreet's back to Boteler's Ford to deal with this peril.[83] Lee's strategy for resuming the campaign was on hold thanks to the Federal pursuit.

Back on the north side of the Potomac, McClellan was feeling secure with his success at Boteler's Ford and soldiers on their way to points upstream and downstream from the ford to anchor the army's flanks on the river. At the river itself, Union soldiers interrogated the Confederate prisoners they recently gobbled up. One chatty Southerner spoke poorly of the state of his army. Already salivating at his captures that evening, Porter proposed to McClellan a morning reconnaissance-in-force to seek opportunities to further exploit his triumph. The commanding general raised no objections.[84]

Portions of two V Corps infantry divisions crossed at the ford shortly after sunrise on September 20. Once across, one column trudged westward and the other due south to search for enemy forces.[85] Nearly one mile from the river, the southward column ran into the vanguard of the Army of

---

82 Emily V. Mason, *Popular Life of Gen. Robert Edward Lee*, 2nd ed. (Baltimore: John Murphy & Co., 1874), 151. In reality, the Federals only captured four guns but that fact was unknown to Pendleton when he made his report to Lee and unknown to Lee when he ordered elements of his army to march away from Williamsport and back towards Shepherdstown.

83 Robert E. Lee to Mary Anna Jackson, January 25, 1866, Lee Family Papers, Virginia Museum of History and Culture.

84 Fitz John Porter to George B. McClellan, September 19, 1862, 9:00 pm, GBM Papers.

85 F. S. Earle to James Barnes, September 20, 1862, *OR* 19, 1:346.

Northern Virginia heading back to the scene of the previous night's action. The Union commander on the field, George Sykes, recognized that the south side of the river, with steep bluffs behind his soldiers overlooking the ford, was no place to fight a defensive battle and ordered his troops back across the river.[86] The westward column was diverted from its trek to deploy atop the bluffs and cover the withdrawal of the rest of the reconnaissance.[87]

As the Unionists shook out into their battle formations, A.P. Hill's Confederate division, in the van of the gray column, began their attack in the face of infantry and artillery fire. Sykes's soldiers stoutly resisted Hill's men. But their purpose was not to defend, only to delay the enemy to facilitate the safe withdrawal of their comrades. Once it was time to do so, the Federals facing Hill's soldiers began their withdrawal.

In the confusion of the moment, one regiment, the green 118th Pennsylvania Infantry, did not heed the order to withdraw. Instead, it briefly stood toe-to-toe against Hill's entire division. Ultimately, the Pennsylvanians' heroics wavered under the pressure from Hill's Confederates. Soon, they broke. The 118th Pennsylvania was the last Federal unit to reach the river's northern shore and suffered dearly for the costly error. A.P. Hill's success erased the enemy threat against the rear of Lee's army but it, coupled with events upriver, had its own consequences.[88]

The columns of the army that moved back to Shepherdstown marched under Lee's personal scrutiny. What the commanding general witnessed did not please him. Straggling and "confusion and hesitation" by the line officers crippled his army's effectiveness. The reversal of the army's march to Shepherdstown exacerbated this situation. To make matters worse, Lee received word from Stuart the next morning that his foothold in Williamsport collapsed under increased Federal pressure—the troops McClellan had dispatched to that area.[89] All of this forced Lee to face the facts that his Maryland Campaign was over. "[T]he condition of our troops

---

86   *OR*, vol. 19, pt. 1, 352.

87   George Sykes to Fitz John Porter, September 20, 1862, 9:15 am, *OR* 19, 2:334-35.

88   An excellent source covering the 118th Pennsylvania's experience at the Battle of Shepherdstown is Mark A. Snell, "Baptism of Fire: The 118th Pennsylvania," *Civil War Regiments* 6, no. 2 (1998): 119-42.

89   Harsh, *Taken at the Flood*, 466.

now demanded repose," he wrote.[90] His plan to reenter Maryland and regain the initiative in order to dictate the pace of the campaign on his own terms was undone by the Army of the Potomac's pursuit to its namesake river and, however ironically, a Confederate victory on the bluffs of Shepherdstown.

Though relatively short in duration, the Maryland Campaign is replete with moments in which the operation's outcome might have changed quickly and dramatically for both army and nation. Despite the conclusions of modern historians, George B. McClellan believed he fought the campaign and battle "splendidly."[91] However, contemporary sources do not always support twentieth century evaluations of McClellan's performance.

One week after the Battle of Antietam, Union surgeon Thomas Ebright wrote home, "Like the great battles of Waterloo, Bunker Hill, Valley Forge or Trenton, [Antietam] is destined to furnish material for volumes in years to come."[92] As more volumes are filled, the debates about McClellan's generalship in western Maryland will continue.

90 *OR*, vol. 19, pt. 1, 152.

91   George B. McClellan to Mary Ellen McClellan, September 18, 1862, 8:00 a.m., *GBM Papers*, 469.

92   "Letter from Dr. Ebright," September 24, 1862, in *Holmes County Farmer* (Millersburg, OH), October 9, 1862.

CHAPTER THREE

What If Great Britain

Had Intervened in the American Civil War?

Dwight Hughes

The people and leaders of Great Britain were horrified, confounded, and conflicted by the conflict raging in North America: horrified by the slaughter, confounded by the reasons for it, and conflicted about what to do. This overseas squabble drastically disrupted their trade and economy, caused rampant unemployment, and set the people against each other. Britons overwhelmingly preferred peace, but having built their huge empire, they were not inclined to tolerate such threats to national interests.

Great Britain had fought Americans twice in the past eighty years; old enmities smoldered from the Revolution and War of 1812. They would go to war again if necessary. Contrarily, powerful humanitarian impulses called for action to stop the carnage among former countrymen with whom they shared so much. Should the world's most powerful nation remain neutral or should she intercede, perhaps forcefully, to stop the war? If so, how?

For over two years, debate raged in the halls of Parliament and throughout the country with insistent voices on both sides. Neutrality prevailed, but it was close. Had British diplomats and arms inserted themselves between the United and Confederate States, the most probable scenarios at the time culminated in the latter's independence.

There was, however, no comfortably neutral position between American combatants, one of whom employed every stratagem to ensnare Great Britain in the dispute while the other insisted they would fight to keep her out. Ancient and thorny arguments resurfaced over the rights and responsibilities of neutral nations in wartime, disturbing echoes of those previous conflicts.

The Confederacy declared itself a legitimate revolutionary movement striving in a fierce civil war to midwife a nation. As such, they demanded international recognition and support. United States President Abraham Lincoln and his Secretary of State, William H. Seward, insisted Confederates were not revolutionaries but rebels engaged in insurrection. It was no one else's business. They hammered these themes into every policy and communication. They were determined to delegitimize the "so-called Confederacy," isolate rebels, and prevent outside interference.

After centuries of bloody war between emerging European nation states, the mid nineteenth century struggled to constrain and to impose humanitarian inhibitions on military violence. In a burgeoning global economy fueled by industrialization and vast trade networks, war was increasingly defined as officially declared conflict between recognized belligerents governed by internationally understood rules.

The rules for inter-state violence resided in heterogeneous collections of treaties, legal decisions, domestic laws, and common practice to protect the vital concerns of non-belligerents—neutrals—in wartime. They also were suitably ambiguous. Effectiveness was grounded in mutual self-interest and bounded by what one could get away with. Neutrals in one conflict could be belligerents in the next.

However, the definition of and rules concerning civil war—intra-state violence—were much less well-defined, particularly the point at which civil war required compliance with the rules and legitimized foreign intervention. These distinctions were (and are) highly subjective, usually clarified only after the fact by the victors.

The new U. S. president's naval strategy—also a key element in Lt. Gen. Winfield Scott's "Anaconda Plan"—was to interdict trade with seceded states, starving them of funds, war materials, and necessities. Advisors proposed that Lincoln simply declare southern ports administratively closed, providing the navy an excuse to turn back merchant vessels under the guise of enforcing customs laws and duties not collectable in rebel-controlled harbors.

During a dinner at the British legation in March 1861, Secretary Seward tested the waters with British Ambassador Lord Lyons, suggesting that warships would be stationed off the coast for this purpose. Lyons responded directly: "If the United States determined to stop by force so important a commerce as that of Great Britain with the cotton-growing States, I could not answer for what might happen. . . . An immense pressure would be put upon Her Majesty's Government to use all the means in their power to open these ports."[1]

Foreign vessels, primarily British, carried most of the South's seaborn trade—especially now that Yankees were out of the business. Obstructing peaceful passage of their merchant vessels was an act of war against them. Lincoln could not strangle the rebellion in this way. He could not even halt the import of weapons and military supplies—legitimate items of foreign commerce—upon which Confederate armies depended.

The alternative was a formal blockade, itself an act of war that tacitly affirmed the combatants as belligerents in international law. Despite this glaring inconsistency, the president officially declared a seemingly impossible, continent-wide blockade on April 19, 1861, just one week after Fort Sumter—his first major strategic decision. The possibility of another war with Great Britain over interrupted trade became real and immediate. Would they respect the blockade or fight it?

On May 13, Queen Victoria officially proclaimed neutrality, formally recognizing the Confederacy as a belligerent. France and other nations followed. With a constitution, a government, an army, a population of nine million people, and effective control over 750,000 square miles of territory, the Confederacy constituted a belligerent power. This was not recognition as an independent nation. However, belligerents were eligible for such recognition by foreign governments—and insurrectionists were not. The Queen's proclamation likewise gave her government sanction to openly discuss which side, if any, to support without being accused of interference in another nation's internal affairs.

Belligerents had three superior rights: the right to halt and inspect suspect ships of all nations on the high seas; the right to confiscate military supplies—contraband—intended for the enemy; and the right to blockade the enemy. Lincoln's declaration of blockade necessarily provided legal justification for interdicting trade with the South. The British declaration necessarily extended protections of neutral status to their merchant vessels, which could not be interfered with so long as they did not carry contraband and respected the blockade.

---

1   Dean B. Mahin, *One War at a Time: The International Dimensions of the American Civil War* (Washington, D.C.: Potomac Books, 1999), 45-48. For additional information, see Chapter 3, "A Powerlessness to Comprehend, British Reactions to the American Civil War."

Blockade running was not illegal, but if caught, seizure or destruction of a British ship and cargo was not contestable, and the British government was not liable for their protection. Risk resided with ship owners, shippers, and ship masters, many of whom were perfectly willing to take it considering the initial porousness of the blockade and immense profits to be made. The capturing power must, however, legitimize their prizes through formal adjudication in a duly constituted admiralty court.

Not appreciating the subtleties of international law and British concerns, Yankees were outraged and Southerners delighted that the Queen had taken what appeared to be a major step toward recognition. Confederates contended that Lincoln's blockade announcement carried *de facto* recognition because countries do not blockade their own ports.

Ironically, the positions of the two nations were historically reversed. As the world's leading maritime power and largest trader, the British tended to restrain ocean commerce of other nations. They dealt harshly with neutrals—primarily the United States—doing business with enemies, most recently during the French wars of revolution and empire. They insisted that neutrals honor blockades of belligerent nations. Americans, meanwhile, clung to the edge of their continent, surviving and prospering on commerce.

Colonial trading rights had been a primary issue in the Revolution. The new nation fought for neutral trade during the Quasi War with France (1798-1800), and in 1812 again declared war with Great Britain on these issues. But the tables were turned. The United States made every effort to impede interaction with and prevent international support for the Confederacy while it became British policy to uphold neutral rights for unrestricted trade of non-contraband goods.

Subsequent events convinced both belligerents that the British flagrantly violated neutrality in favor of the other, leading to the brink of war and generating a great deal of rancor lasting long after 1865. The definition of contraband was restricted to items directly supporting armies but was subject to interpretation. A proper blockade required naval forces outside all affected ports constituting a credible deterrent. This obviously was not the case along Southern coasts in 1861 and was debatable in 1862. Confederates asserted this was just a "paper blockade" and demanded the British ignore it. Powerful British commercial and shipping interests along with elite Southern sympathizers demanded their trade continue unhindered, with Royal Navy protection if necessary.

Under instructions from Secretary Seward, the U. S. Minister to the Court of St. James, Charles Francis Adams, informed his hosts that the Confederacy was an insurgency with no rights under international law. Any movement towards recognition, including failure to respect the blockade, would be considered an unfriendly act towards the United States. From Washington, Ambassador Lyons warned London about Seward: He would be "a dangerous foreign minister."[2]

Seward had talked in the 1850s of annexing Canada and is thought to have planted a *New York Times* article speculating that permanent dissolution of the Union would invariably lead to United States acquisition of that British colony. In February 1861, Seward spoke openly of reuniting North and South in common war against a foreign threat. He suggested that British encouragement of rebels would set a dangerous precedent for Ireland, Scotland, and their widely scattered colonies. Finally, "We will wrap the whole world in flames!" the secretary of state announced, should any foreign power interfere on the rebellion's behalf.[3]

"I do not think Mr. Seward would contemplate actually going to war with us," reported Lyons, "but he would be well disposed to play the old game of seeking popularity here [in the United States] by displaying violence toward us." Seward played the war card frequently and Lincoln allowed it despite his preference for "one war at a time." The president and Ambassador Adams occasionally conspired to soften Seward's bellicose pronouncements. The principle was, however, nonnegotiable: Rebels could not be allowed to finance and supply their armies through unrestricted foreign trade, perhaps protected by British naval might, thereby negating the North's primary advantage in material and production capacity.[4]

Both sides walked a fine line, but in a cautious, wait-and-see approach that would become the pattern, the British chose not to contest the blockade despite powerful political pressure. A long record of insisting that neutral nations honor Royal Navy blockades argued against interference. They

---

2 Mahin, *One War at a Time*, 7.

3 Don H. Doyle, *The Cause of all Nations: An International History of the American Civil War* (New York, 2015), 51

4 Mahin, *One War at a Time*, 7.

were not ready to go to war over this issue and never challenged it thereafter. Blockade runners were on their own.

Another dire threat to the blockade—and to Union survival—was much closer to home. The Supreme Court heard four cases in 1862, collectively called the Prize Cases, challenging the blockade's constitutionality. Northern merchant vessels carrying war materials south were seized by navy blockaders. The owners sued, contending that no state of war had been declared by Congress; therefore, the blockade and seizures were invalid. "If there is no formal war, capturing ships and impounding them is piracy."[5]

The court, in a 5-4 ruling consistent with British interpretations of international law, declared that Southern states were both in insurrection and at war; that a civil war did not have to be declared, but rather existed *de facto* based on judgments of size and scope; and that a belligerent need not be a recognized nation state. By one vote, the blockade was declared constitutionally grounded in the commander-in-chief's emergency powers.

A frustrated President Jefferson Davis and his advisors expected that "King Cotton"—dependence on cotton for the European textile industry— would induce Britain to break the blockade with military intervention. An offer of mediation backed up by force and finally national recognition would naturally follow, or so they thought and many in the North feared. From the Southern perspective, a British policy of inaction violated neutrality as *de facto* support for the blockade and for their enemy.

Confederates took every advantage of their status and insisted on their rights. As a belligerent, the government could contract loans, purchase arms and ships in neutral nations, and commission cruisers with power of search and seizure on the high seas. Ships flying the Confederate flag were to be accorded the same status as those of any other nation, including the United States. They could obtain assistance, supplies, and repairs in neutral ports, but were prohibited from taking aboard military equipment or arms. The United States insisted that rebels had no such rights, opposing them with every diplomatic tool available.

Rebel cruisers became conspicuous international representatives. "Great excitement has been created here by the arrival in our waters this morning of a steamer of war bearing the flag of the Confederate States of

---

5 David Armitage, *Civil Wars: A History of Ideas*, (New York), 125.

America," reported the *London Times* on November 22, 1861. This first such visitor—the CSS *Nashville*—evaded the blockade, dashed across the Atlantic battered by furious storms, and steamed into simmering controversy at Southampton.[6]

Commanded by Lieutenant Robert B. Pegram, *Nashville* was a small side-wheeled costal steamer seized by the Confederate government, lightly armed, and commissioned as a warship. Navy secretary Stephen R. Mallory intended *Nashville* to demonstrate the weakness of the blockade, show the flag, and advance the cause. "A speedy recognition of our Government by the Great European Powers is anticipated," he wrote.[7]

Mallory was confident that his ship and officers would be properly received as representatives of a belligerent power with which the host country desired close commercial relations. He instructed Pegram: "The strictest regard for the rights of neutrals cannot be too sedulously observed; nor should an opportunity be lost of cultivating friendly relations with their naval and merchant services, and of placing the true character of the contest in which we are engaged in its proper light. . . ."[8]

As *Nashville* approached the Irish coast two days before, she encountered the Yankee clipper *Harvey Birch*, bound from Havre to New York. Pegram hoisted his flag, fired a warning shot, demanded her surrender, took crew and passengers aboard *Nashville*, and set her afire. "Before she was lost to our sight her masts had gone by the board and she had burned to the water's edge." He set his prisoners ashore in Southampton. Thus, on Great Britain's doorstep began a devastating four-year campaign against Union commerce by Confederate cruisers. Northerners and many Britons called it piracy. Southampton officials received *Nashville* politely but cautiously, insisting on strict adherence to neutrality regulations.[9]

Union Secretary of the Navy Gideon Welles dispatched the powerful

---

6   Chester G. Hearn, *Gray Raiders of the Sea: How Eight Confederate Warships Destroyed the Union's High Seas Commerce* (Camden, ME, 1992), 45

7   James D. Bulloch, *The Secret Service of the Confederate States in Europe; or, How the Confederate Cruisers Were Equipped*, 2 vols. (Kindle Edition), location 2055.

8   Ibid.

9   R. B. Pegram to Hon. S. R. Mallory, March 10, 1862, in *Official Records of the Union and Confederate Navies in the War of the Rebellion*, 2 series, 29 vols. (Washington, D.C., 1894-1922), series 1, vol. 1, 745. Hereafter cited as *ORN*.

sloop-of-war USS *Tuscarora* to the English coast to catch and destroy *Nashville*. "This wanton destruction of the property of our merchants upon the high seas requires punishment and must receive immediate attention," he instructed Commander T.A.M. Craven. When *Tuscarora* dropped anchor across Southampton harbor from the Rebel ship, authorities parked a British frigate with guns loaded between them.[10]

News arrived in Great Britain five days later, November 27, 1861, that Captain Charles Wilkes in the USS *San Jacinto* stopped the British mail steamer RMS *Trent* near Cuba and forcibly removed Confederate emissaries James Mason and John Slidell, igniting the infamous "Trent affair."

The envoys were bound for Britain and France to press for diplomatic recognition and to lobby for financial and military support. Correctly assuming they would be carrying dispatches, which were contraband, Wilkes determined to seize ship and Rebels. The dispatches, however, had been hidden, so Wilkes concluded without legal precedent that the persons of Mason and Slidell constituted enemy dispatches and thus contraband. He released *Trent* and carried the captives to Boston Harbor to be imprisoned at Fort Warren. Captain Wilkes had no instructions regarding these Confederates and acted entirely on his own initiative.

The British were outraged: this was an egregious violation of neutrality and an insult to national honor. "You may stand for this but damned if I will!" blazed Prime Minister Lord Palmerston to his cabinet. In Southampton, Lieutenant Pegram received numerous and enthusiastic expressions of support for his cause. "There then appeared to be a great probability of an early rupture between England and the United States," he reported.[11]

Northerners celebrated Wilkes as a hero and railed against Britain. Congress passed a unanimous resolution thanking the captain "for his brave, adroit and patriotic conduct" and proposed casting a gold medal for him. Across the Atlantic, a typical British response in the *London Chronicle* admonished, "That spirit of senseless egotism which induces the Americans, with their dwarf fleet and shapeless mass of incoherent squads which they

---

10   Gideon Wells to Commander T.A.M. Craven, December 6, 1861, *ORN* series 1, vol. 1, 230.

11   David Herbert Donald, *Charles Sumner and the Rights of Man* (1970), 31; R. B. Pegram to Hon. S. R. Mallory, March 10, 1862, *ORN* series 1, vol. 1, 745.

U.S.S. *San Jacinto* removed Confederate commissioners James Mason and John Slidell from the British mail steamer *Trent* in old Bahama channel, 8 November 1861. What if the Navy had left the commissioners alone? *Naval History and Heritage Command*

call an army, to fancy themselves the equal of France by land and Great Britain by sea."[12]

Crown law officers advised that the act of forcefully removing passengers from a neutral steamer on an innocent voyage between neutral ports was illegal and unjustified in international law: "Her Majesty's Government will, therefore . . . be justified in requiring reparation for the international wrong which has been on this occasion committed."[13]

Britons soundly rejected the notion that human beings could be contraband, which is ironic considering the Union's application of the concept to fleeing slaves. Also ironic: Wilkes would have been on firmer legal grounds had he retained possession of *Trent* and escorted her into a port of the United States for adjudication as a prize in admiralty court.

12   David Herbert Donald, Jean Harvey Baker, and Michael F. Holt, *The Civil War and Reconstruction* (2001), 315.

13   James P. Baxter 3rd, "Papers Relating to Belligerent and Neutral Rights, 1861–1865," *The American Historical Review*, vol. 34, No. 1 (Oct. 1928), 86–87.

"It looks like war," wrote Foreign Secretary Lord John Russell. Eight thousand troops were readied to reinforce Canada. Export of arms, ammunition, and military stores to the United States was stopped, threatening vital Union supplies. Royal Naval units around the globe prepared to attack American shipping wherever encountered. The North American and West Indies Squadron planned to lift the blockade of Southern ports, establish a blockade of Northern harbors, and be ready to operate in the Chesapeake Bay, perhaps in coordination with Confederate units. The foreign minister directed Lord Lyons to demand an apology with immediate release of Mason and Slidell. Lyons informed Seward that Britons would fight if necessary, but also said they would not be fussy about the form of apology.[14]

Anxious Northerners wavered, fearing a repeat of 1812—trade interrupted, ships and crews lost, bays and harbors invaded, port cities destroyed, economy drastically disrupted—along with a two-front war. Massachusetts Senator Charles Sumner, Chairman of the Foreign Relations Committee and frequent advisor to President Lincoln, was gravely concerned. Southern trade would flow while Northern ports were bottled up and the U. S. Navy driven from the seas. Napoleon III would establish an empire in Mexico and ally with the Confederacy.

Lincoln invited Sumner to a cabinet meeting at 10:00 on Christmas morning, 1861. Consensus was soon reached: the captives must be given up. War with Great Britain, Sumner wrote, would cause "paralysis upon all our naval and military movements against the rebellion." Upon this decision "depended the dearest interest, probably the existence of the nation."[15]

Mason and Slidell were "white elephants," concluded the president. America must stick to her principles, he wrote: "We fought Great Britain [in the War of 1812] for insisting . . . on the right to do precisely what Captain Wilkes has done." He ordered their release; the Confederate emissaries resumed their voyage. Seward issued a halfhearted apology on the excuse that Wilkes had acted without orders while noting that Great Britain had just acknowledged being wrong for sixty years on an issue of neutral rights.[16]

Meanwhile, the CSS *Nashville* completed repairs in a Southampton

14 Donald, *Charles Sumner and the Rights of Man*, 31.

15 Ibid., 33.

16 Mahin, *One War at a Time*, 62.

Royal Navy shipyard. Lieutenant Pegram reported that the authorities "kept a guard constantly on the vessel to see that no alteration was made in the way of strengthening her for warlike purposes. I could make the necessary preparations to render her seaworthy, but no more."[17]

On February 26, 1862, *Nashville* was escorted out of harbor by a Royal Navy frigate under the guns of the USS *Tuscarora*. Captain Craven badgered authorities to have the Rebel impounded as a pirate but could do nothing to capture her in territorial waters. The British were not about to allow another violation of their neutrality. This was the first of many bitter political exchanges over British support for Confederate cruisers.

Nashville set vital precedents in international law. She was the first Confederate ship-of-war to fly the flag in British waters and the first to make a capture in North Atlantic shipping lanes. The cruiser secured belligerent status for their warships in the face of vociferous Union protests. Foreign Secretary Russell stated officially that *Nashville* was not a pirate under the terms of law, but a regularly commissioned ship-of-war with rights to a safe port and repair facilities. To the consternation of the United States, these rulings were crucial to the survival of subsequent raiders.

The thorny questions of intervention and diplomatic recognition pursuant to European interests remained unresolved, however. As fighting intensified and news of the bloody Battle of Shiloh in April 1862 spread, humanitarian considerations also seemed more persuasive. The notion that the international community could intervene in a civil war in the name of human rights was new and untested. It also was, and still is, incompatible with principles of sovereignty and national jurisdiction. British and French governments continued to discuss offers of mediation that they hoped the United States might accept.

Meanwhile from Richmond, Confederate Navy Secretary Mallory dispatched Commander James Bulloch to Liverpool to acquire ships he did not have and could not build at home for his fledgling navy. Mallory's first priorities were ironclads and commerce raiders. "I regard the possession of an iron-armored ship as a matter of the first necessity," he reported in May 1861. The secretary cited a detailed history of rival French and British prototypes to justify ironclads. "Such a vessel at this time could traverse the

---

17 Investigation of the Navy Department, *ORN* series 2, vol. 1, 631.

entire coast of the United States; prevent all blockades, and encounter, with a fair prospect of success, their entire Navy." Northerners soon came to fear these ambitions also.[18]

Great Britain and France had grappled for decades with revolutions in warship construction. France led the way in 1859 with the impressive ironclad frigate *La Gloire*, followed in 1860 by the magnificent British HMS *Warrior*, an all-iron vessel, the epitome of contemporary naval engineering. In August 1861, U. S. Secretary of the Navy Gideon Welles proposed an ironclad building program for a navy that had none. A supporter noted: "England and France will, by the close of this year, have twenty to thirty iron-clad steam ships, each of which could pass into Boston or New York with impunity, and possibly destroy either city."[19]

Iowa Senator James Grimes agreed: "We need a more effective blockade. . . . Scoundrels North, as well as scoundrels South, are carrying on an unlawful trade in fraud of our revenue." Pirates and sea rovers must be captured. Southern harbors and forts must be retaken. Commerce must be protected. Northern harbors must be defended. "Suppose England, in her love for cotton, should . . . attempt to break our blockade, and we should get into trouble with her: what is to become of our northern cities and our cities upon the coast?" Welles's program would produce the revolutionary USS *Monitor* followed by many more Union ironclads.[20]

In March 1862, James Bulloch secretly contracted the Liverpool firm of Laird & Son to construct two powerful, iron-hulled steam warships for the Confederacy, each fitted with two revolving turrets and an iron ramming beak on the bow—the "Laird rams." The Queen's subjects could build merchant vessels for belligerents but were not allowed to build or arm warships for them. So, with the assistance of the sympathetic builders, Confederate involvement was disguised behind false ownership.

Navy Secretary Mallory also desired swift, lightly armed cruisers to scour the globe, capturing and destroying Yankee merchants and whalers wherever found. Powerful Northern commercial interests, many not

18 S. R. Mallory to C. M. Conrad, May 10, 1861, *ORN* series 2, vol. 2, 69.

19 John C. Rives, *The Congressional Globe: The Debates and Proceedings of the First Session of the Thirty-Seventh Congress* (Washington, 1861), 210.

20 Ibid., 256-57.

enthused about the war to begin with, would clamor for peace even at the expense of Southern independence; Union warships would be drawn off the blockade to chase down Rebel raiders. "The enemy's . . . commerce constitutes one of his reliable sources of national wealth no less than one of his best schools for seamen, and we must strike it, if possible."[21]

Against persistent Union espionage and intense diplomatic pressure, Bulloch arranged for the building of a specialized steam screw cruiser that would become the CSS *Florida*, the first of eight such raiders. She departed England on March 22, 1862, in the guise of a merchantman, to be followed in August by the infamous CSS *Alabama*. Both undertook two-year voyages, which, along with their sisters, devastated Union merchant fleets and caused consternation in the North in what was arguably the most cost-effective Confederate campaign of the war.

The most effective of Bulloch's raiders were British built, armed, equipped, largely manned, and surreptitiously sold. Secretary Seward adamantly insisted that rebel vessels had no legitimacy as commissioned men-of-war of a recognized nation—they were pirates. As required by international law, all national warships encountering pirates were obligated to capture them and prosecute officers and crew. The punishment was hanging.

In summer 1862, parliament and the Queen's ministers seriously debated intervention and arbitration, perhaps forcefully. Henry Adams, son and secretary to Ambassador Charles Francis Adams, wrote: "As for this country [Great Britain], the simple fact is that it is unanimously against us and becomes more firmly set every day."[22]

Confederate sympathizers in Great Britain were primarily aristocrats, politicians, and leading businessmen called "the educated million" who constituted public opinion. Working classes, encouraged by opposition politicians, generally supported the Union—even those in textile manufacturing, severely affected by cotton shortages. However, their voices did not coalesce into significant political influence until later in the century as additional political reforms expanded the franchise to the laborer. Many of the educated million became convinced that the North could not prevail, and the United States would split.

---

21   Mallory to Bulloch, August 10, 1864, *ORN* series 2, vol. 2, 701.

22   Sheldon Vanauken, *The Glittering Illusion: English Sympathy for the Southern Confederacy* (Washington, D.C.: Gateway Books, 1989), 2.

Support for the Confederacy did not necessarily imply sympathy for the institution of slavery, which Britons outlawed in 1833. The elite were able to rationalize their support because the Lincoln administration repeatedly stated the war was about Union, not about ending slavery. The Union retained several slave states, and Yankees had been complicit in the illegal slave trade. Most succumbed to Confederate propaganda that slavery would be ended in their own good time, not as forced upon them by northern tyrants.

Lincoln's mystical concept of Union had little resonance for a people with no experience of a written constitution or a federal system. The British constitution consisted of venerated practices and institutions inherited from the mists of time, not a single document or an overarching principle. They were unified by ethnicity, religion, and geography. No society had ever been conceived solely on a principle of individual freedom as claimed by the Americans. They did not appear to be following the ideal in any case. The strange system devised in 1787, based on a complex separation of powers, appeared unworkable.

British opinion also exhibited a growing ambivalence toward their empire flourishing in Africa and Asia. In conflict and commerce, they were undisputed rulers of the waves and of large slices of the globe. While intensely proud of these accomplishments, many concluded that the Declaration of Independence might have been right in some sense. The natural course of civilizing influence in overseas enterprise motivated colonies toward independence in a modern commercial and industrial world.

The United States was a child of Great Britain and an immense success, in which, despite disagreements, they took great satisfaction. It behooved all nations to accept and support this pattern of self-determination, not fight it. The British sympathized with Greek and Italian freedom and supported independence for Spanish American colonies and Belgium, examples that Confederates repeatedly cited in their favor. British experiences in North America and the West Indies demonstrated burdens as well as benefits of colonial rule. Contrarily, the United States continued to grasp at empire by acquiring Louisiana, annexing Texas, warring with Mexico, dispossessing indigenous Americans, and, not coincidentally, threatening British Canada.

So, if slavery was not the issue, Union did not make sense, and independence was a natural consequence of colonial maturity, then this war must be about conquering a people who wished to be left alone. Confederate claims to revolution and secession seemed solid on the principles of 1776.

Southern sympathizers argued for a mutually beneficial commercial relationship with an independent Confederacy, an enhanced balance of power constraining United States territorial, industrial, and maritime ambitions, and respect for legitimate independence movements. A defeat by British arms would induce Union leaders to soften their position and accept mediation. In any case, the war's outcome appeared predetermined for the South that summer of 1862; action to bring about cessation of hostilities was a humanitarian imperative.

The huge Royal Navy overshadowed the controversy. The rapidly expanding United States navy had a few powerful warships but consisted mainly of flimsy converted civilian vessels with a few guns. British leaders grasped, however, that war with Yankees would be difficult. One historian concluded: "Britain's world dominance of the seventeenth and eighteenth centuries had vanished; the Royal Navy, although more powerful than ever, no longer ruled the waves." They had not faced a determined opponent at sea since Napoleon. [23]

The advent of steam made it more difficult even than it had been in 1781 and 1812 to project and sustain naval power across the Atlantic. Despite a major base at Halifax and perhaps aid from Southern ports, coal supplies would be tenuous. Canada was unprepared to thwart a determined invasion even with additional troops, which were delayed until spring 1863. The navy would be unleashed against British shipping worldwide. American grain shipments—a large part of their food supply—would end, as would sales of machinery and supplies to the United States. Great Britain also had pressing concerns with Napoleon III's ambitions in Europe and Bismarck's rise in Prussia.

News of the Union debacle at Second Bull Run reached London in early September. Prime Minister Palmerston scheduled a cabinet meeting for late that month to discuss a mediation proposal, but then decided to wait for further developments in Robert E. Lee's invasion of the North. If Lee prevailed, the proposal would be pursued; if not, they would again wait and see.

Union victory at Antietam provided the opportunity President Lincoln needed to issue the preliminary Emancipation Proclamation,

---

23 Gordon H. Warren, *Fountain of Discontent: The Trent Affair and Freedom of the Seas*, (Northeastern University Press, 1981), 154.

UNCLE SAM PROTECTING HIS PROPERTY AGAINST THE ENCROACHMENTS OF HIS COUSIN JOHN.

From the Library of Congress: "In this 1861 political cartoon, Uncle Sam as a Union soldier resembling Abraham Lincoln unceremoniously routs the English John Bull from an American cotton field. John Bull grasps stolen plants and wears 'Armstrong's Patent' cannon on his legs (an English-made gun sold to Confederates). Wielding a large stick labeled 'Principle of Non Enterference,' Sam warns, 'John, You lost your Non-interfering Principle. I'll lay it on your back again.' A cock representing French Emperor Napoleon III perches on the fence. Lifeless bodies of P. G. T. Beauregard and Jefferson Davis hang from the scarecrow. The plaque reads, 'All Persons Tresspassing These Premisses, will be punished according to Law.'" *Library of Congress*

making abolition an explicit war aim. Among the president's objectives was to discourage talk of intervention. To Lincoln's dismay, however, many Britons concluded that his was not a moral position, but a self-serving act of military desperation that could—perhaps intentionally—start a race war. Seward had warned the president about just this response back in July.

Nevertheless, Britons were induced to pause frantic debates and reconsider as anxiety for intervention receded. Palmerston and Russell tabled the vote on mediation in the cabinet. Henry Adams would later note: "The Emancipation Proclamation has done more for us than all our former victories and all our diplomacy." Confederate reverses at Gettysburg and Vicksburg the next summer accelerated the process.

On December 31, 1862, a huge crowd of textile workers assembled in the Manchester Free-Trade Hall to welcome the new year. Mayor Abel Haywood addressed the assemblage with a message to Lincoln. The victory of the free North "will strike off the fetters of the slave. . . . We joyfully honor you, as the President, and the Congress with you, for . . . exemplifying your belief in the words of your great founders: 'All men are created free and equal.'"[24]

Some conclusions became widely evident: an armistice, whether voluntary or forced, would freeze the *status quo*. During negotiations, the South would reinforce defenses. Should negotiations fail—given waning enthusiasm and increasing anti-war sentiment—the Union would find it exceedingly difficult to resume offensive operations. Mediation implied compromise, but there was none between complete Southern independence and total Union restoration while neither side would accept less. The Confederacy would win by not losing.

Disputes across the Atlantic continued, however. Despite Confederate efforts at secrecy, ownership and purpose of the fearsome Laird rams became obvious to Union agents who vigorously complained to authorities. Virtually impervious to shot and shell, the rams were perceived as a grave threat to the U. S. Navy and to the blockade.

Ambassador Adams and Secretary Seward initiated fierce diplomatic exchanges with Foreign Secretary Russell, finally informing him that delivery of the rams to the Rebels would mean war. In October 1863, a worried British government confiscated the vessels in dubious legal proceedings and took them into the Royal Navy. This was, other than the *Trent* affair, possibly the closest the two nations came to conflict.

British foreign policy during the Civil War was driven by heard-headed strategic and economic interests with no option ruled out if timing was right and incentives outweighed risks. Intervention was seriously considered but increasingly unlikely after January 1863. Americans were acutely aware that British intervention could decide the outcome, but Northerners stood their ground and Southerners failed to make the case.

---

24   James Lander, *Lincoln and Darwin: Shared Visions of Race, Science, and Religion* (Carbondale, 2010), 221.

Without a clear definition of victory and no obvious path to get there, Prime Minister Palmerston and Foreign Secretary Russell eschewed direct involvement—a lesson that might have been more effectively applied in recent history. The Confederacy would sink or swim on its own. Britons weathered economic and social dislocations as they arose and turned their attention elsewhere. Based on a common language and culture, liberal traditions, and flourishing commerce, the two peoples began to sense a "Special Relationship."[25]

---

25 Additional resources consulted for this piece: Howard Jones, *Blue & Gray Diplomacy: A History of Union and Confederate Foreign Relations* (Chapel Hill: University of North Carolina Press, 2010); Frank J. Merli, *Great Britain and The Confederate Navy, 1861-1865* (Bloomington: Indiana University Press, 2004).

CHAPTER FOUR

What If Someone Else

Had Been Offered Command
of the Army of the Potomac?

Frank Jastrzembski

"I was offered command of the Army of the Potomac," Alfred Pleasonton boasted to artist James E. Kelly as he sketched the general's portrait in July 1895. The 71-year-old retired major general had a tendency to inflate his own accomplishments and produce sensationalized battle reports during the Civil War, so something like this coming out of Pleasonton's month was no surprise. But Kelly was intrigued, and he pressed the general for more details. He asked Pleasonton why he turned down such an important command. "I wasn't like Grant," Pleasonton uttered to the inquisitive artist. "I refused to pay the price." That price, according to the pretentious cavalryman, was that the war had to be continued until the Confederacy was crushed, slavery abolished, and President Abraham Lincoln reelected in 1864.[1]

Pleasonton was not the only general who claimed or who was rumored to have been considered for command of the Army of the Potomac during the Civil War. The names ranged from the popular to the relatively unknown. Generals Edwin V. Sumner, Darius N. Couch, Winfield Scott Hancock, John Sedgwick, and William S. Rosecrans were among the more noteworthy ones. Some say the army's *preux chevalier*, Maj. Gen. Philip Kearny, would have risen to command the Army of the Potomac had he not been killed

---

1   William B. Styple, *Generals in Bronze: Interviewing the Commanders of the Civil War* (Kearny, NJ: Belle Grove Publishing Co., 2005), 115-16, 126, 194.

at Chantilly in September 1862. Ironically, the dashing division commander did not see himself as the person to replace Maj. Gen. George B. McClellan. Instead, he had someone else in mind. "The only person to take this place," Kearny told his friend and New Jersey lawyer Cortlandt Parker, "is General C. F. [Charles Ferguson] Smith, in the army in Kentucky. If you have influence with Stanton impress him with this."

One of the strangest names associated with command of the Army of the Potomac was the older half-brother of Maj. Gen. John Buford, Brig. Gen. Napoleon Bonaparte Buford, who Ulysses S. Grant pointed out to Lincoln was "dead weight to carry" and would hardly "make a respectable hospital nurse if put in petticoats." Secretary of War Edwin M. Stanton apparently thought otherwise.[2]

Through an intermediary, President Lincoln offered Robert E. Lee command of Federal forces in April 1861. "[H]ow can I draw my sword upon Virginia, my native state?" Lee replied. After days of troubled deliberation, Lee declined the offer —a decision, said biographer Douglass Southall Freeman, "he was born to make." But was he? What if Lee had accepted Lincoln's offer? *Library of Congress*

Among these dozen or so generals, three stand out as the most intriguing cases: Ethan Allen Hitchcock, Israel B. Richardson, and John F. Reynolds. One was appalled with the thought of taking charge of the Army of the

---

2 Stephen W. Sears, *Lincoln's Lieutenants: The High Command of the Army of the Potomac* (Boston & New York: Houghton Mifflin Harcourt, 2017), 171, 527; Stephen R. Taaffe, *Commanding the Army of the Potomac* (Lawrence: University Press of Kansas, 2006), 49-50, 79; Cortlandt Parker, "Major General Philip Kearny. Part III," in *The Northern Monthly. November 1867—April 1868*, vol. 2, ed. Allen L. Bassett (New Yok & Newark: Allen L. Bassett, 1868), 372; Frank J. Urquhart, *A History of the City of Newark, New Jersey: Embracing Practically Two and a Half Centuries, 1666-1913*, vol. 2 (New York & Chicago: The Lewis Historical Publishing Co., 1913), 694; Philip Kearny, *Letters from the Peninsula*, ed. William B. Styple (Kearny, NJ: Belle Grove Publishing Co., 1988), 20, 205; Ulysses S. Grant to Abraham Lincoln, February 9, 1863, Library of Congress, Washington, D.C.

Maj. Gen. Winfield Scott was one of the finest soldiers America ever produced (left), but by the time of the Civil War (right), he was too old and overweight to take the field. He advocated for a young George B. McClellan to assume command of the Federal armies—a move that would come back to haunt Scott because McClellan stabbed him in the back after getting the job. What if Scott had never petitioned for McClellan in the first place? *Library of Congress*

Potomac; one was offered the position on his deathbed; and one likely turned it down only to be killed weeks later. Each was offered command at a watershed moment in the Army of the Potomac's history: at the start of McClellan's Peninsula Campaign; after McClellan's lackluster showing at Antietam; and on the eve of the battle of Gettysburg.

While we can only speculate how any one of these generals would have performed in the onerous task of leading the Army of the Potomac, we can investigate their backgrounds, qualifications, limitations, why they would have (or why they should not have) been considered as a candidate, and how they may have performed in command of the most politicized and important army during the Civil War.[3]

---

3 Taaffe, *Commanding the Army of the Potomac*, 2; For more on the political activity within the Army of the Potomac see Zachery A. Fry, *A Republic in the Ranks: Loyalty and Dissent in the Army of the Potomac* (Chapel Hill: University of North Carolina Press, 2020).

Revolutionary Stock

President Abraham Lincoln loved to tell stories. One he particularly enjoyed was about Ethan Allen, the leader of the Green Mountain Boys and vanquisher of Fort Ticonderoga during the American Revolution. When Allen visited England after the war, his host thought it would be humorous to tease him about a picture of George Washington he purposely had hung over the toilet. When Allen returned from reliving himself, the Englishman asked if he thought that the picture of his former chief was suitably placed. Allen said it was. Perplexed, the man inquired why. Allen declared, "Nothing will make an Englishman shit so quick as the sight of Washington!" Lincoln relished sharing this anecdote.[4]

Most assumed Ethan Allen's grandson, Ethan Allen Hitchcock, would rival, if not outmatch, his grandfather's deeds and larger-than-life personality. They could not have been more wrong. Young Ethan was unlike his grandfather in almost every regard. While the hero of Fort Ticonderoga was rash and bull-headed, his grandson was cautious and methodical; while the Revolutionary War colonel boasted of his accomplishments, his self-effacing grandson endeavored to remove himself from public attention.[5]

Despite the stark contrasts between grandfather and grandson, Lorrain Peters, Hitchcock's older sister, assumed an army career would be a natural fit for him. She urged her husband, Maj. George P. Peters, to use his influence to get her 16-year-old brother appointed to West Point. In September 1814, Peters wrote to Secretary of War James Monroe and reminded him that his brother-in-law was not any old Vermonter, but the grandson of *the* Ethan Allen, "whose fame he is disposed to emulate." The boy's connection to the war hero led to an appointment to the military college in October of that year.[6]

---

4 Michael Lynch, "Lincoln's Ethan Allen Story," *Past in the Present* (blog), November 25, 2012, https://pastinthepresent.wordpress.com/2012/11/25/lincolns-ethan-allen-story/. This anecdote is shared most famously in Steven Spielberg's film *Lincoln*.

5 William S. Randall, *Ethan Allen: His Life and Times* (New York: W.W. Norton & Company, 2011), xiii. For more on Ethan Allen see John Duffy and H. Nicholas Muller III, *Inventing Ethan Allen* (Lebanon, NH: University Press of New England, 2014).

6 Ethan Allen Hitchcock, *Fifty Years in Camp and Field: Diary of Major-General Ethan Allen Hitchcock, U.S.A.*, ed. by William A. Croffut (New York, NY: Putnam, 1909), 40; Joshua Shepherd, "Patriot Raid on Fort Ticonderoga," *Military Heritage* (November 2017): 43.

From the beginning, Hitchcock expressed his aversion to his chosen profession. "I did not go to the Military Academy because I deliberately made choice of a military profession," he divulged in his diary. "I went because, being a grandson of Ethan Allen, some of the friends of our family thought it appropriate." Nonetheless, he continued with his studies and successfully graduated in July 1817.[7]

Added to his reluctance to pursue an army career, Hitchcock suffered from poor health most of his life. The U.S.-Mexican War was especially hard on his body. He endured bouts of diarrhea that "prevailed with increased virulence"; troublesome bone aches, fatigue, and hemorrhoids; and discomfort in his right shoulder and arms, accompanied by numbness to his left hand. The paralysis became so bad that whenever he stretched his head backwards, he lost feeling in both arms. He applied for extended leave in 1848 and traveled abroad to London, Vienna, and Constantinople, visiting Turkish baths in the hope that they would provide some relief, but his symptoms only persisted.

After 40 years in the army, Hitchcock resigned his commission in October 1855. He hoped to put his career as a soldier behind him for good, choosing to dedicate his remaining years to scholarly research and writing. "I have been a student all my life, even when I was a soldier by an education involuntarily received," he declared. "I served forty years. Is not that long enough?" Just as Hitchcock was thrust into a profession that he was unenthusiastic about, he was drawn into a civil war he wanted no part of.

Hitchcock detested the rebellion, but he had no desire to take up arms. He was in no physical condition to handle the rigors of army life. "As to going into the army, I have no particular wish for it," he admitted. "In the first place, I am past 63, and, though my general health is good, I keep it so by a regularity of living which campaign life would hardly permit me to keep up." He would let younger, more energetic men do the fighting. He decided to sit this one out.[8]

Although he wished to remain in voluntary exile, politicians and generals came knocking at his door requesting his service—among them Joseph

---

7 Hitchcock, *Fifty Years in Camp and Field*, 437.

8 Jack D. Welsh, *Medical Histories of Union Generals* (Kent, OH: Kent State University Press, 1996), 169-170; Hitchcock, *Fifty Years in Camp and Field*, 203-204, 210-11, 215-22, 437, 433, 358.

Holt, William S. Harney, Henry Halleck, and Winfield Scott. "Many friends urge my return to the army," he stated. "But I have no heart for engaging in civil war. I cannot think of it." His link to Ethan Allen further added pressure to come out of retirement. On September 20, 1861, the governor of Vermont, John N. Pomeroy, wrote to him affirming that "the Grandson of Ethan Allen should be the man" to lead a volunteer regiment of Green Mountain Boys. Hitchcock replied to Pomeroy five days later, turning the offer down and declaring that he "hoped to remain unseen and unknown." Governor Pomeroy was the least of his worries.[9]

To ask "What if Maj. Gen. Ethan Allen Hitchcock channeled his famous Revolutionary War ancestor" is to ask for a fundamentally different Hitchcock. *Library of Congress*

On February 8, 1862, Maj. Gen. Henry Halleck suggested to McClellan that Hitchcock be commissioned a major general of volunteers and appointed to command of the Department of Mississippi. Halleck telegraphed Secretary of War Edwin M. Stanton the same day, telling him that Generals William T. Sherman, John Pope, Ulysses S. Grant, Samuel R. Curtis, Stephen A. Hurlbut, Franz Sigel, Benjamin M. Prentiss, and John A. McClernand were unwilling and incapable of serving under one another. "If Brig Gen E. A. Hitchcock could be made Major Genl of vols & assigned to this Dept., it would satisfy all & reconcile all differences," Halleck assured Stanton. "If it can be done there should be no delay, as an experienced officer of high rank

9 Marshall True, "A Reluctant Warrior Advises the President: Ethan Allen Hitchcock, Abraham Lincoln and the Union Army, Spring, 1862," *Vermont History* 50 (1982): 143-44; Hitchcock, *Fifty Years in Camp and Field*, 430-33, 435-36; "The Howard Guard," *Burlington Free Press* (Burlington, VT), April 19, 1861; Ethan Allen Hitchcock Papers, 1793-1888, Ethan A. Hitchcock to John N. Pomeroy, September 20, 1861, Library of Congress, Washington, D.C. Note: Hitchcock's correspondence from the Library of Congress will be thereafter cited as EAH, LOC.

is wanted immediately on the Tennessee line." Halleck obviously valued not only Hitchcock's ability to act as an arbitrator between these generals, but also his four decades of military experience.[10]

Halleck's admiration for Hitchcock must have attracted Stanton's attention, who requested the aging officer to travel from Missouri to Washington for a "personal conference." Hitchcock left St. Louis for Washington on the evening of March 7. On the train ride, he suffered a severe nosebleed when he reached Pittsburgh, the sixth or seventh he experienced within a three-week period. He feared it was an omen of something far more serious.

Three days after leaving Missouri, he arrived at the War Department. President Lincoln and Secretary of War Stanton were preoccupied at the time, so Assistant Secretary of War Peter H. Watson suggested that Hitchcock check into Willard's Hotel until summoned by Stanton.[11] When he arrived at Willard's, Hitchcock suffered another serious nosebleed. It took two physicians to finally contain the bleeding. Hitchcock was so exhausted from the whole ordeal that he could hardly make it up the stairs to his hotel room. The next morning, Stanton called on Hitchcock and pressed him to accept a position as his personal advisor. Hitchcock declared that Stanton made "all sorts of assurances that he would 'put no more upon me than I could bear.'" He turned down the offer, maintaining that his poor health, which had been a recurring issue since the Mexican War, would never allow it.[12]

On his way to New York City to seek treatment for the hemorrhages, Hitchcock had second thoughts, perhaps feeling an urgency to do his duty, maybe feeling that he was missing a chance in a lifetime, or for some other reason. He returned to Washington on March 15. There he met with President Lincoln and reiterated to him, as he had to Stanton, that he only intended to remain in the advisory role "for contingent purposes." He felt that

---

10   Hitchcock, *Fifty Years in Camp and Field*, 434-35; Ulysses S. Grant, *The Papers of Ulysses S. Grant. Volume 4: January 8-March 31, 1862*, ed. John Y. Simon (Carbondale: Southern Illinois University Press, 1972), 196-97.

11   Ethan A. Hitchcock to Mrs. Mann, March 15, 1862, EAH, LOC; William Marvel, *Lincoln's Autocrat: The Life of Edwin Stanton* (Chapel Hill: The University of North Carolina Press, 2015), 172.

12   Welsh, *Medical Histories of Union Generals*, 170; Ethan Allen Hitchcock to Henry Hitchcock, March 10, 1862, Missouri Historical Society Archives, St. Louis, Missouri. Note: Hitchcock correspondence from the Missouri Historical Society will be thereafter cited as EAH, MS. Ethan A. Hitchcock to Mrs. Mann, March 15, 1862, EAH, LOC; Hitchcock, *Fifty Years in Camp and Field*, 437-38; Ethan A. Hitchcock to Edwin M. Stanton, March 11, 1862, EAH, LOC.

serving as an advisor shielded him from the stresses of a field command and would allow him to serve his country without risking his health. Likewise, Hitchcock wished to avoid the intrigue that existed between senior generals vying for an independent command. Despite dismissing numerous appeals to return to service, Hitchcock yielded to Stanton's and Lincoln's pressure. "I am here against my will and almost against my judgment," he wrote to his nephew Henry Hitchcock, "and feel much as if I had a bandage over my eyes." As events unfolded, he had every reason to harbor these reservations.[13]

What transpired next nearly gave Hitchcock the greatest hemorrhage of all. Stanton pulled him aside and bluntly asked if he would replace McClellan as the commander of the Army of the Potomac. Behind closed doors, Stanton revealed his distrust and reservations for McClellan's capability to command the army. There was dissatisfaction among McClellan's enemies—generals Philip Kearny, Joseph Hooker, David Birney, and others—and discontent festered within the army's ranks. The relationship between Stanton and McClellan hit such a low point that the commanding general bypassed the secretary of war and communicated directly with the president, breaking the chain of command. Stanton, for his part, was vindictive of men who stood in his way, and a harsh critic to those he saw as enemies of the U.S. McClellan became his mortal enemy, and Stanton set out to destroy him.[14]

Hitchcock was both shocked and bothered with Stanton's proposal, but he declined to reveal the specifics of the secret meeting. "I can not recite them," he wrote afterward. "[B]ut the Secretary stated fact after fact, until I felt positively *sick*—that falling of the heart which excludes hope." Hitchcock had grudgingly come out of retirement with the promise of a quiet advisory role far away from any battlefields or the burden of responsibility. Now he was being offered command the most important field army. "I was amazed, and told him at once that I could not," he wrote. Hitchcock knew that he was incapable of enduring the physical and mental rigors of commanding

---

13 Ethan A. Hitchcock to Lorenzo Thomas March 17, 1862, EAH, LOC; Ethan A. Hitchcock to Henry Hitchcock, March 17, 1862, EAH, MS; Ethan Allen Hitchcock to Henry Hitchcock, March 15, 1862, EAH, MS; Ethan A. Hitchcock to Mrs. Mann, March 15, 1862, EAH, LOC.

14 Taaffe, *Commanding the Army of the Potomac*, 20-21, 28-9, 56; Jack C. Mason, *Until Antietam: The Life and Letters of Major General Israel B. Richardson, U.S. Army* (Carbondale: Southern Illinois University Press, 2009), 164; Francis C. Barlow, *"Fear Was Not in Him": The Civil War Letters of Major General Francis C. Barlow, U.S.A.*, ed. Christian Samito (New York: Fordham University Press, 2004), 99; Robert L. Crewdson, "Edwin M Stanton and the Lincoln Assassination" (master's thesis, College of William and Mary, 1986), 38-41, 54-5.

an army. "I know the terrible responsibility," he jotted down with anxiety in his journal that evening. "What if I should suffer physical collapse while at the head of an army?"[15]

It is hard to believe that Hitchcock would have executed the war any more vigorously than McClellan if he had agreed to this proposition. Despite a firm belief that the rebellion should be crushed, Hitchcock's idea of how the war should be waged did not align with the administration's vision. He reasoned that the war should be "against the rebellious party as a part, and not against the South as a people." Hitchcock even wrote to Winfield Scott a month before Confederate forces fired on Fort Sumter urging Lincoln to withdraw Maj. Robert Anderson and his garrison to "remove the occasion for a conflict." Total war was not Hitchcock's cup of tea.[16]

By the time Hitchcock had been offered command by Stanton, Lincoln had already stripped McClellan of his duties as commander-in-chief of the U.S. Army at the urging of Stanton and other Radical Republicans, although the administration still prodded the general to take action. McClellan devised a bold plan to transport the Army of the Potomac up the Virginia Peninsula, land at Fortress Monroe, and advance on the Confederate capital. Stanton offered Hitchcock command of the army right around the time McClellan began moving troops and supplies to the southern tip of the Peninsula. Had Hitchcock accepted Stanton's offer and replaced McClellan at this time, he would have taken charge of army at the opening phase of a major campaign. It is doubtful Hitchcock would have carried out a plan of another man's design with confidence and enthusiasm. Besides, one could only wonder how Hitchcock would have fared when pitted against the hard-hitting Lee at the head of the Army of North Virginia (assuming the battle of Seven Pines was fought and Gen. Joseph E. Johnston wounded). Then again, maybe Hitchcock would have stunned his critics like "Granny Lee" did during the summer of '62. Stranger things happened during the war.[17]

The stresses of responsibility of commanding the Army of the Potomac and taking the field would have easily crushed Hitchcock's fragile health.

15 Hitchcock, *Fifty Years in Camp and Field*, 435, 438-40, 474; Henry Hitchcock to Doctor Samuel G.J. DeCamp, May 9, 1862, EAH, MS.

16 Hitchcock, *Fifty Years in Camp and Field*, 431; Ethan A. Hitchcock to Winfield Scott, March 1861, EAH, LOC.

17 Fry, *A Republic in the Ranks*, 34-5.

Typhoid fever crippled McClellan for three weeks from December 1861 to the middle of January 1862. The "Chickahominy Fever" festered in McClellan's army during the course of his campaign in Virginia. Disease contracted on the Peninsula killed brigadier generals William H. Keim and Charles D. Jameson. Typhoid fever, dysentery, measles, malaria, and other infectious diseases took the lives of thousands during the war. What are the odds that a man 28 years McClellan's senior, already in shaky health, would have been able to stay healthy? Hitchcock would have been a prime host for the many diseases rampant among both armies during the war.[18]

So why would have Stanton considered Hitchcock as a suitable replacement for McClellan? While it appears as if Stanton was simply acting out of desperation (which was likely the case), there may have been some logic behind selecting Hitchcock. The general had spent 40 years in the army, and like Halleck and others, Stanton must have valued this experience. Another factor may be that Hitchcock posed no military or political threat to Lincoln or Stanton, unlike the ambitious and troublesome McClellan. Humble in nature, Hitchcock desired no department or army command, and hardly considered himself to be a great war chief. He possessed a reputation for integrity and modesty, compared to the temperamental and egocentric "Little Napoleon." He undoubtably would be far easier to work with and to control at the head of the army than McClellan.[19]

But Hitchcock proved to be less easy to manipulate than Stanton probably anticipated. He advised against Maj. Gen. John C. Frémont being given a command of the Mountain Department, was dissatisfied with McClellan's plan to take Yorktown, and was irritated that Lincoln and Stanton had not heeded his warning to avoid moving troops out of the Shenandoah Valley. Frustrated and annoyed, Hitchcock tried to resign on numerous occasions. Lincoln and Stanton refused to allow it since his abrupt departure would

---

18   Judkin Browning and Timothy Silver, "Nature and Human Nature: Environmental Influences on the Union's Failed Peninsula Campaign, 1862," *Journal of the Civil War Era* 8, no 3. (September 2018): 401-403; Sears, *Lincoln's Lieutenants*, 132; Welsh, *Medical Histories* of *Union Generals*, 183, 189.

19   Marvel, *Lincoln's Autocrat*, 172; Taaffe, *Commanding the Army of the Potomac*, 7, 56-7, 60-62; T. Harry Williams, *Lincoln and His Generals* (New York, NY: Alfred A. Knopf, 1952), 150; Hitchcock, *Fifty Years in Camp and Field*, 431, 433, 439-41, 473, 482; Ethan Allen Hitchcock, *A Traveler in Indian Territory: The Journal of Ethan Allen Hitchcock, Late Major-General in the United States Army*, ed. Grant Foreman (Norman: University of Oklahoma Press, 1996), 10-12, 232; Cohen, I. Bernhard, "Ethan Allen Hitchcock: Soldier, Humanitarian, Scholar," *American Antiquarian Society Proceedings* 61 (1951): 35-7.

have led to public suspicion that he was dissatisfied with the conduct of the war—which to some degree was true. On November 15, 1862, Stanton assigned Hitchcock as commissioner for the exchange of prisoners, shifting him to a new position to likely avoid the embarrassment of a senior general in the administration's inner circle quitting.

Hitchcock survived the war and was permitted to live out his retirement as he had intended until disrupted by pesky generals and politicians begging for him to take up the sword.[20]

Michigan's Cincinnatus

In May 1861, Michigan Governor Austin Blair summoned the 1st Michigan Infantry's colonel, Orlando B. Willcox, to his office to inquire about a retired captain and farmer from Pontiac, Michigan, seeking a commission in the 2nd Michigan Infantry. Residents from Pontiac alleged that the ex-army officer was mentally unstable. But Blair had been attracted to the man's modesty, a rare quality among the men lobbying for commissions.

Blair valued Willcox's opinion, so he asked if he had heard of a soldier named Israel B. Richardson. The colonel admitted that he did not personally know him but did recognize the name. Richardson had graduated from West Point and made a name for himself in Mexico. At the battle of Cerro Gordo on April 18, 1847, the 5th U.S. Infantry lieutenant earned the sobriquet "Fighting Dick" for his bravery. By the end of the war, he was brevetted captain and major for "gallant and meritorious" service.[21]

The governor requested that Willcox meet with Richardson before he offered him a commission in the 2nd Michigan. Willcox agreed to. When

---

20 True, "A Reluctant Warrior," 146-48; Hitchcock, *Fifty Years in Camp and Field*, 440-45.

21 Abby Maria Hemenway, *The Vermont Historical Gazetteer: A Magazine, Embracing a History of Each Town, Civil, Ecclesiastical, Biographical and Military*, vol. 2 (Burlington, VT: Published by Miss A.M. Hemenway, 1871), 188; Mason, *Until Antietam*, 49; Charles K. Gardner, *Dictionary of All Officers Who Have Been Commissioned or Have Been Appointed and Served, in the Army of the United States, Since the Inauguration of Their First President in 1789, to the First January 1853,—With Every Commission of Each;—Including The Distinguished Officers of the Volunteers and Militia of the States, Who Have Served in Any Campaign, or Conflict With an Enemy, Since That Date; and the Navy and Marine Corps, Who Have Served With the Land Forces: Indicating the Battle, in Which Every Such Officer Has Been Killed, Or Wounded,—and the Special Words of Every Brevet Commission* (New York: G.P. Putnam & Company, 1853), 379.

talking over the war with Mexico and the impending civil war with Richardson, Willcox "found him clear and alert and up to the occasion." Within 15 minutes, the colonel was able to "size him up" and determined that he was "sound as a nut." Willcox returned to Blair and confidently reported, "That is your man, not for major, but for colonel, the man to drill your Second regiment."[22]

Richardson was named after his father, who was himself named after the famed Revolutionary War general Israel Putnam. In July 1835, at the age of 19, Richardson was admitted to West Point. After graduating, he saw service in most of the major battles during the Mexican War. While stationed in El Paso, Texas, after the war,

During the battle of Antietam, Maj. Gen. Israel Richardson's men broke through the Confederate center at the Sunken Road, but cannon fire directed by his old friend, James Longstreet, struck him down as he tried to push his men forward. His mortal wounding robbed the attack of its momentum. What if Richardson had not been shot? *Library of Congress*

he courted Rita Stephenson, the daughter of Hugh Stephenson, a wealthy Kentucky-born miner. The army officer converted to Catholicism and married her on August 3, 1850. Tragically, she died a year later while in childbirth. Six months later, the child followed her to the grave.[23]

---

22 Orlando B. Willcox, *Forgotten Valor: The Memoirs, Journals, & Civil War Letters of Orlando B. Willcox*, ed. by Robert G. Scott (Kent, OH: Kent State University Press, 1999), 250.

On September 30, 1855, Richardson resigned his army commission after 20 years of service and joined his family in Michigan. Looking to start a new life, he followed his mother, father, sister Susan, and her husband, Joseph A. Peck, to Pontiac, Michigan, and became a farmer. He would have probably continued managing a portion of his brother-in-law's fields for the rest of his life had not civil war erupted. He promptly offered his service to Michigan's governor when Confederate forces fired on Sumter.[24]

After consulting Willcox, Blair told Richardson that he would be made colonel of the 2nd Michigan instead of major. Richardson fell silent for a moment upon receiving this news. "I did not expect anything higher in the regiment than the majority," he told Blair. "I think it is all that I am capable of. I do not think I am fit to command a regiment of men, and would rather decline the colonelcy." This kind of humility is what attracted Blair to Richardson in the first place. Richardson did end up accepting the commission, and quickly rose from a colonel of a regiment to a major general in command of a division within 14 months.[25]

General Richardson's outwardly appearance did not inspire confidence like his colleagues, such as George B. McClellan, Fitz John Porter, and others, did. The sunbaked farmer paced about camp wearing an old straw hat, a citizen's coat without any insignia, and torn trousers with his hands thrust into his pockets. He looked more like a teamster or farmer than a major general. Even Willcox, who had a high opinion of him, described Richardson as "slouchy and slovenly," comparing his look and mannerisms to that of "Stonewall" Jackson. A soldier even likened Richardson to Zachary Taylor, stating that it was as if "old Rough and Ready was reproduced in his

23 Mason, *Until Antietam*, 4, 65-6, 72; Jamie M. Starling, "'He Does Not Profess, Until Today, any Religion': Catholic Clergy and Intermarriage in Paso del Norte during the Nineteenth Century," *American Catholic Studies* 126, no. 1 (Spring 2015): 43-61; Archives of the Cathedral of Ciudad Juarez, 1671-1945, Roll 3, Frame 250-51, Israel B. Richardson and Rita Stephenson seek permission to marry. Signed by R. Ortiz and Agustin Fischer, July 29, 1850, Microfilm Collection, The University of Texas at El Paso University Library, El Paso, Texas.

24 *The Daily Dispatch* (Richmond, VA), November 14, 1855; *The Daily Union* (Washington, D.C.), November 13, 1855; Mason, *Until Antietam*, 76-78; Oakland, Pontiac Village, Michigan, United States Census, 1860, *FamilySearch*, https://www.familysearch.org/ark:/61903/3:1:33SQ-GBS3-T3Z?wc=73BR-4ZF%3A1589428970%2C1589429382%2C1589430515&cc=1473181.

25 John Robertson, *Michigan in the War* (Lansing, MI: W.S. George & Co., State Printers & Binders, 1882), 187, 203-204; *Journal of the Executive Proceedings of the Senate of the United States of America, From December 1, 1862, to July 4, 1864, inclusive*, vol. 13 (Washington, D.C.: Government Printing Office, 1887), 205.

person." This casual appearance and easygoing personality caused some to question his aptitude for high command.[26]

Whatever doubts his colleagues had, they quickly dissipated during the Peninsula Campaign. "He is no holiday soldier," one newspaper noted of Richardson. He knew that "war is earnest business, in which man must shoot and be shot, and not a mere opportunity to wear fine clothes and disport in the bravery of evening parades." Richardson desired to be where the gunfire was the thickest, instead of remaining in the rear, out of touch with his frontline troops. This leadership style regularly placed him in harm's way, but his men loved him for it. After numerous close calls, his soldiers began to think he was bulletproof. Brigadier General Oliver O. Howard, who initially had his doubts about Richardson, changed his estimation of the old army soldier when observing him in action on the battlefield. "[I] learned to prize him for his pluck and energy that came out in battle and on an active campaign," Howard stated. "In the fight he was a capital leader, very cool and self-possessed."[27]

"Fighting Dick" caught the attention of President Abraham Lincoln early in the war. "The President is a great friend of mine," Richardson wrote to his sister Susan in November 1861. "[S]ays I am honest and faithful, and tells people that if there is to be any fighting to be done, he expects me to be among the first." If Richardson called on Lincoln, he boasted, the president

---

26   Robert I. Girardi, *The Civil War Generals: Comrades, Peers, Rivals-In Their Own Words* (Minneapolis, MN, Zenith Press, 2013), 146; Josiah Marshall Favill, *Diary of a Young Officer Serving with the Armies of the United States During the War of the Rebellion* (Chicago: R. R. Donnelly & Sons, 1909), 103; D. G. Crotty, *Four Years Campaigning in the Army of the Potomac* (Grand Rapids, MI: Dygert Bros. & Co., 1874): 33-34; Charles B. Haydon, *For Country, Cause and Leader: The Civil War Journal of Charles B. Haydon*, ed. Stephen W. Sears (New York: Ticknor & Fields, 1993), 151; "General Richardson," *Orleans Independent Standard* (Irasburg, VT), April 4, 1862; Willcox, *Forgotten Valor*, 250; Mason, *Until Antietam*, 80, 83, 148, 165-66; Jacob H. Cole, *Under Five Commanders, or a Boy's Experience with the Army of the Potomac* (Paterson, NJ: News Printing Company, 1906), 86; Oliver O. Howard, *Autobiography of Oliver Otis Howard, Major General, United States Army*, vol. 1 (New York: The Baker & Taylor Co., 1907), 208; Oliver Otis Howard Papers, 1833-1912, Oliver O. Howard to Eliza G. Howard, March 23, 1862, George J. Mitchell Department of Special Collections & Archives, Bowdoin College Library, Brunswick, Maine. Note: Howard's correspondence at the Bowdoin College Library will be thereafter citied as OOHP. Oliver O. Howard to Lizzie Howard, April 4, 1862, OOHP.

27   "General Richardson," *Orleans Independent Standard* (Irasburg, VT), April 4, 1862; Nelson A. Niles, *Serving the Republic: Memoirs of the Civil and Military Life of Nelson A. Miles, Lieutenant-General, United States Army* (New York: Harper & Brothers Publishers, 1911), 46; Mason, *Until Antietam*, 104, 165-66; Howard, *Autobiography of Oliver Otis Howard*, 208.

would see him first. Lincoln was likely attracted to the same modesty, frankness, common sense, and fighting reputation Richardson possessed, which also endeared him to a fellow Midwesterner, Ulysses S. Grant. Besides, Richardson was a Republican. It was no chance that Lincoln found an ally in this Republican division commander fighting in an army under the command of a Democrat. When he was promoted to division command, Richardson desired to take his old brigade with him, so he directly petitioned Lincoln to interject on his behalf. A telegram from Lincoln, signed by Secretary of War Edwin M. Stanton, was sent to McClellan requesting that Richardson's wish be granted. McClellan, incensed not only that Lincoln was meddling in the army's organization, but that Richardson was going over his head, rejected the request.[28]

Richardson's finest performance during the war was also his last. At the battle of Antietam on September 17, 1862, his division struck Maj. Gen. Daniel Harvey Hill's gray-clad troops at the Sunken Road. He had an opportunity to slice Gen. Robert E. Lee's Army of Northern Virginia in two—and nearly did. "I looked over my right shoulder and saw that gallant old fellow advancing on the right of our line, almost alone, afoot and with his bare sword in his hand, and his face was as black as a thunder cloud," Lt. Thomas L. Livermore of the 5th New Hampshire Infantry wrote of Richardson. "I shall never cease to admire that magnificent fighting general who advanced with his front line, with his sword bare and ready to use, and his swarthy face, burning eye, and square jaw, though long since lifeless dust, are dear to me." Richardson never asked his men to go where he was not willing to go himself.[29]

Richardson was on the front line directing the fire of the six 12-pounders of Capt. William M. Graham's Battery K, 1st U.S. Artillery, within 300 yards of a Confederate battery. Ironically, his old friend, Maj. Gen. James Longstreet, ordered his staff to man Capt. Merritt B. Miller's four guns and return fire. Richardson's assistant adjutant general, Capt.

---

28   Mason, *Until Antietam*, 123; Israel B. Richardson to Abraham Lincoln, June 7, 1862, Library of Congress, Washington, D.C.; Abraham Lincoln, *The Collected Works of Abraham Lincoln*, vol. 5, ed. Roy P. Basler (New Brunswick, NJ: Rutgers University Press, 1953), 159, 360; Abraham Lincoln to Carl Schurz, November 24, 1862, Library of Congress, Washington, D.C.

29   Sears, *Lincoln's Lieutenants*, 398; Thomas L. Livermore, *Days and Events, 1860-1866* (Boston & New York: Houghton Mifflin Co., 1920), 137-38.

John M. Norvell, was nearby when the general fell mortally wounded by an artillery shell. "[I] was on my horse beside him, he being dismounted at the time receiving an order from him to deliver to General McClellan a message," Norvell recalled, "when he was struck by a piece of shell, a piece of same shell struck my horse, which knocked me about 10 feet." With Richardson down and no one to take charge and press the attack, this rare opportunity to shatter Lee's army quickly sputtered out. McClellan called a hasty conference among his commanders to consult them if they should renew the offensive. He decided to call off the attack. It was one of the many missed opportunities that day.[30]

Richardson was evacuated to a three-story gristmill, serving as a field hospital, less than a mile from the Sunken Road. "[N]o one but a soldier can understand our sorrow at seeing him carried off the field," Livermore declared as he watched his beloved commander pass to the rear. The general was then transported by an ambulance to the home of Elizabeth and Philip Pry and placed in an upstairs bedroom. When he visited the house two days later to check on Maj. Gen. Joseph Hooker, Col. Charles S. Wainwright observed that Richardson "seemed in great pain as I could hear his groans the whole time I was in the house."[31]

McClellan dispatched the Army of the Potomac's medical director, Dr. Jonathan Letterman, and one of his assistants, to evaluate the severity of Richardson's wound. Both doctors concluded that the general's chance of survival was one in twenty. Despite their despairing prognosis, Richardson's personal surgeon and his division's medical director, Dr. John Howard Taylor, fought to save his life. Richardson's wife Frances and sister Marcella headed for the battlefield as soon as word reached them that he had been wounded. "He is very much depressed, not at all like himself," Frances described in a letter to her sister-in-law Marcia from his bedside. "[He is] inclined to look at the dark side, much more than is good for him."

---

30 Mason, *Until Antietam*, 185-87; *The War of the Rebellion: A Compilation of the Official Records of the Union and Confederate Armies. Series I—Volume 19—In Two Parts. Part I—Reports* (Washington: Government Printing Office, 1887), 343-44; John E. Norwell, "A Memoir of John Mason Norwell's Civil War Service," *Military Collector & Historian* 68, no. 2 (Summer 2016): 161; Taaffe, *Commanding the Army of the Potomac*, 46.

31 Livermore, *Days and Events, 1860-1866*, 143-44; Charles S. Wainwright, *A Diary of Battle: The Personal Journals of Colonel Charles S. Wainwright*, ed. Allan Nevins (New York: Harcourt, Brace & World, Inc., 1962), 104.

Emaciated and weak, "Fighting Dick" lost the will to live and expired on the evening of November 3, 1862.[32]

A month before Richardson's death, President Lincoln arrived at the Antietam battlefield and paid a visit to his old acquaintance at the Pry House. Captain Charles S. Draper, Richardson's aide-de-camp, who had been shot through the right leg below the knee by a Minié ball that passed through both legs, lay wounded in the same room as the general. Eavesdropping on the conversation that took place between Lincoln and the mortally wounded general, the young officer claimed that the president promised Richardson command of the Army of the Potomac when he recovered.[33]

According to Dr. Jack C. Mason in *Until Antietam: The Life and Letters of Major General Israel B. Richardson* (2017), the only biography written on Richardson, Draper's account was recorded by Winifred Lee Lyster, wife of Dr. Henry F. L. Lyster, assistant surgeon of the 2nd Michigan Infantry, in a 1907 article titled "Michigan, My Michigan," written by Lt. Colonel Frederick Schneider of the same regiment. Schneider claimed that in the sixth verse of the song Mrs. Lyster "alludes to the much-lamented death of that eminent and heroic Michigan soldier, Major General Israel B. Richardson . . . with President Lincoln at his bedside, who, according to the late Charles Stewart Draper, aide-de-camp on General Richardson's staff and also wounded at this battle, and also present, was assured by the president that had General Richardson lived he would undoubtedly have been selected as General McClellan's successor as commander of the army of the Potomac." This mention of Draper's account by Schneider is the only evidence that Lincoln offered Richardson command of the Army of the Potomac.[34]

---

32   Israel B. Richardson, Military Pension Records, National Archives and Records Administration, Washington, D.C.; Samuel W. Durant, *History of Kalamazoo County, Michigan: with Illustrations and Biographical Sketches of its Prominent Men and Pioneers* (Philadelphia: Everts & Abbot, 1880), 114; Hemenway, *The Vermont Historical Gazetteer*, 188; Mason, *Until Antietam*, 126, 191-93, 196, 199; Israel B. Richardson Papers, Fannie Richardson to Marcia Richardson, October 1862, U.S. Army Military Institute, Carlisle Barracks, Pennsylvania; Rachel Moses, "'[A]s he lived for others, so did he die:' The Life of Israel B. Richardson," *National Museum of Civil War Museum*, February 4, 2019, http://www.civilwarmed.org/richardson/#_ftnref5.

33   Ward Hill Lamon, *Recollections of Abraham Lincoln, 1847-1865*, ed. by Dorothy L. Teillard (Washington: The Editor, 1911), 148; Mason, *Until Antietam*, 195-96.

34   Winifred Lee Lyster's sister was Eleanor Carroll (Brent) Poe, who was the wife of Brig. Gen. Orlando M. Poe. Mason, *Until Antietam*, 218; *Historical Collections: Collections and Researches Made By the Michigan Pioneer and Historical Society*, vol. 35 (Lasing, MI: Wynkoop Hallenbeck, Crawford Company, State Printers, 1907), 157, 162.

If Draper's account of the conversation between Lincoln and Richardson was not misconstrued, or had not been fabricated, why would have the president considered a division commander only promoted to major general a few months before to succeed McClellan in command of the Army of the Potomac? Richardson had never commanded more than a division, and this rapid ascent would have certainly infuriated his fellow division and corps commanders who had seniority.

It is possible, being a friend of Richardson's, Lincoln made a promise he had no intention of keeping. He had to know how desperate Richardson's wound was and could have used this promise simply to bolster the spirit of a dying man.[35]

However, Lincoln may have had more calculated motives for considering Richardson for this command. He knew he had a political ally. A Republican, Richardson was closely aligned with the Radical Republican senator from Michigan, Zachariah Chandler. Both men, while friendly, used each other for their own gains: Richardson used Chandler for his political influence, and Chandler used Richardson to collect damning evidence to demonstrate McClellan's incompetence. While Richardson was not as an outspoken critic of McClellan, his displeasure with the general was published in some Republican newspapers and expressed in his official report after the Peninsula Campaign. There was no hiding that Richardson did not think highly of McClellan. Replacing McClellan with Richardson would have firmly put the Army of the Potomac in control of a loyal Republican for the first time during the war.[36]

Had Richardson recovered in time, he would have likely assumed command of the Army of the Potomac after Lincoln relieved McClellan. Instead, he died two days before Lincoln appointed Maj. Gen. Ambrose E. Burnside to replace him. While much friendlier to the administration than McClellan, the politically moderate Burnside did not want the job and only agree to take it to avoid his principal rival and Republican operative, Maj. Gen. Joseph Hooker, from taking control of the army. Richardson could have been the one leading the Army of the Potomac during the winter of

---

35 Taaffe, *Commanding the Army of the Potomac*, 12; Favill, *Diary of a Young Officer,* 196; Oliver O. Howard to Lizzie Howard, September 26, 1862, OOHP.

36 Mason, *Until Antietam*, 111, 118-19, 124, 164-67. Chandler served as one of Richardson's pallbearers at his funeral and later advocated an increase to his widow's pension.

1862 rather than Burnside. There might have never been more than 12,000 lives sacrificed at Fredericksburg.

Or, had he taken a few more months to recover from his wounds, Richardson may have replaced Burnside. Lincoln instead took a gamble with Hooker in January 1863, willing to overlook his flaws because he knew Hooker was a brave and skillful soldier, confident in himself, and most importantly, a fighter. But Richardson was the better version of Hooker Lincoln was seeking. Lincoln had to settle for less.[37]

Would have Richardson have been willing to wage total war against the rebellious south? While he remained cordial to old army cronies fighting against the country he spent 20 years protecting, Richardson demonstrated that he held nothing back in battle. His affection toward old friends is not enough to indicate he would not have waged a hard war against his enemies if placed at the head of the Army of the Potomac. Unfortunately for Lincoln, he never had a chance to find out, and would have to endure two more years of disappointment in the Eastern Theater before he found a fighting general to steer the war effort in the right direction and keep it that way: south into Virginia, relentlessly and confidently at Lee's army.[38]

"Reliable as Steel!"

"It is the wish of the 1st Corps, I mean the whole corps, men and officers, to pay a small tribute to his memory," Captain Robert W. Mitchell wrote to John F. Reynolds's sisters, whose brother had been killed two months before while leading the Union 1st Corps at Gettysburg. "I was selected as one of a committee + asked to write to you, begging you to allow us the privilege, I mean the honor, to place over our General a monument, which would be done without any public demonstration, + which would please the officers and men of the old Corps." Perhaps no other corps commander held the confidence in the Army of the Potomac

---

37   Fry, *A Republic in the Ranks*, 71; Jeffrey W. Green, *McClellan and the Union High Command, 1861-1863: Leadership Gaps That Cost a Timely Victory* (Jefferson, NC: McFarland & Co., Inc., 2017), 129.

38   James Longstreet, *From Manassas to Appomattox Memoirs of the Civil War in America* (Philadelphia: J.B. Lippincott Co., 1896), 59.

that John Reynolds did during the summer of 1863.[39]

At the age of 16, John Fulton Reynolds received an appointment to West Point with the help of his father's good friend and future fifteenth president of the United States, James Buchanan. He graduated in the middle of his class—ranked 26th of 50 cadets— four years later in 1841. Despite his average class rank, Assistant Professor Henry L. Kendricks was impressed with the cadet's "clear and independent thinking, his even temperament, and by his courtesy." The Pennsylvanian seemed to have something special about him.[40]

He had chance to demonstrate what that was during the Mexican War. As a young first lieutenant in the 3rd Artillery, Reynolds performed well on the battlefield. At the battle of Buena Vista in

Maj. Gen. John Reynolds was killed early on the first day of the battle of Gettysburg, July 1, 1863. What if he had lived? *Library of Congress*

February 1847, Reynolds directed his guns with "coolness and firmness," according to his superior officer, Capt. Thomas W. Sherman, helping to

---

39   Reynolds Family Papers, 1765-1934, Captain R.W. Mitchell to Eleanor Reynolds, September 16, 1863, Franklin & Marshall College Archives & Special Collections, Lancaster, Pennsylvania. Note: Reynolds' correspondence from the Franklin & Marshall College Archives & Special Collections will be thereafter cited as JFR, FM. Marsena R. Patrick, *Inside Lincoln's Army: The Diary of Marsena Rudolph Patrick, Provost Marshal General, Army of the Potomac*, ed. David S. Sparks (New York: Thomas Yoseloff, 1964), 237.

40   Edward J. Nichols, *Toward Gettysburg: A Biography of General John F. Reynolds* (University Park: Pennsylvania State University Press, 1958), 11, 18; *Reynolds Memorial: Addresses Delivered Before the Historical Society of Pennsylvania Upon the Occasion of the Presentation of a Portrait of Maj.-Gen. John F. Reynolds, March 8, 1880* (Philadelphia: J.B. Lippincott & Co., 1880), 12.

secure an American victory. The battle was one bloodiest of the war, and probably the closest the American forces came to being defeated. But they persevered, in a large part to the Americans' tenacity and the leadership of Gen. Zachary Taylor.

The impressionable lieutenant afterward praised Taylor's leadership style during this desperate fight. He observed that Taylor "only becomes the greater the more difficulties thicken around him"—even when the battle seemed to be going awry. The 63-year-old career army officer exposed himself to Mexican cannon and rifle fire to calm and inspire his army composed predominately of green volunteers. "I never saw him so perfectly cool and determined in my life before," Reynolds wrote home in admiration. "He was in a good humor the whole fight and appeared perfectly certain of gaining the day." The Pennsylvanian would go on to mirror Taylor's coolness and confidence during the Civil War.[41]

While many of his colleagues left the army in the interwar years, Reynolds stayed put. He campaigned against the Mormons in Utah and the Rogue River Indians in the Pacific Northwest. In September 1860, he replaced Col. William J. Hardee as commandant of cadets at West Point, continuing in this assignment until June 1861, two months after Confederate Brig. Gen. P. G. T. Beauregard's guns fired on Fort Sumter.[42]

But as early as March 1861, Gen. Winfield Scott offered Reynolds a position on his staff as an aide-de-camp when it became clear that civil war was imminent. "Several years ago I said to you that I should offer you the first vacancy for an aide-de-camp that might occur in my staff," Scott affectionately wrote to Reynolds. "I now have the pleasure of saying that I shall be glad if you will accept it. I have thought of no one else for the place." Reynolds turned down Scott's generous offer, hoping to receive a field command rather than a desk job in the looming conflict.

---

41 Nichols, *Toward Gettysburg*, 43-44. Admiration for Brig. Gen. Zachary Taylor was shared by many other future Civil War generals, most notably Ulysses S. Grant.

42 George W. Cullum, *Biographical Register of the Officers and Graduates of the U.S. Military Academy at West Point, N.Y. From Its Establishment, In 1802, to 1890 With the Early History of the United States Military Academy. Third Edition. Vol. 2. Nos. 1001 to 2000* (Boston & New York: Houghton, Mifflin & Co., 1891), 91-92; John P. Nicholson, Lewis Eugene Beitler, and Paul L Roy, eds., *Pennsylvania at Gettysburg: Ceremonies at the Dedication of the Monuments Erected by the Commonwealth of Pennsylvania to Major-General George G. Meade, Major-General Winfield S. Hancock, Major-General John F. Reynolds and to Mark the Positions of the Pennsylvania Commands Engaged in the Battle*, vol. 2 (Harrisburg, PA: W.S. Ray State Printers, 1914), 990; Nichols, *Toward Gettysburg*, 70-71.

Five months later his wish was granted when he was appointed a brigadier general of volunteers. General George B. McClellan, impressed with his resume, used his influence to get Reynolds yanked from Maj. Gen. John E. Wool's Department of Virginia and reassigned to a brigade of Pennsylvania Reserves—a state-organized division of all-Pennsylvania troops—in the newly formed Army of the Potomac.[43]

Reynolds impressed many with his soldierly appearance and disposition on and off the battlefield. Thin and erect, the veteran army officer possessed piercing black eyes, dark hair, and cheeks tanned from years of service on the frontier. "He was a superb-looking man," Col. Frederick Lyman Hitchcock recalled, "dark complexioned, wearing full black whiskers, and sat his fine horse like a Centaur, tall, straight, and graceful, the ideal soldier." But most of all, he dazzled those surrounding him with his confidence and resourcefulness. "A strict disciplinarian, attention to the wants of his men, and a brave and fearless commander combined," First Sgt. W. Hayes Grier of the 5th Pennsylvania Reserves noted, "united our hearts in willing action to his commands." Brigadier General Charles Devens described Reynolds most succinctly: "Modest and simple, in manner: with no trace of affectation or boasting: reliable as steel!"[44]

Following the battle of Gaines's Mill on June 27, 1862, Reynolds and his assistant adjutant general were captured by pickets of the 4th Virginia Infantry. He returned to the Army of the Potomac in August after being exchanged. He received glowing praise for his performance at the Second Battle of Bull Run in August 1862, where he seized the colors of the 2nd

---

43   Nichols, *Toward Gettysburg*, 75-76; Winfield Scott to John F. Reynolds, March 7, 1861, JFR, FM; Sears, *Lincoln's Lieutenants*, 92-93; George B. McClellan, *George B. McClellan's Own Story: The War for the Union, the Soldiers Who Fought It, the Civilians Who Directed It, and His Relationship to It and Them* (New York: Charles L. Webster & Co., 1887), 140.

44   *Reynolds Memorial*, 32-3; Henry A. Hazen and S. Lewis B. Speare, eds., *A History of the Class of 1854 in Dartmouth College, Including Col. Haskell's Narrative of the Battle of Gettysburg* (Boston: Alfred Mudge & Son, Printers, 1898), 74; Nicholson, Beitler, and Roy, *Pennsylvania at Gettysburg*, 995-96; Frederick L. Hitchcock, *War from the Inside: The Story of the 132nd Regiment Pennsylvania Volunteer Infantry in the War for the Suppression of the Rebellion* (Philadelphia: Press of J.B. Lippincott Co., 1904), 101-102; Nichols, *Toward Gettysburg*, 75-77, 147, 163, 184; George Meade, *The Life and Letters of George Gordon Meade, Major-General United States Army*, vol. 1 (New York: Charles Scribner's Sons, 1913), 346; Girardi, *The Civil War Generals*, 145-46; "General Meade and the Battle of Gettysburg. An Oration, Delivered by Major-General Charles Devens, Junior, at the Re-Union of the Army of the Potomac, at New Haven Connecticut, May 14, 1873," *The Historical Magazine* 2, no. 1 (July 1873): 20; W. Hayes Grier to Catherine (Cate) Reynolds, August 21, 1863, JFR, FM.

Pennsylvania Reserves from of a color-bearer and rode up and down the line, waving it above his head to inspire his division, which helped to save Pope's army from destruction. Five days before the battle of Antietam, Governor Andrew Curtin of Pennsylvania requested that Stanton assign Reynolds to organize and lead the Pennsylvania militia during Lee's invasion of Maryland, despite the fervent protest of McClellan and his corps commander, Joseph Hooker. This caused Reynolds to miss the bloody engagement. When he returned at the end of September, McClellan gave him command of the I Corps, although nine other generals outranked the Pennsylvanian. He would remain in command of the corps for roughly 10 months until his death.[45]

The Army of the Potomac's corps commanders nearly mutinied during the spring of 1863. Generals Darius N. Couch, Henry W. Slocum, George G. Meade, John F. Reynolds, and others lost confidence in Hooker's ability to command after his abysmal performance at Chancellorsville. By May 10, Couch, Slocum, and John Sedgwick all pledged to serve under Meade of the V Corps, who had ended the campaign with an enhanced reputation. Meade and Reynolds, meanwhile, had expressed concerns over Hooker's ability to lead the army to Governor Curtin, who in turn reported their sentiments to Lincoln. Both Couch and Slocum traveled to Washington and called on Lincoln to condemn Hooker and petition for his removal. Couch even resigned his commission rather than having to endure another battle under Hooker's leadership.[46]

On May 31, 1863, Reynolds followed Couch's and Slocum's example and left for Washington to meet with Lincoln. Major General John Gibbon

---

45   Elmer R. Woodard, III, *A Bloody Day at Gaines' Mill: The Battlefield Debut of the Army of Northern Virginia, June 27, 1862* (Jefferson, NC: MacFarland & Co., Inc, 2018), 224; *Reynolds Memorial, 32;* Tobias B. Kaufman, *Tobias's Story The Life and Civil War Career of Tobias B. Kaufman,* ed. Doug Kauffmann (Xlibris Corporation, 2012), 39; Nichols, *Toward Gettysburg,* 96-9, 100, 126-28; Charles Lamborn to Eleanor Reynolds, July 18, 1862, JFR, FM; Taaffe, *Commanding the Army of the Potomac,* 48-9.

46   Darius N. Couch, "The Chancellorsville Campaign" in *Battles and Leaders of the Civil War,* vol. 3 (New York: The Century Co., 1888), 171; Taaffe, *Commanding the Army of the Potomac,* 101-4; Christopher S. Stowe, "'The Longest and Clearest Head of Any General Officer' George Gordon Meade as Corps Commander, December 1862-June 1863," in *Corps Commanders in Blue: Union Major Generals in the Civil War,* ed. Ethan S. Rafuse (Baton Rouge: Louisiana State University Press, 2014), 112-155; Green, *McClellan and the Union High Command, 1861-1863,* 166-67, 174; Sears, *Lincoln's Lieutenants,* 520-26; Meade, *The Life and Letters of George Gordon Meade,* 372, 379-81; John Sedgwick, *Correspondence of John Sedgwick, Major-General,* vol. 2, ed. George W. Curtis (New York: Printed for Carl & Ellen Battelle Stoeckel by the De Vinne Press, 1903), 125-27.

later recalled that Reynolds "was the picture of woe and disgust" over how Hooker had been outgeneraled. While he despised politicians interfering in army affairs, he felt compelled to speak up. But this meeting reportedly went differently than Lincoln's meeting with Couch and Slocum. In August 1913, Reynolds' sister, Eleanor, claimed in a letter to her nephew, Lt. Col. John F. Landis, that on the night of June 2, 1863, her brother revealed that he had been offered command of the Army of the Potomac during the meeting with Lincoln. He had declined since Lincoln could not assure him that Washington would not meddle in the army's operations.[47]

Other officers corroborated Eleanor Reynolds's claim that her brother had been offered command of the army in the summer of 1863. On June 28, 1863, Col. Charles S. Wainwright wrote that, "General Reynolds told me today that the command of this army was offered to him when he was summoned to Washington a month ago; but he refused it, because, to use his own expression, 'he was unwilling to take Burnside's and Hooker's leavings.'" Captain Stephen M. Weld of Reynolds's staff indicated the general had confided to him "that the command had been offered to him, but that he had refused it," but did not provide a reason why like Wainwright. Reynolds even told his friend and colleague, George G. Meade. Meade wrote to his wife Margaretta and said that a friend—likely Governor Curtin—warned Reynolds that he was being considered for command of the Army of the Potomac, causing him to hurry to Washington to tell Lincoln that "he did not want the command and would not take it."[48]

From these varying accounts, one theme stands out: Reynolds did not want command of the Army of the Potomac, whether it was offered to him or not. On the morning of June 28, Lincoln convened his cabinet and showed them a telegram from Hooker requesting to be relieved. According to Secretary of the Navy Gideon Welles, Sedgwick's, Meade's, and Couch's names came up as potential replacements, but Reynolds's name was

---

47 Taaffe, *Commanding the Army of the Potomac*, 102; Nichols, *Toward Gettysburg*, 182, 220-21. It is worth noting that this letter from Eleanor Reynolds is missing from Franklin & Marshall College. This may still be in possession of Reynolds's descendants.

48 Wainwright, *A Diary of Battle*, 229; Nichols, *Toward Gettysburg*, 223; Stowe, "'The Longest and Clearest Head of Any General Officer' George Gordon Meade as Corps Commander, December 1862-June 1863," 141-42; Oliver J. Keller, "Soldier General of the Army: John Fulton Reynolds," *Civil War History* 4, no. 2 (June 1858): 124; "Gen. Reynolds," *Rutland Weekly Herald* (Rutland, VT), July 9, 1863.

excluded. Welles surmised that Lincoln simply asked his cabinet members' opinions "as a feeler to get an expression of opinion—a committal—or to make it appear that all were consulted." Meade had already been placed in command and Hooker relieved by the time the meeting was held. But it is interesting that Reynolds's name did not come up as a potential candidate, indicating that either he had communicated to Lincoln that he wanted nothing to do with army command or that he was not being considered for some other reason.

Colonel James A. Hardie arrived with orders to place Meade in command of the Army of the Potomac on the morning of June 28. "General Meade had shared the opinion of the whole army, that if General Hooker were to be superseded, General Reynolds, commander of the First Corps, should and would be appointed to the chief command," Hardie recalled. "[A]nd as they were devoted friends, his anxiety to confer with Reynolds was intense, but he had to give way to the imperative order to assume command of the army at once."[49]

Of his seven corps commanders, Meade placed the greatest confidence in Reynolds during the opening phase of the battle of Gettysburg. Reynolds's performance and the events on July 1, 1863, are well-known, and have become revered in Gettysburg lore. Reynolds quickly grasped the importance of the field, and his prompt and resolute course of action allowed Meade's army to gain the high ground, significantly contributing to the Union success in the subsequent two days of battle.[50] It was a pyrrhic high point for Reynolds, though. A Confederate infantryman's musket ball struck him in back of the neck near Herbst Woods, killing him. (There is some debate about who killed him and the manner of his death.) Like Richardson at Antietam, he died at the apex of his military career. Staff officers rescued his body from

49   Nichols, *Toward Gettysburg*, 220-23. See "Reynolds and the Army of the Potomac Command" in the appendix of Nichols's book. Green, *McClellan and the Union High Command, 1861-1863*, 173; Gideon Welles, *Diary of Gideon Welles, Secretary of the Navy Under Lincoln and Johnson, Volume 1, 1861—March 30, 1864*, Edgar T. Welles, ed. (Boston: Houghton Mifflin, 1911), 347-48; James A. Hardie, *Memoir of J.A. Hardie, Inspector-General, U.S. Army*, ed. Charles F. Benjamin (Washington: Printed for Private Circulation, 1877), 40.

50   Michael G. Klingenberg, "Of Cupolas and Sharpshooters: Major General John Fulton Reynolds and Popular Gettysburg Myths," *Gettysburg Magazine* 59 (July 2018): 49-65; Survivors' Association, *History of the 121st Regiment Pennsylvania Volunteers* (Philadelphia: Press of the Catholic Standard and Times, 1906), 224; D. Scott Hartwig, "John Reynolds' Recklessness Shaped Victory at Gettysburg," *HistoryNet*, October 7, 2019, https://www.historynet.com/john-reynolds-recklessness-shaped-victory-at-gettysburg.htm.

the field and transported it to Baltimore, where it was embalmed. A metallic coffin holding his remains rested at his sister's home for viewing until its burial in Lancaster, Pennsylvania, on July 4, 1863.[51]

It is probable that placing Reynolds in command of the Army of the Potomac came up as a topic of discussion during Lincoln's meeting with him on June 2. But why would have Lincoln considered the general as a candidate to succeed Hooker?

For one, Reynolds was highly regarded for his capability as a soldier and leader. Winfield Scott, George B. McClellan, Darius N. Couch, Joseph Hooker, Winfield Scott Hancock, George G. Meade, William T. Sherman, and other senior officers praised him. This also included the lower ranks. "From soldiers, cadets, and officers, junior and senior," Maj. Gen. Oliver O. Howard declared, "he always secured reverence for his serious character, respect for his ability, care for his uniform discipline, admiration for his fearlessness, and love for his unfailing generosity." Some thought he, not Meade, should have had led the Army of the Potomac after Hooker was relieved. "[I]n the opinion of many," Maj. Gen. Carl Schurz revealed, "it was he that ought to have been put at the head of the Army of the Potomac."[52]

No one probably thought more highly of Reynolds than the man who ended up replacing Hooker. "[W]hen he fell at Gettysburg, the army lost its right arm," Meade soberly declared. He also grieved that at Gettysburg, "I lost, not only a lieutenant most important to me in his services, but a friend and brother." After speaking with Meade, Maj. William Riddle told Reynolds's sister, Eleanor, that the general claimed, "he would 'rather have lost twenty thousand men, for the country's sake, than Reynolds.'" A

---

51   Charles H. Veil to David McConaughy, April 7, 1864, JFR, FM; "The Great Battle Near Gettysburg—Latest from the Battlefield," *Wilmington Journal* (Wilmington, NC), July 9, 1863; "Arrival of the Body of Gen. Reynolds," *Daily National Republican* (Washington, D.C.), July 3, 1863; *Alexandria Gazette* (Alexandria, D.C.), July 8, 1863; Scott Mingus, "Eyewitness described death of Lancaster's General Reynolds at Gettysburg," *Cannonball* (blog), June 10, 2015, https://yorkblog.com/cannonball/eyewitness-death-lancasters-general-reynolds-gettysburg/.

52   Sears, *Lincoln's Lieutenants*, 536; Joseph Hooker to John F. Reynolds, April 3[0?], 1863, JFR, FM; Darius N. Couch to James L. Reynolds, July 3, 1863, JFR, FM; McClellan, *McClellan's Own Story*, 140; William T. Sherman to Samuel Reynolds, February 16, 1883, JFR, FM; Howard, *Autobiography of Oliver Otis Howard*, 402; Carl Schurz, *The Reminiscences of Carl Schurz, 1863–1869*, vol. 3 (New York: The McClure Co., 1908), 6; *Reynolds Memorial*, 94.

captured Confederate lieutenant remarked that the Confederacy could far better spare "Stonewall" Jackson than the Federals could spare Reynolds.[53]

In the months following Gettysburg, there is no doubt that Meade was hurting due to the loss of Reynolds, Hancock, and other senior leaders. This was especially the case during the Mine Run Campaign, where he was deficient of resourceful and aggressive corps commanders. Reynolds's death not only robbed Meade of a resourceful subordinate, but also Ulysses S. Grant during the campaigns of 1864–65.[54]

But the seemingly unassailable general had two major flaws: He was a McClellanite and Democrat. Reynolds was one of the first officers McClellan appointed to the Army of the Potomac and remained loyal to him throughout the war. Despite his political ideology, Reynolds had the unwavering confidence of Republican Governor Andrew G. Curtin, one of Lincoln's most avid supports. Curtin thought highly enough of Reynolds to specifically request that he be sent to command the Pennsylvania militia on the eve of McClellan's clash with Lee at Antietam and "praised his zeal, spirit, and ability" in that role. It certainly helped that Reynolds was a political moderate, unlike some of his fellow corps and division commanders.[55]

One also has to at least consider if Reynolds would have adopted waging a hard war against the Confederacy. When he found out that Reynolds had become a prisoner of war following Gaines's Mill, Fredericksburg's mayor, Montgomery Slaughter, and dozens of citizens from the city sent a letter to Confederate Secretary of War George W. Randolph "invoking for him now a prisoner of our Government a treatment as kind and considerate as was extended by him to us," since Reynolds had "sav[ed] our citizens from the countless ill[s], which an unbridled and licentious soldiery might inflict on a helpless population" during his 16-day tenure as military governor. Reynolds, the letter continued, "conserve[ed] and protect[ed] as far as

---

53   George G. Meade, *The Life and Letters of George Gordon Meade*, vol. 2 (New York: Charles Scribner's Sons, 1913), 315; Frank A. Haskell, *The Battle of Gettysburg* (Madison: Wisconsin History Commission, Democrat Printing Co., 1908), 14; *Reynolds Memorial*, 31; Keller "Soldier General of the Army: John Fulton Reynolds," 128; William Riddle to Eleanor Reynolds, August 6, 1863, JFR, FM; Charles Lamborn to Eleanor & Harriet Reynolds, July 7, 1863, JFR, FM.

54   Taaffe, *Commanding the Army of the Potomac*, 128-9.

55   *Reynolds Memorial*, 89-92; Andrew G. Curtin to John F. Reynolds, September 26, 1862, JFR, FM; Andrew G. Curtin to James L. Reynolds, July 3, 1863, JFR, FM; Fry, *A Republic in the Ranks*, 71, 102.

practicable, the personal rights and domestic comfort of the citizens; and thus to mitigate, so far as his action could avail, the evils and annoyances which are incident to such an occupation." Reynolds differed from Grant and Sherman in that he believed that a war should be waged against enemy soldiers, not property or civilians.[56]

What probably alarmed Lincoln the most about John Reynolds would have been his contempt for the administration's interference with the Army of the Potomac. As far back as the Mexican War, Reynolds chastised President James K. Polk for stripping Zachary Taylor of his troops due to the general's growing popularity on the home front and viability as a political rival. Reynolds had voiced his distaste for Lincoln's and Stanton's interference in the Army of the Potomac's operations on numerous occasions. He was of the option that just as soldiers should fight other soldiers and not civilians, politicians in Washington should not meddle with army operations. For instance, he was outraged when Burnside left the Army of the Potomac after the fiasco at Fredericksburg and traveled to Washington to confer with the president. This desire for a disconnect from Washington could have alarmed Lincoln. For the time, Lincoln needed a general whom he could keep a close eye on and efficiently manage as Lee's troops marched freely across Pennsylvania.[57]

If Reynolds had received command instead of Meade, he would have taken over during one of the most important campaigns of the war. Perhaps things would have played out differently had he led the army instead of the more cautious Meade. He committed his corps to a fight at Gettysburg on July 1, only to be killed. He may have decided to take strong offensive action against Lee's army on either July 2 or July 3 had he been at the helm of the army. The battle may have even been fought somewhere else instead of Gettysburg. But the biggest question is if Reynolds would have relentlessly pursued Lee's battered army after the battle. While soft on civilians and property, he was not forgiving to enemy combatants. Would Reynolds have

56 Taaffe, *Commanding the Army of the Potomac*, 48; Montgomery Slaughter and citizens of Fredericksburg, Virginia, to George W. Randolph, July 2, 1862, JFR, FM; Nichols, *Toward Gettysburg*, 85-6.

57 Nichols, *Toward Gettysburg*, 34-6; John F. Reynolds to Eleanor Reynolds, June 10, 1862, JFR, FM; John F. Reynolds to My Dear Sisters, August 25, 1862, JFR, FM; John F. Reynolds to My Dear Sisters, June 23, 1863, JFR, FM; Taaffe, *Commanding the Army of the Potomac*, 105-106; Sears, *Lincoln's Lieutenants*, 532.

delivered the knockout blow to the Army of Northern Virginia that Meade failed to do? One has to wonder if that thought crossed Lincoln's mind as Lee's army slipped back into Virginia.

*   *   *

We can only estimate how Hitchcock, Richardson, or Reynolds would have fared at the head of the Army of the Potomac. What we do know is that Lincoln spent four frustrating years trying to find the right general to lead the most important army in the field, leading to a lack of continuity at the head of the army. The inability of McClellan, Burnside, and Hooker to find success—and their subsequent oustings—led to a great effort on the part of Lincoln's administration to remedy this leadership problem, which was a problem in itself. The turmoil and politicizing surrounding this senior position led to rumors, conjectures, jealousies, and backstabbing among its corps commanders. Politics was always a central part of the Army of the Potomac and was directly responsible for numerous setbacks. The appointment of Democrat George B. McClellan in 1862 kicked it off and it continued well into 1864. For the first ten months of his tenure as army commander, Meade spent as much time worrying about political machinations in his rear as he did the Confederates in his front.

But at last, in March 1864, Lincoln found a man to bind together the fragile egos and unique personalities in the army when Grant arrived east. While he could not completely quell the political rumblings within the army, the political moderate and victor from the Western Theater brought with him stability and finally put these rumors of who would be in charge of the Army of the Potomac to rest for good.[58]

---

58 Fry, *A Republic in the Ranks*, 142-43.

CHAPTER FIVE

What If Stonewall Jackson

Had Not Been Shot?

Kristopher D. White

I have endured the phrase countless times: "If Stonewall Jackson hadn't been shot . . . the Confederacy would have won the battle of Gettysburg. . . . Jackson, unlike Ewell, would have taken Cemetery Hill . . . the South would have won the Civil War . . . the League of Nations wouldn't have been a failure . . . and the last episode of *Game of Thrones* would not have been such an utter disappointment."

The vast number of Monday morning quarterbacks who love to play the "What If" game when it comes to the exploits of Lt. Gen. Thomas J. "Stonewall" Jackson is staggering. Many history buffs view the exploits of Jackson in a hermetically sealed vacuum—a roughly eight-week span of time that covers his wounding at Chancellorsville and his death at Guinea Station, to the end of July 1, 1863, when his successor Richard Ewell failed to secure Cemetery and Culp's hills at Gettysburg.

It is essentially the same game every sports fan, unsuccessful politician, or failed general plays after a loss: the "What If" game. What if we had one more first down, campaigned harder in a swing district, or taken that hill? These types of assumptions can be very dangerous because folks knock over all of the dominos at once to find the outcome they want to have happened, rather than look at the next one, three, or five dominos down the line, as they veer off in all directions.

The assumption that all of the ills of the failing Southern Confederacy

According to historian William C. Davis, to ask "What if Stonewall Jackson was at Gettysburg" is to ask "the oldest and most often asked 'what if' question of the Civil War." First, Jackson would have had to survive his wounding. One-armed or two-, he would have then had to survive pneumonia. *ECW collection*

would have been cured had one man, Thomas J. "Stonewall" Jackson, not been shot or died of pneumonia is extraordinarily shortsighted. Jackson was not an Alexander of Macedon, Frederick the Great, or Napoleon Bonaparte. These men were the embodiment of the states of which they were leaders. Their respective political, economic, and military spheres revolved around each of them.[1] For instance, Prussian military theorist Carl von Clausewitz dubbed Napoleon the "God of War himself."[2] Clausewitz was not so much

1   Adam Zamoyski, *Napoleon: A Life* (New York; Basic Books, 2018), 262-265, 400-414.

focusing on Napoleon's fifty-three military victories, but rather focusing on the idea that Napoleon was the embodiment of the state and military.[3] As emperor, Napoleon could wage war as he sought fit, not having to contend with the strictures of a chain of command. Napoleon, too, could call upon his levee *en masse* to refill his ranks year after year. He could also dictate who led men under him and which commanders were assigned to his respective theaters of war, among the many powers that he wielded.

Thomas J. Jackson was not Napoleon, nor was he even at the top of the pecking order of the southern chain of command. Generals such as Samuel Cooper, Robert E. Lee, Joseph Johnston, P. G. T. Beauregard, and others ranked Jackson. He was not even the second-in-command of the famed Army of Northern Virginia. In an era where the date of rank and a rigid seniority system dominated the Union and Confederate armies, Jackson could not have hoped to leap over numerous senior leaders to head a vital army such as the Army of Northern Virginia or Army of Tennessee.[4] When lower-ranking John Bell Hood was thrust into command of the latter army over the top of more-senior generals, it was in a time of great desperation for the Confederacy, and Hood had worked hard to stroke the ego of Jefferson Davis in an effort to receive an army command.[5]

Jackson was not Hood, just as he was not Napoleon. He was merely a corps commander who ceased having a broad impact on the strategic level of the Eastern Theater of the American Civil War once his troops were folded into Lee's army full time in early December of 1862, just prior to the battle of Fredericksburg. Moving into 1863, Jackson could only have an impact on the tactical and at times the operational level of a battle or campaign, and they are not the levels at which a full-scale war are always won or lost. Thus,

---

2 Carl von Clausewitz, *On War*, Translated and Edited by Michael Howard and Peter Paret (Princeton, NJ.: University of Princeton Press, 1989), 583.

3 Andrew Roberts, *Napoleon: A Life* (New York, Viking Press, 2014), xxxiv.

4 Given Jackson's personality and his rigid adherence to military protocol, he most likely would have balked at usurping senior leaders in the chain of command.

5 Rick Atkinson, *An Army at Dawn: The War in North Africa, 1942-1943* (New York, Henry Holt and Company, 2002), 6-18, 42-46. The United States Army would not truly break their away from its structured nature of seniority until the cusp of World War II, when junior officers were promoted overtop of more senior leaders. Dwight Eisenhower and Mark Clark are just two examples of this promotional line jumping.

those assuming Jackson would have been an all-powerful deity on a strategic level, who would have been given vast amount of authority necessary to wage a full-scale war of annihilation had he lived, are both shortsighted and sadly mistaken. Lee himself was not even granted full operational authority of his theater until he assumed command of all Confederate armies in January of 1865. He, too, had to lobby Davis and the Southern high command for the opportunity to carry the war north into Pennsylvania. Not having operational authority is a fact Jackson himself grudgingly accepted during the winter of 1862-63.[6] Until Davis—who was his own worst enemy as a strategist—granted Jackson a truly independent command akin to what he'd had during the 1862 Shenandoah Valley Campaign, and a large army to support his efforts, the hyper-aggressive Jackson would languish, relegated to a subordinate role, in what was quickly becoming the non-decisive theater of the Civil War.[7]

While the above argument would appease some, it will not stand the fervor of the most ardent Jackson apologists. So, for the sake of argument, let's quickly retrace the steps that led us to the brink of Jackson's May 2, 1863, wounding at the hands of his own troops—a wounding that he is as much at fault for as Maj. John Berry of the 18th North Carolina, who ordered the destructive volley. Following, we will then dissect some of the countless possibilities of what could have happened had Jackson not been struck by three bullets and died eight days later of pneumonia.

The Chancellorsville Campaign

In April of 1863, the strategic initiative in the three decisive theaters of the Civil War lay squarely in Federal hands.[8] In the Eastern Theater, Maj.

---

6   Francis Augustin O'Reilly, *The Fredericksburg Campaign: Winter War on the Rappahannock* (Baton Rouge, LA.: Louisiana State University Press, 2006), 40.

7   Jackson's impact on the Federal prosecution of the Peninsula Campaign should have been minimal, but George B. McClellan allowed Jackson's small force to have an oversized impact on Federal operations near Richmond by begging to have more reinforcements sent to the Peninsula. By the time the Federal reinforcements started moving toward the Peninsula, the operational situation had changed, with Jackson fully undertaking his Valley Campaign, which necessitated holding the I Corps in the Fredericksburg area until the formation of the Army of Virginia.

8   The three major theaters are the Eastern, Western, and Trans-Mississippi Theaters.

Gen. Joseph Hooker had reorganized and reinvigorated President Abraham Lincoln's principal army in the theater, the Army of the Potomac. Hooker set his nearly 135,000-man army in motion on April 27. A wing moved on a circuitous route to the north and west, eventually doubling back to the south and east cutting through a dense second- and third-growth forest known locally as the "Wilderness," arriving 12 miles to the west of Lee's army stationed at Fredericksburg, Virginia. On April 29, another wing moved across the Rappahannock River below Fredericksburg to hold Lee's attention. The last piece of Hooker's puzzle, his mounted wing, rode hard to the west, south, and east in an effort to disrupt Lee's supply and communication lines.

Lee countered the Federal movement by splitting his army into two pieces. The Confederate commander held a force at Fredericksburg to ascertain the Federal intentions in that sector, while dispatching his de facto second-in-command, Jackson, west toward the Wilderness to assume command of the Confederate forces in that sector, where a second Federal force had materialized.[9]

Stonewall stonewalled the Union offensive to the west, then counterattacked. In the process, the Confederates wrestled the initiative away from the Federals. By the evening of May 1, the bulk of the Rebel army was at or near the Chancellorsville front, and the Confederate high command was formulating a plan of action for May 2. That plan of action involved Lee splitting his army for a second time. Jackson, with some 28,000 men, would march to the southwest, and eventually swing north to strike the Federal army on its right flank. Meantime, Lee would hold the Federals' attention with a force of some 14,000 men.

Jackson's soldiers trudged along the backroads of Spotsylvania County to their jumping-off point. The march consumed most of the day and was slowed at one point by Federal cannon shelling the road and at another when Jackson's column was forced to fight a rear-guard action with the Union III Corps even as Lee's holding force engaged elements of the Federal XII Corps. In the process, the Federals opened a one-mile gap in their main

---

9 Lee's army was outnumbered two-to-one, and his second in command, James Longstreet, along with two divisions of the First Corps were operating in the area of Norfolk and Suffolk, Virginia.

defensive line, which ran parallel to the Orange Turnpike, isolating the Union XI Corps, which was the smallest in the army.

At 5:15 p.m., Jackson's column was still strung out, but two of his three divisions were in position to launch his assault on the Union right flank. Jackson gave the order, and roughly 16,000 gray and butternut soldiers surged forward, with another 12,000 trailing along backcountry roads. The Confederate juggernaut caught the Federal XI Corps on its flank and largely unawares. Within one hour, the majority of the isolated XI Corps was set to flight, with Confederates in pursuit.

Contrary to popular belief, the XI Corps was not swept from the field in one fell swoop. At least 5,000 soldiers manned a defensive line that slowed the Rebel advance for roughly 30 minutes. Also contrary to popular belief, Jackson's men were not surging forward in an unbroken line. In fact, his line came apart almost immediately, and unit cohesion suffered tremendously. This was due to the failure of a division commander to move forward at once, the nature of the ground—dense woods, creeks, hollows, and rolling hills—and the fact that not all of the enemy were standing and fighting—many were fleeing.

It was in pursuit of the XI Corps, and into the gap created by the forward movement of the III and XII Corps earlier in the day, that Jackson and his third and final division strode sometime between 7:30 and 8:00 p.m. on May 2. If we followed the course of history, one hour later Jackson would be felled by three bullets. However, since we are deviating from that timeline for a moment, let us examine what Jackson was up against near 8:30 p.m. on May 2, 1863.

Jackson's final orders to A.P. Hill were along the lines of either "Press them, Hill! Press them and cut them off from the United States Ford."[10] Or, "General Hill, as soon as you are ready, push right forward. Allow nothing to stop you. Press on to United States Ford."[11] Regardless of how he stated it, Jackson was looking to slice deep into the heart of the Army of the Potomac's position around the Chancellorsville crossroads and cut it off from its route of escape.

---

10   James I. Robertson, Jr., *General A. P. Hill: The Story of a Confederate Warrior* (New York: Vintage Books, 1987), 185-186.

11   Joseph G. Morrison, "Stonewall Jackson at Chancellorsville," in *Confederate Veteran Vol. 13, No.5*, 231.

To reach a blocking position, Hill had two options. The first was to swing his 12,000-man division to the left and cut in a northeasterly direction utilizing the Bullock Road. The second option was to move directly east along the Orange Turnpike, which Jackson had been using as his axis of advance throughout the flank attack, then link with the River Road to swing northeast toward United States Ford. While the Bullock Road offered the shortest distance and easiest access to the Federal rear and the blocking position Jackson desired, a change of front to the Bullock Road would expose Hill's right flank and rear to the Federals, while also forcing Hill's men to maneuver into unforgiving terrain. The latter option of moving down the Orange Turnpike seemed to be the option that Hill was going to utilize, as he was swinging his brigades from a marching column into a line of battle facing due east. Without a doubt, this was the worst decision Hill and Jackson could have made.

Hill's Light Division would enter a kill zone of nearly unequaled proportions in the Civil War. While the XI Corps had been swept from the field, sustaining 2,400 casualties in the process, the remnants of the corps were being rallied on the left flank of the Federal army. Joe Hooker, too, was hard at work trying to right the situation. Initially, due to an acoustic shadow, he had not been able to hear the opening battle raging on his flank. Not until a mass of blue soldiers broke into the Chancellor and Fairview clearings did the Federal commander realize something was amiss there. Hooker reacted in a cool and calm manner. Less than a mile from Hill's front line, he ordered the thirty-four cannon on the open farm of Melzi Chancellor, "Fairview," to face west. Commanded by the able Capt. Clermont Best, these guns formed the backbone of the Fairview defense. Bolstering Best's guns was Hooker's old III Corps division, commanded by Maj. Gen. Hiram Berry. Hooker ordered Berry not to fire a shot and to "receive the enemy on your bayonets."[12] Knowing that panic in an army can quickly turn into an epidemic, Hooker even manned a cannon himself, leading by example. He also called upon Maj. Gen. John Sedgwick, whose VI Corps was still in the Fredericksburg area, having forced a crossing on April 29 below the

---

12   Stephen W. Sears, *Chancellorsville* (New York: Houghton Mifflin Company, 1996), 285. Swinton, Campaigns of the Army of the Potomac: A Critical History of Operations in Virginia, Maryland, Pennsylvania From the Commencement to the Close of the War (New York: Charles Scribner's & Sons, 1882), 288.

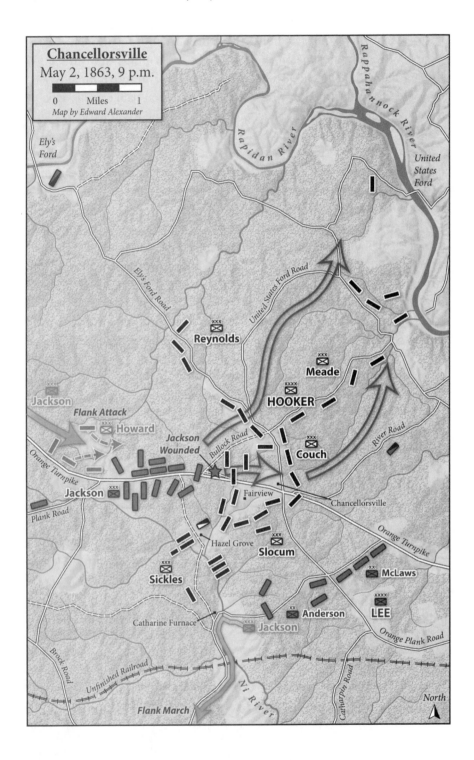

Chancellorsville
May 2, 1863, 9 p.m.

0   Miles   1
Map by Edward Alexander

Ely's Ford

Rapidan River

Rappahannock River

United States Ford

Ely's Ford Road

United States Ford Road

Reynolds

Meade

HOOKER

Jackson

Flank Attack

Howard

Jackson Wounded

Bullock Road

Couch

River Road

Orange Turnpike

Jackson

Plank Road

Fairview

Chancellorsville

Orange Turnpike

Hazel Grove

Slocum

McLaws

Sickles

Anderson

LEE

Catharine Furnace

Jackson

Orange Plank Road

Brock Road

Unfinished Railroad

Ni River

Catharpin Road

North

Flank March

Chancellorsville On May 2, 1863, Lt. Gen. Thomas "Stonewall" Jackson led a crushing attack against the Federal right flank at Chancellorsville. For all its initial success, the Virginia Wilderness sapped the assault of much of its momentum after just a couple of hours. Jackson determined to use his reserves—the division of Maj. Gen. A. P. Hill—to renew the assault even as darkness fell on the battlefield. Jackson urged Hill to cut the Army of the Potomac off from its route of escape to United States Ford. To do so, Hill would have had two options: a straightforward push or a direct swing to the northeast. Either route would have taken Confederates directly into the jaws of the Union army, with significant bodies of veteran troops on either side of them. Jackson's wounding brought a halt to any advance, most likely to the eventual advantage of the Confederates, who otherwise would have found themselves in dire peril.

city. Sedgwick and his force of 28,000-plus men—with fifty-six cannon— represented a threat Lee would have to deal with sooner rather than later.

The Federal commander also recalled the four divisions of III and XII Corps troops he had earlier dispatched to the south. These troops, and at least thirty-seven pieces of artillery, pressed north toward the Orange Turnpike and threatened the flank and rear of Hill's column, assuming a position in the open fields of Fairview. Reinforcing this force was one brigade of the XI Corps, commanded by the capable but xenophobic Francis Barlow, and regiments of Col. Thomas Devin's cavalry brigade—one of the best cavalry officers in either army.[13]

To Hill's left arrived elements of the Union I Corps, who had done more marching than fighting up to this point of the campaign. These troops were bolstered by the Federal V Corps. Two of the three V Corps divisions had yet to see heavy action, and their corps commander, George G. Meade, was not only Hooker's most trusted corps commander on the field, he was the best combat leader in the Army of the Potomac. Meade's corps also boasted some of the best division commanders in the army. These two venerable corps sat on Hill's left and rear.

Then, at the Chancellor clearing, stood two of the three divisions of the Federal II Corps, reinforced by more artillery in and north of the clearing.

To add one final element to the scene, late on May 2, Daniel Sickles's III Corps, located around Hazel Grove to Hill's immediate right, moved northward with aggression—so much so that some Federal units charged one another in the dark, confusing forest.

---

13   John Buford once said of Tom Devin that there was not anything he could teach Devin about cavalry that the capable officer didn't already know.

While Lee's undersized force of 14,000 men stood on the eastern side of a strangely shaped salient, Lee and Jackson could not directly communicate. As the crow flies it was roughly three miles between Lee and Jackson's command posts, but any courier would have to ride more than twice that distance to deliver a message, wait for a response, and then ride back—in the middle of the night and in a forest, no less. Thus, support from Lee could not be counted upon, and to even reach Jackson's wing of the army, his men would either have to execute a flank march of their own, or crash headlong into an aroused enemy readying itself for a fight.

The two men heading divisions close enough to support Hill were entering their first battles as division commanders. Adding to their worries, these men, Robert Rodes and Raleigh Colston, were still trying to untangle their divisions from the forest and each other. Rodes had shined thus far; Colston had not.

Around 9:00 p.m., Jackson was severely wounded in a friendly fire incident that also led to the wounding of A. P. Hill a few minutes later. Cavalryman Jeb Stuart would assume command of the Confederate troops on that front. At 5:15 a.m, May 3, Stuart would attack down the Turnpike, but by that time, the tactical situation had changed. Because the Confederates didn't immediately press him, and allowing his uncertainty over the Confederate plans to haunt his own battle directives, Hooker abandoned his strong position at Hazel Grove and withdrew most of the men and thirty-seven guns by the time the Stuart made his assault. And by late morning, Hooker was suffering the effects of a concussion.

But with Jackson and Hill unwounded in our scenario, Jackson was marching his largest and best division into an utter deathtrap—in the dark forest, without proper reconnaissance, and after a march of 17 or so miles. Marching 12,000 men into the heart of enemy that could muster 60,000 men and more than 70 cannon on both your flanks and rear, not to mention your front, through a dark and forbidding forest where command and control was at many times non-existent above a company level, was the makings of a bloodbath on a Pickett's Charge scale.[14]

Jackson's wounding potentially saved the Army of Northern Virginia from Stonewall Jackson.

---

14 Hill's assault and Pickett's assault would have consisted of roughly the same number of assault troops.

Illness and Court-Martial

So, next, let us assume that Jackson was not shot and, as in reality, the Rebels were victorious at Chancellorsville. What would the Army of Northern Virginia be facing?

First and foremost, Lee would have to contend with the Confederate high command in Richmond, much like he had to in May of 1863 when the question of reinforcing Vicksburg was a hot-button issue. As history played out, Lee deftly dodged this issue by proposing a northern offensive of his own. With Jackson alive, though, what would this have looked like?

Since Lee assumed command of the Army of Northern Virginia in June of 1862, he had worked hard to make his fighting force as efficient as possible. He transferred leaders of lesser ability out of the army, and he replaced the wing system with a corps system in late 1862. He, too, revitalized the artillery by placing guns of the same make into sections or batteries with one another, and he introduced the battalion system, which effectively massed guns to bear on the enemy. With a series of victories spanning back to the Peninsula, interrupted only by the loss at Antietam, Lee's army seemed to be firing on all cylinders.

Lee did worry, though, that the two corps now headed by James Longstreet and Thomas Jackson were too large and unwieldy. "I have for the past year felt that the corps of this army were too large for one commander," Lee wrote to Davis on May 20, 1863. "Nothing prevented my proposing to you to reduce their size & increase their number, but my inability to recommend commanders. . . . The loss of Jackson from the command of one-half the army seems to me a good opportunity to remedy this evil."[15] With Jackson alive, would Lee have reorganized his army into three corps? The answer is most likely yes. In our scenario where Jackson was not wounded by friendly fire in our scenario, he was still sick.

Throughout the Chancellorsville Campaign, Jackson displayed signs of pneumonia. He wore multiple layers of clothing on warm days. He sat close to the fire at night. He slept more than usual. Witnesses described him vomiting at least twice along the flank march. Had Jackson survived

---

15   Robert E. Lee, *The Wartime Papers of R.E. Lee*, Edited by Clifford Dowdey and Louis H. Manarin (New York; Bramhall House, 1961), 488-489.

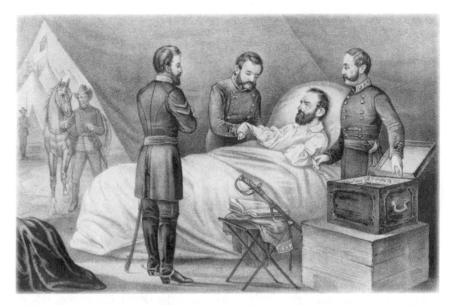

What if Stonewall Jackson had returned to the Army of Northern Virginia following his wounding? Admirers assume the one-armed Jackson would have otherwise been his old fiery self, but looking at the performance of other aggressive leaders who returned after serious injuries, the record suggests otherwise. There's also the question of whether the army would see the Jackson of the 1862 Valley Campaign or the Jackson of White Oak Swamp during the Seven Days. *Library of Congress*

Chancellorsville, there is little doubt he still would have had to contend with pneumonia. After all, it was ultimately the disease and not the lead thrown downrange by the 18th North Carolina that killed Stonewall Jackson. The trauma of not being wounded surely would have improved his chances of surviving the disease, but we cannot assume this with utter certainty. Then comes the question of recovery time if Jackson does survive the disease. How long would he have been sidelined, and what would the short-term effects have been on his vigor and judgement?

Assuming that Jackson survives, and Lee does indeed reorganize the army, who then becomes the full-time commander of the newly created Third Corps, and who assumes temporary command of the Second Corps? Here, one must consider the terrible relationship between Stonewall Jackson and A. P. Hill. It was no army secret that the two men loathed one another. Jackson was a man who saw the world starkly in black and white, with no gray. Largely humorless, overly demanding, and a stickler for protocol, Jackson seemed to make a sport out of seeking out charges to level against superiors and subordinates alike. His old army career ended in a feud with fellow officers. His Confederate career was nearly cut short by the handling of his officers and men during the Romney Expedition early in the war. Jackson's most recent feud revolved around A. P. Hill and dated to the late summer of 1862, although it had recently come to a head when Hill refused to back down. Hill even ordered a courier not to report directly to Jackson, but rather through Hill first. Stonewall spent much of the winter and early spring weeks finalizing a court martial case against Hill. Hill, in turn, was preparing his defense. "I suppose that I am to vegetate here all the winter under that crazy old Presbyterian fool," wrote Hill to Jeb Stuart in November of 1862. "I am like the porcupine all bristles, and all sticking out too, so I know that we shall have a smash up before long . . . . The Almighty will get tired of helping Jackson after a while, and then he'll get the damndest thrashing—and the shoe pinches, for I shall get my share and probably all the blame, for the people never blame Stonewall for any disaster."[16]

As the Chancellorsville campaign opened, the hatred these two men had for one another was reaching a crisis point. Lee, who rarely dealt with conflict among his subordinates well or directly, seemed to hope all of it would blow over.[17] It wasn't going to. The battle lines between Jackson and Hill had been drawn. Thus, as Hill entered the fight at Chancellorsville, he was well aware that the man ordering him and his division to their potential demise would end his career with the Army of Northern Virginia one way or the other.[18] One has to ask, how hard would you fight for, or work for, a boss that wants to end your career?[19]

---

16   AP Hill to Jeb Stuart Nov 14, 1862. Ernest B. Furgurson, *Chancellorsville 1863: The Souls of the Brave* (New York: Vintage Books, 1993), 83.

17   James I. Robertson, Jr., *Stonewall Jackson: The Man, The Soldier, The Legend* (New York; Macmillan Publishing, 1997), 626-627, 692-693. Douglas Southall Freeman, *Lee's Lieutenants: Cedar Mountain to Chancellorsville, Vol. 2* (New York: Charles Scribner's Sons, 1971), 510-511. Also see Robertson, *General A.P. Hill: The Story of a Confederate Warrior*.

18   The author is not implying that Jackson was ordering Hill to his death in a suicidal charge. Jackson lacked the operational knowledge on the ground at the time of his orders to Hill.

19   The author does not feel that Hill's heart was in this battle. A few minutes after Jackson fell wounded, Hill was grazed on the back of his legs by a shell that bruised him. Hill removed himself from command, but as soon as the Army of the Potomac was across the river and the campaign was over, Hill made a miraculous recovery and was again at the head of his troops.
     For a similar case in point, see Mark Snell's excellent book covering the life of Maj. Gen. William B. Franklin, *From First to Last: The Life of William B. Franklin.* Franklin was threatened with a court martial that would follow the Fredericksburg Campaign. The threat

Maj. Gen. A. P. Hill had fractured relationships with both of the Army of Northern Virginia's corps commanders. If Jackson had survived his wounding, his court-martial charges against Hill would certainly have gone forward. What if Lee sent Hill to the western theater as a way to circumvent that trouble? *Library of Congress*

With Jackson still alive after the battle, there is no doubt he would have pursued the charges against Hill to their fullest. An army split apart from the inside cannot withstand the enemy for long. Given Lee's track record of transferring officers from his army rather than dealing with their incompetence or court-martials head on, it is likely that the charges against Hill would have been sidelined, but Hill would have been transferred to another theater of the war to rid Lee and his army of this internal headache—even though the headache was not so much from Hill as from Jackson. Who would be the next officer to fall into Stonewall's poor graces? Jubal Early? Robert Rodes? The possibilities seem limitless.[20]

While history has shown that Hill was a stellar division commander, he was a very poor corps commander. The often ill and ill-tempered hypochondriac in all likelihood would have found himself in Braxton Bragg's Army of Tennessee (with most likely similar caustic results), or with Joseph Johnston at Jackson, Mississippi, in the hopes of breaking the siege of Vicksburg.

---

stemmed from Maj. Gen. Henry W. Halleck, who was at that time the general-in-chief of the Union Army. Halleck, using the recent case against Maj. Gen. Fitz John Porter as an example, told Franklin that when they were done with Porter that he was next. Franklin throughout the Battle of Fredericksburg showed little initiative or outside the box thinking, not wanting to fuel the case against him.

20 If history dictates anything, it is that the number of officers that were or would be charged by Jackson would only grow.

The Pennsylvania Campaign

With no A.P. Hill in the picture, Third Corps would go to Lt. Gen. Richard S. Ewell, and assuming that Jackson would return to the army after his illness, Second Corps would temporarily go to its senior division commander, Maj. Gen. Jubal A. Early.

The Pennsylvania Campaign then, in theory, would play out in much the same way that it had through its early stages at Brandy Station and in the drive down the Shenandoah Valley toward the Potomac River. Ewell's now-Third Corps victories at Martinsburg and Second Winchester would open the Confederate route into Maryland and south-central Pennsylvania. Even had Jackson rejoined the Army of Northern Virginia mid-campaign, Ewell would have pressured the capital of Pennsylvania, Harrisburg, helping to draw the Army of the Potomac up and out of Maryland and into the Keystone State.

In this scenario, with Maj. Gen. George G. Meade assuming the command of Lincoln's principal army, and Confederate forces approaching Gettysburg, Pennsylvania, from the north and west, what role would Jackson play in the battle? A. P. Hill allowed one of his division commanders, Henry Heth, to initiate the battle, and then Hill did not bother to approach the front. If Jackson's Second Corps assumes the role of Third Corps, it is likely that Gettysburg is simply a skirmish. Jackson, ever the aggressor, engages with two-thirds of John Buford's cavalry division, and Maj. Gen. John F. Reynolds's Left Wing of the Army of the Potomac is forced to engage with Jackson south of the town or south of the Mason-Dixon Line. The battle of Gettysburg is hardly a battle, but rather a footnote in the larger campaign.

Gettysburg July 1, 1863

But, let's take a role-reversal approach to this paradigm and examine the aspect of the battle that most Jackson apologists love to argue: the fact that he would have taken Culp's and Cemetery Hill on the evening of July 1, 1863. To get to this point, we would have to ignore everything that we have examined thus far and assume everything played out as it had in history, sans the fact that Jackson is sick or dead.

Early on the morning of July 1, 1863, Confederate infantry and artillery were pushing east along the Chambersburg Pike toward the crossroads

If we parachute Stonewall Jackson into the scenario of July 1, 1863, at Gettysburg (seen in the distance on the left), he would arrive just as Richard Ewell did on Oak Hill (see in the distance on the right). Events would ultimately bring him to Benner's Hill, where he would notice unoccupied Culp's Hill (where this photo was taken from). When Ewell told Jubal Early to take the hill, Early demurred. What if Jackson had been there, instead, to tell Early to take the hill? *Chris Mackowski*

town of Gettysburg. Two Federal cavalry brigades engaged in a delaying action with the Confederates, and by late morning, Federal infantry of the I Corps arrived to reinforce the cavalry brigades of John Buford. More Union and Confederate soldiers arrived in the vicinity of Gettysburg. By noon, assuming that Jackson made every exact decision that Richard Ewell historically made, the Second Corps of the Army of Northern Virginia arrived on the north side of town, its line of battle spanning across Oak Hill, spilling down into the large open plain below. Bungled Confederate assaults and poor coordination between the Second and the new Third Corps cost the Confederates in time and lives as the Second Corps bloodied itself against the Federal position on Oak Ridge. Sometime near 3 p.m., the Confederates got their act together and launched the assault that drove the Union I and XI Corps back through the streets of Gettysburg and to their last resistance point at Cemetery Hill.

Assuming that the battle would play out this way is an extremely flawed paradigm. Jackson was both a veteran and aggressive commander. While Ewell was aggressive, too, he lacked the authority and command experience of Jackson. There is no doubt that the Federal line along Oak Ridge could have been Rodes's division's undoing under Jackson, just as it was under Ewell, given Jackson's aggressiveness in the face of troops so well positioned to shred his flank. Jackson rarely micromanaged his subordinates when they deployed, so if they deployed for him the way they deployed for Ewell, the outcome would be the same—but it remains another of the countless dominos that could fall in all directions had Jackson lived. Thus, when confronted with the task of wrestling Cemetery Hill from the hands of the Federals, it could be argued that this is a scenario that may never have happened, or at least not on the traditional timeline. Yet, we trudge onward.

Faced with the traditional timeline, Jackson would have confronted the same conundrums as Ewell. By 4 p.m., most Federal troops would have abandoned their position to the north and west of the town and made their way to the Cemetery Hill sector. The Confederate Third Corps would have been battered, given the heavy losses sustained in the fighting at the Herbst Woods, McPherson Ridge, and Seminary Ridge. Second Corps would deal with rounding up Union prisoners in the town and restoring their own unit cohesion. Longstreet's First Corps would be caught in the epic traffic jam that was the Chambersburg Pike, and the Federals would be taking up positions south of the town.

Atop, behind, and along the hills and ridges south of Gettysburg, the Federals were assuming a stout defensive position. After the death of John Reynolds, command devolved to XI Corps commander Oliver O. Howard. The "pious but vapid" Howard was not the man you wanted in charge of a crisis of this nature, some of which he was accountable for creating. Arriving on the scene from army headquarters was Federal II Corps commander Maj. Gen. Winfield Scott Hancock. Hancock "the Superb," as he was known, was the right man for the job.[21] Meade had ordered Hancock to the front to assume command of the Union forces at Gettysburg. Hancock was not the only new Federal arrival at Gettysburg, either. Much of the III Corps and XII Corps arrived on the Federal left and right, respectively.

Hancock carried with him knowledge of Meade's intentions. In contrast, no Confederate officer was privy to Lee's plan of action for July 1 until the Confederate commander suggested Cemetery Hill be taken.

Meade planned for both the best- and worst-case scenarios. In the worst case, his army would fall back to Pipe Creek in Maryland. There,

21 O'Reilly, 87.

at predesignated locations, Meade would assume a defensive position that would block the Rebel approaches to Baltimore and Washington, D.C. In the worst case, the Federals would have a running battle to Pipe Creek, but in the best case, Lee would attack Meade on ground of Meade's own choosing. Hancock, privy to this information, had the authority to keep giving battle north of the Mason Dixon Line or to withdraw the elements of the Federal Army now north of the line into Maryland. Much rested on this junior corps commander's shoulders.

With the bulk of two fresh infantry corps approaching Gettysburg, Hancock set up a defensive line centered around Cemetery Hill, where three roads ran over or adjacent to the heights. Bolstering his defensive line were stone walls, one fresh brigade of XI Corps infantry, and at least 41 cannon commanded by two of the best gunners in either army, Col. Charles Wainwright and Maj. Thomas Osborne.

Swinging wide to the east of Gettysburg was the veteran XII Corps division of Brig. Gen. Alpheus Williams. Williams's bluecoats assumed a position on the extreme Union right along the Hanover Road. This force would have to be contended with in some way if the Confederates were to take Cemetery or Culp's Hill.

Also complicating Jackson's attempt to take Cemetery Hill would be a lack of Confederate cavalry. While some Confederate horsemen were on the field, they were not being utilized properly by any of the infantry commanders, nor were they being utilized properly by Lee himself. In addition, Jackson would be confronted by the fact that Third Corps was roughly handled by the Union I Corps and could offer no assistance in any assault. Regardless of these many factors, Jackson fans around the world are convinced that had Jackson attacked Cemetery Hill at this point, it would have not only been successful, but the battle of Gettysburg would have been a Confederate victory, and the Union would have fallen shortly thereafter.

Assuming that this paradigm is true, what battle of Gettysburg would Jackson have won? Like many historians whose war ends the same day that Jackson dies, the Jackson apologists who like to play the "What If" game often end their war on the evening July 1. In their game of dominos, Cemetery Hill falls, Lincoln just gives up Washington and the Federal war effort, Vicksburg is saved by A. P. Hill and others, and Braxton Bragg is remembered as a great general to history. None of this would have come about with the fall of Cemetery Hill and the minor tactical victory it would have given to the Confederates on July 1. Even in defeat at Gettysburg, Lee's army fights on for another twenty months—so why wouldn't the Army of the Potomac? Rarely does a war of this magnitude end in one fell swoop of a battlefield victory. The Western Way of Warfare paradigm of "one battle wins an entire war" is flawed, especially considering that this all took place in the third summer of the Civil War. It took seven coalition wars to take down Napoleon and the French Empire; one hill in south-central Pennsylvania would not have felled the American republic overnight, if at all. Ending the battle of Gettysburg on July 1 would have amounted to a minor Confederate victory, and the two armies would have sustained some 15,500 casualties, with both sides moving on to fight another day, elsewhere.

Consider, too, that while two Federal infantry corps were roughly handled, the losses in Buford's division were rather light.[22] Add to that the fact that Meade both had a fallback position at Pipe Creek, and he had two of his best rearguard generals on the field. On May 3 at Chancellorsville, with the Federal army falling back to its last defensive position, the Union high command called on Hancock, who was a division commander at the time, and XII Corps commander Henry W. Slocum to cover the withdrawal of the army. Hancock, Slocum, and others fought an impressive rearguard action with a determined enemy closing in on three sides. At Gettysburg, had the Federals decided to—or been forced to—withdraw to Pipe Creek, the Confederates would once again have had to deal with the some of the best officers and men in the Union army covering the retreat.

With Jackson taking Cemetery Hill and the Federals withdrawing to Pipe Creek, the battle of Gettysburg would not have been the ultimate major action in the Pennsylvania Campaign; rather, it would have been the penultimate action, with the real battle of the campaign taking shape south in Maryland. Even if Cemetery Hill fell, the war would continue in the Eastern Theater, the Western Theater, and the Trans-Mississippi Theater. Who knows what the ultimate outcome would be, but my money would still be on ultimate Federal victory with or without Jackson or Cemetery Hill.

---

22   John W. Busey and David G. Martin, *Regimental Strengths and Losses at Gettysburg* (Highstown, NJ: Longstreet House, 2005), 144.

Conclusion

The premise that the war would have been different had Stonewall Jackson lived is not an incorrect premise. Everything would have been different, much like a temporal shift episode in *Star Trek* dealing with the ripple effect in the space-time continuum if the crew does one thing or another when traveling through time. It is the assumption by those playing the "What If" game that the timeline would have played out exactly as it did, whether he had been shot or not, carrying the Army of Northern Virginia to the foot of Cemetery Hill, where Jackson would have attacked and everything after that point would have been different—that's the assumption that is truly flawed. This line of thinking is akin to selective memories. You want to believe what you want to be true regardless of the evidence that everything would be different one way or another.

Jackson was a man as flawed and fallible as the rest of us. Placing him on a marble pedestal and assuming he would have done what you wanted him to do is both shortsighted and selfish. We have no idea what Lee, Jackson, Grant, or Captain Kirk would have done given a different timeline. All we can focus on is the evidence we have.

The fact that Lee and Jackson were bleeding the Army of Northern Virginia from within due to outrageous battlefield casualties over an 11-month span, from the Seven Days through Gettysburg, is evidence enough that the Confederate army would eventually collapse. Grant played the same game of warfare and attrition arithmetic as the coaltions that took down Napoleon, Kaiser Wilhelm II, and Adolph Hitler. It's the long game—attrition—that brings most major wars to an end. While average fans of warfare yearn for the cult of the offensive, like that one big NFL pass wins a Super Bowl, it's normally the armies grinding it out that ultimately decide the fate of wars.

To quote the esteemed time traveler Dr. Emmett L. Brown from *Back to the Future*, "Your future hasn't been written yet. No one's has." So why waste so much time or energy on what could have been, rewriting Jackson's "future"?

CHAPTER SIX

To Go Around to the Right?

Longstreet's Great What If at Gettysburg

Dan Welch

In one of the many iconic moments in the 1993 movie *Gettysburg*, Lt. Gen. James Longstreet, commander of the Army of Northern Virginia's First Corps, arrives at a Confederate field hospital in search of one of his subordinates. As darkness sets on the scene, he finds Maj. Gen. John Bell Hood. Earlier that afternoon, July 2, 1863, Hood led Longstreet's corps into the second day of fighting. Hood was a hard-hitting division commander and a trusted subordinate. Yet, as surgeons prepare to perform an operation on Hood's arm for wounds he received at the start of the attack, he once again protests the orders for his earlier assault. He had wanted to go "around to the right," in order to avoid a frontal assault on the Union position and the broken, rock-strewn terrain that faced his troops opposite their position along Warfield Ridge. Longstreet reassures him that the argument is moot at this point, urges him to rest easy, and reassures him that his men performed well—that they had accomplished their objectives.

The moment depicted in the film was lifted from the pages of history. Hood's appeal to Longstreet—and Longstreet's earlier request of Lee to "go around to the right"—has been one of the battle's most enduring counterfactual questions, relished and debated by generations of historians and enthusiasts. Although we cannot determine the answer to the question, we *can* evaluate the reasons why Longstreet and Hood made their request. Further still, by assessing real-time intelligence from July 2, 1863, we can deflate some of the myths that obscure the battle, creating a clearer understanding of what actually occurred and why.

The Reconnaissance

Intelligence is a key ingredient to success on the battlefield. Understanding thoroughly the strengths and weaknesses of your own position—as well as the enemy's position—are vital to strategic and tactical planning. There are numerous other factors to be considered as well, including local road and railroad networks, terrain, enemy strength, movements within your theater of operations, and—if going on the offensive—the route or approach of attack. All of this, as well as much more, can be ascertained with thorough reconnaissance. Dennis Hart Mahan, a noted American military theorist of the nineteenth-century, contended, "There are no more important duties . . . than those of collecting and arranging the information . . . upon which . . . [the] daily operations of a campaign must be based."[1] For Generals Lee and Longstreet, several reconnaissance missions on July 2 not only led to Lee's plan of attack, but also initiated Longstreet and Hood's desire to go around the Union army from the Confederate right flank.

Throughout the evening of July 1 and into the early hours of July 2, outfits from both armies continued to march toward Gettysburg. As these units arrived and more distinct battle lines took shape, Lee needed more intelligence before making his next move. In the predawn darkness, Lee ordered Capt. Samuel R. Johnston to make a reconnaissance of the Federal left flank. At approximately 4 a.m., Johnston and the three to four men that accompanied him began their mission.[2] Johnston's reconnaissance took approximately three hours to complete. However, Johnston was not the only Confederate officer making a reconnaissance that morning. Brig. Gen. William Nelson Pendleton wrote in his official report of the battle that Col. Armistead Long, Captain Johnston, Col. Reuben L. Walker (commander of the artillery reserve for the Third Corps), and himself, "soon after sunrise,"

---

1   D. H. Mahan, *An elementary treatise on advanced-guard, out-post, and detachment service of troops and the manner of posting and handling them in presence of an enemy. With a historical sketch of the rise and progress of tactics, & c., & c. intended as a supplement to the system of tactics adopted for the military service of the United States, and especially for the use of officers and volunteers* (New York: John Wiley, 1861),105.

2·   Richard A. Sauers, "Confederate Movements on the Right Flank At Gettysburg, July 2, 1863" (History 544, May 18, 1981), 13.

examined the Federal left.[3] According to Lee biographer Douglas Southall Freeman, the Gray Fox himself conducted a personal reconnaissance of the Union position opposite the Confederate right on the morning of July 2.[4]

Of all these early morning intelligence-gathering operations, however, Lee used only one to plan the Confederates' second day of operations at Gettysburg. "The reconnaissance with the most impact on Lee's thinking appears to have been conducted by Captain Samuel Richards Johnston," writes Karlton Smith,

Lt. Gen. James Longstreet, here sketched by Alfred Waud, may have been Lee's "Old Warhorse," but after the war, he became a Confederate scapegoat—in part because he dared to speak frankly about his opinions of Lee. Things only went downhill for Longstreet from there. He was essentially written out of Confederate histories of the war or, if included, vilified. What if Longstreet had not laid the defeat of Gettysburg at Lee's feet during the postwar era? *Library of Congress*

longtime National Park Service ranger and historian at Gettysburg National Military Park.[5] Indeed, based upon Johnston's report, Lee planned for his army to resume the offensive of the previous day. The plan called for a main thrust against the federal army's left flank and a simultaneous feint against the Union right. The attack on the federal right would pin down troops that Maj. Gen. George G. Meade might otherwise shuttle to his embattled left. Sometime around 10 a.m., having returned to his headquarters along the Chambersburg Pike west of Gettysburg,

3   U. S. War Department, *The War of the Rebellion: A Compilation of the Official Records of the Union and Confederate Armies* (Washington, D.C.: U. S. Government Printing Office, 1880 – 1901), Series I, 27(2): 350. (Hereafter cited as OR)

4   Dr. Douglas S. Freeman, "Headquarters Army of Northern Virginia, Chambersburg Pike, Near Gettysburg, Pa., July 2, 1863 (10 p.m.)," *The Evening Star,* July 2, 1938, A-4.

5   Karlton D. Smith, "'To Consider Every Contingency' Lt. Gen. James Longstreet, Capt. Samuel R. Johnston, and the factors that affected the reconnaissance and countermarch, July 2, 1863," in *"The Most Shocking Battle I Have Ever Witnessed": The Second Day at Gettysburg. Papers of the 2006 (11th) Gettysburg National Military Park Seminar. April 8-9, 2006* (Gettysburg: Gettysburg National Military Park, 2008) 102.

Lee revealed his plan for the day's offensive. "[A]fter discussing the ground for some time he determined I should make the main attack, and at eleven o'clock gave me the order to prepare for it," Longstreet wrote.[6] Before the two divisions of the Confederate First Corps could attack, however, they had to get into position.

Longstreet's deployment of his two divisions along Seminary and Warfield Ridges did not go as smoothly as either he or Lee had planned. Hoping to rustle his troops into position in secrecy, Longstreet's column was forced to retrace its steps in a vexing and frustrating countermarch when Union signal corpsmen stationed on Little Round Top detected its movements. Following the reversal of the column's order of march, and with McLaws's division in the lead, Longstreet, riding with Hood and his division, grew impatient with the accordion nature of the marching column. "Finally, Longstreet, considerably irritated by the long delays, took matters into his own hands and led Hood's division directly to its position even though the route was in full view of the enemy," related historian E.T Downer in 1958.[7] As Longstreet's divisions got into position, Longstreet, his staff, and his subordinate unit commanders began to make their own reconnaissance of the area.

Perhaps the most determined reconnaissance in Longstreet's command was conducted by Texans in Hood's division. Lieutenant Colonel P. A. Work, commanding the 1st Texas Infantry, wrote of the immediate need to reconnoiter of the area. "As soon as [we] reached the battlefield," Work reported, "[I] sent William H. Barbee and Charles Kingsley to reconnoiter Little Round Top."[8] Hood himself later wrote that he had ordered these enlisted men, whom he called "mounted couriers," to inspect his position and the area of operations. At approximately the same time Hood had ordered this reconnaissance, Brig. Gen. Evander Law, commanding a brigade of Alabama soldiers in Hood's division, nodded several enlisted men forward to scout the position to his front. "In order to gain information on this important point, I sent out a detail of six picked men as scouts, with

---

6   James Longstreet, "Lee in Pennsylvania," in *The annals of the war written by leading participants north and south* (Philadelphia: The Times Publishing Company, 1879) 437.

7   E. T. Downer, "Gettysburg-July 2, 1863: The Case for Longstreet," January 20, 1958, Gettysburg National Military Park Vertical File - Lee-Longstreet Controversy, 9.

8   Dr. John O. Scott, "Heroic Acts in Texas History," in *Hood's Texas Brigade*, 311.

instructions to move as rapidly as possible to the summit of Round Top," remembered Law after the war.[9] The objective for these men was to find the federal left flank.

Thus, the results of each reconnaissance done that day, both for Lee and Longstreet, shaped these commanders' answers to the question and validity of moving around the Union army from the Confederate right flank.

Results, Decisions, and Proposals

Longstreet disagreed with Lee on his strategy beginning on July 1. In 1938, Sears Wilson Cabell wrote of Longstreet's objection to Lee's strategy on the battle's first day. "When General Longstreet first met General Lee on the field, about 4:00 p.m., on the 1st, and viewed the Federals in their position on Cemetery Hill," Cabell wrote, Longstreet remarked to Lee, "We could not call the enemy to a position better suited to our plans. All that we have to do is to file around his left and secure good ground between him and his capital."[10] Lee disagreed, but Longstreet's objection to his commander's offensive strategy in Pennsylvania and at Gettysburg did not end there.

"At daylight on the morning of the second day," noted W. H. Swallow in an 1886 article for *Southern Bivouac*, "General Longstreet went to General Lee's headquarters and submitted his plan to the commanding General. It was 'That General Ewell should withdraw his corps from Cemetery Hill and swing around to our extreme right and then unite with my (Longstreet's) corps flanked by A.P. Hill's.'"[11] Once Longstreet's Corps joined Ewell's, the two corps would move south and east of the current battlefield, somewhere between the Army of the Potomac and Washington, D.C.

A veteran of the Army of Northern Virginia, reading a copy of Walter Taylor's *Four Years with General Lee* upon its release, concurred with Longstreet's understanding of the strategic and tactical situation on the

---

9 Evander M. Law, "The Struggle for 'Round Top,'" in *Battles and Leaders of the Civil War*, edited by Robert U. Johnson and Clarence C. Buel, (New York: The Century Co., 1888): 3:321.

10 Cabell, *The "Bulldog" Longstreet at Gettysburg and Chickamauga*, 7. James Longstreet, *From Manassas to Appomattox: Memoirs of the Civil War in America* (Philadelphia: J.B. Lippincott Company, 1896), 358.

11 W. H. Swallow, "The Second Day at Gettysburg," *Southern Bivouac*, January 1886, 491.

Gettysburg   After the fighting at Gettysburg on July 1, Confederate general James Longstreet, in command of the Army of Northern Virginia's First Corps, proposed a strategic turning movement against the Army of the Potomac. The plan included withdrawing the army from its current position, marching it to the south and east, and selecting a new field of battle more advantageous to the army between the Army of the Potomac and Washington, D. C. Several times Longstreet presented this idea to army commander Robert E. Lee, each rebuffed by the general. By the afternoon of July 2, one of Longstreet's division commanders, John Bell Hood, presented his own idea for a turning movement. Hood felt that a tactical turning movement of the Army of the Potomac's left flank during the planned Confederate assault that afternoon would significantly lessen casualties in his ranks and increase the results of his ferocious assault. Longstreet would rebuff Hood much like Lee had rebuffed Longstreet.

---

field. Writing in the margins of the book, Benjamin G. Humphreys noted, "He wanted to flank to the right through Emmitsburg and to force Meade to attack him in his own chosen position. . . ."[12] Historian Karlton Smith viewed Longstreet's plan as "a 'wide tactical development' against the Army of the Potomac's left flank."[13] No matter how Longstreet's proposed movement was labeled in the post-war era, Longstreet believed that the intelligence gleaned on July 1, and now on the morning of July 2 from Johnston's reconnaissance, dictated a wide movement to the right.

Lee's interpretation of the situation on the field led him to assume a course of action completely opposite that of Longstreet's proposal. Johnston's reconnaissance efforts had fortified Lee's conviction that maintaining the operational offensive would secure victory. Lee's tactical plan—and subsequent orders—was for an attack on the Union army's left flank and rear, reported by Johnston to be unanchored, unsupported, and weak. There would not be a need to move around by the Confederate right flank because the Federal left was in a precarious state; a bold attack would drive the Yankees from the field. Thus, Lee called on two divisions of Longstreet's corps to mount an assault; portions of the Third Corps would support Longstreet as the Second Corps made its diversionary effort.

By the time Longstreet's two available divisions moved into position along Seminary and Warfield Ridge, however, Lee's plan and Longstreet's

---

12   Frank E. Everett, Jr., "Delayed Report of an Important Eyewitness to Gettysburg—Benjamin G. Humphreys," *The Journal of Mississippi History* Volume XLVI, no. 4 (November 1984): 313.

13   Smith, "To Consider Every Contingency," 100.

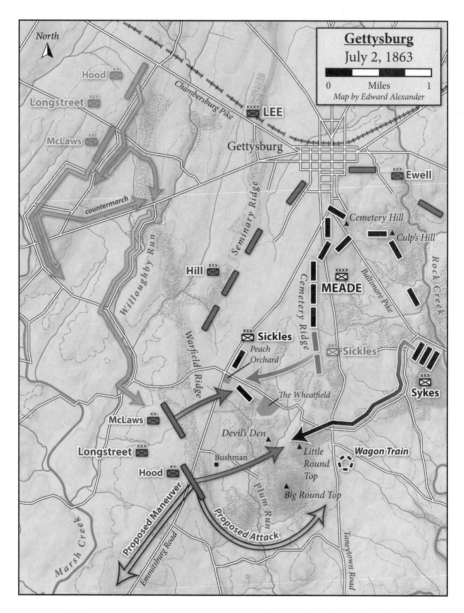

proposal, like their intelligence, was woefully outdated. As Hood's division trudged toward their assigned position, the general sent out his own "picked Texas scouts." Hood also sent out pioneers to take down fences and clear the front of his assigned position all the way to the Emmitsburg Road. All of this was standard operating procedure. The scouts would gather intelligence on what was in front of the division's position, and the pioneers would prepare a route of march for the attack. Ultimately, the reconnaissance the scouts performed and the intelligence they and the pioneers gathered brought Hood squarely into the debate between Lee and Longstreet on the best strategy and tactics to be employed—particularly a movement to the right.

Hood's Reconnaissance

The "picked scouts" that Hood sent out as his division moved into position probed eastward towards the Round Tops opposite his front. Although the exact route of this reconnaissance has not been discovered, the results of what Hood's scouts reported had a significant impact on their commander's thoughts about the best tactics to use to accomplish the strategic objective. Dr. John O. Scott, a veteran of Hood's division, recalled after the war that William H. Barbee and Charles Kingsley, two of the scouts sent forward to reconnoiter Little Round Top, "soon returned with the valuable information that the mountain and the space to the rear was then unoccupied by the Federal troops."[14] Not only was this area devoid of federal troops, but so too was the approach toward the left flank and rear of the Army of the Potomac. This intelligence was likewise confirmed by Law. As Law and his troops awaited further orders, he noticed several men moving near the Emmitsburg Road. Law immediately nodded forward a detachment to discover their identities. This detail ended up capturing several Union soldiers. The Yankees alerted their captors to the collection of barely-guarded federal wagons parked behind the Round Tops, pointing out a farm road that led from Law's right flank to that area. Law immediately rode off to report this new intelligence to Hood. As he sought out Hood, he encountered a messenger from the scouting party he had dispatched earlier. They confirmed what the enemy prisoners had told him.[15]

The area around the Round Tops "was open," Hood recalled. "I could march through an open woodland pasture around Round Top, and assault

---

14   Scott, "Heroic Acts in Texas History," 311.

15   Law, "The Struggle for 'Round Top,'" 3:321.

the enemy in flank and rear."[16] Reconnaissance efforts had revealed the location of the Federal army's left flank. To the surprise of Hood—and certainly that of McLaws—the Federal army's left flank was not where army headquarters had reported it to be. Johnston's report to Lee had not given the exact location of the Federal army's left flank, but rather outlined where he did and did not see Federal troops. Lee used that information to infer that the Federal army's left flank rested near the termination of a ridge that extended southward from Cemetery Hill. Lee's tactical plan for the day rested on this belief. In the eight-hour span since Johnston had returned to army headquarters, though, the Federal position had changed.

As McLaws nudged his division into position along Seminary and Warfield Ridges, the Federal army's position was opposite his front. Hood's scouts completed the picture, reporting that "the Union flank was no farther south than Big Round Top. . . ."[17] This placed the Federal army's left flank much farther south, at least to Little Round Top, by the time the scouts reconnoitered this area between 3 and 4 p.m. These scouts reported exactly what Law's men had discovered and reported earlier: the alluring presence of a lightly guarded park of Federal supply trains, "massed in an exposed position behind Cemetery Ridge."[18] With this new intelligence in hand, and his division completing their march into position, Hood had limited time to suggest and perhaps alter his orders based upon this reconnaissance.

With the Federal army's left flank far further to the south than reported, Hood's tactical orders from Lee and Longstreet to attack almost due north up the nearby Emmitsburg Road would not work. It would expose Hood's own right flank to the new Federal position. This also held true for McLaws and his division, who was to support Hood's effort on Hood's left. Hood wrote as much after the war, noting that "it was unwise to attack up the Emmetsburg [sic] road, as ordered."[19] With time dwindling

---

16   John Bell Hood, *Advance and Retreat: Personal Experiences in the United States and Confederate States Armies* (Reprint: Kessinger Publishing), 57-58.

17   Col. Harold B. Simpson, *Hood's Texas Brigade: Lee's Grenadier Guard* (Waco: Texian Press, 1970), 267.

18   Ibid.

Confederates ended up attacking across the northwest face of Big Round Top (and a pair of regiments even went up over it). What if Hood had moved around to the south of the hill and approached the Federal position from the flank and rear? *Daniel T. Davis*

before his orders to attack arrived, Hood began to send the first of several staff officers to report this new intelligence to Longstreet. Hood believed that the results of this latest reconnaissance demonstrated that both of his commanders were wrong. Lee's tactical plan needed to be altered because of the new line of battle the Army of the Potomac had assumed and the potentially devastating impact it could have on the Confederate attack as Lee outlined. With regard to Longstreet's plan for moving the entire Army of Northern Virginia in a wide movement to the right, placing it on a new battlefield between the Union army and Washington, D.C., it would not be necessary, as this latest intelligence suggested an opportune point of attack for Hood.

"... Around to the Right"

The first staff officer Hood sent to Longstreet was Capt. James Hamilton, who had been present when Law came to Hood to voice his opposition

---

19 Hood, *Advance and Retreat,* 57-58.

(based on the new intelligence) to the attack order as written. Hood turned to Hamilton and asked him to repeat what he had just heard. Confident that Hamilton could recite Law's intelligence and objections, Hood ordered Hamilton to find Longstreet and report this to him immediately. When Hamilton returned, he repeated Longstreet's reply in earshot of Law: "General Longstreet orders that you begin the attack at once."[20] Law went to prepare his command to open the assault.

Hood next sent two more staff officers to convey the latest intelligence to Longstreet. These staff officers found the Old War Horse with Lee not far down the line from Hood's position somewhere on Warfield Ridge. In addition to the fresh intelligence on Hood's front, the staff officers were to "request to be allowed to make the [Hood's] proposed movement" around the Union flank and into their rear via the discovered open route.[21] When both of these scouts returned, they reported the same response from Longstreet each time: "General Lee's orders are to attack up the Emmetsburg [sic] road."[22]

Feeling the urgency of getting the orders amended before the attack went forward, Hood next sent Maj. W. H. Sellers to see Longstreet. Sellers was also to relay the intelligence gathered from the scouts, and to propose Hood's change to the plan of attack. Sellers was to "'go as fast as your horse can carry you and explain all this to General Longstreet, and ask him to permit me to move by the right flank, so as to be able to envelop that knob,' pointing to Little Round Top, 600 or 800 yards in the distance. . . ."[23] Hood perhaps believed that the weight of this information would have more of an effect on Longstreet if delivered by his adjutant general, rather than a staff officer.

Sellers did not absent himself long, suggesting Longstreet was still rather close to Hood's position. When he returned, though, he told Hood, "General Longstreet replied that General Lee had already given the order of battle and it could not be changed."[24] As Sellers reported his conversation to

---

20 Law, "The Struggle for 'Round Top,'" 3:322.

21 Ibid., 58-59.

22 Ibid.

23 Dr. John O. Scott, "Hood's Texas Brigade at Gettysburg," in *Hood's Texas Brigade*, 339.

24 Scott, "Heroic Acts in Texas History," 311.

Hood, Maj. John W. Fairfax, an aide on Longstreet's staff, rode up. Fairfax repeated what Hood's three earlier messengers had already said: "Tell General Hood to attack."[25]

But the situation gave Fairfax pause. Perhaps further remonstrations from Hood or a view of the current federal position changed his mind; we may never know. Whatever the case, Fairfax "asked [Hood] to please delay his attack until I could communicate to General Longstreet, that he can turn the enemy—pointing to a gorge in the mountain, where we would be sheltered from his view, & attack by his Cavalry." Writing more than three decades later, Fairfax recalled, "General Hood, slapped me on the knee and said—'I agree with you—bring General Longstreet to see for himself.'"[26] The major raced back to Longstreet. However, the general's reply remained firm: "It is General Lee's order — the time is up — attack at once." Fairfax "lost no time in repeating the same to Gen'l Hood and remained with him to see the attack, which was made instantly."[27]

Hood, ever the dutiful soldier, nodded the attack forward. Within moments he was wounded by an exploding artillery round somewhere in the vicinity of the Michael Bushman farm. The combination of conceding to the attack plan as ordered—much as Longstreet had yielded to Lee—and his serious wounding ensured that no movement around to the right would be made. Although there is no definite way to predict what would have happened had Hood taken his division around to the right, or if Longstreet had convinced Lee to shift the whole army to the right, we can explain why these two movements did not occur.

Not "What If," but "Why Not"?

No safe movement for an army or portion thereof can be made without reconnaissance. On the late afternoon of July 1 and into the early morning hours of July 2, General Lee and numerous others scouted their perch along Seminary and Warfield Ridge, the enemy position extending

---

25 John Walter Fairfax to General James Longstreet, Nov. 12, 1897, VHS Manuscript MSS1f1613a1.

26 Ibid.

27 Ibid.

southward from Cemetery Ridge, and the area around the Army of the Potomac's left flank and rear. As the federal position changed throughout July 2, owing to the movements of Maj. Gen. Daniel Sickles's Third Corps, new pieces of ground were also reconnoitered, albeit with limited time to process the intelligence gathered. One of the principal reasons the Army of Northern Virginia and later, Hood, was not allowed to go around the right of the Union left flank was because of the intelligence gleaned from these reconnaissance efforts.

As previously noted, the reconnaissance with the most impact on General Lee was the one completed by Captain Johnston. Although Johnston's reconnaissance has historically raised more questions than answers, it convinced Lee both to remain at Gettysburg and to press his attack. For Lee, the intelligence that Johnston provided led him to believe that launching an offensive on the Union left would deliver a battlefield victory. Once he had made his decision, Lee sought to organize his attack as quickly as possible. General Longstreet, in an 1893 newspaper interview, recalled Lee's temperament during this moment. "He (Lee) chafed at inaction; always desired to beat up the enemy at once and have it out. He was too pugnacious. His impatience to strike, once in the presence of the enemy, whatever the disparity of forces or relative conditions, I consider the one weakness of Gen. Lee's military character," Longstreet contended. These leadership weaknesses, according to Longstreet, afflicted Lee on July 2. "It was at Gettysburg," the First Corps commander believed, "where Gen. Lee's pugnacity got the better of his strategy and judgment and came near being fatal to his army and cause."[28] Further still, it was this trait, at this tension-filled time on July 2, that would not entertain suggestions by Longstreet or Hood.

Despite the difference of military opinions based on the intelligence received through reconnoitering, there are those who felt it was Longstreet's duty to challenge Lee. Lieutenant Colonel D.B. Sanger came to Old Pete's defense in 1936. "We know that Longstreet proposed a movement around Meade's left to interpose between the Union Army and Washington; or, if a different construction is put on Longstreet's words, to envelop Meade's left tactically," Sanger wrote. Yet, "His intimate relation with Lee was in itself

---

28 Leslie J. Perry, "Gen. Longstreet as a Critic," *Washington Post*, June 11, 1893, 10.

sufficient to justify such recommendations, not to mention his official position as Lee's senior corps commander."[29] Thus, Longstreet's proposed movement to go around the right of the Army of the Potomac, somewhere between it and Washington D.C., offered a divergent path forward for the Army of Northern Virginia at Gettysburg. Both generals had the same intelligence based on numerous reconnaissance missions, but each interpreted the best possible results differently, placing Lee and Longstreet at odds.

General Longstreet never yielded on the wisdom of his proposal to move around the right. Writing to his former division commander Lafayette McLaws in 1877, he wielded some compelling historical evidence: "Gen Meade telegraphed to Gen Halleck at 3.P.M. on the 2nd. 'If the enemy interposes between me and Washington, I shall fall back on my supplies at Westminster.'" Longstreet pointed out that this communication from Meade to Halleck "was just 30 minutes before our battle of the 2nd was opened, and is conclusive of the effect of the move that I proposed to interpose between him and Washington and show that we should have won the position at Gettysburg by a simple flank movement and without a blow."[30] Writing just several years later in *Southern Bivouac*, W.H. Swallow agreed: "Now if Longstreet's advice had been taken it is certain, beyond a doubt, that the whole Union army would have been completely maneuvered out of its position. Had this been done the Army of Northern Virginia, with Round Top and [L]ittle Round Top in its possession, could, by moving on its flanks, have compelled the Federal army to abandon its line of defense without difficulty."[31] Even northern historians and military officers speculated on the possible results Longstreet could have achieved if he had been allowed to move around to the right. General Meade wrote in a letter in 1870, "Longstreet's advice to Lee was sound military sense. It was the step I feared Lee would take."[32]

---

29   Lieutenant Colonel D.B. Sanger, "Was Longstreet a Scapegoat?" *Infantry Journal*, Volume XLIII, no. 1 (January-February, 1936): 39.

30   General James Longstreet to General McLaws, November 12, 1877, Lafayette McLaws Papers, Southern Historical Society Collection, University of North Carolina at Chapel Hill. Underline in the original. Longstreet and McLaws's relationship had soured greatly during the war, particularly after Gettysburg. Those tensions eased in the years after the war as can be witnessed in the increase in their correspondence towards the end of the 1870s.

31   Swallow, "The Second Day at Gettysburg," 491.

Hood at Odds with Longstreet

Lee's temperament at Gettysburg, the intelligence that led to his orders for the army on July 2, and his position as commanding general of the Army of Northern Virginia all led to his firm decision not to move the army or portions thereof to a new position between the Army of the Potomac and Washington, D.C. Lee clearly disagreed with Longstreet's strategic proposition. But why did Longstreet not allow Hood to change tactics to accomplish Lee's strategic goals? Hood's reconnaissance clearly demonstrated an opportunity to exploit the Federal left flank and rear, just as Jackson had eight weeks earlier at Chancellorsville.

Longstreet had already been denied by Lee several times in suggesting the army move around to the right. One can only imagine the conversations between the two as Longstreet continued to suggest a movement away from the battlefield at Gettysburg. Certainly, Longstreet would have to gain Lee's approval for Hood's maneuver—particularly in this case, as it overlapped Longstreet's strategic and tactical suggestion. Lieutenant Colonel Sanger, in his 1936 article exploring whether Longstreet was truly a scapegoat for Gettysburg, painted the picture thusly: "Can anyone fail to visualize Lee's reactions had Longstreet again approached him with a suggestion that had been twice rejected—the last time in anger?"[33]

This was not the only consideration to deny Hood's request to move his division around the right. At such a late hour, nearing 4 p.m., to get Hood's division into position for an assault against the Federal flank and rear would have taken an immense amount of time. Hood's redeployment "would have necessitated another march into position of at least a mile and a half. This would have required at least another hour to two hours to get the troops into position, not to mention having to move the artillery support. This would have moved the attack time back to about 6 P.M. and would have given Longstreet's men less than two hours of daylight to launch an attack and to try to exploit any gains." "This," historian Smith argued, "would have meant no attack at all on July 2."[34] Lee's "pugnacity" on July

---

32   George G. Meade, *The Morning Journal-Courier,* August 11, 1886.

33   Sanger, "Was Longstreet a Scapegoat?" 40.

Longstreet's attack on July 2 went in strong, but when the *en echelon* wave rippled up to A. P. Hill's front, poor communication between the corps resulted in a loss of momentum even as the assaults peaked. Was this lack of coordination the result of bad blood between Hill and Longstreet, which traced its origins all the way back to the Seven Days? What if the two men had enjoyed a better relationship? *Library of Congress*

2 would never have allowed his freshest troops on the field to not follow up the attacks and successes of July 1.

In the end, Hood went forward, but not around to the right. So too did the rest of Longstreet's corps on July 2 and 3, respectively. Perhaps Lee had a better read on the intelligence gathered on July 1 and 2 than did Longstreet, or perhaps he just read his new opponent Meade better. Just over a month after the battle, the *Times* of London wrote in support of Lee's decision not to allow Longstreet, and thus Hood, to move around to the right. "To attempt to march around these sugar-loaf pimmacles would have exposed the Confederates to the danger of weakening their forces so greatly as to make it easy for the Federals to advance and cut off the flanking forces," the *Times* reported.[35]

Both Lee and the *Times* were correct. As the final acts of July 2 played out across General Longstreet's front, the largest reinforcements for the Army

34 Smith, "To Consider Every Contingency," 113.

35 The *Times* of London, August 18, 1863.

of the Potomac arrived on the battlefield. The Sixth Corps arrived behind the "sugar-loaf pimmacles" between 4:30 and 5 p.m. in the precise place where Hood had hoped to move his division. Thus, as the *Times* suggested, Hood's "flanking forces" would have been "cut off."

Confederates continued to refight their decisions of those fateful days and how the battle ultimately played out. By 1876, the counterfactual was already so vigorously debated that Confederate veteran Armistead Long sounded a note of wearied vexation when asked to comment. "The only feeling I have in the matter," he remarked, "is that of regret at beholding a controversy among such distinguished members of the [A]rmy of Northern Virginia."[36]

36 A. L. Long reply to James Longstreet, April 19, 1876, Southern Historical Collection, UNC at Chapel Hill.

CHAPTER SEVEN

What If Jefferson Davis
Had Not Been So Loyal to Braxton Bragg?

Cecily N. Zander

> *"Mr. Davis thinks he can do a great many things*
> *other men would hesitate to attempt. For instance,*
> *he tried to do what God failed to do. He tried to make*
> *a soldier of Braxton Bragg, and you know the result.*
> *It couldn't be done."*
> — *Joseph E. Johnston, 1864*

Historians invariably describe the Confederate high command in the Civil War's Western Theater with one word—dysfunctional.[1] Initially assigned to General Albert Sidney Johnston and his Army of Mississippi, the region spent much of the war under the command of General Braxton Bragg, whose Army of Tennessee tallied only one victory under his leadership— Chickamauga—between 1862 and 1863. Historians have questioned why Confederate President Jefferson Davis did not act sooner to relieve Bragg of his command, especially because positive battlefield results in the West could have helped sustain his fledgling nation in the face of superior resources and manpower on the part of the United States.[2] Bragg's irascibility and

---

1 See, for example, James M. McPherson, *Embattled Rebel: Jefferson Davis as Commander in Chief* (New York: Penguin, 2014), 115; William Glenn Robertson, *River of Death—The Chickamauga Campaign Volume 1: The Fall of Chattanooga* (Chapel Hill: University of North Carolina Press, 2018), 68; Craig L. Symonds, "A Fatal Relationship: Davis and Johnston at War," in *Jefferson Davis's Generals*, ed. Gabor S. Boritt (New York: Oxford University Press, 1999), 25-6.

Davis's stubbornness combined to produce decidedly negative results for the Confederacy. This essay analyzes how Davis's support of Bragg proved injurious to Confederate hopes for independence after the latter's failed invasion of Kentucky, in the wake of the disastrous loss of Middle Tennessee in the Tullahoma campaign, and following Bragg's failure to consolidate his victory at Chickamauga—leading to his defeat in the battle for Chattanooga.

The collective failures of Braxton Bragg dealt the Confederate war effort three substantial blows: the loss of Kentucky and its agricultural capacity;

What if Joe Johnston, Jefferson Davis, or God himself had been able to make a soldier out of Braxton Bragg? *Library of Congress*

the loss of Tennessee, which allowed Union armies to penetrate the Confederate heartland along riverine routes; and, finally, helping to elevate Ulysses S. Grant's reputation as the preeminent Union military commander. The decision to maintain Braxton Bragg after each of his failures should be given significant weight in historical judgements of Jefferson Davis's leadership ability. Unlike Abraham Lincoln, who recognized the successes of his Western generals and promoted them to important command positions, Davis treated the Western Theater as a dumping ground for some of the

2   The most notable volume to tackle the question of Davis's retention of Bragg is Steven E. Woodworth, *Jefferson Davis and His Generals: The Failure of Confederate Command in the West* (Lawrence: University of Kansas Press, 1990).

most cantankerous and incompetent officers in the Confederacy.[3] Taking each of these failures in turn, this essay confirms that events in the Civil War's Western Theater may not have determined which side ultimately won or lost the war, but that Jefferson Davis's management failures—and loyalty to Braxton Bragg—did become a hindrance to the Confederate fight for independence.[4]

On paper, Jefferson Davis far outqualified Abraham Lincoln in experience with organizing and commanding armies. By 1861, Davis had demonstrated his military competency through years of association with the Regular Army and the office of the secretary of war. As historian Frank E. Vandiver observed, "[Davis] trusted himself and meddled much, sometimes to detriment, sometimes to success." Vandiver noted that Davis "knew wars and generals and found it hard to leave the field to others . . . some he liked and trusted as himself, and these were favored long and overwell."[5] The first name on Vandiver's list of officers whom Davis supported for too long was Braxton Bragg. Like Vandiver, Davis's contemporaries often noted the effects his loyalties had on Confederate military operations. "I speak advisedly when I say Mr. Davis prided himself on his military capacity," Ulysses S. Grant explained in his memoirs, "he says so himself, virtually, in his answer to the

---

3   One notable example is Daniel Harvey Hill, who was dismissed from the Army of Northern Virginia and told to report to Braxton Bragg and the Army of Tennessee, where he promptly began fomenting a rebellion against Bragg's leadership. See Woodworth, *Jefferson Davis and His Generals* for analysis of troublesome eastern generals being shifted to the Western Theater.

4   The question of the relative importance of the Civil War's two largest theaters has been extensively debated by historians. This essay accepts the conclusion that most nineteenth-century Americans would have focused their attention on the war's Eastern Theater and the fighting that raged (for the most part) between the two national capitals—Richmond and Washington DC—due in no small part to the presence of Robert E. Lee, whose battlefield triumphs could often be directly correlated to Confederate morale. See, for example, Gary W. Gallagher, "The Idol of His Soldiers and the Hope of His Country: Lee and the Confederate People," in Gallagher, ed., *Lee and His Generals in War and Memory* (Baton Rouge: Louisiana State University Press, 1998). Despite the focus of popular attention on the East, however, most military historians of the war accept the strategic importance of the West when considering how the North won or why the South lost. See Williamson Murray and Wayne Wei-Siang Hsiesh, *A Savage War: A Military History of the Civil War* (Princeton, NJ: Princeton University Press, 2016) and Earl J. Hess, *The Civil War in the West: Victory and Defeat From the Appalachians to the Mississippi* (Chapel Hill: University of North Carolina Press, 2012) for two recent treatments of the Western Theater's geographic and strategic importance to the war.

5   Frank E. Vandiver, "The Shifting Roles of Jefferson Davis," in Gary W. Gallagher, ed., *Essays on Southern History: Written in Honor of Barnes F. Lathrop* (Austin: The General Libraries of the University of Texas, 1980), 123.

notice of his nomination to the Confederate presidency."[6] From day one, Davis intended to take charge of the Confederacy's military operations.

By way of a brief example, the controversies involved in the appointment of the first four full generals of the Confederacy reveal Davis's politicking at work. The first target of Davis's Civil War meddling was career army officer Joseph Eggleston Johnston. Though he was among the highest ranking officers of the antebellum army's staff command (Quartermaster General), Joseph E. Johnston fell behind Colonel Samuel Cooper, Colonel Albert Sidney Johnston, and Colonel Robert E. Lee in the line of superiority in the new Confederacy. In March 1861 the fledgling Confederate Congress authorized the appointment of five officers to the grade of brigadier general. The law stipulated that "the relative rank of officers of each grade shall be determined by the former commissions in the U.S. Army."[7] The measure did not distinguish between staff and line rank in the antebellum force, therefore Johnston believed he should be the senior officer in the new Confederate national army. Davis ignored this provision and bristled at Johnston's repeated objections to being passed over—writing "insubordinate" repeatedly on the Virginian's official correspondence.[8] The incident served as a bellwether for Davis's obstinance when dealing with his commanding generals and indicated that the Confederate president would not attempt to hide his personal preferences when handing out military assignments.

Braxton Bragg inherited command of the Army of Tennessee after General Pierre G. T. Beauregard defied Jefferson Davis by taking medical leave without permission following the siege of Corinth.[9] Bragg had little

---

6 Ulysses S. Grant, *Personal Memoirs of U. S. Grant,* 2 vols. (New York: Charles L. Webster & Company, 1885), 2:88.

7 Kristopher D. White, "The Cresting Tide: Robert E. Lee and the Road to Chancellorsville," in Chris Mackowski and Kristopher D. White, ed. *Turning Points of the American Civil War* (Carbondale: Southern Illinois University Press, 2018), 111.

8 Davis's bitterness toward Johnston lasted for the remainder of the Confederate president's life. In 1874 Davis wrote to William Preston Johnston (son of Albert Sidney) upon the appearance of *A Memoir of the Life and Public Service of Joseph E. Johnston,* about the long list of Confederate officers who excelled where Johnston had failed as a commander, including Cooper, Sidney Johnston, and R. E. Lee. See Jefferson Davis to William Preston Johnston, June 13, 1874 in Haskell M. Monroe, Jr., James T. McIntosh, Lynda Caswell Crist, et. al., *The Papers of Jefferson Davis,* 14 vols. (Baton Rouge: Louisiana State University Press, 1971-2015), 13:221 [hereafter *PJD*]; for Davis's insubordinate comments see *PJD,* 7:335.

9 The *Montgomery Advertiser* accused the president of gratifying his spleen at Beauregard's expense; *The Montgomery Advertiser,* July 9, 1862.

more than his relationship with Davis and his Mexican War reputation to recommend him over other prominent Confederate officers available for the post, most notably Joseph E. Johnston. Still, Bragg, an 1837 graduate of West Point, brought a respectable military record to the Civil War. Though he left the Regular Army in 1856—telling Secretary of War Jefferson Davis he could not see the use in chasing "Indians with six-pounders"—Bragg was considered a hero by many of his countrymen for his actions at the Battle of Buena Vista in 1847.[10] Two critical interventions carried the day for Zachary Taylor's forces in that Mexican-American War fight—Bragg's employment of artillery against the Mexican defenders of the city and the defense of the American army's extreme left flank by Jefferson Davis's Mississippi Riflemen.[11]

Although he commanded one the Confederacy's largest armies for nearly two years, Bragg has not been a favorite subject of biographers. The lack of attention to Bragg is probably due in large part to a lack of substantial collections of papers generated by the general. Though he helped found the Southern Historical Society Papers—which created much of the Lost Cause mythologization of the war—Bragg never wrote for the publication, or any other, about his wartime experiences. There are four biographical treatments of Bragg worth consulting on the subject of the North Carolinian's generalship, though almost all agree that Bragg never grasped the tactical and strategic intricacies of the war on the same level as some of his contemporaries.[12] Most assessments do note, however, that Bragg often excelled in military administration.[13] In the spring of 1863, for instance, General Leonidas Polk recommended that Bragg become inspector general of the Confederacy because of his "peculiar talent" for the difficult

---

10 William Tecumseh Sherman, *Memoirs of General W.T. Sherman*, 2 vols. (New York: D. Appleton and Company, 1889), 163.

11 See K. Jack Bauer, *The Mexican War, 1846-1848* (New York: Macmillan Publishing Company, 1974), 209-17.

12   In order of publication they are: Dan C. Seitz, *Braxton Bragg: General of the Confederacy* (Columbia, S.C.: The State Company, 1924); Grady WcWhiney, *Braxton Bragg and Confederate Defeat: Volume 1* (New York: Columbia University Press, 1969); Judith Lee Hallock, *Braxton Bragg and Confederate Defeat: Volume 2* (Tuscaloosa: The University of Alabama Press, 1991); Earl J. Hess, *Braxton Bragg: The Most Hated Man of the Confederacy* (Chapel Hill: University of North Carolina Press, 2016).

13 Other accounts suggest that even administrative tasks were difficult for the cantankerous Bragg. The oft-repeated story of Bragg's argument with himself over supplies at a western post while in the Old Army can be found in Grant, *Personal Memoirs*, 2:87.

and disagreeable tasks of organization and discipline.[14] In other words, Bragg could organize the materials an army needed, but not convince his officers and soldiers to fight.

The 1862 Confederate invasion of Kentucky offered Bragg his first opportunity to aid the Confederate cause. Of all of the border states, Kentucky held the most value to both Jefferson Davis and Abraham Lincoln—who had both been born in the Bluegrass state. In a letter to Orville Browning written just days after Union victory in the battle of Antietam prevented the loss of Maryland to the Confederacy, Lincoln explained, "I think to lose Kentucky is nearly the same as to lose the whole game. Kentucky gone, we can not hold Missouri, nor, as I think, Maryland. These all against us, and the job on our hands is too large for us."[15] Lincoln had good reason to watch Kentucky closely in the early fall of 1862—simultaneously with Robert E. Lee's invasion of Maryland, Braxton Bragg launched a campaign to install a Confederate government in Kentucky and inspire the state's citizens to rise up against what he characterized as their Union oppressors. Bragg proclaimed to Kentucky's citizens that his army came "not as conquerors or as despoilers, but to restore to you the liberties of which you have been deprived by a cruel and relentless foe . . . to punish with a rod of iron the despoilers of your peace."[16]

The Kentucky Campaign began positively for the Confederates. Bragg had two primary goals in mind for his late summer foray into the Bluegrass state. First, he hoped to induce Kentuckians to rise to Confederate banners as his troops liberated them from Lincoln's oppressive yoke. Second, Bragg needed to relieve Union military pressure on Northern Alabama and Tennessee, whose railroad network was increasingly under threat— especially after the capture of forts Henry and Donelson earlier in the year. By moving north he hoped to draw the Union army with him, thus releasing the pressure that had been building since the battle of Shiloh. Marching from

---

14 U.S. War Department, *The War of the Rebellion: A Compilation of the Official Records of the Union and Confederate Armies*, 127 vols. index and atlas (Washington: GPO, 1880-1901), 23(2): 729.

15 Roy P. Basler, Marion Dolores Pratt, and Lloyd A. Dunlap, eds., *The Collected Works of Abraham Lincoln*, 9 vols. (New Brunswick, NJ: Rutgers University Press, 1953), 4:533.

16 *O. R.*, 16(2):822; the message was nearly identical to Lee's in Maryland, which promised "to enable [citizens] to again enjoy the inalienable rights of free men, and restore independence and sovereignty to your State." [*O. R.*, 19(2):601-2].

Chattanooga, Tennessee, Bragg and the Army of Mississippi encountered little resistance in the initial stages of the invasion. After Confederate general Edmund Kirby Smith gained a success at Richmond, Kentucky in late August, Bragg hoped Smith's Army of Kentucky would join his larger force and strike a decisive blow against Don Carlos Buell's Union Army of the Ohio, which had moved north out of Tennessee to mirror the invading Confederate column. By September 2, Bragg learned that Buell and his force of fifty thousand men had reached Louisville and were reinforcing.

As the two armies maneuvered around one another in the opening weeks of September, Bragg vacillated over whether to take the offensive and attack Buell before he could be fully reinforced. Bragg, however, expected his own reinforcements, either from Smith's army to his east or from Earl Van Dorn's army to his south—the latter supposed to be moving north to retake the vital railroad junction of Corinth, Mississippi, while Bragg operated in Kentucky. As the Confederates struck north out of Glasgow, they encountered a Union garrison on the Green River at Munfordville and demanded its surrender. Union colonel John T. Wilder refused to give up his position and Bragg's army laid siege to the city for two days. Don Carlos Buell responded quickly and marched his men south the meet the Confederates. Before they could arrive, however, a final Confederate push for surrender succeeded and Bragg counted the capture of 4,000 Union soldiers as his first great prize in Kentucky. Rather than stay to fight Buell, Bragg burned the railroad bridge and moved toward Bardstown, where he installed a Confederate government on September 28. Buell retreated to Louisville.

Bragg surrendered the initiative of the campaign to Buell when he refused to give battle at Munfordville. Instead, Bragg waited for his army to be united with Kirby Smith's force, allowing Buell the opportunity to interpose his Union army between the two Confederate forces operating in Kentucky. On October 7, 1862 Buell reached the crossroads town of Perryville where he encountered Confederate skirmishers. Both armies were lacking a full complement of troops and waited overnight for reinforcements. On October 8, the battle of Perryville commenced with the arrival of Brigadier General Lovell Rousseau's Union troops on the Springfield Pike. Major General William J. Hardee responded by dispatching Benjamin F. Cheatham's Confederate division into the Union left flank, who withstood several substantial attacks before being routed. Confederates overwhelmed Alexander M. McCook's I Corps troops and Buell failed to deploy any

"I hope God is on our side, but I must have Kentucky," President Lincoln said. The border state tried to maintain neutrality, although the Confederates made several plays for it during the war, culminating in their victory at Perryville (above)—which was quickly followed by a withdrawal from the commonwealth. What if Kentucky had gone one way or the other? *Chris Mackowski*

reinforcements along the Union left, due, in part, to an acoustic shadow that prevented him from hearing that a battle had been joined. Brigadier General Phillip H. Sheridan attempted a counter-attack late in the afternoon, but failed to breach the Confederate defense of the city. By the time darkness fell, Bragg could reasonably claim a tactical victory as his troops held a substantial portion of the day's battlefield.

Still, the result at Perryville was not a decisive battle for possession of Kentucky. Bragg, realizing that his troops could not sustain another day of fighting—let alone more campaigning while desperately short of supplies and water—determined to withdraw during the night and retreat from the Bluegrass state. In possession of intelligence that Earl Van Dorn had been badly defeated in an attempt to recapture Corinth on October 3–4 and knowing he was outnumbered nearly two to one, Bragg could evince little hope in his fortunes improving. His retreat, nevertheless, created an uproar among his subordinates and the Confederate press. *The Richmond Whig* lamented that Bragg's movement into Kentucky "turned out to be simply a fizzle," while the *Memphis Appeal* commented that Bragg's retreat was a "sad finale" to a campaign which had been expected to bring about the "redemption" of Kentucky. "Of what good result are such victories productive," the editors wondered "if straightway we must relinquish the State to the occupancy and possession of the enemy?"[17]

It would be difficult to quantify what the loss of access to Kentucky cost the Confederacy. A few scattered figures help to give some sense of the economic blow occasioned by Bragg's retreat. In June of 1861, just weeks after the war had begun in earnest, the Louisville and Nashville Railroad reported $252,000 worth of freight sent to the South.[18] E. A. Pollard, an early historian of the Confederacy, estimated that "Tennessee alone had secured wheat and flour enough to feed the state troops for a year, or that 1,200,000 pairs of shoes had gone South, or that the meat products represented by 3,000,000 hogs had been shipped to the rebels before Kentucky had [been] abandoned."[19] Though Pollard wrote from a Lost Cause perspective, his numbers still give a sense of the agricultural and manufacturing value of products that Kentucky produced. While Kentucky never officially declared for either of the belligerents during the war, abandoning the state to Union occupation in 1862 (save for the occasional Confederate cavalry raid in the years that followed) was not an ideal outcome for the already outnumbered and out-supplied Rebel armies.

Press criticism of Bragg and the complaints voiced by the commander's subordinates raised questions in Jefferson Davis's mind about Bragg's suitability for command. On October 23 the War Department summoned Bragg to Richmond to give an account of the campaign. In Richmond, Bragg attempted to shift the blame for the Kentucky debacle on his great

17 *Richmond Daily Whig*, October 20, 1862; *Memphis Daily Appeal*, October 29, 1862. The *Whig* rated Bragg's campaign from beginning to end as "a brilliant blunder and a magnificent failure." In his essay for Battles and Leaders of the Civil War, Confederate cavalryman Joseph Wheeler defended Bragg, saying that the Confederacy "hoped for more from their generals and armies than could reasonably be accomplished." Wheeler maintained, at a distance of two decades, that Bragg had no choice but to retreat after the battle of Perryville. See Clarence Clough Buel and Robert Underwood Johnson, ed., *Battles and Leaders of the Civil War*, 4 vols. (New York: The Century Company, 1884-1888), 3:19.

18 Sr. Mary Raphael Hayden, "The Importance of Kentucky in the Civil War," MA Thesis, Loyola University of Chicago (1937), [54].

19 Edward A. Pollard, *The Lost Cause: A New Southern History of the War of the Confederacy* (New York: E. B. Treat and Co., 1866), 491.

adversary Leonidas Polk, but, unfortunately for Bragg, Polk also stood high in the president's estimation.[20] The animosity that Bragg's subordinates expressed toward their commander largely derived from the incompatibility of personalities in the high command of the war's Western Theater. As Earl J. Hess put it, "It is probable that no army commander of either side in the Civil War had to deal with such insubordinate corps and division commanders as did Bragg."[21] Even worse for Bragg, Polk had also been summoned to Richmond. Reporting that Bragg had lost the confidence of his generals, Polk recommended that Joseph E. Johnston supersede Bragg in command of the Confederacy's western army. Writing to Edmund Kirby Smith after the meeting, Davis argued, "[O]f the Generals, Cooper is at the head of the Bureau, Lee in command of the army in Va., Johnston still disabled by the wound received at seven [sic] Pines, [and] Beauregard was tried as commander of the Army of the West." In defense of Bragg, Davis continued, "[He] succeeded to command, organized the army, and marched to your support with efficient troops."[22]

Unwilling to believe that Bragg was as incompetent as he was widely reputed to be, Davis took the halfway measure of placing Joseph E. Johnston in command of a new department that included the commands of Bragg, Smith, and John Clifford Pemberton, and sent Bragg back to the field to establish his headquarters at Murfreesboro, Tennessee.[23] In November Bragg renamed his force the Army of Tennessee and absorbed many of Edmund Kirby Smith's troops when Davis dissolved Smith's Department of

---

20 Inability to take responsibility for the failure of his subordinate stands out in stark contrast to Robert E. Lee's conduct following the battle of Gettysburg, when the commander of the Army of Northern Virginia explained to Jefferson Davis that he was entirely responsible for the defeat of his army and would not allow blame to be placed on the heads of any of his subordinates. R. E. Lee to Jefferson Davis, July 31, 1863 in Robert E. Lee, *The Wartime Papers of R. E. Lee*, ed. Clifford Dowdey and Louis H. Manarin (Boston: Little, Brown, 1961), 564-5.

21 Hess, *Braxton Bragg*, 279.

22 Jefferson Davis to Lieutenant General E. Kirby Smith, October 29, 1862, in William J. Cooper, Jr., ed., *Jefferson Davis: The Essential Writings* (New York: The Modern Library, 2004), 265-6.

23 Confederate war clerk J. B. Jones recorded on October 28, 1862 that Bragg "succeeded in getting away with the largest amount of provisions, clothing, etc., ever obtained by an army, including 8,000 beef cattle, 50,000 barrels of pork, and a million yards of Kentucky cloth." J. B. Jones, *A Rebel War Clerk's Diary at the Confederate States Capital*, 2 vols. (Philadelphia, J. B. Lippincott and Co., 1866), 1:176.

East Tennessee. The army's two wings were commanded by Leonidas Polk and William J. Hardee, with Nathan Bedford Forrest as the highest-ranking cavalry officer. The new arrangement proposed by Davis failed to bolster the Confederate war effort west of the Mississippi, and lapsed after the fall of Vicksburg, but not before Bragg added Middle Tennessee to his roster of ground lost by the largest Confederate army in the West.

The late-December battle of Stones River and the campaign that followed the next summer did little to restore Braxton Bragg's reputation in the minds of the press, his subordinates, or his soldiers—but seemingly did nothing to damage the North Carolinian in the estimation of Jefferson Davis. By the time Bragg confronted Union general William Starke Rosecrans in Murfreesboro on December 31, 1862, and January 2, 1863, he was on the verge of losing control of his army. Though his men fought hard and defended the city for two days in the face of their numerically superior federal foes, Bragg withdrew his army in the days following the battle. The latent hostility of Leonidas Polk, William J. Hardee, and Benjamin F. Cheatham turned to full-blown mutiny in early January, after Bragg abandoned the city of Murfreesboro to Federal troops—following up another tactical victory with a retreat.[24] The intrepid British observer James Arthur Lyon Fremantle noted that the commander of the Army of Tennessee appeared "sickly, cadaverous, [and] haggard" in the aftermath of the battle. His observation was hardly a ringing endorsement of Bragg's strength in the midst of a physically grueling campaign.[25]

Despite Bragg's decision to retreat, Davis refused to doubt the ability of his chosen commander. Instead of acting decisively to remove Bragg, Davis dispatched Joseph Johnston to assume command of the North Carolinian's army, if Johnston felt the situation between Bragg and his corps commanders had become unredeemable. "[T]hough my confidence in General Bragg is unshaken," Jefferson Davis wrote to Joseph Johnston upon

---

24 Historian Larry J. Daniel points to Stones River as an example of Bragg's failure as a tactician. "Despite having been at Murfreesboro for six weeks, he overlooked the most strategic geographic feature on the Stones River battlefield," Daniel explained, "McFadden's Hill, a hill subsequently occupied by the Federals that proved pivotal. The subsequent assault plan on December 31 was actually Polk's; Bragg had wanted to attack up the center." See Larry J. Daniel, *Conquered: Why the Army of Tennessee Failed* (Chapel Hill: University of North Carolina Press, 2019), 51.

25 Arthur James Lyon Fremantle, *Three Months in the Southern States* (Edinburgh: William Blackwood and Sons, 1863), 145.

dispatching the Virginian to investigate the troubles in the high command of the Army of Tennessee after its disastrous retreat from Murfreesboro, "it cannot be doubted that if he is distrusted by his officers and troops, a disaster may result which, but for that cause, would have been avoided."[26] Davis's unwillingness to condemn Bragg, combined with his failure to give Johnston clear authority to remove Bragg if necessary, set the stage for the abandonment of Middle Tennessee in the spring of 1863.

Joseph Johnston compounded the Confederacy's problems when he proved reluctant to assume command of the Army of Tennessee, despite knowing how little faith Bragg's subordinates had evinced in their commander. As Colonel David Urquhart, who served on Bragg's staff, recalled for *Battles and Leaders*, "Johnston's arrival was hailed with joy, for our army specially wanted him as their commander . . . this result quieted the bad feeling somewhat, but did not restore harmony between the corps commanders and their commanding general."[27] Johnston assessed the situation and explained to Davis that he could not effectively command the armies of Bragg and Pemberton simultaneously—nor did he want to do so. He stressed that Bragg's army was much closer to Robert E. Lee's in Virginia than it was to Pemberton's in Vicksburg, Mississippi, meaning Davis's plan to centralize military authority in the expansive Western Theater made little geographic sense.[28] Bragg, consequently, would be left to his own devices in the campaign that followed.

Union general William Starke Rosecrans reinforced his army for nearly six months before launching into the Tullahoma Campaign, which achieved a long held Federal ambition—clearing Middle Tennessee of a substantial Confederate presence. The combination of Rosecrans's maneuvering around Bragg's army toward Chattanooga and Ulysses S. Grant's investment of the last Confederate bastion on the Mississippi River at Vicksburg were two major positives for the United States in the summer of 1863. Both were essential for completing General Winfield Scott's Anaconda Plan, which aimed to encircle the seceded states and cut off their access to resources

26   *O. R.*, 23(2): 613-4.

27   Buel and Johnson, ed., *Battles and Leaders of the Civil War*, 3:608-9.

28   Bradley T. Johnston, ed., *A Memoir of the Life and Public Service of Joseph E. Johnston* (Baltimore: R. H. Woodward and Company, 1891), 96.

and transportation, especially major riverine transportation networks. Unfortunately for the Confederacy, rivers were one of the most convenient avenues for the United States to use to penetrate rebel territory. If the Confederates failed to hold Middle Tennessee, Union troops could converge by land and river on major railroad depots—especially Nashville, on the Cumberland River.

In the face of Rosecrans's brilliant maneuvering through the Tennessee mountains, Bragg felt he had no choice but to retreat to the city of Chattanooga, where he could reprovision and reinforce his army. Luckily for Bragg, General James Longstreet and his First Corps from the Army of Northern Virginia were on their way to Tennessee. As Longstreet's chief artillerist pointed out in his memoirs, however, instead of waiting for the full complement of troops from Virginia to arrive and support his army, Bragg brought on a battle with Rosecrans while five of Longstreet's brigades remained out of range of the fight. Still, Edward Porter Alexander saved most of his ire for Bishop Leonidas Polk, who "the Lord had not" made a general.[29] Instead of attacking when ordered, Polk waited almost four hours before engaging the federals. It was only through a catastrophic error on the part of William Rosecrans—whose efforts to reinforce his flanks opened up a gap in the middle of his lines—that James Longstreet was able to win the day for Bragg's army.

Despite what was, finally, a decided victory for the Confederates, Bragg allowed Rosecrans to fall back into Chattanooga while his army looked down on the city atop the high bluffs of Missionary Ridge. He had not consolidated the prize and mutiny threatened his command once again. In the days and weeks that followed the battle rancor rippled through the army. Confederate cavalry general Nathan Bedford Forrest refused to serve under Bragg any longer. Lieutenant General James Longstreet wrote to Secretary of War James Seddon arguing that the situation in Tennessee would remain hopeless unless Davis replaced Bragg. Most of Bragg's division and corps commanders met in secret and wrote and signed a petition to Jefferson Davis asking that Bragg be removed.[30] Jefferson Davis could not ignore the

---

29 Gary W. Gallagher, ed., *Fighting for the Confederacy: The Personal Recollections of General Edward Porter Alexander* (Chapel Hill: University of North Carolina Press, 1989), 289.

30 See Hess, *Braxton Bragg*, 177-8.

Take your pick: What if Bragg had gotten along better with any of these subordinates (or all of them): John C. Breckenridge, William Hardee, Daniel Harvey Hill, James Longstreet, and Leonidis Polk. At various times, Bragg clashed with each—and all—of them, as well as others. Departmental commander General Joseph E. Johnston had been empowered to solve the Gordian knot that was the high command of the Army of Tennessee and chose not to. President Jefferson Davis also personally intervened in the situation but failed to act decisively. What if the government had acted more definitively on any of these occasions? *photo illustration by Chris Mackowski from photos at the Library of Congress*

situation any longer and got on a train bound from Richmond to Tennessee. The meeting that followed has become a core part of the narrative of the Army of Tennessee's dysfunction, as Davis gathered Bragg and his subordinates in the army's headquarters and asked each officer present to provide his assessment of Bragg's leadership—while Bragg was in the room.

The meeting did not go in Bragg's favor. Every officer present told Jefferson Davis that Bragg lacked the capacity to command the Army of Tennessee. Hal Bridges, biographer of Confederate general and Bragg antagonist Daniel Harvey Hill, noted that "Bragg listened passively to the successive statements that he was incompetent, saying not a word but looking as [Major General Simon B.] Buckner remembered it 'a little confused.'"[31] The entire situation encapsulated Davis's management failures as commander in chief. Prior to the council, Bragg had informed Davis of his willingness to resign, which should have eliminated the need for a referendum on Bragg's leadership. When the preponderance of opinion suggested that Bragg should be removed, Davis ignored the considered opinions of some of his most experienced officers and stood firmly in favor of retaining Bragg. Davis again claimed that he had no viable alternatives for

---

31 Hal Bridges, *Lee's Maverick General: Daniel Harvey Hill* (1961; reprint, Lincoln, NE: Bison Books, 1991), 238.

the post, passing over Beauregard, Johnston, and Longstreet in favor of his friend. The only personnel decision Davis made was removing the irascible D. H. Hill and suggested John Pemberton, who had become a Confederate pariah following the surrender of Vicksburg, as a replacement.

In Chattanooga, meanwhile, William Rosecrans's days were numbered. On October 17, 1863, Rosecrans was relieved of command of the Army of the Cumberland and replaced by Major General Ulysses S. Grant. The latter officer's rise in the Western Theater had produced signal victories at Forts Henry and Donelson and at Vicksburg. Removing the Confederate threat at Chattanooga would allow the Union army to establish a supply hub and operate deep into Georgia and Alabama. Without Chattanooga the March to the Sea would have been far less likely to succeed and without Chattanooga Grant may not have finally convinced the Lincoln administration that he was the man most likely to turn the tide against Robert E. Lee. All Grant had to do was dislodge Braxton Bragg—and he did so by exhibiting the "bulldog" qualities that would come to the fore during the Overland Campaign the following spring.[32] As he recalled in his memoirs, "The victory at Chattanooga was won against great odds, considering the advantage the enemy had of position, and was accomplished more easily than was expected by reason of Bragg's making several grave mistakes."[33] Bragg's personal exhortations that his men make a stout defense at Missionary Ridge, moreover, fell on deaf ears in the midst of battle. Not only had Bragg failed militarily, but he had also failed to convince his soldiers that he was the best man to lead them.[34] In the wake of the battle for Chattanooga Jefferson Davis finally recognized that Bragg was not up the task of commanding his army and accepted Bragg's proffered resignation on November 29, 1863.

Both Bragg and Grant found themselves bound for their respective national capitals in the months that followed the battle—Bragg to serve as a military advisor to Jefferson Davis and Grant to assume command of all Union

32   Roy P. Basler, Marion Dolores Pratt, and Lloyd A. Dunlap, eds., *The Collected Works of Abraham Lincoln*, 9 vols. (New Brunswick, NJ: Rutgers University Press, 1953), 7:499.

33   Grant, *Personal Memoirs*, 2:85.

34   Bragg's ineffective rallying cry stands out in sharp contrast from the response to Robert E. Lee's appearance in the Widow Tapp field on the second day of the battle of the Wilderness, which inspired exaltations from his troops and spurred them on to victory—saving the army's right flank. See Gordon C. Rhea, *The Battle of the Wilderness, May 5--6, 1864* (Baton Rouge: Louisiana State University Press, 2004), 300-1.

armies. Based on his track record of victories, "Lincoln bet his presidency" that Grant could be the man to finally defeat Lee—in the combat theater that mattered most for morale and public opinion (and Lincoln's chances for re-election).[35] Davis's stubbornness in retaining Bragg in October yielded disaster in November and established the conditions for Lincoln to finally decide to put the Civil War in the hands of Ulysses S. Grant. If Davis had removed Bragg sooner Grant might have faced a more recalcitrant opponent (Grant believed his friend James Longstreet would have been a superior choice) and the Confederacy might not have lost Chattanooga and thrown open the gates to Georgia.

It should briefly be noted, in defense of both Davis and Bragg, there may have simply been no better option for the Confederate president to choose. "A *General* in the full acceptation of the word is a rare product, scarcely more than one can be expected in a generation," Davis wrote in May of 1863, "but in this mighty war in which we are engaged there is need for a half dozen."[36] Davis certainly never found his half dozen, and in the war's Western Theater, especially after the death of Albert Sidney Johnston, he could hardly find one. Apart from Bragg, who Davis clearly trusted, there was Joseph Johnston or P. G. T. Beauregard, who had both been given chances to command armies and disappointed Davis. There was Leonidas Polk, "a basically incompetent general," or William J. Hardee, who shied away from assignments larger than corps command.[37] The fact that none of Bragg's successors improved upon his record underscores the point that it was a lack of talent across the board that heavily influenced Jefferson Davis's decision making when it came to picking commanders.

At every critical moment during his tenure in command of the Army of Tennessee, Braxton Bragg failed to achieve victory. Under his leadership the Confederacy lost access to Kentucky, effectively abandoned Tennessee, and helped to convince the Lincoln administration to trust Ulysses S. Grant with command of the Union military effort. More stubborn resistance at any point might have given the Confederacy an agricultural or economic

35   Joan Waugh, *U. S. Grant: American Hero, American Myth* (Chapel Hill: University of North Carolina Press, 2009), 74.

36   *PJD*, 9:166-7.

37   Woodworth, *Jefferson Davis and His Generals*, 156; Nathaniel Cheairs Hughes, *General William J. Hardee: Old Reliable* (Baton Rouge: Louisiana State University Press, 1965).

lifeline, protected the fledgling nation's most valuable advantage—a vast and difficult to occupy geography—or done more to cast doubt over the military abilities of the man who would eventually turn the tide of the war in favor of the Union—Ulysses S. Grant. Jefferson Davis's high estimation of his own abilities as a military leader and Braxton Bragg's lack of tactical sense and determination to avoid battles he might have easily won proved to be a losing combination. What if Jefferson Davis hadn't been so loyal to Braxton Bragg? The war in the West might not have been so easily lost and the fate of the Confederacy might have hinged on the fortunes of more than one army and more than one commander. As it turned out, Robert E. Lee had to make a stand for his adopted nation with his Army of Northern Virginia alone. In the Civil War's Western Theater, Braxton Bragg and Jefferson Davis helped to ensure Confederate defeat.

CHAPTER EIGHT

What If Robert E. Lee

Had Struck a Blow at the North Anna River?

Chris Mackowski

Ulysses S. Grant hadn't expected any visitors on the evening of May 25, 1864, but the old woman who approached him and his staff seemed harmless enough. They sat outside Grant's headquarters tent, set up near Quarles Mill along the north bank of the North Anna River. The woman lived in a small house nearby and, "not lacking in the quality of curiosity," came out to see the commander who'd brought the Federal horde southward. "She wore an old-fashioned calico dress about six inches too short with sleeves rolled up to the elbows," wrote Grant's chief of staff, Horace Porter. "She had a nose so sharp that it looked as if it had been caught in the crack of a door, and small gray eyes that twinkled and snapped as she spoke." When she did, her voice "squeaked like the high notes of an E-flat clarinet with a soft reed."[1]

The woman pulled up a chair and, in good-humored tones, struck up conversation. "I'm powerful glad General Lee has been lickin' you-all from the Rapidan cl'ah down h'yah, and that now he's got you jes wh'ah he wants you," she told Grant.[2]

Grant seemed mostly amused by the exchange, which lasted for some minutes. At the end, he sent one of his orderlies off with the woman to protect her house while the army remained encamped nearby. Grant could afford magnanimity: over the course of the previous three weeks, Federal forces

---

1   Horace Porter, *Campaigning with Grant* (New York: Mallard Press, 1991), 147-8.

2   Ibid., 148.

had driven Lee thirty miles from the Rapidan River, more than halfway to the Confederate capital of Richmond. The commanding general didn't seem too worried about being pinned down "jes wh'ah Lee wanted him," although he later conceded it had been a near thing. Lee had set a perfect trap for the Union army, and Grant had walked blindly into it—but then, for no apparent reason, Lee didn't spring the trap. "[H]e did not attempt to drive us from the field," Grant later marveled.

Why didn't he, Grant wondered. And might he yet? What if Lee tried?

The Federal commander had no way of knowing that, on the south side of the river, Lee had lain delirious in his tent, wracked by a dysenteric fever. Even as Grant first realized his precarious position on the afternoon of May 24, Lee pleaded to his staff officers, "We must strike them a blow. . . . We must strike them a blow!" He tried to send orders to his officers, but as his aide, Charles Venable, said, "Lee confined to his tent was not Lee on the battlefield."[3]

Writing years later for the Southern Historical Society, the Confederate staff officer admitted, "I know it is unprofitable now to consider what might have happened," but he nonetheless couldn't help himself. "I cannot refrain from venturing to express the opinion that had not General Lee been physically disabled, he would have inflicted a heavy blow on the enemy. . . ." If not at North Anna, the blow might have come on the march from the Pamunkey River to the Chickahominy. "[T]he opportunity was offered for this blow near Haw's shop . . ." Venable said. "However that may be, Grant found Lee always in his front whenever and wherever he turned."[4] Venable was speaking specifically about the march to Cold Harbor and, more generally, referring to the entire 1864 Overland Campaign, but his statement held just as true for the May 21-23 lead up to the confrontation at North Anna.

We remember the fiery horrors of the Wilderness, the up-close slaughter at Spotsylvania's Bloody Angle, that final assault Grant ever-after regretted at Cold Harbor—these features define the 1864 Overland Campaign. The

---

3   Charles Venable, "Campaign from the Wilderness to Petersburg," *Southern Historical Society Papers*, vol. 14, 535.

4   Ibid., 13-14.

campaign's third "epoch," as the veterans called it, usually gets overlooked or, when we do remember it, we remember the formidable, ingenious V-shaped defense Robert E. Lee created—so strong it discouraged the kind of massive assault that would have made the confrontation along the North Anna River regrettably more memorable. "To make a direct attack . . ." Grant told the War Department, "would cause a slaughter of our men that even success could not justify."[5]

Because of the North Anna's generally anticlimactic nature, we forget about the very things that made the third phase of the Overland Campaign so dramatic and so fascinating: the many missed opportunities both armies had to strike a blow. For the Army of Northern Virginia (ANV), those missed opportunities carried magnified weight because the armies were as numerically matched in size during the North Anna phase of the campaign as they ever were during the spring of 1864—indeed, as they would ever be during the entire rest of the war.

Lee began the campaign that spring with 66,000 men in the Wilderness, but fighting through Spotsylvania whittled him down to only 40,000. However, new additions that joined his army as it moved toward the North Anna brought the ANV back up to about 53,000 men: Maj. Gen. John Breckinridge's 3,200-man army from the Shenandoah, fresh off its win at New Market; Maj. Gen. George Pickett's 6,000-man division, fresh off its win at Drewry's Bluff; the 1,600-man North Carolina brigade still known as "Hoke's Brigade," now commanded by Lt. Col. William Lewis; and Col. Bradley Johnson's 2,100-man "Maryland Line"—veterans all, with high morale.

Grant, meanwhile, started with roughly 120,000 men. The fighting through Spotsylvania brought him down to 84,000, and an ill-conceived cavalry jaunt by Maj. Gen. Philip Sheridan beginning on May 8 took as many as 12,000 more men off the board. Expiring enlistments, sickness, and detachments to protect the ever-extending supply line all siphoned off even more men, although Grant gained some 17,250 replacements by stripping soldiers from the Washington, D.C., defenses and ordering them to the

---

5 Ulysses S. Grant, *Ulysses S. Grant: Memoirs and Selected Letters* (New York: Library of America, 1990), 569, quoting from the OR.

What if Grant had won the race to the North Anna River?
Chris Mackowski

Army of the Potomac. He also took into the army some 1,800 new draftees. All told, Grant's strength stood at just over 68,000 effectives, with nearly all the new men green behind the ears.[6]

The new additions to Grant's army began arriving just as he began making plans to leave Spotsylvania after twelve days of stalemate fighting. Grant needed to lure the Confederates out of their trenches, and to do this, he determined to move around Lee's right, just as he had done at the end of their fight in the Wilderness. The paths of the two armies would eventually converge on the banks of the North Anna River, although Grant had not initially set out with that objective in mind. "Had Grant originally started his movement as a race for the North Anna, having the initiative, he might have easily won it," mused Confederate artillerist E. Porter Alexander.[7] But Alexander's "might" offers only the possibility of a tantalizing "what if" rather than any certain judgment.

But what if Grant *had* reached the North Anna first? The Federal

6   The sizes of armies going into the Wilderness are statistics that come from the NPS, as are the final army sizes going into North Anna. Statistics on the various unit sizes come from Mark Miller's *The North Anna Campaign: "Even to Hell Itself" May 21-26, 1864* (Lynchburg, VA: H.E. Howard, 1989).

7   Edward Porter Alexander, *Fighting for the Confederacy: The Personal Recollections of General Edward Porter Alexander*, Gary Gallagher, editor (Chapel Hill: University of North Carolina Press, 1989), 387.

position south of the river would have cut Lee off from his supply line along the Richmond, Fredericksburg, and Potomac Railroad. It also would have denied Lee access to supplies from the Valley along the Virginia Central Railroad, also on the south bank of the river. Such a dire consequence would have precipitated a crisis for the Army of Northern Virginia and forced Lee to action, either to dislodge Grant by force or somehow maneuver to get around him.

To draw Grant out, Lee might have tried a sharp move northward in a feint toward Washington. That might force Grant to pursue, but it would also draw Lee away from his own source of supplies. Grant, unpanicked, had confidence in the fortifications around the Federal capital, which is why, a week before, he'd begun drawing troops from those fortifications to replenish his own dwindling numbers. Finally, Grant could have shifted Maj. Gen. Franz Sigel's recently defeated army from the Shenandoah Valley toward D.C. in an effort to intercept Lee. To the north, then, lay only diminishing possibilities.

However, it's doubtful Lee would have made a headlong attempt to get across the North Anna, which offered significant topographical advantages as a defensive position. Lee understood this well and had cast his eye there as early as the fall of 1862. When Ambrose Burnside replaced George McClellan in command of the Army of the Potomac, Lee had initially planned to fall back to the North Anna to contest Burnside's advance on Richmond; only a presidential edict from Jefferson Davis forced him to defend Fredericksburg along the Rappahannock River instead.[8]

Running west to east, the river had sharp, steep banks that obstructed southward movement. A bridge, a railroad trestle, and a couple of fords dominated by the south riverbank offered the only easy crossings. Ordinarily, the water didn't run deep, but the river's narrow gorge filled up quickly when it rained, adding potential difficulties to any crossing.

Certainly Grant would have welcomed any attempt by Lee to force a crossing, and indeed, it's likely Grant would have tried to coax Lee into an attack. Alternatively, Grant could have made a dash at the Confederate capital in the spirit of the early war's "On to Richmond" campaigns, but

---

8 For an in-depth discussion of this, see decision #3, "Robert E. Lee Decides to Defend Fredericksburg" in *Decisions at Fredericksburg: The Fourteen Critical Decisions that Defined the Battle* by Chris Mackowski (Knoxville, TN: University of Tennessee Press, 2021).

Grant had decided at the outcome of the campaign that Lee, not Richmond, was the strategic objective.[9]

Lee's only real option would be to adopt the same policy Grant had followed in the Wilderness and at Spotsylvania: try to move around the enemy's flank. This would not be an entirely impossible option for Lee, either, considering the limited cavalry support Grant enjoyed at the time—although that advantage would evaporate by May 24 when Sheridan's troopers rejoined the army.

The exact route of any flanking move would be impossible to guess without knowing Grant's own dispositions. A move around Grant's right would risk running into Sheridan's returning cavalry; a move even farther to the right would bring the Army of Northern Virginia into the range of Federal gunboats operating on the upper reaches of the Pamunkey River (formed by the juncture of the North and South Anna Rivers). A move around Grant's left would at least put Lee back in contact with the Virginia Central Railroad as a possible source of resupply while offering a quick route to the South Anna River, where a crossing would offer relative safety. Of course, with Lee, there's always the possibility of a sudden, unexpected strike at some vulnerable part of Grant's army once Confederates got around its flank.

As intriguing as all these possibilities are, history unfolded differently. Instead of dashing straight toward the North Anna on the night of May 20, Grant sent Maj. Gen. Winfield Scott Hancock's II Corps on a wide southward arc toward Bowling Green, Milford Station, and if practicable, across the North Anna River to the vital Confederate rail hub at Hanover Junction.[10] Dangling out there as bait, the II Corps would ideally entice the aggressive Lee to make a move against them, at which time Grant would strike with the rest of the army. He detailed his V Corps, under Maj. Gen. Gouverneur K. Warren, as the tip of the spear.

Instead, the aggressive Lee acted out of character—not for the last time during this phase of the campaign—and rather than striking at Hancock, he

9   Charles S. Wainwright, *A Diary of Battle: The Personal journals of Colonel Charles S. Wainwright, 1861-1865*, Allan Nevins, editor (New York: De Capo, 1998), 338.

10   Gordon Rhea, *To the North Anna River: Grant and Lee, May 13-25, 1864* (Baton Rouge: LSU, 2000), 239.

opted to try and get in front of the Federal column. As he had in 1862, Lee looked to the North Anna once again.

Hancock's route took his II Corps far enough to the east that it left open the closer Telegraph Road (modern-day Route 1), which offered a straight shot southward toward the river. Lee sent his own Second Corps, under Lt. Gen. Richard Ewell, to capture an intersection at Mud Tavern that would secure access to the road and the direct route south.

Like Lee, Grant also began acting out of character. During the battle of the Wilderness, at the height of the action on May 6, as staff officers began to fret about the many ways Robert E. Lee might bedevil Federal forces, Grant had snapped, "I am heartily tired of hearing what Lee is going to do. Some of you always seem to think he is suddenly going to turn a double somersault, and land on our rear and on both our flanks at the same time. Go back to your command, and try to think what we are going to do ourselves, instead of what Lee is going to do."[11] The fifteen days since, though, had taught Grant some hard lessons about Lee, and on May 21, he began to worry very much about what the Old Gray Fox might do. The II Corps, dangling as bait, suddenly looked more vulnerable than tantalizing out there all on its own, and spotty communications between Hancock and army headquarters—disrupted by Confederate cavalry—made the link feel even more tenuous.

Here, the absence of Sheridan proved debilitating. What if he had returned in time to assist with the movement? A strong cavalry presence on May 21 and 22 would have secured Grant's lines of communications, screened his movements, and provided vital information about Lee's whereabouts. Grant could have moved with confidence, and Lee would have had a more difficult time getting past him. The dynamics of the entire day would have changed dramatically.[12]

But with his confidence shaken, Grant changed his plan and ordered

---

11 Porter, 70.

12 Although beyond the scope of this essay, imagine this: What if Sheridan had done his job and soundly defeated Wade Hampton's Confederate cavalry outside of Richmond? Although the raid led to the mortal wounding of Jeb Stuart on May 11 at Yellow Tavern, Sheridan's entanglements with Hampton, Stuart's successor, kept him detached from the army far longer than he should have been—with drastic consequences for Grant's men. (With thanks to Kris White for posing this question.)

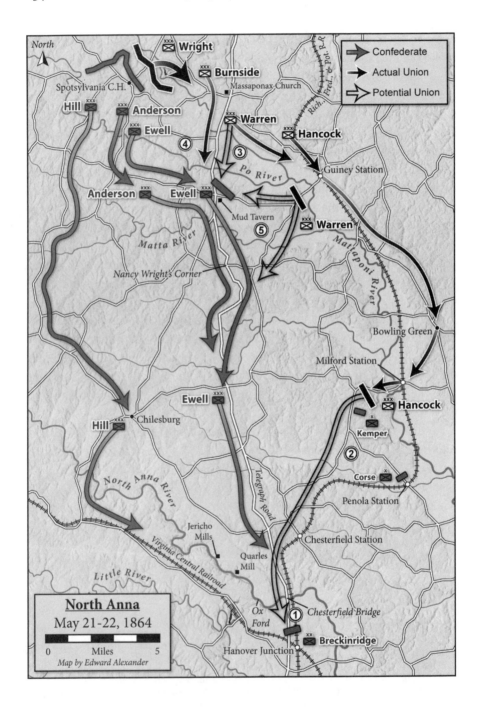

North

Confederate
Actual Union
Potential Union

Wright

Burnside

Spotsylvania C.H.

Massaponax Church

Hill

Anderson

Ewell

Warren

Hancock

④

③

Po River

Guiney Station

Anderson

Ewell

Mud Tavern

⑤

Warren

Matta River

Mattaponi River

Nancy Wright's Corner

Bowling Green

Milford Station

Ewell

Chilesburg

Hancock

Hill

Kemper

②

Corse

Penola Station

Telegraph Road

Chesterfield Station

North Anna River

Jericho Mills

Virginia Central Railroad

Quarles Mill

Little River

North Anna
May 21-22, 1864

0   Miles   5

Map by Edward Alexander

Ox Ford

① Chesterfield Bridge

Hanover Junction

Breckinridge

North Anna   On the march to the North Anna River, the Federal II Corps under Winfield Scott Hancock could have raced directly down the Telegraph Road and secured the river crossing. Instead, Hancock had orders to take a more roundabout route through Bowling Green. Although he stopped just beyond Milford Station, he did have permission to march all the way to the river and Hanover Junction beyond (1), where he would have run into John Breckinridge's division. Breckinridge, for his part, could have answered a summons by Confederate cavalryman Wade Hampton and marched up to help confront Hancock at Milford Station (2). Meanwhile, the Federal V Corps under Gouverneur K. Warren was initially supposed to march south on the Telegraph Road but was redirected to follow Hancock (3). Ambrose Burnside's Federal IX Corps was instead directed down the Telegraph Road, where he ran into Confederate opposition that he chose not to contest (4). Either advance by Warren or Burnside to Mud Tavern would have caused trouble for Confederates. Warren also had a chance later to advance on Confederates from the east (5) but chose to take a defensive posture instead.

Warren to follow Hancock in support. Major General Ambrose Burnside's IX Corps and Maj. Gen. Horatio Wright's VI Corps remained in place to cover the Army of the Potomac's withdrawal from Spotsylvania, but were to later disengage and move south with the first two corps, striking out along the Telegraph Road.

What if Grant had stuck with his original plan? Warren would have advanced down the Telegraph Road where, just a few miles south at Mud Tavern, he would have found the exact kind of scenario Grant had originally hoped for: a portion of Lee's army, drawn out by Hancock's movement, isolated and vulnerable to attack.

Would Warren have attacked? The personal presence of Grant, traveling with the V Corps that morning, almost certainly would have inspired a vigorous response. However, if left to his own devices, Warren's own reflexive nature was to hunker down on the defense—as demonstrated, for instance, by past actions at Gaines's Mill, Second Manassas, and Bristoe Station. More recently, on the first morning of the fight in the Wilderness, Grant ordered Warren to immediately pitch into any part of the Confederate army if an opportunity presented itself; instead, the cautious Warren took time to create a fallback position for his men before sending them into battle.[13] His piecemeal attacks at Spotsylvania on May 8 and uncoordinated attacks on May 10 only underscored his lack of talent on offense, and by the morning of May 12, Grant grew so frustrated with Warren's delay in

---

13   Grant to Meade, 5 May 1864, O.R. XXXVI, Pt. 2, 403.

attacking and the feeble character of his assaults," he even authorized Meade to relieve Warren if necessary.[14] In the week since, Grant's opinion had not changed, nor had Warren done anything that might inspire such a change. On May 21, it's hard to see the cautious V Corps commander pitching into a foe along the Telegraph Road he would not have been expecting to find.

Ewell's position at the Mud Tavern intersection that morning was the most exposed spot occupied by anyone in either army. He had the Federal II Corps to his rear and the now-in-motion V Corps in position to bear down on him from the north. Had Warren pushed the V Corps toward Ewell's position, the Federal IX and VI corps could have arrived on the scene as reinforcements faster than the Confederate First and Third corps. Hancock's II Corps would have been too far to lend immediate aid and, after their morning march and an afternoon counter-march, would have been too exhausted on their eventual arrival to do more than serve as reserves, but they would have arrived as any battle would have been reaching its crescendo and so still would have added much-needed weight at a crucial moment.

But rather than move south along the Telegraph Road, the Federal V Corps followed Hancock's earlier route east-southeast toward Guiney Station. Grant later admitted this might not have been his best move because, by that afternoon, his forces were strung out over a twenty-five-mile arc, from Spotsylvania Court House to Milford Station. What if the ANV had jumped on the opportunity Grant presented?

"Lee now had a superb opportunity to take the initiative," the Federal commander wrote in his memoirs, "either by attacking Wright and Burnside alone, or by following by the Telegraph Road and striking Hancock's and Warren's corps, or even Hancock's alone, before reinforcements could come up. But he did not avail himself of either opportunity."[15] In Grant's retrospective mind, this moment represented Lee's last best hope of the war. "He never again had such an opportunity of dealing a heavy blow," Grant wrote.[16]

Lee did not recognize the opportunity Grant unwittingly presented, though.

14 Porter, 108.

15 Grant, 562.

16 Ibid., 563.

Even as Confederate cavalry kept him abreast of Hancock's movement, Lee had to keep probing Union lines at Spotsylvania to see what portions, if any, of Grant's army remained there. As he explained to Confederate President Jefferson Davis the next day, "[T]he reports of movement were so vague & conflicting that it required some time to sift the truth."[17]

What if Lee had a more dependable intelligence-gathering apparatus at this critical juncture? The bulk of his cavalry, under Maj. Gen. Jeb Stuart, had been lured away by their Federal counterparts on May 9, and Stuart had been mortally wounded at the subsequent battle of Yellow Tavern on May 11. "He never brought me a piece of false information," Lee said when he heard the news.[18] But what if Stuart had not been killed in action? What if he and his invaluable eyes and ears had not been lured away?

It would not be until after 7:00 p.m. on May 21 that Lee would feel confident enough about Grant's withdrawal to release his First Corps, under Lt. Gen. Richard Anderson, to follow Ewell's route to Mud Tavern. He simultaneously ordered Hill's men to withdraw and follow a route southward that ran parallel to, and within supporting distance of, Anderson and Ewell.

Even as Lee struggled to see a clearer picture of the situation, he knew Spotsylvania no longer remained tenable for him. As artillerist E. P. Alexander noted, "Hancock's movement had the merit of being a turning operation if it did not act as a trap."[19] To counter Federal movements as he imperfectly understood them, Lee directed Ewell by early afternoon to move south on the Telegraph Road, still with the hope of intercepting Hancock before the Federal II Corps made it across the North Anna.

Before departing, Ewell advanced pickets a mile northward from Mud Tavern to block the Telegraph Road where it crossed the Po River, one of several narrow but steep-banked waterways that flow west-to-east through the region (just as the North Anna did). Ewell also sent pickets eastward to watch the road from Guiney Station, then he sent his Second Corps south.

By late afternoon, Ambrose Burnside's IX Corps, making its exit from Spotsylvania, finally appeared on the Telegraph Road, taking the southward

---

17 Robert E. Lee, 22 May 1864 dispatch to Davis, *The Wartime Papers of Robert E. Lee.* Clifford Dowdey and Louis Manarin, editors (New York: De Capo, 1961), 746.

18 Robert E. Lee, Jr., *Recollections and Letters of Robert E. Lee* (New York: Doubleday, Page, & Co., 1904), 125.

19 Alexander, 387.

"Unsure of the enemy's strength, [Burnside] did not attempt to force a crossing . . ." says a state historical marker along the Po River. What if Burnside had acted more aggressively? *Chris Mackowski*

march originally intended for Warren. "[W]e were to move down the road to . . . the Po River," Burnside wrote, "and effect a crossing there, if it could be done without too great opposition." From there, Burnside was to continue southward.[20] On the Po's south bank, though, waited elements of Brig. Gen. John R. Chambliss's cavalry, advanced there by Ewell as sentinels, as well as a detail of Confederate engineers sent to fortify the position. By the time Burnside's vanguard arrived on the Po's north bank late in the afternoon, the engineers had built impressive earthworks along the high south bank.

The commander of Burnside's lead brigade, Col. John J. Curtin, could see the earthworks but couldn't tell just how many Confederates waited in them. Then a Confederate battery arrived and "opened a lively shell fire," and Curtin's skirmishers "were very briskly engaged along the riverbank,"

---

20 Burnside report, O.R. XXXVI, pt. 1, 911.

Curtin's division commander, Brig. Gen. Robert B. Potter, later reported.[21] Potter ordered additional reconnaissance that bore no fruit. As the rest of the IX Corps bottlenecked behind him, the division commander sought instructions from Burnside.

What if Burnside forced a crossing of the Po? Despite the noise Confederates made, scant forces occupied the south bank—enough to alert Lee and Ewell of any Federal crossing but not enough to actually stop one. By this point, Lee had ordered the rest of his troops to evacuate Spotsylvania, with Anderson's corps on the road to Mud Tavern but not yet near there. Anderson might have been able to hurry reinforcements forward but, more likely, Burnside would have captured the key intersection and either caught Anderson strung out on the march or forced Anderson to backtrack on himself, risking an entanglement with Hill's corps, which was also trying to evacuate Spotsylvania. Ewell, farther south, would have been cut off from the rest of Lee's army. Had Ewell's corps backtracked north to engage Burnside, it would have had to move across the front of Warren's Federal V Corps, exposing itself to danger. Had Ewell's isolated corps stayed in place, it would have had to contend with Hancock's II Corps, with Warren's V Corps in position to fall on Ewell from the rear.

As it was, Burnside did not like what he saw in the gloaming. Confederate resistance at the river seemed too strong. "[I]t was not deemed advisable to attempt carrying the ford by assault," he decided, "as it would have resulted in a very great loss even if it should be successful. . . ."[22] Instead, using the discretion his orders gave him, Burnside turned his column around and headed north on the Telegraph Road toward the Guiney Station Road to follow in Warren's footsteps. This, in turn, delayed Wright's movement south because he had to wait while Burnside filed by.

As the corps of both armies shifted across the map on May 21, Hancock—whose corps had triggered all the movement to begin with—froze in place. The far-flung II Corps, preceded by a new cavalry detachment under Brig. Gen. Alfred Torbert, had rolled through Bowling Green beginning at 7:00 a.m. and moved on to Milford Station four miles to the south. Grant expected

---

21 Potter report, O.R. XXXVI, pt. 1, 929.

22 Burnside report, O.R. XXXVI, pt. 1, 911.

Hancock to push as far as he could "toward Richmond on the line of the Fredericksburg railroad," going as far as he could and "fighting the enemy in whatever force he may find him."[23]

The pesky Confederate cavalry that had harassed him all morning notwithstanding, Hancock finally found an enemy force to fight at Milford Station. When Torbert's cavalry rode into the hamlet at the vanguard of the column, they were met by an unexpected Confederate volley. Torbert's men tried to charge, but the Confederates rebuffed them, leading to some back and forth that finally went Torbert's way because of his superior numbers and firepower. He brought some 2,000 men to the fight compared to only about 500 Confederates, successfully driving his opponents across the nearby Mattaponi River. Federals captured the village, the train station, and a bridge across the Mattaponi that Confederates tried unsuccessfully to torch.

Prisoners revealed that the Confederates came from Kemper's brigade, the first elements of Maj. Gen. George Pickett's division—one of several groups of reinforcements being shuttled to Lee. The division had played a role in rebuffing Federals at Bermuda Hundred outside Richmond on May 16, then had been reassigned to resume their former place with the Army of Northern Virginia. The 500 men Torbert had tangled with represented only the lead elements of that full division; a second brigade, under Brig. Gen. Montgomery Corse, was set to join Kemper's and, together, the two were to march to Spotsylvania, unaware that Lee was even then contemplating his evacuation of that place.

Hancock learned of Torbert's tussle by 10:30 a.m., and by noon, the II Corps commander marched into Milford Station at the head of his infantry. Using the bridge Torbert captured, Hancock deployed three of his divisions on the west side of the Mattaponi, keeping his fourth on the east bank as a reserve. Spotting a ridge a mile beyond the river crossing, Hancock ordered his men to deploy there and dig in. Hancock the Superb became Hancock the Stationary.

Capturing prisoners from an army *not* Lee's raised all sorts of questions for Hancock, chief among them, how many Confederates were still to come and from what direction(s)? Brushing away part of an undersized brigade was one thing, but the II Corps commander could easily envision getting enmired

---

23   Grant to Meade, O.R. XXXVI, pt. 2, 865.

in a fight that could prove more than he bargained for. With an unreliable communications chain back to army headquarters—and thus, no sure way of calling on reinforcements if things got out of hand—Hancock felt exposed. "Considering . . . that he was alone, on the extreme left flank of the army, across an important stream, and not knowing but that some accidental or treacherous discovery . . . might bring down upon him the whole weight of Lee's army, General Hancock set his troops to intrenching," wrote Francis Walker, a staff officer who would later become the II Corps's historian.[24] Hancock's men spent the next day and a half "throwing up heavy breastworks in anticipation of severe fighting in this area," wrote Thomas Francis Galwey of the 8th Ohio. "Miles of breastworks were constructed during the course of the day, seeming to cross one another in almost every direction."[25]

What if Hancock had pushed onward? The II Corps had already trekked some twenty-five miles that day, "a long, weary, dusty march," as one Massachusetts officer described it.[26] The North Anna River crossing at Chesterfield Bridge remained another thirteen miles distant, Hanover Junction another three miles beyond that. Waiting at the junction was the small "army" of Maj. Gen. John C. Breckinridge, fresh from its May 15 victory at New Market. While Hancock's men would have outnumbered Breckinridge's, they would have been exhausted and Breckinridge would have likely contested any river crossing using the same topographical advantages Lee himself so envied. With Ewell's corps descending the Telegraph Road, Hancock might have found himself pinned against the North Anna, deep in the very kind of trouble he feared.

Before Hancock could even get that far, though, he would have first had to contend with the rest of Kemper's brigade, which had finally come north along with Corse's brigade. Both bodies of troops arrived midafternoon at Penola Station, the rail stop immediately south of Milford. Learning of Hancock's presence, Corse positioned himself to block a Federal advance toward Hanover Junction. The evening arrival of Confederate cavalryman Wade Hampton provided additional strength and coordination, and the

24 Walker, 492.

25 Thomas Francis Galwey, *The Valiant Hours,* W. S. Nye, ed. (Harrisburg, Pennsylvania: Stackpole Company) , 221.

26 Report of Capt. James Fleming of the 28th Massachusetts, OR XXXVI, Vol. 1, 389.

two halves of Kemper's brigade reunited. "We would have played thunder with a brigade and a half fighting the whole Yankee army," wrote one of Corse's soldiers.[27]

Hampton saw opportunity. "This party [Hancock] . . . could be cut off unless they are much larger than I suppose," he wrote to Breckinridge late on May 21. "I am sure that I could burn the bridge behind them, and an attack in front would destroy them. . . ." What if Breckenridge sent him additional infantry? "Could you send any more troops up to effect this?" Hampton asked. "I know this country thoroughly, and I think that a good blow might be struck."[28] Breckinridge, helping to keep marauding Federal cavalry out of Hanover Court House and away from vital Confederate supplies at Hanover Junction, had no men to spare. Instead, Confederate forces had to content themselves with blocking the roads from Milford Station westward, which ultimately proved a huge service because it protected Ewell's southward march along the Telegraph Road.

Ewell got within nine miles of the North Anna before finally resting for the night. It was 10:00 p.m. They would finish their march the next morning, crossing the river at 8:00 a.m. Anderson, whose last units left Spotsylvania just after 8:00 p.m., marched hard to close the gap. The First Corps's overnight route took it through the Mud Tavern intersection and straight down the Telegraph Road—and straight across the front of the Federal V Corps, encamped for the night along a network of roads just to the east. "Warren's cavalry outpost . . . had heard the noise of troops passing along the Telegraph road all night," the Army of the Potomac's Chief of Staff, Andrew Humphreys, later reported, "and some part of the trains that accompany troops were in view. . . ."[29]

Warren initially expected the Federal IX Corps—uninformed about Burnside's change in plan—so news of the Confederate presence spooked him. "My force is quite insufficient to hold the position against a determined attack . . . " worried Col. J. Howard Kitching, commanding one of the units

---

27 Quoted in Rhea 239.

28 Hampton to Breckinridge, 21 May 1864, O.R. XXXVI, pt. 3, 816.

29 Andrew Humphreys, *The Virginia Campaign, 1864 and 1865* (New York: De Capo Press, 1995), 125.

closest to the Confederate column.[30] In the event of such an attack, any support Warren might get would "have to be brought round"—meaning the same roundabout route he had just taken—rather than straight down the Telegraph Road.[31]

Sometime after 11:15 p.m., Warren received permission to pull his units "as far back as necessary" to create a more consolidated, and thus defensible, position.[32] Even then, Warren seemed frozen. "The command will be prepared to move to-

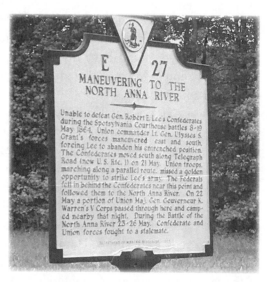

You know it's bad when a state highway marker rubs it in: "Union troops, marching along a parallel route, missed a golden opportunity to strike Lee's army." This sign appears along U.S. 1 in Thornburg, Virginia. *Chris Mackowski*

morrow by 4 a.m.," he replied, "the object being to take up at that time a defensive position in this vicinity to receive an attack of the enemy should he advance in this direction." Warren made sure to lay the blame on Burnside for not "getting into the position assigned him."[33]

What if Warren had thought aggressively instead of defensively? While that would have required an offensive turn of mind likely beyond him, Warren did have two avenues of advance—the road to Mud Tavern and, just a few miles south of it, the road from Nancy Wright's Corners— he could have used to thrust himself into the unsuspecting flank of the Confederate column. Lee had used a similar tactic in the Wilderness, spearing into Warren's marching column along two parallel roads. Here

30 Kitching to Warren, O.R. XXXVI, pt. 3, 6.

31 Humphreys to Warren, O.R. XXXVI, pt. 3, 58.

32 Humphreys to Warren, O.R. XXXVI, pt. 3, 59.

33 V Corps Orders, O.R. XXXVI, pt. 3, 59.

in Caroline County, Federals on the offense would have had more open ground for maneuver and better roads for movement and support. Picking the fight, though, might have invited exactly the kind of "heavy blow" Grant had begun to fret over that afternoon, with his forces flung so widely across the countryside.

So it was that Lee and his army marched, fully exposed, right past the Union army—a rookie mistake attributable only to Lee's utter exhaustion and the onset of the dysentery that would plague him for the next few days.

By midmorning on May 22, Wright had closed with Warren, and the two began a combined move south. Warren directed half of his column to the Telegraph Road, with the other half marching a parallel route a mile to the east. Federals scooped up stragglers from the Confederate First Corps and, according to Humphreys, "The rear of Longstreet's corps [Anderson] was reported to be but three miles distant"—all a reminder of the larger opportunity the Federals had missed.[34] Humphreys saw the days of march and maneuver as wasted. "The chief object of Hancock's circuitous movement was not accomplished," he admitted. "There would probably have been more chance of success had Hancock moved by the Telegraph Road on the night of the 20th, followed by Warren. . . . [T]hat would perhaps have brought on a collision before Lee could intrench on new ground."[35]

Remarkably, though, Lee did not direct his army to entrench when it first crossed the river, although by this point in the campaign, such entrenching had become second nature to them. A. P. Hill had learned a hard lesson on the morning of May 6 when he had refused the night before to allow his men to entrench after the first day's fighting in the Wilderness. Federals opened the second day of battle by wiping Hill's unprotected corps *en masse* from the battlefield. Thereafter, Confederates entrenched any chance they got. However, on May 22, Lee had come to believe Grant was swinging east with an intent to cross the Pamunkey River, the name of the waterway downriver from the point where the North and South Anna merged. The race to the North Anna had exhausted his infantry, and the army commander opted to let them rest rather than dig in, expecting they'd have to pivot

34 Humphreys, 126.

35 Humphreys, 127.

downriver soon enough in another attempt to block Grant. Either overconfident or dulled by his exhaustion and illness, Lee made an entirely slipshod call.

It's worth here recalling a comment made by one of Lee's favorite division commanders, Maj. Gen. John Brown Gordon. In his hyperbolic memoir, Brown described a so-called superpower often ascribed to Lee: "He read the mind of the Union commander, and developed his own plans accordingly. There was no mental telepathy in this. Lee's native and tutored genius enabled him to place himself in Grant's position to reason out his antagonist's mental

When fighting opened along the North Anna River, Robert E. Lee was standing on the front porch of the Fox House when a cannonball came screaming in and hit the doorframe next to him. What if Lee had been standing a little closer to the door? *Chris Mackowski*

processes."[36] However, time and time again in the Overland Campaign, Lee demonstrably failed to read Grant's mind, and May 22 proved no different.

Grant showed up on the far riverbank on the afternoon of May 23. "The enemy had followed us up much more closely than we seemed to expect," Confederate artillerist E. Porter Alexander wrote, "& he announced himself as if he was in a hurry & meant business."[37] However, Lee held on to his belief so strongly that, when he took the time to inspect the Federal appearance, he announced, "This is nothing but a feint. The enemy is preparing to cross below." A. P. Hill, encamped several miles upstream after

36 John Brown Gordon, 297.

37 Alexander, 388.

crossing at Jericho Mill, sent a courier to Lee informing him of a Federal presence there.[38] "Go back and tell General A. P. Hill to leave his men in camp," Lee reassured him.

Poor cavalry work by Lee's son, Rooney, initially led Hill to believe he faced only two brigades of Federal cavalry, when in reality, the entire V Corps was crossing the river, with the VI Corps waiting in line right behind it. Despite Lee's order, Hill decided to investigate. As Grant incorrectly recounted in his memoirs, "The whole of Hill's corps was sent against Warren's right before it had got in position."[39] In fact, Hill sent only the division of Maj. Gen. Cadmus Wilcox, who attacked the Federals even as they were still deploying. Wilcox achieved early success, but the weight of Federal numbers eventually worked against him. A second of Hill's divisions, Maj. Gen. Henry Heth's, arrived too late to effect a reversal. "General Hill, why did you let those people cross here?" Lee later scolded Hill. "Why didn't you throw your whole force on them and drive them back as Jackson would have done?"[40]

As one of Jackson's successors, Hill was a proven disappointment, and to have Lee invoke Jackson in such a way must have been particularly galling to Hill—he and Jackson had detested each other. While there was no chance of the martyred Stonewall returning to take his place on the line, Lee did have Maj. Gen. Jubal Early in his back pocket. In fact, from May 8-21, Hill had been on medical leave prompted by a recurring illness, so for the entirety of the fight at Spotsylvania, Early had successfully commanded the Confederate Third Corps. Hill had returned to duty just in time to stumble through the debacle at Jericho Mill. What if Early had remained in charge?

Early had a solid record of independent thinking, with particularly important results at Fredericksburg, Second Fredericksburg, and Mine Run. For this reason, Lee continued to give Early opportunities for increased responsibility. Lee nearly tapped him to take over as First Corps commander when James Longstreet was wounded in the Wilderness and then gave him

---

38 "Mill" or "Mills"—that is the question. The name appears both ways, but the American Battlefield Trust, which purchased the land in 2014, and Richmond National Battlefield, which now owns and operates the land, both use the singular "Mill." For consistency, I'm following their lead.

39 Grant, 564.

40 "The Maneuvers on the North Anna River," *Confederate Military History*, vol. III, edited by Clement A. Evans (Atlanta: Confederate Publishing Company, 1899), 460.

temporary helm of the Third Corps at Spotsylvania; it would also eventually earn Early command of the Second Corps and independent assignment to the Shenandoah Valley in the summer and fall of 1864. Had Early still commanded the Third Corps on May 23 and received word of a Federal presence massing along the river, it's reasonable to believe he would have taken some sort of initiative.

It's likely, too, that Early would not have trusted the job to Wilcox alone. At Salem Church on May 3-4, 1863, Early and Wilcox had failed to coordinate attacks against an isolated Federal force.[41] With that memory in mind, Early would at the very least have gone with Wilcox's division to Jericho Mill to offer a steadying hand, and he likely would have sent a second division—probably his own—as back-up.

Lee's invocation of Jackson notwithstanding, the "what if" he implied— "What if Hill had thrown all his troops against the Federals?"—was just one of several questions that arise from action at Jericho Mill. What if Lee had properly read the situation when he first saw skirmishing on the far side of the river? What if Rooney had provided better intelligence? What if Hill had sent more than Wilcox's division? What if Hill himself had come to the field to oversee action?

As Hill's sympathetic biographer James Robertson pointed out, "After Lee's statement that the Federal movement at Jericho Mill was a feint, Hill cannot be faulted for sending only one division on his own initiative to investigate. . . . How much difference Hill would have made had he been on the field and personally directing the action is conjectural."[42] For that matter, it's even conjectural to assume that if Hill was on the field he would have been personally directing the action, as students of Hill's July 2, 1863, (in) action at Gettysburg can attest.

Had Hill directed the battle in person, and had he thrown more than Wilcox into the fight, it's likely he could have forced the V Corps back into the river. Wilcox performed credibly, but he lacked the weight for a definitive push, and so the V Corps held on long enough for the tide of

---

41   For the full scoop, see *Chancellorsville's Forgotten Front: The Battles of Second Fredericksburg and Salem Church* by Chris Mackowski and Kristopher D. White (Savas Beatie, 2013).

42   James I. Robertson, *General A. P. Hill: The Story of a Confederate Warrior*, First Vintage Edition, (New York: Random House, 1992), 276.

battle to turn. The added weight of Confederate reinforcements would have made an immediate difference had they come up behind Wilcox and driven into the Federal line, which was just barely holding on (topographically, because the battle was fought in a bend of the North Anna , there would have been no room for reinforcements to deploy on Wilcox's left or right). Warren, in contrast, would not have been able to funnel reinforcements from the VI Corps across the river in numbers enough to counter a heavier push from Hill.

As it was, with the V Corps lodgment secure on the south bank, Lee's left flank was suddenly, seriously threatened. Compounding the problem, Hancock secured a crossing several miles downriver at the Chesterfield Bridge, with direct access from there to Hanover Junction. At first, these developments seemed disastrous for the Army of Northern Virginia, but they inspired one of Lee's best improvisations of the war. Under the advice of his chief engineer, Maj. Gen. Martin Luther Smith, Lee repositioned his lines so that they formed a "V," with the apex anchored on the commanding bluff above Ox Ford. Hill's corps fell into a line that made up the western leg of the "V," while Anderson's corps made up the eastern Leg; Ewell's corps made a juncture with Anderson's and extended dog-leg style to the east, where it made a right turn south to protect Hanover Junction. Grant's aide, Horace Porter, described Lee's formation as "exceedingly strong." "It had one face turned toward Hancock, and the other toward Warren," Porter explained. "The lines were made exceedingly formidable by means of strong earthworks with heavy obstacles planted in front, and were flanked on the right by an impenetrable swamp, and on the left by Little River."[43]

The most insidious aspect of the formation manifest itself as both Warren and Hancock advanced. The "V" forced the two Federal wings father apart; to reinforce each other, they would have had to backtrack six miles and cross the North Anna twice to do so. Lee, meanwhile, had the Virginia Central Railroad as an interior line to shuffle his reinforcements— Pickett and Breckenridge—from one part of the line to another as necessary.

Grant, emboldened by his successes on May 23, ordered everyone forward the next morning, blundering into vulnerability exactly as Lee expected. Only Burnside at Ox Ford could not cross. "The prospects of success are not all that flattering," the IX Corps commander warned, "but I think the attempt can be made without any very disastrous results, and

---

43 Porter, 145.

we may possibly succeed."[44] Or not. And they didn't. Hancock, meanwhile, found himself under enfilading artillery fire along his right flank from Anderson's leg of the "V." Soon thereafter, he finally ran into Ewell's infantry, although he first mistook them for just skirmishers. Warren, on the far side of the battlefield, advanced for miles unmolested, getting farther and farther out of position to help Hancock or be helped himself. "We were, for the time, practically two armies besieging," Grant later realized.[45]

Here's when Lee's unruly bowels took command of the Army of Northern Virginia. He became so sick he could not leave his tent, and he grew delirious for part of the day. Unable to take the field, he could not strike the blow he so desperately yearned to. Nor did he trust any of his subordinates to strike it on his behalf. Hill had disappointed Lee the previous day at Jericho Mill, and as his underwhelming performances at Gettysburg and Bristoe Station demonstrated, he needed closer supervision than Lee could, at that moment, provide. Anderson, only two weeks in his post, anchored the whole position and so couldn't really move. Ewell, second in command of the army, was also coming down with dysentery, but more damning, he had lost Lee's confidence after poor performances on May 10, 12, and 19 at Spotsylvania. "Had Ewell possessed more boldness and independence, he might have initiated an attack on his own responsibility," Ewell biographer Donald C. Pfanz suggests—but, alas, the bolder Ewell who had once served under Stonewall Jackson no longer existed.[46]

Whether covering up Lee's indelicate state or Lee's lack of confidence in his corps commanders, Walter Taylor, Lee's faithful adjutant, later tried to explain away his commander's inaction by prescribing it to the disparity of numbers between the armies. "If [Lee's] army had been of even reasonable proportions in comparison with that of his adversary, his movement would have been of another character, and one of the two wings of the Federal army would have been assailed while on the south side of the river."[47] However, Grant only outnumbered Lee at this point by about 15,000 men, something

---

44   Burnside to Grant, *OR* XXXVI, pt. 3, 166.

45   Grant, 567.

46   Donald C. Pfanz, *Richard S. Ewell: A Soldier's Life* (Chapel Hill: University of North Carolina Press, 1998) 396.

47   Walter Taylor, *Four Years with General Lee*, James I. Robertson, ed. (Bloomington, IN: Indiana University Press, 1966), 133.

Taylor knew at the time he wrote his defense, making his rationale sound especially lame.

It took almost all afternoon for the full danger of the situation to come into focus for Grant. First, he stripped divisions from Burnside to try and bolster his two wings. Eventually keen to the full extent of his vulnerability, he ordered everyone to hunker down. "Lee's position from the strength and location of his intrenchments and the defensive character of the country, was impregnable, or at least it could not be carried by assault without involving great loss of life," Porter admitted.[48] The II Corps' Walker carried that scenario one step further: "Lee, after administering a bloody repulse, [could] assume the aggressive and throw nearly his whole force on one or the other wing of the Union army. Indeed, the Confederate commander has been severely criticized for not taking advantage of the position in which Grant's forces had been placed, to deal a crushing blow."[49]

Federals, unaware of Lee's illness, expected an attack all day. "Contrary to all expectation, the Confederates didn't disturb us although we were within easy range of their guns," wrote John Haley of the 17th Maine, pinned down among Hancock's men near the Fox House. "Perhaps they had no ammunition left to spare."[50] Haley spoke for many who expected Lee's other shoe to drop at any minute. "[I]t was expected the Rebs might strike after dark," he wrote the next day. "We weren't at all sorry that they chose not to. . . . They could have massed a heavy force in front under cover of a dense growth and rushed us before we could duck them."[51]

By then, though, Lee's opportunity had slipped away. Sheridan returned to the army with his cavalry, bolstering Federal forces by some 12,000 men. Warren and Wright consolidated their position, presenting a strong defense of their own. Hancock had dug in securely. Even then, mused Humphreys, Lee might have raised trouble. "Some persons, indeed, have thought that Lee should have left a small part of his force to hold the intrechments of

---

48   Porter, 149.

49   Walker, 496.

50   John W. Haley, *The Rebel Yell & the Yankee Hurrah: The Civil War Journal of a Maine Volunteer*, Ruth L. Silliker, ed. (Camden, ME: Down East Books, 1985), 162.

51   Haley, 163.

his left and attacked Hancock with the rest of his army," he wrote.[52] Porter, in his wonderings about the moment, said, "There was the possibility, also, that Lee might mass his artillery on his left flank, and try to hold it by this means and with a minimum of his infantry, and with the bulk of his army move out on his right in an attempt to crush Hancock's corps. This is exactly what Grant himself would have done under similar circumstances. . . ."[53]

But everybody knew that Lee knew better. "Hancock was intrenched, and Lee knew well the advantage that gave," Humphreys concluded, "and he could not afford the loss that he would have inevitably suffered in such an attack." Hancock, along with Potter's IX Corps division, consisted of perhaps 24,000 men, Humphreys estimated, while Lee might have brought to bear as many as 36,000 men. "[B]ut intrenchments make up for greater differences than that in numbers," Humphreys added, echoing the very philosophy that underlay Lee's own defensive position.[54]

On the 25th, Grant received word that Lee was falling back on Richmond. "This proved not to be true," he deadpanned. Lee remained in full view before him. "But we could do nothing where we were unless Lee would assume the offensive," Grant said.[55] When Lee didn't, Grant opted to once more move toward Richmond around Lee's flank. "[A] withdrawal in the face of a vigilant foe, and the crossing of a difficult river within sight of the enemy, constitute one of the most hazardous movements in warfare," Porter wrote.[56] Sheridan's cavalry provided a screen, faking a movement to Lee's left, allowing Grant to withdraw and slide downriver toward the Pamunkey, exactly as Lee first predicted.

Lee's inaction at the North Anna did not seem to puzzle Grant, although it should have. The Army of Northern Virginia had come at the Army of the Potomac aggressively in the Wilderness and showed no lack of fighting spirit at Spotsylvania, where Lee repeatedly looked for a chance to go on the offense. The first three weeks of the campaign alone should have established

---

52 Humphreys, 132.

53 Porter, 149.

54 Humphreys, 132.

55 Grant, 568.

56 Porter, 149.

a track record to make Grant wary. Instead, he came to exactly the wrong conclusion. "Lee's army is really whipped," he wrote to Washington. "The prisoners we now take show it, and the action of his army shows it unmistakenly [sic]. Our men feel that they have gained the morale over the enemy, and attack him with confidence. I may be mistaken, but I feel that our success over Lee's army is already assured."[57]

What if Grant knew of Lee's illness—that Lee had been all too willing to strike a blow, but the flesh had been too weak? Would Grant have come to the same conclusion about the Confederate army's inaction? About its morale? About his own chances of success? Would he have marched so boldly south, attacking with such confidence when he finally came to Cold Harbor? For it was there, in the fateful, fruitless charges Grant ordered on June 3, that the true legacy of North Anna realized itself, much to Grant's ever-after regret.

To ask "What if Lee had not gotten sick" is to invite a complete reimagining of the entire third epoch of the Overland Campaign. It would be tempting to limit the question to the possibilities inherent in the inverted "V" formation, but to hypothetically erase Lee's illness means giving him physical health and mental clarity that, at the very least, would have impacted his decision-making on May 22 when he first crossed the North Anna if not back to May 21 when he tried to decide what to do about Hancock. If Lee had not gotten sick, the inverted "V" might never have existed in the first place.

Lee might have indeed been lickin' the Federals "from the Rapidan cl'ah down h'yah" to the North Anna, as Grant's visitor said on the evening of May 25, but after the lost opportunity at the North Anna, Lee never again had the Federals "jes wh'ah" he wanted them. The campaign had robbed him of the initiative, forced him into an uncomfortable and unaccustomed defensive posture, unable to strike a blow.

57 Grant, 569.

CHAPTER NINE

"Rally the Loyal Men of Missouri"

What If Sterling Price's 1864 Missouri Expedition Had Been Successful?

Kristen M. Trout

In early December 1864, Confederate victory had once again slipped from the grasp of Maj. Gen. Sterling Price. Having just approached the Arkansas-Texas border near Laynesport, Price's bold expedition into his home state of Missouri had finally come to its miserable end. Price's Army of Missouri—once 12,000 men strong at the start of the campaign and now just over 3,000—had crossed 1,400 miles in just over three months, making the 1864 Missouri Expedition one of the longest cavalry campaigns of the Civil War. "Old Pap" Price's—and the Confederacy's—last-ditch attempt to liberate Missouri from years of Federal occupation and control was over.

The Army of Missouri was merely a skeleton of its original self at that point, and there was no doubt Price reflected on his audacious and failed campaign. What were the Confederacy's strategic and political goals for the expedition? What events or decisions led the army into the jaws of defeat? Was this expedition's success even possible? And, finally, what if Price had succeeded? To answer these questions, particularly *what if it were successful,* it is necessary to analyze *what* the Confederate military and political goals were for the campaign and *why* they were not successfully achieved.

Taking place west of the Mississippi River, Price's 1864 Missouri Expedition has long been overlooked and misunderstood in the annals of Civil War history. In fact, if Price had been successful, the campaign would

What if Sterling Price had never been routed from Missouri in the first place? *Library of Congress*

have delivered Missouri to the Confederacy and struck a crushing blow to Lincoln as he sought re-election. Price hoped to foment a general uprising of Missouri's pro-Confederate civilians; seize the vital city of St. Louis, including its well-stocked federal arsenal; capture the state capital of Jefferson City; and gather as many recruits and supplies as possible. In order to understand why these goals— and the campaign—ultimately failed in the fall of 1864, it is imperative to understand what happened and how it came to a crushing halt.

More than four decades before Price moved into Missouri in 1864, Missouri joined the Union as a slave state. Her major natural waterways, vitamin-rich soil, budding railroad system, and growing urban and agricultural economies incentivized migrants. Over the course of the following decades, Missouri became home to nearly 1.2 million people (including 114,000 enslaved persons) by 1860. Instead of being socially, politically, and culturally "Southern" by the outbreak of the Civil War, Missouri was more of a borderland comprised of Southern-born whites, German and Irish immigrants, and the enslaved. As historian Adam Arenson has argued, St. Louis—and ultimately, Missouri—was "the beacon of moderation in border-state politics."[1]

By the start of the Civil War, Missourians were largely reluctant to support secession, even though the majority supported the protection of slavery. Missourians also wanted to preserve the Union, which the

---

1   Adam Arenson, *The Great Heart of the Republic: St. Louis and the Cultural Civil War* (Columbia: University of Missouri Press, 2011), 6.

Missouri State Convention demonstrated when it voted overwhelmingly to remain with the Union in March 1861. Even Sterling Price, who would later command the Army of Missouri during its expedition in 1864, was a conditional Unionist until the controversial Camp Jackson Affair. On May 10, U.S. Army Captain Nathaniel Lyon forced a bloodless surrender of Missouri Volunteer Militiamen near St. Louis, in order to protect the vital federal arsenal in the city, which he believed was under immediate threat by the southern-sympathizing militia. Shortly thereafter, Lyon paraded these prisoners through the streets of St. Louis toward the arsenal for confinement. However, when confused and angry crowds began to surround Lyon's column, a shot was fired and Lyon's own men opened fire on the crowd, killing nearly thirty civilians and injuring dozens more. The Camp Jackson Affair then became the pivotal event that tore the state apart and pitted Missourians against one another. The state sat at the cultural and physical border of East, West, North, and South economically, politically, and socially. As a borderland, Missouri would become a hotbed of violence and bloodshed before and during the Civil War.

In the first year of the war, Missouri witnessed significant bloodshed. The state rapidly mobilized between the pro-secessionist Missouri State Guard and pro-Union Federal and state volunteers after the Camp Jackson Affair. Though there were attempts to maintain neutrality and discourage the escalation of violence, the situation in Missouri quickly deteriorated. Throughout the summer, Brig. Gen. Nathaniel Lyon's Union Army of the West maneuvered through central and southern Missouri, securing the Missouri River, the strategic lifeline of the Pacific Railroad, and the state capital at Jefferson City. Maj. Gen. Sterling Price's Missouri State Guard successfully combined with Brig. Gen. Ben McCulloch's Confederate volunteers and Arkansas State Troops. About a dozen miles outside Springfield, Missouri, at Wilson's Creek on August 10, 1861, these two armies clashed, resulting in Lyon's death and a Confederate victory. Another Southern victory emerged at Lexington, Missouri, the following month, where Price's troops defeated the Federal garrison there. However, with a growing Federal military force at St. Louis, the Missouri State Guard could not follow up on their victories. Though Missouri's exiled legislature voted to secede in late 1861, the departure of the pro-Confederate force and the fleeing of the "rump" legislature from Missouri to Texas set the stage for the next two years.

This political cartoon, according to the Library of Congress, shows "an exultant view of the rout by Union forces commanded by Capt. Nathaniel Lyon of troops under Gen. Sterling Price and Claiborne F. Jackson at Boonville, Missouri, in June 1861. Jackson, the secessionist governor of Missouri, had been driven from the state capital, Jefferson City. He and other members of his government retreated along with Confederate commander Price and his troops. Overtaken by Lyon at Boonville on June 17, they were then forced to flee in separate directions. The artist makes a play on a commonplace of the time: the public notice of strayed animals. Jackson is the subject of this notice. He is portrayed here as an ass, strayed 'from the neighbourhood of Boonville, Mo. on the 18th inst[ant] a mischievous JACK who was frightened and run away from his Leader by the sudden appearance of a Lion.' The notice continues 'He is of no value whatever and only a low Price can be given for his capture. [Signed:] Sam.' On the outskirts of the city, the ass stands on top of a small rise, clearly alarmed by the approach of federal troops led by a lion (Lyon). On the right a terrified General Price crouches (apparently defecating) as his panicked troops flee in the background." *Library of Congress*

Engulfed in war for over three years and under Federal occupation and control, Missouri found itself in the throes of an increasingly savage irregular war. Most of Missouri's Federal and Confederate ground troops had been incorporated into the various Western and Trans-Mississippi armies, which included the Federal Army of the Tennessee and the Army of the Cumberland, as well as the Confederate Army of Tennessee. Back in Federal-occupied Missouri, however, it was the pro-Union state militia organizations that patrolled, guarded, and protected virtually every one of the state's counties from invading Confederate troops and rampant insurgency. Though Rebel cavalry raids into the state endeavored each year to recruit volunteers, sow chaos, and attack Federal units, it had always been the goal for Missouri's Confederates to take the state by force and overthrow the increasingly radical Union government from Jefferson City.

As a former governor of Missouri, congressman, and a Mexican War hero, Sterling Price focused his attention on his adopted home state. Since late 1861, following his victories at Wilson's Creek and Lexington, and the subsequent retreat into Arkansas, Price had made it a priority to re-enter Missouri. This sentiment by Price was reflected in a declaration to his Missouri State Guardsmen after he accepted a Confederate general officer's commission, that he "may sooner lead you back to the fertile prairies, the rich woodlands, and majestic streams of our beloved Missouri."[2] Price wanted to advance into Missouri as soon as able, but his larger role in Confederate operations west—and even east—of the Mississippi River took priority.

Soon after they were formally accepted into Confederate service in the immediate wake of their defeat at Pea Ridge, Arkansas, on March 8, 1862, Price and his Missouri division were merged into Maj. Gen. Earl Van Dorn's command and sent east of the Mississippi River, per orders of Gen. Albert Sidney Johnston. Back home in Missouri, many of the state's well-trained and armed Union volunteer units had been transferred east to Tennessee and Mississippi. Additionally, Missourians in the northern region of the state began to rise against Union authorities over registration requirements and militia enrollment. In his eyes, Price was convinced that a Confederate offensive into Missouri was needed. By June, "Old Pap" was able to travel to Richmond to meet with the Confederate president.

In Richmond, greeted by crowds of cheering citizens, Price's meetings with President Jefferson Davis were initially successful. Writing a memorandum about his wishes, Price argued for an independent department of the Trans-Mississippi, for the president to place him in command, and that a "movement should be made immediately in the direction of Missouri."[3] According to Price's adjutant Major Thomas Snead, Van Dorn "generously urged the President to assign General Price to that command."[4] Even so,

2   Sterling Price to Soldiers of the State Guard, General Orders, No. 79, in *The War of the Rebellion: A Compilation of the Official Records of the Union and Confederate Armies,* ser. 1, vol. 13, (Washington, DC: 1880-1901), 814. (Hereafter, cited as *OR*)

3   Memorandum from Sterling Price to George W. Randolph, June 19, 1862, in *OR*, ser. 1, vol. 13, 838.

Davis had already placed Maj. Gen. John B. Magruder in command of the Trans-Mississippi Department, frustrating Price into offering his own resignation. Though Davis initially accepted the resignation, he soon retracted it, knowing the influence Price had on Confederate Missourians. Instead, Davis "would instruct Bragg to send the Missourians to the trans-Mississippi as soon as it could safely be done."[5]

When Price rejoined his division in July, he was given overall command of the Army of the West. Despite the fact that Davis and Gen. Braxton Bragg promised at their "direction, to return to the west of the Mississippi River," by the fall of 1862, Price's command had not been transferred west even after he and his Missourians fought courageously at Iuka and Corinth.[6] Under pressure by his own men, many of whom threatened mutiny, Price needed to return to Richmond to once again demand the transfer of his command.

Instead of Price, Missouri Confederate Governor Thomas C. Reynolds resolved to go on his own in January 1863 to confer with Davis. Even though both of the Missouri Confederate leaders aspired to bring the state into the Confederacy, Reynolds questioned Price's loyalty to the greater Confederacy. According to Reynolds, Price "vehemently insisted on the transfer not only of himself, but of all the Missouri troops in Confederate service, and at the same time as himself."[7] In addition, and most relevant to this analysis, both Price and Reynolds hoped to stress their "desire that the Confederate States should as soon as practicable send an army into Missouri, and that [Price] should command it."[8] Though strategically impractical while Vicksburg was so severely threatened, Secretary of War James Seddon agreed that "a simultaneous move would be made up each bank of the Mississippi River to recover Missouri and Kentucky, and perhaps bring about a peace."[9] A deal

---

4 Thomas Snead, "With Price East of the Mississippi", *Battles and Leaders of the Civil War*, vol. II (New York: The Century Co, 1914), 723.

5 Snead, 725.

6 Letter from Braxton Bragg to Samuel Cooper, July 12, 1862, in *OR*, ser. 1, vol. 17, pt. 2, 645.

7 Thomas Reynolds, *General Sterling Price and the Confederacy*, ed. Robert G. Schultz (St. Louis, MO: Missouri History Museum, 2009), 55. Note: This manuscript by Reynolds was written in the wake of the failed Missouri Expedition, in which he was highly critical of Price. Quotes used by Reynolds in this piece are taken with this bias in mind.

8 Ibid., 52.

between Reynolds, Price, and Davis's administration allowed Price to return west of the river. However, a major advance into Missouri would not arrive until the following year.

Much to the Missouri rebels' dismay, not only would the subsequent fall of Vicksburg and the ousting of Confederate presence on the Mississippi cause their leaders to put aside any possibility of a major advance into Missouri, there was also concern with Price himself among the Confederate high command. According to his critics, Price was more of a politician than an army commander. He repeatedly put Missouri, his own men, and his own ego ahead of what was best for the Confederacy. In combination with his stellar record as governor and a war hero, Price himself was affectionately nicknamed "Old Pap" by his own men. However, it was not the same with his superiors, who believed that "no reliance could be placed upon his obedience to an order unless it chimed in with his own plans and fancies."[10] Davis and Reynolds, in particular, were suspicious of Price's motives, believing that he was not completely devoted to the Confederate cause. Additionally, Davis himself reportedly said that Price was the "vainest man he had ever met" during the meetings in Richmond.[11] Over the course of the first half of 1864, though, it seemed more clear to the Trans-Mississippi Department commander, Gen. E. Kirby Smith, that Price might be the only commander that could lead an offensive operation into Missouri.

In the late spring and early summer of 1864, the larger Confederacy was under widespread pressure from simultaneous Union operations in Virginia, Maryland, and Georgia, all three under the supervision of General-in-Chief Ulysses Grant. Farther west, larger Union efforts to surround and capture the strategic port city of Mobile, Alabama had failed, significantly due to Lt. Gen. Richard Taylor's successful defense of Louisiana's Red River. Under the overall command of Smith, Confederate success in Louisiana was in part due to their effectiveness in stopping Union Maj. Gen. Frederick Steele's columns in Arkansas from moving south and uniting with

9 Reynolds, 58.

10 Letter from Edmund Kirby Smith to R.W. Johnson, January 15, 1864, in *OR*, ser. 1, vol. 34, pt. 2, 870.

11 Reynolds, 53.

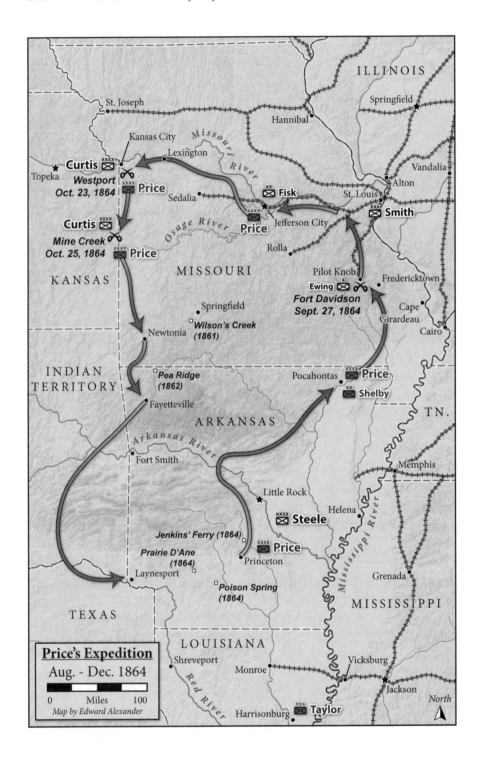

Price's Expedition
Aug. - Dec. 1864

0   Miles   100
Map by Edward Alexander

Price's Expedition Ever since leaving Missouri earlier in the war, Maj. Gen. Sterling Price had his eyes focused on a return to his home state. In the fall of 1864, he had an opportunity to lead an offensive and finally bring Missouri into the Confederacy. With approximately 12,000 men in his Army of Missouri, Price hoped to take St. Louis and the state capital at Jefferson City, but bypassed both after realizing the Federal defenses were too strong. Unable to fulfill his promise to bring the state into the Confederacy, Price's 1864 Missouri Campaign became more of a raid marked by notable battles, such as Fort Davidson, Westport, and Mine Creek.

---

additional Federal forces under Maj. Gen. Nathaniel Banks in Louisiana. Smith's troops, including Price's District of Arkansas, played a crucial role in defeating Steele at Prairie D'Ane, Poison Spring, and Jenkins' Ferry, leading to the worst overall Federal defeat of the war in Arkansas. When Banks had retreated to the Mississippi River and no longer posed a threat, Smith—having reclaimed the strategic initiative—was now able to focus on a movement northward to bolster the Confederate war effort.[12]

On the grand strategic level, a northward push into Missouri would assist "in relieving Tennessee . . . even if compelled to return, it might gain time for us in Georgia or avert an attack on Mobile by compelling the enemy to send large forces to Missouri."[13] With critical threats to numerous Confederate armies, particularly in the eastern half of the Confederacy, an advance in the west could force Grant to pull troops from Virginia or Georgia. But no less important was the strategic situation on the ground in Missouri, where Union forces were spread thin.[14] Confederate cavalry raids had routinely looped into Missouri to collect supplies, disturb lines of supply and communication, and incite fear among the state's Unionist population. In his 1863 cavalry raid into Missouri, Brig. Gen. Jo Shelby demonstrated to Price that Federal authorities were unable to protect and defend the state's civilians from hit-and-run cavalry actions. Federal outposts and garrisons scattered throughout the Department of Missouri's five districts were vulnerable to a fast-moving cavalry column.[15] Pro-Confederate guerrillas,

---

12 Thomas Cutrer, *Theater of a Separate War* (Chapel Hill, NC: The University of North Carolina Press, 2017), 406.

13 Letter from Thomas C. Reynolds to Sterling Price, July 18, 1864, in *OR*, ser. 1, vol. 41, pt. 2, 1011.

14 Louis Gerteis, *The Civil War in Missouri: A Military History* (Columbia, MO: University of Missouri Press, 2012), 180.

"more numerous and bold than ever" by 1864, were invigorated by the prospects of an offensive into Missouri.[16]

"Old Pap"—believing the state was dominantly pro-Confederate—was convinced that an expedition into the state would incite a state-wide uprising to liberate Missouri from Federal control. In a letter to Reynolds on July 22, Price believed that, "the people of Missouri are ready for a general uprising."[17] Brigadier General Jo Shelby reflected this sentiment, that "the unparalleled tide of Southern victories has so inflamed the minds of a vast proportion of its inhabitants, stimulated by three years of crime and desolation, that they have risen . . . they call for organized help from the South."[18] Price was also convinced that by possessing portions of the state and consolidating the various pro-Confederate factions, "the least sanguine seem to think will amount to not less than 30,000" recruits.[19] There is little doubt that both Price and Shelby were aware of the small-scale uprisings in northern Missouri over the state Militia Act that required military-aged males to join the Union militia. Further, Price and former Governor Claiborne Jackson were able to recruit several thousand troops during the 1861 campaigns. The only chance they had at recruiting these numbers was if they could achieve battlefield victories and remove Union forces during the expedition.

In addition to inciting a large-scale uprising in Missouri, a successful expedition would provide a glut of supplies and munitions. Perched on the central-eastern border of the state, along the Missouri and Mississippi rivers, sat St. Louis. The home to the largest Federal arsenal of any of the slave states, along with well-supplied military stores, hospital complexes, and businesses, St. Louis was a prime target for Price's expedition. In addition to St. Louis, the army could take advantage of the lack of Union volunteer troops in the state, which, according to Shelby, left "depots of

15 Mark A. Lause, *Price's Lost Campaign: The 1864 Invasion of Missouri* (Columbia, MO: University of Missouri Press, 2011), 13.

16 Letter from A.M. Lay to Early, July 23, 1864, in *OR,* ser. 1, vol. 41, pt. 2, 941.

17 Letter from Sterling Price to Thomas C. Reynolds, July 22, 1864, in *OR,* 1020.

18 Letter from Jo Shelby to Lt. Col. J.F. Belton, July 27, 1864, in *OR,* 1027.

19 Letter from Sterling Price to Gen. E.K. Smith, July 23, 1864, in *OR,* 1023.

supplies unguarded."[20] Similar to the Liberty Arsenal, which was seized by pro-secessionist forces in April 1861 and provided much-needed weaponry to the Missouri State Guard, the acquisition of military supplies could continue to arm the Trans-Mississippi Confederates. However, with the want of supplies—and booty—would come the need for strict discipline of invading troops, something Price drastically undermined.

On top of strategic goals, political objectives played a major role in the planning the operation. As in other major military campaigns of the spring, summer, and fall of 1864, eyes were certainly on the fall presidential election. A major Confederate victory west of the Mississippi River could offset setbacks in the east and impact the elections. More immediately in Price's gaze, however, was Missouri's capital at Jefferson City. If his army captured Jefferson City or St. Louis for long enough, the state could hold a general election to elect a new governor and legislature. Instead of the Unionist Missouri Constitutional Convention, which held the majority of power in Jefferson City, a pro-Confederate government would be installed, and Missouri would consequently vote to secede. Purportedly, Snead was arranging elections set for January 1865, with the hope that Price would be elected governor.[21] There was no doubt that a successful raid constituted much more than just securing Missouri for the Confederacy. Nonetheless, the high expectations by Price for Missouri hampered his overall ability to think critically and realistically about his influence over the state's pro-Confederate population.

It was not until July 30 that Smith had officially made up his mind to order an offensive into Missouri. Throughout the month of July, he had been under pressure from both Davis and Lee to send ten thousand reinforcements east, as well as from Price, who argued that, "the time was never more propitious for an advance of our forces into Missouri."[22] On August 4, Smith officially, yet reluctantly, placed Price in command of "the entire cavalry force" of the District of Arkansas and issued the official orders

20 Letter from Jo Shelby to Lt. Col. J.F. Belton, July 27, 1864, in *OR*, 1027.

21 Kyle Sinisi, *The Last Hurrah: Sterling Price's Missouri Expedition of 1864* (Lanham, MD: Rowman & Littlefield, 2015), 20.

22 Letter from Sterling Price to Thomas C. Reynolds, July 22, 1864, in *OR*, 1020.

of the campaign: "Rally the loyal men of Missouri, and remember that our great want is men." He added, "Make Saint Louis the objective point of your movement, which, if rapidly made, will put you in possession of that place, its supplies, and military stores, and which will do more toward rallying Missouri to your standard than the possession of any other point." Smith also ordered Price to "restrain your men" and "avoid all wanton acts of destruction and devastation." Finally, if he had to retreat, "make your retreat through Kansas and the Indian Territory, sweeping that country of its mules, horses, cattle, and military supplies of all kinds."[23] With his influence over the people and troops of Missouri, as well as to effectively transfer him from the District of Arkansas, Price was selected over other Confederate leaders in the Trans-Mississippi, including Taylor and Lt. Gen. Simon Bolivar Buckner. In the meantime, Price assembled his 12,000-man cavalry force at Princeton, Arkansas.

One of the principal *what ifs* of Price's 1864 Missouri Expedition centers on 10,000 reinforcements under Taylor that were sent eastward by Smith. Though Price's expedition would be staffed by cavalry or mounted infantry, Taylor's troops were predominantly infantry and could have been used to support Price's advance as he moved on St. Louis and Jefferson City. However, on August 19, less than two weeks before Price embarked north from Princeton, Davis cancelled the transfer of Taylor's troops, who were two hundred miles away from Price at Harrisonburg, Louisiana. Smith, though, was inclined to keep Taylor's reinforcements near the Arkansas-Missouri border, to react quickly to any renewed attacks or movement north of Federal troops by Steele. Nonetheless, these reinforcements, "would be at hand to help Price extricate himself in case of failure or disaster."[24] There is little doubt that Smith's reluctance to reinforce Price with those 10,000 troops was caused by inter-departmental politics and his lack of confidence in Price's ability to achieve victory in the campaign.[25] This critical error by the high command undoubtedly set the Missourians up for failure.

At Princeton, Price took command of the bulk of his "Army of Missouri,"

23 Letter from E.K. Smith (via W.R. Boggs) to Sterling Price, August 4, 1864, in *OR,* 728.

24 Letter from E.K. Smith to Jefferson Davis, August 21, 1864, in *OR*, ser. 1, vol. 41, pt. 1, 113.

25 Scott E. Sallee, "Missouri! One Last Time: Sterling Price's 1864 Missouri Expedition, 'A Just and Holy Cause,' in *Blue & Gray Magazine,* June 1991, 12.

which was split into three mounted divisions. These divisions were under the command of three of the Trans-Mississippi theater's senior ranking officers: Maj. Gen. James Fagan, Brig. Gen. John S. Marmaduke, and Brig. Gen. Joseph O. Shelby. The only division not at Princeton was Shelby's, which was causing disruption of Federal lines of supply in northeastern Arkansas to divert attention from the main body's movements. Fagan's and Marmaduke's divisions were mounted infantry. Due to delays in obtaining proper ordnance, weapons, money, and supplies, Price's advance from Princeton to rendezvous with Shelby at Pocahontas did not begin until August 30. On September 14, Price's column arrived at Pocahontas. There, he organized the Army of Missouri, a force of 12,000 men, and prepared it for the invasion into Federal-occupied Missouri. Several issues plagued the Army of Missouri from the get-go. Unsurprisingly, there was friction between Price, Fagan, and Marmaduke over performance issues during the Red River Campaign. Price considered Fagan and Marmaduke to be untrustworthy, incompetent, and self-serving. Of their force, one-third of the men were unarmed, 1,000 did not have horses, supply wagons were in poor condition, and the majority of arms were outdated or had various ammunition requirements. However, in just four days, the Army of Missouri made all the preparations for the march it could and embarked for Missouri in three distinct columns on the morning of September 19. It is surprising that Smith, aware of the manpower and supply issues the Army of Missouri faced when it departed Pocahontas, had not already planned to reinforce Price with Taylor.

While it is unnecessary to recount the entire expedition battle for battle, it is necessary to analyze the specific moments in the campaign that ultimately led to the failure of Price's 1864 Missouri Expedition. These decisive events include Pilot Knob (Fort Davidson) and the abandonment of the plan to occupy both St. Louis and Jefferson City, which stripped the campaign of its strategic and political goals. Underlying these events were chronic issues with the equipage and the physical state of the army, wanton physical destruction, a large wagon train that significantly slowed the army, and the federals' deliberate and effective response. Overall, blame rested with Price's leadership as a military commander. He made decisions to abandon key targets, yet continued to pursue his goal of taking Missouri. A succinct analysis of Pilot Knob, Price's reluctance to attack and occupy St. Louis and Jefferson City, and the consequences are imperative.

When Price's force entered Missouri on September 19, there was hope that they could take advantage of the lack of experienced and well-trained Union manpower defending the state. Major General William S. Rosecrans, commander of the Department of Missouri, had slightly more than 17,500 troops and fifty artillery pieces for the entire state. Moreover, these troops were scattered across the state manning defensive works at Rolla, St. Louis, and Springfield.[26] Under suspicion that a Confederate advance into Missouri was imminent, Rosecrans made precautions to raise several regiments of one-year volunteers. In addition to more federal units to protect Missouri, he was able to convince Maj. Gen. Henry Halleck to redirect Maj. Gen. Andrew J. Smith's Right Wing of the XVI Corps back to Missouri to assist in repulsing Price. By September 17, Smith had 4,500 of his troops south of St. Louis at Jefferson Barracks. Even though Rosecrans was unaware of where Price was going, he was able to dispatch militia to protect vital supply depots and railheads across southern Missouri.

Price's columns steadily arrived at Fredericktown beginning on September 23, first with Shelby, then Fagan and Marmaduke. On September 24, Rosecrans confirmed the Confederate presence in eastern Missouri. In the days prior, reports had trickled into his St. Louis headquarters that Shelby's division was operating virtually all across southeastern Missouri with no definitive numbers. With the potential for "4,000 or 5,000 men" in one division, Rosecrans dispatched Brig. Gen. Thomas Ewing, Jr. and a brigade from Smith's wing to Fort Davidson at Pilot Knob, where he could help protect the vital St. Louis & Iron Mountain Railroad line there that sat just under ninety miles from St. Louis.[27] Ewing arrived at Fort Davidson at noon on September 26 and took command of an assortment of state militia and Union volunteer troops.

Though Price knew Rosecrans's forces had detected his army's proximity to St. Louis, he was unaware of the rapid concentration of Union troops in the state and the immediate region. There was immediate concern when Price discovered that Maj. Gen. Andrew Jackson Smith's troops, "composed of about 8,000 infantry," had been redirected to St. Louis from

26 Sinisi, 49-50.

27 Letter from W.S. Rosecrans to Governor Hall, September 24, 1864, in *OR*, ser. 1, vol. 41, pt. 3, 342.

Cairo, Illinois to meet this threat and reinforce Rosecrans.[28] Smith's strength Price feared "far exceeded my own two to one."[29] St. Louis was also heavily fortified with at least ten fortifications, each armed with siege guns and manned by state militia. He needed more time and more men before even thinking about advancing on the Gateway City.

As a result, the Army of Missouri would attack a more vulnerable target: Fort Davidson at Pilot Knob, Missouri. In his eyes, a victory at Fort Davidson could be enough to spark the uprising Price had hoped for. But when Price gave up on attacking St. Louis, he had abandoned what E. Kirby Smith had stressed most importantly—that capturing the Gateway City "will do more toward rallying Missouri to your standard than the possession of any other point."[30] Nevertheless, Price eyed the opportunity at Fort Davidson. Victory there could also mean more recruits, enough to successfully attack and hold St. Louis. Before he could attack the fort, Price ordered Shelby's division "to destroy the railroad there and the bridges after effecting that object to fall back in the direction of Gen. A. J. Smith from re-enforcing the garrison."[31] In other words, Shelby's division would destroy portions of the St. Louis & Iron Mountain Railroad line that connected St. Louis with Pilot Knob and the Arcadia Valley. On the morning of September 26, Price and both Fagan's and Marmaduke's divisions marched from Fredericktown toward Pilot Knob.

A hexagonal earthen fort and armed with sixteen guns (four 32-pound siege guns, three 24-pound howitzers, three 12-inch mortars, and six 12-pound field guns), Fort Davidson looked entirely formidable against attacking infantry. However, the fort sat at the bottom of the Arcadia Valley, surrounded by mountains, making it truly vulnerable to an attack from above. Price himself was under the impression "the place could be taken without great loss," which proved much more difficult than he believed.[32] After securing Pilot Knob and Shepherd Mountain, two of the largest

28 Report of Sterling Price, December 28, 1864, in *OR*, ser. 1, vol. 41, pt. 1, 628.

29 Ibid., 630.

30 Letter from E.K. Smith (via W.R. Boggs) to Sterling Price, August 4, 1864, in *OR*, 728.

31 Report of Sterling Price, December 28, 1864, in *OR*, ser. 1, vol. 41, pt. 1, 628.

32 *Ibid.,* 629.

mountains overlooking the fort, on September 27, Price ordered an artillery bombardment followed by a quick assault. In fact, due to his poor physical fitness, Price was unable to scale the mountains to survey the situation, which forced him to make the tactical decisions virtually blind. One of the critical errors he made was trusting a group of civilians who implored him to call off the artillery bombardment, for they incorrectly feared their loved ones had been corralled into the fort by Ewing. Without verifying the information or observing the situation from his own troops' positions, Price called off the bombardment and ordered just a frontal attack with 4,700 men at 2:00pm.

A combination of rough terrain, disorganized lines of battle, heavy and steady enemy fire, and an inability to successfully cross the moat that surrounded the fort forced Price's attacking force to retire. Though his troops were humiliated and exhausted, Price renewed his orders to attack the next day. A victorious Ewing had other plans, however. In his eyes, "with all its dangers, the policy of retreat was clearly best, and preparations for it began at midnight." To prevent the fort's magazine from being captured by Price's men, Ewing "had Colonel Fletcher arrange for having the magazine (which was large and filled with every variety of ammunition) blown up in two hours after we left, or as soon as our exit should be discovered by the enemy."[33] At 3:30am, the magazine detonated, with Ewing's troops well ahead of the enemy en route northwest. The Battle of Fort Davidson had come to an end, however the strategic troubles for Price's Army of Missouri were just beginning.

In combination with his moderate losses sustained in combat, estimated between 500 and 1,200 casualties, as well as the confirmation of A.J. Smith's force at St. Louis, Price decided to officially abandon the plan to attack and occupy St. Louis. There is a common myth that Price abandoned his plan to attack St. Louis because the casualties nearly destroyed his army at Fort Davidson. In fact, Price only lost approximately 6 percent of his fighting force there.[34] Price then resolved "to move as fast as possible on Jefferson City, destroying the railroad as I went, with the hope to be able to capture that city with its troops and munitions of war."[35]

---

33 Report of Thomas Ewing, Jr., October 20, 1864, in OR, ser. 1, vol. 41, pt. 1, 449.

34 Sinisi, 85-86.

35 Report of Thomas Ewing, Jr., October 20, 1864, in *OR*, ser. 1, vol. 41, pt. 1, 449.

As Price maneuvered his way west toward Jefferson City, he continued to raid Unionist towns, destroy lines of communication and supply, and acquire needed supplies. Both extensive looting and the significant increase in wagon trains drastically slowed the army's movement, though. Most importantly for Price, by early October his army was virtually at the doorstep of Jefferson City and the dominantly pro-Confederate Boonslick region was just beyond it to the west. With these prospects, Price was undoubtedly hopeful to make his political mark soon.

Approximately one week after departing Pilot Knob, Price's army was just miles outside the capital city. On October 6, Shelby's column pushed through Union cavalry guarding the crossings over the Osage River just six miles south of Jefferson City. The following day, also positioned to the south of the city, Fagan successfully forced Federal troops back along the Moreau River. After pushing the Federals into the city's defenses, Price's army was perched on the heights overlooking the Jefferson City defensive works.

In command at Jefferson City was Brig. Gen. Clinton Fisk, who had worked to bolster the capital city's defenses. By the time Price had arrived at their doorstep, the formidable Federal defenses were being fed with an additional seven thousand Federal troops. Five new earthen forts had been built to repulse attacks from either direction. In response to reconnoitering the Jefferson City defenses, Price "determined to move my forces two miles south of the city," where he "received positive information that the enemy were 12,000 strong in the city, and that 3,000 more had arrived on the opposite bank of the river." After consulting with his division commanders, "I determined not to attack the enemy's intrenchments, as they outnumbered me nearly two to one and were strongly fortified."[36] To Price, it would have been an utter waste of his men's lives to attack such fortified positions. On October 8, Price's main column departed the outskirts of Jefferson City and moved west through the Boonslick toward Kansas City.

When Price abandoned the idea of attacking and capturing Jefferson City, he gave up another major target of his expedition. Whereas St. Louis would have provided supplies, munitions, and a significant strategic center, Jefferson City was both the physical and symbolic seat of power in the state

36 *Ibid.,* 631.

of Missouri. If Price had successfully taken the city and held it long enough to install a new pro-Confederate government, the state of Missouri may very well have seceded. For his own aspirations, a victorious Price could have been elected governor under Confederate control. A Confederate Missouri in 1864 would have significantly changed the war west of the Mississippi River.

The rest of the 1864 Missouri Expedition was largely a foot chase between Price and Federal cavalry that pursued the Confederates from east and west, as Price moved toward the Kansas border. After moving west from Jefferson City, the chances for Price to achieve victory in Missouri were largely dashed. His army gradually dwindled in size and strength. By the time Price arrived at Westport with just 8,500 men, he was decisively defeated on October 23 by Maj. Gen. Samuel R. Curtis's Army of the Border and Maj. Gen. Alfred Pleasonton's cavalry division. One of the largest battles fought west of the Mississippi, Westport effectively ended Price's 1864 Expedition and any hope for a strategic victory. It significantly hurt the effectiveness of Price's fighting force, compelling the Confederates to retire south. Just days after Westport, at the Battle of Mine Creek in Linn County, Kansas, two of Price's divisions were virtually destroyed. By the time Price crossed the Arkansas-Texas border in early December of 1864, he had just 3,500 men in his starved, exhausted, and disintegrated army. Price's war-long goal of returning to Missouri and securing it for the Confederacy was finally over.

In the annals of Civil War history, Price's 1864 Missouri Expedition is perhaps the most understudied major campaign of the entire war. The fact that it was west of the Mississippi River and did not make a considerable difference in the war effort may contribute to why we have largely overlooked this campaign–one that deserves much more attention than it has. But, based on the Confederacy's bold strategic and political goals for this campaign into Missouri, there was opportunity for Price and his army to significantly impact the war. While Price failed to take St. Louis and Jefferson City and did not incite a general uprising in Missouri—indeed, the state remained under federal control for the balance of the conflict—the campaign serves as a powerful reminder that the war was replete with lost opportunities and alternative endings.

So, what if Price had been successful?

CHAPTER TEN

A New Endorsement of Abraham Lincoln

Could Lincoln Have Won Reelection without Sherman's and Sheridan's Successes?

Jonathan A. Noyalas

On October 4, 1864, Thomas Holliday Barker, a member of the executive committee of the Union and Emancipation Society in Manchester, England, penned a letter to William Lloyd Garrison.[1] Throughout the years, Barker and the leading abolitionist communicated frequently about matters related to American politics and efforts to destroy slavery. From the other side of the Atlantic it seemed to Barker that, one month prior to the presidential election, Lincoln was well poised to triumph as a result of General William T. Sherman's capture of Atlanta and General Philip H. Sheridan's twin victories nearly three weeks later at Winchester and Fisher's Hill. "The capture of Atlanta, and the splendid victory in the Shenandoah Valley," Barker estimated, "have so changed the situation and prospects of the struggle, that the famous Peace Platform at Chicago, and its equally famous War or Peace General, must by this time have become somewhat small by degrees, and beautifully less. By the 8th [of] November,

---

1 Thomas H. Barker to William Lloyd Garrison, October 4, 1864, quoted in *The Liberator*, November 4, 1864. For further discussion of Barker see Walter M. Merrill and Louis Ruchames, eds., *The Letters of William Lloyd Garrison: 1868-1879* (Cambridge, MA: The Belknap Press of Harvard University, 1981), 6: 66-67; *Papers Relating to Foreign Affairs, Accompanying the Annual Message of the President to the Second Session Thirty-Eighth Congress, Part II* (Washington, D.C.: Government Printing Office, 1865), 205.

I expect that they will be *nowehere*."[2] Sentiments such as Barker's echoed throughout newspapers, letters, and diaries in the weeks leading up to the election and following Lincoln's victory over Democratic challenger George B. McClellan.

In the decades since, dozens of historians have posited a causal relationship between Sherman's and Sheridan's battlefield feats and Lincoln's reelection. For example, Charles Carleton Coffin, a wartime correspondent for the *Boston Journal*, wrote twenty-five years after the war's conclusion that the Union victories in the late summer and early autumn of 1864 significantly boosted Lincoln's chances at the polls. "We are to remember that in November the people were to elect a President. . . . If the Union armies were defeated, the chances were that McClellan might be elected," Coffin wrote.[3] Historian Stephen Oates echoed the perspective of many historians in his classic biography of Lincoln. Union control of the "queen city of the cotton states," coupled with "good news from the Shenandoah . . . seemed to kick the bottom out of the Democratic platform," Oates concluded.[4]

While countless contemporary statements and observations from historians reiterate the importance of Sherman's and Sheridan's successes to Lincoln's reelection, I have often been asked if Lincoln (who soundly defeated McClellan in the electoral college by a vote of 212 to 21, but who notched a narrower popular vote margin), could have won the presidential election of 1864 absent Sherman's and Sheridan's victories.[5] Historical judgements, particularly those involving what-if scenarios, are difficult. While it is impossible to determine how the election of 1864 might have fared differently had Sherman and Sheridan not delivered such timely battlefield successes, a

---

2   Thomas H. Barker to William Lloyd Garrison, October 4, 1864, quoted in *The Liberator*, November 4, 1864.

3   Charles Carleton Coffin, *Freedom Triumphant: The Fourth Period of the War of the Rebellion from September, 1864, to its Close* (New York: Harper & Brothers Publishers, 1890), 31.

4   Stephen B. Oates, *With Malice Toward None: A Life of Abraham Lincoln* (New York: Harper Perennial, 1994), 397.

5   Charles Bracelen Flood, *1864: Lincoln at the Gates of History* (New York: Simon & Schuster, 2009), 372.

close examination reveals the extent to which individuals at the time believed Sherman's and Sheridan's victories impacted the presidential election of 1864.

By the early summer of 1864 Democrats seemed hopeful that the inability of Union forces to secure meaningful victories—coupled with Confederate general Jubal A. Early's success in the Shenandoah Valley and his push to Washington, D.C.'s outskirts—would bode well for McClellan.[6] Reports from various political advisers and allies portrayed Lincoln's political situation as dire. On August 22, 1864, one week before the Democratic convention convened in Chicago, Thurlow Weed, a powerful Republican who disagreed with Lincoln's decision to issue the Emancipation Proclamation, penned a rather pessimistic note to Secretary of State William Henry Seward about the likelihood of Lincoln winning in November. Lincoln's "re-election was an impossibility," Weed wrote bluntly. "Nobody here doubts it; nor do I see any body from other States who authorizes the slightest hope of success," Weed continued despondently.[7] Henry J. Raymond, the chair of the National Republic Commitee, wrote President Lincoln in similarly gloomy terms on the same day: "I am in active correspondence with your staunchest friends in every state and from them all I hear but one report. The tide is setting strongly against us."[8] Raymond informed Lincoln that his prospects looked bleak in Pennsylvania, New York, and Illinois.[9] Indiana appeared to be a toss-up. Raymond advised Lincoln that Governor Oliver P. Morton believed Lincoln could win the Hoosier State only through "the most strenuous efforts."[10]

In addition to these abysmal projections from Weed and Raymond, newspapers carried similarly negative perspectives. "Mr. Lincoln's Re-election is now considered an impossibility. There is an overwhelming gathering of political elements against him," warned a correspondent in

---

6   Jonathan W. White, *Emancipation, the Union Army, and the Reelection of Abraham Lincoln* (Baton Rouge: Louisiana State University Press, 2014), 99.

7   Thurlow Weed to William Seward, August 22, 1864, quoted in Roy P. Basler, ed. *The Collected Works of Abraham Lincoln* (New Brunswick, NJ: Rutgers University Press, 1953), 7: 514.

8   Henry J. Raymond to Abraham Lincoln, August 22, 1864, quoted in ibid., 517-518.

9   Ibid., 518.

10   Ibid.

Millersburg, Ohio, nearly one month prior to Weed's and Raymond's woeful letters.[11] Even more disturbingly, some newspapers reported that Lincoln's popularity with Union soldiers had waned. A correspondent for the *Detroit Free Press* allegedly overheard an exchange between a Republican and Democrat discussing the probability of Lincoln's defeat. While the Republican ceded that McClellan would likely win "the home vote," the Lincoln supporter adamantly believed that "the soldiers will nearly all go for Lincoln." Supposedly, a wounded Union soldier who had lost a leg in battle overheard the conversation and intervened. The unidentified veteran informed the Republican that approximately 700 wounded Union soldiers took an informal poll as to whom they would support in the upcoming election. "There was not a single vote for Lincoln," the soldier snapped.[12]

The various reports that trickled into Lincoln's office made him confront the seemingly stark reality that he would not win a second term. In early August, Schuyler Hamilton, the grandson of Alexander Hamilton who had served on the staffs of Generals Winfield Scott and Henry Halleck, spoke candidly with the president. "As things stand at present," he began, "I don't know what in the name of God I could say, as an honest man, that would help you. Unless you . . . do something with your army, you will be beaten overwhelmingly." Aware of the challenges he confronted, Lincoln told Hamilton: "You think I don't know I am going to be beaten, *but I do* and unless some great change takes place *badly beaten*." As the conversation continued, Lincoln clearly explained to Hamilton that he understood his political fortunes were tethered to the fortunes of the Union armies. "The people promised themselves when Gen. Grant started out that he would take Richmond . . . he didn't take it, and they blame me, they hold me responsible," Lincoln explained.[13]

Prepared to confront the possibility of defeat, Lincoln gathered his

---

11 *Holmes County Farmer* (Millersburg, OH), July 28, 1864.

12 This exchange in the *Detroit Free Press* was reported in various newspapers. This account was taken from *The Burlington Weekly Sentinel* (Burlington, VT), September 16, 1864.

13 Conversation between Schuyler Hamilton and Abraham Lincoln recounted in *Private and Official Correspondence of General Benjamin F. Butler during the Period of the Civil War* (Norwood, MA: The Plimpton Press, 1917), 35. For further discussion of Schuyler Hamilton's military service see Ezra J. Warner, *Generals in Blue* (Baton Rouge: Louisiana State University Press, 1992), 200-201.

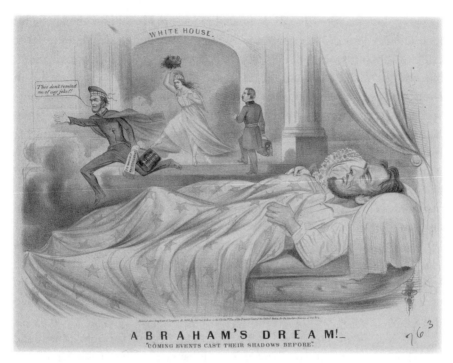

"Abraham's Dream," produced by Currier and Ives a few months prior to the election, depicts Lincoln being pushed out of the White House by Liberty while McClellan enters. *Library of Congress*

cabinet on August 23, 1864, and had them sign "the back of a paper." He did not reveal the contents of the document, which he folded and stowed away. The cabinet secretaries obliged the president, but it was not until November 11, after McClellan had been defeated, that Lincoln revealed the memorandum's contents. "This morning," Lincoln began the brief missive, "as for some days past, it seems exceedingly probable that this Administration will not be re-elected." Although apparently resigned to his political fate, Lincoln, who pledged "to so co-operate with the President elect," was also determined to save "the Union between the election and the inauguration" because the president knew that the Union could not be saved after the inauguration because his Democratic successor "will have secured his election on such ground that he can not possibly save it afterwards."[14]

14   Basler, ed, *Collected Works*, 7: 514; Flood, *1864*, 272.

Four days prior to Lincoln's unusual request to his cabinet, the president met with Frederick Douglass at the White House. Douglass, an often-fierce critic of Lincoln's who did not initially support Lincoln's bid for reelection, did not go "most gladly" to his meeting on August 19. Lincoln, who, in Douglass' estimation, "spoke with great earnestness and much solicitude" and appeared "troubled by the . . . growing impatience there was being manifested through the North at the war," spoke with Douglass about his fears of what a Democratic victory might mean for the fate of emancipation. Fearful that a Democratic president would "leave still in slavery all who had not come within" Union lines, Lincoln hoped Douglass could assist him in developing "the means most desirable to be employed outside the army to induce the slaves in the rebel States to come within Federal lines."[15] Lincoln's comments to Schuyler Hamilton, his blind memorandum, and the conversation with Douglass revealed his fatalism about his political fortunes; still, the president remained determined to do all in his power to preserve the Union and strengthen the Emancipation Proclamation's reach if his days in office were truly numbered.

While Lincoln prepared for the worst, soldiers in the field considered for whom they would cast their ballots. Perspectives about the candidates varied.[16] A Wisconsin soldier refused to vote for Lincoln because he believed like "most of the soldiers now-a-days . . . that Lincoln never can put down this rebellion."[17] Conversely, Charles Jeffords, a veteran of the 14th Pennsylvania Cavalry, wrote a friend from Sandy Hook, Maryland, in a "camp of about 3,000 men of different regiments . . . there is but very few that talk [a]bout voting for McClellan. . . . Old Abe . . . is the safe horse. . . .

---

15 Douglass wrote that this meeting had transformed his view of Lincoln. "What he said on this day showed a deeper moral conviction against slavery than I had even seen before in anything spoken or written by him. I listened with the deepest interest and profoundest satisfaction." For further discussion see Frederick Douglass, *The Life and Times of Frederick Douglass, From 1817 to 1882, Written by Himself* (London: Christian Age Office, 1882), 312-313; David W. Blight, *Frederick Douglass: Prophet of Freedom* (New York: Simon and Schuster, 2018), 428-437.

16 It is not the intent of this essay to provide a detailed, nuanced examination of the varying perspectives of Union soldiers on the election. For further discussion of the varying perspectives of Union soldiers and what prompted them see White, *Emancipation*, 105-116.

17 Letter from unidentified Wisconsin soldier quoted in *The Charleston Mercury*, September 14, 1864.

LITTLE MAC TRYING TO DIG HIS WAY TO THE WHITE HOUSE
BUT IS FRIGHTENED BY SPIRITUAL MANIFESTATIONS._

McClellan tries to dig his way into the White House, but Liberty opposes him because the nation regards him as a traitor. "You betrayed me. . . . You shall rise no more to any position," Liberty tells the general. *Library of Congress*

I can't vote for [McClellan] and do justice to the oath I have taken for Uncle Sam." Jeffords implored his friends and family, "for God's sake and for the sake of our country and for the sake of thousands of poor soldiers who are suffering every privation and risking their lives to save our government from shame and dishonor [to] do all you can for Old Abe."[18] Some, such as Colonel Charles Russell Lowell, who commanded a cavalry brigade in the Shenandoah Valley, committed their support to Lincoln in early August after Lincoln approved the appointment of General Philip H. Sheridan to command of the newly-established Middle Military Division, popularly known as the Army of the Shenandoah. Lowell, who was mortally wounded at the Battle of Cedar Creek as part of Sheridan's army, wrote his wife from Halltown, Virgina, "It was a lucky inspiration of Grant's or Lincoln's to

18   Charles Jeffords to Friend Barnes, November 6, 1864, Miscellaneous Civil War Letters Collection, Shenandoah University's McCormick Civil War Institute, Winchester, VA.

make a Middle Military Division and put him in command of it; it redeems Lincoln's character and secures him my vote."[19]

Sheridan's appointment to command of the Army of the Shenandoah during the first week of August illustrates that despite the president's own pessimistic outlook, Lincoln and his closest allies hoped to nullify that plank of the Democratic platform which declared Lincoln's effort "to restore the Union by the experiment of war" a "failure."[20] Aware that Union victory in the Shenandoah Valley—a region that had long been a bugbear for war planners in Washington, and a place that offered significant provender for Confederate troops operating in the Old Dominion—could greatly improve Lincoln's chances for reelection, they also understood that another defeat in the Valley could hamper Lincoln's campaign. On August 5, Secretary of War Edwin M. Stanton impressed upon Sheridan the political and military importance of the Army of the Shenandoah's task.[21] "After we left the White House," Sheridan remembered, Stanton "conversed with me freely in regard to the campaign I was expected to make, seeking to impress on me the necessity for success from the political as well as from the military point of view."[22] It became eminently clear to Sheridan that he had to fight and defeat Jubal Early's Army of the Valley, but that he should not strike Early unless he could be assured of success. Aware of the catastrophic consequences battlefield defeat could inflict on Lincoln's presidential campaign, Sheridan took a pragmatic approach. "I deemed it necessary to be very cautious; and the fact that the Presidential election was impending made be doubly so," Sheridan wrote. "The authorities at Washington having impressed upon me that the defeat of my army might be followed by the overthrow of the party

19 Charles Russell Lowell to wife, August 9, 1864, quoted in Edward Waldo Emerson, ed., *Life and Letters of Charles Russell Lowell: Captain, Sixth United States Cavalry, Colonel Second Massachusetts Cavalry, Brigadier-General, United States Volunteers* (Boston: Houghton Mifflin Company, 1907), 322.

20 Democratic Party 1864 Platform quoted in Samuel M. Schmucker, *The History of the Civil War in the United States: Its Cause, Origin, Progress and Conclusion* (Philadelphia: Jones Brothers & Co., 1865), 317.

21 Philip H. Sheridan, *Personal Memoirs of P.H. Sheridan* (New York: Charles L. Webster & Co., 1888), 1: 463.

22 Ibid., 464.

in power, which event, it was believed, would at least retard the progress of the war, if, indeed, it did not lead to the complete abandonment of coercive measures. Under circumstances such as these I could not afford to risk a disaster," Sheridan explained.[23]

While Sheridan's superiors might have initially approved of his pragmatic approach, Lincoln became impatient by the second week of September. On September 12 Lincoln sent an inquiry to Grant. "Sheridan and Early are facing each other at a dead lock. Could we not pick up a regiment here and there, to the number of say ten thousand men, and quietly, but suddenly concentrate them at Sheridan's camp and enable him to make a strike," Lincoln asked.[24] Lincoln's patience waned not only because inactivity from the largest Union force ever assembled in the Shenandoah Valley might prove nearly as detrimental as a defeat, but because Lincoln understood that elsewhere, the Union war effort had begun to turn in his favor.

Ten days before Lincoln wrote Grant, General Sherman's armies achieved what they had been trying to do since late July: they took Atlanta.[25] Sherman's success revitalized Lincoln's campaign and made moot the Democratic Party's claim that the war effort had been a "failure."[26] One impudent Lincoln supporter who wrote under the nom de plume Sir Lucius O'Trigger mocked the Democratic platform in the wake of Atlanta's fall. "General Sherman has taken Atlanta without consulting the patriotic Democratic party," O'Trigger taunted. He urged the Democrats to reassure Jefferson Davis "that they emphatically disapprove of this new measure of coercion and aggression, and pledge the entire Northern Democracy to make restitution and apology as soon as they shall get into power."[27] Lincoln-

---

23   Ibid., 499-500.

24   Basler, *Collected Works*, 548.

25   For an overview of Sherman's campaign for Atlanta see Gary Ecelbarger, *The Day Dixie Died: The Battle of Atlanta* (New York: St. Martin's Press, 2010); John F. Marszalek, *Sherman: A Soldier's Passion for Order* (New York: Free Press, 1993), 276-287; Richard M. McMurry, *Atlanta 1864: Last Chance for the Confederacy* (Lincoln: University of Nebraska Press, 2000), 113-176.

26   Stephen W. Sears, *George B. McClellan: The Young Napoleon* (New York: Ticknor and Fields, 1988), 377.

27   *The Pittsburgh Daily Commercial*, September 5, 1864.

William T. Sherman (center) finally took Atlanta in September, but in the early months of the campaign, he had been on track to capture the city much sooner. General Joseph E. Johnston, commander of the Confederate Army of Tennessee, had favored a strategy of giving up ground in order to preserve the fighting effectiveness of his army. In July 1864, officials in Richmond, distressed at the real estate Johnston had given up, replaced him with Gen. John Bell Hood, who refused to give up ground. What if Johnston had not been replaced? Would he have given up Atlanta sooner than Hood did? How would that have impacted Lincoln's reelection prospects? *Library of Congress*

friendly newspapers throughout the North celebrated Sherman's victory and believed it would help secure Lincoln a second term. "We cannot overlook the political effect of the fall of Atlanta. Lincoln's chances of reelection are improving," wrote one correspondent from Brooklyn, New York.[28] Secretary of the Navy Gideon Welles believed that Sherman's triumph, coupled with Admiral David G. Farragut's victory at Mobile Bay in early August, improved Lincoln's chances. "The success of Sherman at Atlanta, following on that of Farragut at Mobile," has very much discomposed the opposition. They had planned for a great and onward demonstration for their candidate and platform, but our . . . successes have embarrassed them exceedingly."[29] Lincoln's personal secretary John Nicolay, who chastised

28 *Times Union* (Brooklyn, NY), September 5, 1864.

those who characterized Lincoln as "a beaten man," believed that the "Atlanta victory alone ought to win the Presidential contest for us. . . . The political situation has not been as hopeful for six months past as it is just now. There is a perfect revolution in feeling . . . our friends . . . are hopeful, jubilant, hard at work and confident of success."[30] General Sherman believed that his "victory was most opportune" and that his army's "brilliant success at Atlanta . . . made the election of Mr. Lincoln certain."[31]

Sherman's capture of Atlanta unnerved Confederates, but some clung to the hope that it would not derail McClellan's chances. Walter Taylor, a member of General Robert E. Lee's staff, pondered the effect of Atlanta's fall on the northern electorate. "Some think it will impede the progress of the peace sentiment and injure the prospects of the McClellanites," he remarked. "It may, however, have the contrary effect," Taylor wrote hopefully.[32] Taylor's optimism proved somewhat naïve.

Less than three weeks after Atlanta fell, Sheridan's Army of the Shenandoah, which had been spurred into action partly as a result of Lincoln's message to Grant on September 12, began to turn the tide in the Shenandoah Valley.[33] Sheridan's victories at the Third Battle of Winchester on September 19 and at Fisher's Hill on September 22 increased momentum in Lincoln's favor.[34] As Sheridan's star rose in the wake of these twin

29 Gideon Welles, *Diary of Gideon Welles* (Boston: Houghton Mifflin Company, 1911), 2: 140.

30 John Nicolay to Theodore Tilton, September 6, 1864; John Nicolay to Therena Bates, September 11, 1864, quoted in Michael Burlingame, ed., *With Lincoln in the White House: Letters, Memoranda, and Other Writings of John G. Nicolay, 1860-1865* (Carbondale: Southern Illinois University Press, 200), 158. For further discussion of the impact of Farragut's victory at Mobile Bay see Arthur W. Bergeron, Jr., *Confederate Mobile* (Jackson: University Press of Mississippi, 1991), 138-151.

31 William T. Sherman, *Memoirs of General William T. Sherman* (New York: D. Appleton and Co., 1886), 2: 109-110.

32 Walter Herron Taylor, *General Lee: His Campaigns in Virginia, 1861-1865, with Personal Reminiscences* (Norfolk, VA: Nusbaum Book & News, 1906), 262-263.

33 For further discussion of this see Jonathan A. Noyalas, "That Woman was Worth a Whole Brigade," *Civil War Times* 52 (June 2012): 43-49.

34 For further discussion of the Third Battle of Winchester see Scott C. Patchan, *The Last Battle of Winchester: Phil Sheridan, Jubal Early, and the Shenandoah Valley Campaign, August 7-September 19, 1864* (El Dorado Hills, CA: Savas Beatie, 2013). For an examination of the Battle of Fisher's Hill see Jonathan A. Noyalas, *The Battle of Fisher's Hill: Breaking the Shenandoah Valley's Gibraltar* (Charleston, SC: History Press, 2013).

victories, newspapers piled on praise reminiscent of that received by Sherman after Atlanta. For example, Philadelphia's *Press* mused in the aftermath of Fisher's Hill that the "value of Gen. Sheridan's new victory is not to be measured by prisoners, standards, and guns. . . . It is a . . . victory for the supporters of the Union over the real foes and the false friends of the country." The *Press* believed the success on September 22 served as "a new endorsement of Abraham Lincoln, thundered in the Shenandoah Valley" and that "these grand victories inspire the nation with new ardor, and make the platform on which General McClellan stands its laughing stock."[35] General Grant believed that Sheridan's "decisive victory" at Fisher's Hill proved "the most effective campaign argument made in the canvass."[36] Several days after the battle, approximately 30,000 Lincoln supporters gathered at New York's Cooper Institute and offered a resolution that lauded Sheridan's latest tactical achievement. Cognizant of how triumph at Fisher's Hill benefited Lincoln, the resolution offered "the thanks of the nation . . . to Sheridan, who . . . fights Early . . . up the Valley of the Shenandoah 'striking and doubling up the left flank of the enemy' at Fisher's Hill . . . and apparently without a single compunction of conscience, routed the whole rebel army."[37]

Less than one month later, on October 19, 1864, the Army of the Shenandoah's come from behind victory at the Battle of Cedar Creek generated even more optimism among Lincoln and his supporters. Overjoyed, Lincoln wrote Sheridan after the battle: "With great pleasure I tender to you and your brave army the thanks of the nation." Lincoln not only celebrated Sheridan's victory at Cedar Creek, but the string of battlefield successes Sheridan's army achieved during the past month. Lincoln extended his "own personal admiration and gratitude" to Sheridan "for the month's operations in the Shenandoah Valley."[38] Two days after Cedar Creek, Lincoln supporters held a torchlight parade in the nation's capital. Republican allies utilized the event to hail Lincoln, honor Sheridan,

35 *The Press*, September 24, 1864, September 27, 1864.

36 Ulysses S. Grant, *Personal Memoirs of U.S. Grant* (New York: Charles L. Webster & Co., 1886), 2: 332.

37 *Daily Evening Bulletin*, September 28, 1864.

38 John G. Hay and John Hay, eds., *Complete Works of Abraham Lincoln* (New York: Francis D. Tandy, 1905), 10: 251.

When Confederates initially attacked at Cedar Creek, Federal commander Maj. Gen. Phil Sheridan
had been in Winchester, ten miles away. After an intense horseback ride, he arrived at Cedar Creek
as the tide of battle was turning after Confederates had paused their attack. What if Sheridan had
been on the field at the start of the battle? *Library of Congress*

and defame McClellan. A group of Lincolnites from New Jersey carried a
sizable portrait of McClellan in the parade with the words "Great Failure
of the War" emblazoned across it.[39] When the parade ended at the White
House, Lincoln's followers demanded the president offer some remarks.
Lincoln urged his supporters to not cheer for him, but instead to acclaim
the general who had so dramatically improved their mood. "I propose that
you give three hearty cheers for Sheridan," Lincoln informed the audience.[40]

Lincoln's devotees not only touted Sheridan's victory at Cedar Creek
to further destroy the Democratic Party's claim that the war had been a
"failure," but utilized the Army of the Shenandoah's recent triumph to

39   Margaret Leech, *Reveille in Washington: 1860-1865* (New York: Harper and Brothers,
1941), 351.

40   Basler, *Collected Works*, 8: 58-59.

remind undecided voters that success on the battlefield was one index of Lincoln's effectiveness as commander-in-chief. On election day the *New York Tribune*, a strong advocate of Lincoln's reelection, published Thomas Buchanan Read's poem "Sheridan's Ride."[41] The poem, "a ringing, thrilling, dramatic" depiction of Sheridan's ride from Winchester astride his horse Rienzi to Middletown's northern outskirts to turn the battle's tide, significantly elevated Sheridan's legacy and proved a useful tool for Republicans on election day.[42] While impossible to ascertain the impact Read's poem had on undecided voters, Republicans certainly believed it offered a powerful reminder of why voters should support Lincoln.[43]

Clearly, Lincoln's supporters believed Sherman's and Sheridan's victories greatly boosted Lincoln's chances for reelection, but the question remains: could Lincoln have won without them? Historian Stephen W. Sears argued in his seminal treatment of McClellan that while Atlanta, Winchester, Fisher's Hill, and Cedar Creek "effectually removed the 'failure of war' issue from the Democratic campaign," Sherman's and Sheridan's triumphs were not by themselves "necessarily fatal to the party's chances in November."[44] Other factors, including McClellan's rejection of the Democratic Platform's plank proclaiming the war a failure, worked against McClellan because it incensed Peace Democrats.[45] When McClellan formally accepted his party's nomination on September 8, he wrote from his home in Orange, New Jersey, that he "could not look in the face of my gallant comrades of the army and navy who have survived so many bloody battles, and tell them that their labors and the sacrifices of so many of our slain and wounded brethren,

---

41   John Fleischman, "The Object at Hand," *Smithsonian* 27 (Nov. 1996): 30.

42   "The Murdoch Testimonial Last Night: Tuesday, November 1, 1864," Thomas Buchanan Read Papers, Beinecke Rare Books and Manuscripts Library, Yale University, New Haven, CT. For additional discussion of Sheridan's Ride see Jonathan A. Noyalas, "'Its' Thrill will Never Die': Sheridan's Ride in War and Memory" in *"We Learned that We are Indivisible": Sesquicentennial Reflections on the Civil War Era in the Shenandoah Valley*, eds., Jonathan A. Noyalas and Nancy T. Sorrells (Newcastle upon Tyne, UK: Cambridge Scholars, 2015), 143-167.

43   Fleischman, "The Object at Hand", 30.

44   Sears, *McClellan*, 377.

45   John C. Waugh, *Lincoln and McClellan: The Troubled Partnership Between a President and His General* (New York: Palgrave, 2010), 206.

THE CHICAGO PLATFORM AND CANDIDATE.

This Currier and Ives image of "The Chicago Platform and Candidate" depicts a two-faced McClellan with various figures surrounding him, including a soldier shouting, "It's no use, General." *Library of Congress*

had been in vain; that we had abandoned the Union for which we have so often periled our lives."[46] While McClellan and his supporters, including soldiers such as the 8th Vermont's Willard Smith, who believed "Abe will loose [sic]," undoubtedly hoped McClellan's repudiation of the failure plank would garner significant support from Union soldiers; it did not.[47] Lincoln won the soldiers' vote.[48] Perhaps Captain Henry Newton Comey,

46 *Official Proceedings of the Democratic National Convention, Held in 1864 at Chicago* (Chicago: The Times Steam Book and Job Printing House, 1864), 60.

47 Willard G. Smith to Friends at Home, October 23, 1864, quoted in Jeffrey D. Marshall, ed., *A War of the People: Vermont Civil War Letters* (Hanover, NH: University Press of New England, 1999), 276.

48 White, *Emancipation*, 171. White's study challenges the conventional wisdom on the soldier vote margin secured by Lincoln. Traditionally, scholars have reported that Lincoln earned 78% of the soldier vote. White suggests that by factoring in soldiers who did not vote—by considering suppressed ballots and voter intimidation in the ranks—historians have overestimated rank and file support for the president.

2nd Massachusetts Infantry, who fought in the Shenandoah Valley in 1862 and was part of Sherman's army in 1864, most succinctly explained why McClellan failed to attract the soldiers' support. "No decent man in the army supports him [McClellan] and his former warmest friends are bitter against him . . . They do not have so much against McClellan as they have against the platform he represents and the company he keeps," Comey explained.[49]

Considering the overwhelming support Lincoln garnered among Union troops, it is hard to imagine that he would have lost it to McClellan had Sherman not taken Atlanta and Sheridan not defeated Early in the Shenandoah. Theodore Lyman, a member of General George Meade's staff, wrote five days before Sheridan's victory at Cedar Creek, "The soldiers . . . are said to show five to one for the Administration, which tells me that they identify it with the support of the war; for the troops in their private thoughts make the thrashing of the Rebs a matter of pride, as well as of patriotism."[50]

If one subscribes to the idea that Sherman's and Sheridan's successes made no substantial impact on the voting behavior of Union troops, it follows that assessing the impact of Sherman's and Sheridan's victories rests on the voters at home. Hugh McCulloch, a Hoosier who in 1865 became Lincoln's secretary of the treasury, certainly believed all that transpired on the battlefield between early September and mid-October swung the pendulum in Lincoln's favor among northern civilians. "There scarcely ever was a greater change effected in the public mind . . . the . . . successes in the field have put a new aspect on our public affairs. The rebellion is staggering under the blows," McCulloch explained to his wife.[51]

Although it is not explicitly clear that Sherman's and Sheridan's victories altered the political perspectives of Corporal James Thatcher's father and brother, something prompted the kinsmen of the New York artillerist to suddenly switch their support from McClellan to Lincoln shortly before

49   Lyman Richard Comey, ed., *A Legacy of Valor: The Memoirs and Letters of Captain Henry Newton Comey, 2nd Massachusetts Infantry* (Knoxville: University of Tennessee Press, 2004), 197.

50   George R. Agassiz, ed., *Meade's Headquarters 1863-1865: Letters of Colonel Theodore Lyman from Wilderness to Appomattox* (Boston: Atlantic Monthly Press, 1922), 245.

51   Quoted in Jennifer L. Weber, *Copperheads: The Rise and Fall of Lincoln's Opponents* (Oxford: Oxford University Press, 2006), 181-182.

election day. Less than one week before the election, Corporal Thatcher chastised his brother for supporting McClellan. "I suppose you will vote for Mc[Clellan] next Tuesday. Well that is your privilege but he don't get my vote. . . . I don't see what a man can be thinking of that will vote for him," Thatcher wrote.[52] Much to Thatcher's surprise, about two weeks after the election, he learned that his father and brother at the last moment opted to cast their ballots for Lincoln. The "conversion of our father & brother," Thatcher explained to his sister on November 20, satisfied him tremendously.[53]

Certainly, the Confederates believed Sherman's and Sheridan's triumphs bolstered Lincoln's chances for reelection. The Confederacy's supporters understood, as Jonathan W. White observed, that "battlefield victories and losses determined the outcome of the election more than anything else."[54] In the summer of 1864, when Lincoln believed his chances for reelection slim, the rebels understood the value of limiting Union military success. On March 5, 1864, months before the parties formally nominated their candidates, Confederate general James Longstreet wrote to General Alexander Lawton that if "we can break up the enemy's arrangements . . . and throw him back, he will not be able to recover his position nor his morale until the Presidential election is over, and we shall then have a new President to treat with. If Lincoln has any success . . . he will be able to get more men and may be able to secure his own re-election."[55] Edward Pollard, the editor of the *Richmond Examiner* and one of the architects of the Lost Cause, wrote bluntly "that the military successes of the two or three preceding months secured the re-election of President Lincoln on the 8th of November."[56]

There is no doubt that Lincoln confronted various obstacles during his

---

52   James Thatcher to Brother, November 2, 1864, Al MacLeod 9th NYHA Collection, Shenandoah University's McCormick Civil War Institute, Winchester, VA.

53   James Thatcher to Sister, November 20, 1864, in ibid.

54   White, *Emancipation*, 102.

55   U.S. War Department, comp., *War of the Rebellion: A Compilation of the Official Records of the Union and Confederate Armies* (Washington, D.C.: Government Printing Office, 1880-1901), ser. 1, vol. 32, pt. 3, 588. For additional discussion of this sentiment see Allen C. Guelzo, *Robert E. Lee: A Life* (New York: Knopf, 2021), 338-339.

56   Edward A. Pollard, *Southern History of the War* (New York: The Fairfax Press, 1990), 412.

bid for reelection—stalemate on the battlefield, dissension his party, and charges of overstepping the boundaries of his Constitutional authority—but McClellan confronted those obstacles, too. Chief among them was, as Stephen W. Sears noted, "the distance between" McClellan and "both his platform and his running mate," the Ohio Peace Democrat George H. Pendleton.[57] Historian Jennifer Weber concurred that the dissension between McClellan and the Democratic platform benefited Lincoln. "To be sure, the Democrats helped Lincoln enormously. With their peace plank and Copperhead nominee for vice president, the Democrats had hurt themselves irreparably," Weber concluded.[58] Richard McMurry, in his study of the Atlanta Campaign, argued that while Sherman's capture of Atlanta put "McClellan in a most ticklish situation" and Sheridan's victories "conspired against McClellan and the Democrats," a majority of Northern voters would have supported Lincoln regardless, because they "had to come to believe that slavery had caused the war, and that if the institution were not destroyed, it would lead to similar problems in the future."[59]

While one could theorize that Lincoln could have secured reelection without the capture of Atlanta and Sheridan's victories in the Shenandoah Valley, perhaps by a much closer margin in the Electoral College, there is no denying that what transpired between September 2-October 19, 1864, significantly solidified Lincoln's chances. Battlefield triumphs, as Secretary of State William Seward noted, "would cause" the "signs of discontent and faction . . . to disappear."[60] Needless to say, Sherman's capture of Atlanta made, as a correspondent for the *London Times* observed, "Mr. Lincoln's reelection possible"; the "victory gained by Gen. Sheridan . . . rendered it almost certain."[61]

---

57 Sears, *McClellan*, 374.

58 Weber, *Copperheads*, 182.

59 McMurry, *Atlanta 1864*, 180.

60 William H. Seward to Home, August 16, 1864, quoted in Frederick W. Seward, *Seward at Washington as Senator and Secretary of State: A Memoir of His Life, With Selections from His Letters 1861-1872* (New York: Derby and Miller, 1891), 240.

61 Observation from *London Times* quoted in *The Liberator*, November 4, 1864.

CHAPTER ELEVEN

What If Robert E. Lee

Had Waged a Guerrilla War with His Army of Northern Virginia in April 1865?

Barton A. Myers

Just after sunrise on Palm Sunday, April 9, 1865, Brig. Gen. Edward Porter Alexander, a zealous and highly proficient young artillery commander in the Army of Northern Virginia, was two miles away from Appomattox Court House, Virginia when he encountered Gen. Robert E. Lee. Sitting on an oak log, Lee discussed the strategic situation facing his army with the young artillerist. With only two infantry divisions (Charles Field's and William Mahone's) in fighting condition and the route of retreat blocked by Maj. Gen. Philip Sheridan's Union cavalry, Lee was left with a desperate decision. The story of what actually happened is well known. Robert E. Lee elected to surrender his remaining force to the Army of the Potomac and Lt. Gen. Ulysses S. Grant. On that morning, however, Alexander was emotional and understandably angry. The Confederacy's most successful army, and with it, its political survival, was on the edge of defeat. In his memoir, the artillerist described how he proposed to his commander a different strategic course than the one Lee ultimately chose.[1]

Alexander considered several paths for himself in his own mind: escape to Brazil, link up with Confederate Gen. Joseph E. Johnston's Army of Tennessee, and options for a continued military struggle. He ultimately proposed, hypothetically to Lee, that if the Confederate army did not

---

1 Gary W. Gallagher ed., *Fighting for the Confederacy: The Personal Recollections of General Edward Porter Alexander* (Chapel Hill: Univ. of North Carolina Press, 1989), 530-533.

This CDV of Robert E. Lee wearing a presentation sword comes from an 1864 sitting with photographer Julian Vannerson. The signature is real. Lee has been called "The Marble Man" because of the reverence with which his partisans viewed him during the war and since. That view allowed Lee to successfully lead his men into a peaceful surrender at Appomattox, but unfortunately, it later helped fuel Lost Cause mythology. What if his admirers had taken a more realistic view of him over the years? How might that have impacted the overall way we understand the Civil War? *Washington and Lee University Special Collections*

surrender it might "be ordered to scatter in the woods & bushes & either to rally upon Gen. Johnston in North Carolina, or to make their way, each man to his own state, with his arms & to report to his governor." In response, Lee diagnosed the strategic situation facing his army quickly and clearly, arguing that there were only about 15,000 men with muskets and that even if 10,000 got away "their numbers would be too insignificant to accomplish the least good." Lee did not believe foreign military aid would be forthcoming, and he believed few of the men would go to Johnston, even if ordered. To Alexander, he clearly asserted that the Confederacy had "failed." Furthermore, Lee believed that if the soldiers were ordered to go to their homes by dispersal, "The men would have no rations & they would be under no discipline. . . . They would have to plunder and rob to procure subsistence. The country would be full of lawless bands in every part, & a state of society would ensue from which it would take the country years to recover." "Then," Lee continued, "the enemy's cavalry would pursue in the hopes of catching the principal officers, & wherever they went there would be fresh rapine & destruction." He then explained to a visibly agitated Alexander his last major strategic military decision. "And as for myself, while you young men might afford to go bushwhacking, the only proper & dignified course for me would be to surrender myself & take the consequences of my actions." The Confederacy's general-in-chief then outlined his hope that once he surrendered the Army of Northern Virginia to Grant later that morning, the men of the army would be able to return home unmolested in order to plant crops and "begin to repair the ravages of war." Lee summed up by arguing that he believed that Grant would offer "honorable terms" not "unconditional surrender," a comment meant to ease Alexander's worst fears.[2]

General Robert E. Lee's rejection of his subordinate's alternative military strategy hinged on the negative impact of Alexander's "bushwhacking" alternative for the Confederate civilian population. Lee, ultimately, chose an end to the Army of Northern Virginia as a fighting force and not a conversion of that force into small bands of irregulars, one that was a critical message to the Confederate population about the end of the struggle for an independent nation-state. And, though Alexander's alternative military plan was far from being a fully developed strategy for an insurgency, Lee certainly understood his suggestion as the use of widespread guerrilla warfare to "delay" and continue the military struggle. This conversation has been the root of much historical and pop-historical speculation on the question of an 1865 "guerrilla option" for the Confederacy or for Lee's Army, specifically.[3] This essay offers some insight into the possibilities of what might have happened if Lee had chosen a different path that April, but it more importantly clearly explains why he did not choose this strategy rooted in his own history and the Confederate experience with using irregular warfare. As a result, it briefly explores the internal problems with the Confederate military and government's use of guerrilla warfare and irregular tactics as part of its own overall strategy to win independence between 1861 and 1865. It also offers an overview of Lee's views on the use of guerrillas, partisan rangers, raiding regular cavalry, and irregular war as a strategy during the American Civil War.[4]

First, it is worth carefully considering the immediate military situation facing the Army of Northern Virginia, if it had chosen Alexander's potential path that fateful morning in April 1865. The enemy also gets a vote in

2 Ibid., 532-533.

3 Ibid., 532.

4 On definitions related to irregular warfare during the American Civil War, see "Guerrilla Warfare's Place in the History of the American Civil War," in Brian D. McKnight and Barton A. Myers, *The Guerrilla Hunters: Irregular Conflicts during the American Civil War* (Baton Rouge: Louisiana State Univ. Press, 2017),

war. In this case, Lee's enemy was a confident and determined Ohioan named Ulysses S. Grant, the industrial machine and logistical proficiency orchestrated by the Georgia-born U.S. Army Quartermaster General Montgomery Meigs, and the significant white manpower advantage of the loyal Border South and Northern states, augmented by large numbers of newly recruited United States Colored Troops. In an occupation and counter-irregular effort, those would also have been advantages in defeating irregular forces. Five years later, Grant successfully selected commanders during his U.S. Presidency that virtually eradicated Ku Klux Klan activity in South Carolina in the early 1870s, an indication of how he might have handled an immediate guerrilla-converted A.N.V. threat. Grant and the Union army truly despised the successful partisan leaders like Virginia's John Singleton Mosby, commander of the Forty-third Battalion of Virginia Cavalry, an authorized partisan ranger command. For Grant, the possibility of northern Virginia and the Shenandoah Valley's guerrilla conflict proliferating further would have fueled his collective efforts to counter the Confederate military, knowing there were more potential Gray Ghosts on the loose. Furthermore, Mosby himself might have continued his own effort as opposed to disbanding his unit as he actually did in 1865 following news of Lee's surrender at Appomattox. Mosby never formally surrendered his unit to the Union Army.[5]

When the challenges of guerrilla warfare emerged for Grant during the war in Tennessee and Virginia, he chose a determined and consistent, hard-war military policy. In the eastern theater, Grant had selected Philip Sheridan to address the problems of Virginia's guerrillas in late 1864 and early 1865. And, it is necessary to keep in mind, Phillip Sheridan's cavalry, with generals George Custer and Wesley Merritt as brigade commanders, were the lead pursuing elements of Lee's retreating force. The most mobile, adept Union anti-guerrilla force was already on the scene for the surrender, and Sheridan had a wealth of experience in facing partisan tactics and warfare in a civilian context in Virginia the previous fall. Given Sheridan's stern stance at Appomattox on the 9th of April, it would have clearly led to greater loss of life for recalcitrant Confederate soldiers or "die-hard rebels" who were

---

5   Russell F. Weigley, *Quartermaster General of the Union Army: A Biography of M.C. Meigs* (New York: Columbia Univ. Press, 1959); Ron Chernow, *Grant* (New York: Penguin Press, 2017).

captured or attempted to continue as "bushwhackers."[6] Nevertheless, if we speculate on Alexander's suggestion that two-thirds of the A.N.V. might get away, it is worth considering what a wider dispersal of this size/number of troops would have resulted in at that point. Here it is also worth noting Phillip Sheridan's success after the war as a highly efficient prosecutor of numerous wars against Native Americans using mobile tactics of hit-and-run in the American West.[7]

Lee pointed his army's retreat toward Lynchburg and the Blue Ridge mountains during the Appomattox Campaign. If any portion of the army had made it to the mountains and over into the Shenandoah Valley, it might have been possible for them to have linked up with smaller groups like John S. Mosby's. Mosby's military organization had grown considerably by the end of the war. He was a magnet for more and more men from the home front that were melting away from the regular army or convalescing from battle wounds and illness.[8] An A.N.V.-sponsored guerrilla strategy would have been, as Lee suggested to Alexander, an expensive endeavor for the population of the Confederacy in both blood and treasure. A region that was stripped of supplies by Union Army military operations in fall 1864 would have been difficult to find food supplies in spring 1865, and further Union Army counter-irregular operations would have again targeted the population's homes, civilians, and barns in order to root out the resisting Confederates.[9]

Lee made two critical strategic decisions that April. First, he decided to surrender the A.N.V., the most successful Confederate fighting force and, second, he decided to not endorse an irregular war strategy personally. His example was ignored by some in the years following Appomattox, but it was listened to by most of his officers in the days immediately following the surrender of the Army of Northern Virginia. That is a critical point for

---

6   Jason Phillips, *Diehard Rebels: The Confederate Culture of Invincibility* (Athens: Univ. of Georgia Press, 2010).

7   *Fighting for the Confederacy*, 537; Roy Morris, Jr., *Sheridan: The Life and Wars Of General Phil Sheridan* (New York: Crown, 1992).

8   James A. Ramage, *Gray Ghost: The Life of Col. John Singleton Mosby* (Lexington, KY: Univ. Press of Kentucky, 1999).

9   *Fighting for the Confederacy*, 532-533.

Robert E. Lee (right) gathered with his commanders, including James Longstreet, Fitzhugh Lee, and John Brown Gordon, for a final council of war on the evening of April 8, 1865. What if corps commanders Richard Ewell and/or Richard Anderson—and the men they commanded who were captured days earlier at Sailors Creek—were still available to Lee at Appomattox? *ECW collection*

understanding the end of the regular Confederate conventional military effort in 1865.

In February 1865, Confederate President Jefferson Davis gave a speech in Richmond promoting the use of mobile warfare to continue the fight.[10] Davis and Robert E. Lee's actions on the topic of irregular warfare and Confederate strategy in 1865 can also be examined in light of Davis's 4 April 1865 speech, after Lee's army retreated from Richmond. It was a moment where the Confederate President advocated for a "new phase" of Confederate strategy, but scholars have debated the speech's meaning. In the most relevant section of his proclamation, Davis wrote that the Confederate forces in the field were now "Relieved from the necessity of guarding cities and particular points, important but not vital to our defence with our army free to move from point to point, and strike in detail the detachments and garrisons of the enemy." "Operating in the interior of our own country," Davis hoped that, "where supplies are more accessible, and

---

10 William B. Feis, "Jefferson Davis and the "Guerrilla Option": A Reexamination," Brooks D. Simpson and Mark Grimsely, eds., *The Collapse of the Confederacy* (Lincoln, NB: Univ. of Nebraska Press, 2001), 104-127.

where the foe will be far removed from his own base, cut off from all succor in case of reverse, nothing is now needed to render our triumph certain, but the exhibition of our own unquenchable resolve. Let us but will it, and we are free." At this point, Davis was striking the most optimistic tone in the context of a desperate military situation.[11]

What Davis almost certainly envisioned was a more mobile version of Lee's Army of Northern Virginia fighting in the interior of the South, not defending a city in a siege or raiding *en masse* into the Northern and Border South states, as his army had done when it invaded Maryland in 1862 and Pennsylvania in 1863.[12] This was an advocacy of Gen. George Washington and Nathaniel Greene's Fabian strategy during the American War for Independence, which relied upon battle avoidance, delay, and occasional battle framed toward pyrrhic British battle victories.[13] Davis and Lee both knew that the Army of Northern Virginia had repeatedly tried to lure U.S. Grant's and George Meade's Army of the Potomac into a trap during the Overland Campaign in 1864, but Lee's army remained prisoner to defending both Richmond and the long supply line/railroad network at Petersburg, Virginia. The "new phase" was freedom from that strategic prison. In hindsight, what Lee was attempting to do as

---

11   Jefferson Davis, 4 April 1865, *The War of the Rebellion: A Compilation of the Official Records of the Union and Confederate Armies* (Washington: Government Printing Office, 1894), ser. 1, vol. 46, 1382-1383.

12   Scholar William B. Feis in an excellent piece on the proclamation's meaning also argues convincingly that Davis's proclamation was not an advocacy of a disbanded guerrilla strategy in 1865 but one of a mobile, conventional army freed of protecting cities. Emory M. Thomas, *Robert E. Lee: A Biography* (New York: W.W. Norton, 1995), 362-363 and William C. Davis, *An Honorable Defeat: The Last Days of the Confederate Government* (New York: Harcourt, Inc., 2001), 78-82 have taken a more traditional view that the Davis speech did advocate for a guerrilla strategy. American Civil War scholars writing in the post-Vietnam era often used the phrase "guerrilla strategy" fairly broadly and uncritically to represent mobile armies like Ho Chi Minh's fighting in the countryside. Davis and Thomas use the term in this sense. William C. Davis argues that Jefferson Davis's very general speech would have inevitably led to a small unit guerrilla strategy as an outcoming. Nevertheless, there is a clear distinction between Washington's army in the Revolution's later phase (mobile, conventional force engaged in a war of delay), uncontrolled guerrilla bands in the American Civil War, and the combination of both small unit warfare and large mobile units in the Vietnam War. Without careful explanation of terminology, nuance with examples, discussion of the strategic practices, it is a scholarly conversation that quickly becomes opaque.

13   Joseph Ellis, *His Excellency: George Washington* (New York: Alfred A. Knopf, 2004). For a fuller analysis of George Washington's understanding of military strategy specifically on the topics of *grande* and *petite guerre* (small war), see John W. Hall, "An Irregular Reconsideration of George Washington and the American Military Tradition," *The Journal of Military History*, vol. 78, no. 3, 961-993.

he retreated and pointed his army toward the mountains in Virginia was precisely that, an army unencumbered by protecting Jominian strategic points on a map (*guerre de poste*) and one free to engage in a war of delay. Lee's rejection of Alexander's proposal was a rejection of guerrilla bands and division of his army as a viable strategy for winning independence in 1865. What Davis's proclamation did not advocate was a small-unit dispersal of troops into guerrilla bands (like Missouri and Arkansas's internal civil war of incessantly proliferating bushwhackers) or even a people's uprising like the one promoted by Gen. John Hunt Morgan in Kentucky during the Civil War. After all, neither Davis nor Lee in that final week even mentioned the Confederacy's twenty-two month long experiment with the partisan ranger military policy that had sanctioned controlled units using irregular tactics to augment the regular, conventional army struggle.[14]

The Confederacy's tortured history with localized guerrilla warfare and the use of authorized partisan rangers as military policy, an experiment that, despite some notable, tactical successes, ultimately failed strategically between 1862 and 1864, also illuminates the 1865 decision by both Lee and the Confederate government's senior leadership to not choose further diffuse guerrilla conflict by converting its conventional forces. By dispersing the manpower of the Confederate armies into small units, control by the planter-elite would have been weakened considerably, and in all likelihood, ceded completely to charismatic guerrilla band leaders who may or may not have been successful practitioners at a time when even the most ethical partisan rangers like John Mosby were suspect in the eyes of Union Army commanders like Phil Sheridan and U. S. Grant. This loss of elite control over the poor whites and yeomen fighters of the South that made up the Confederate armies in 1865 was not something senior leaders would have been willing to accept or inflict on the white Southern population, especially in the midst of a crumbling slave-based society. A final dimension to this issue was the emergence of slaves as both informants and counter-irregulars during the war. This element of the population already played an important role in directing Union Army forces toward disloyal Confederates during

---

14 *Official Records*, ser. 1, vol. 46, 1382-1383; James A. Ramage, *Rebel Raider: The Life of General John Hunt Morgan* (Lexington, KY: Univ. Press of Kentucky, 1986).

military occupation between 1861 and 1865. This would have only grown in importance.[15]

What Americans ultimately witnessed during the post-Appomattox military occupation of the former Confederate states by the U.S. Army would have almost certainly been even worse if Lee had promoted or encouraged continued violent struggle in any form, including using the tactics and strategy of irregular warfare with his symbolically powerful Army of Northern Virginia.[16] With Lee's forces continuing a struggle in the eastern theater, the post-1865 irregular conflicts of the American South would have ramped up in earnest and in violence chronologically sooner. It is also possible that the punitive efforts of the Union Army would have been more extreme and the number of extra-legal and legal executions in the field by Union officers would have increased. It would have almost certainly led to more trials for murder among Confederates than what actually occurred in 1865-1866. Irregular wars have heightened animosity and deepened bitterness. This is not to say there was not bitterness already, there certainly was a great deal of anger and violence that continued, but it would have made the process of white Northern and Southern reconciliation and healing even more difficult for the country, perhaps lasting decades longer than what the period of reconciliation did. Scholar Aaron Sheehan-Dean has recently argued in his *The Calculus of Violence* that, as bad as the American Civil War's death toll was, it could have been even worse given comparative historical examples. A promotion of continued struggle personally by Lee, even if it was militarily unsuccessful for Lee's army from a strategic standpoint, would have deepened animosity and likely led to protracted violence in an even greater way following 1865. If that had happened, the United States as a country restored whole—with functioning freely elected governments representing newly enfranchised African Americans—could

---

15　Daniel E. Sutherland, *A Savage Conflict: The Decisive Role of Guerrillas in the American Civil War* (Chapel Hill: Univ. of North Carolina Press, 2009), includes a deep analysis of guerrillas and their use throughout the war.

16　Scholars who have argued that the war and violence of the American Civil War continued post-Appomattox surrender include Gregory P. Downs, *After Appomattox: Military Occupation and the Ends of War* (Cambridge, MA: Harvard Univ. Press, 2015); Dan T. Carter, *When the War Was Over: The Failure of Self-Reconstruction in the South* (Baton Rouge: Louisiana State Univ. Press, 1985), 6-23; George C. Rable, *But There Was No Peace: The Role of Violence in the Politics of Reconstruction* (Athens, GA: Univ. of Georgia Press, 1984), 1-15; "The Myth of the 'Great' Conventional Battlefield War," in Wesley Moody, ed., *Seven Myths of the Civil War* (Indianapolis, IN: Hackett Publishing, Inc., 2017), 75-102.

have taken decades longer. This continued violence and hatred might have weakened the country going into the twentieth century, and even on the eve of World War I, it could have left bitterness that might have allowed for European powers to have inflamed those feelings on the American home front and weakened the American war effort in World War I.[17]

Historical experiences with insurgencies and irregular wars offer some lessons for what have constituted both successful and unsuccessful struggles using irregular strategies and tactics. To be effective, guerrilla warriors require a strong, domestic civilian supply line and/or an external support system from a foreign state. The Confederate population might have provided this in 1861. Yet, it was drained from four years of internecine civil war by 1865. This made the prospect of a guerrilla resistance against the North far less viable by April 1865. Foreign support from Europe was not a viable option either at this point. There would be no new French military alliance nor Dutch financial lifeline for the Confederacy in 1865 as there had been for the Patriots during the War for Independence. Neither Mexico or Canada were places for military supply or support in 1865 either. Though many ex-Confederates ended up fleeing to Mexico and Latin America at the end of the Civil War, these states were not anxious to invade in 1865 to support the Confederate nation-state, which sought to protect the institution of slavery and which faced an awakening industrial and manpower behemoth in the form of the Union Army.[18]

The wrongheaded notion that guerrilla warfare won the American Revolution has also led some readers to believe that Lee's Army of Northern Virginia might have won with a guerrilla strategy. This idea ignores and overlooks a huge amount of American Civil War history and literature on guerrilla warfare and the Confederacy's experimentation with it during the 1861-1864 period. Romantic visions of the American Revolution's irregular leaders in Virginia and South Carolina, who were fighting in their own interior (with a civilian population roughly eighty percent in support of the Patriot effort) and facing a British army focused on a traditional European conventional war strategy for most of the war, were not an apt comparison

---

17 Aaron Sheehan-Dean, *The Calculus of Violence: How Americans Fought the Civil War* (Cambridge, MA: Harvard Univ. Press, 2018).

18 On domestic and foreign support during the course of irregular wars, see Anthony James Joes, *America and Guerrilla Warfare* (Lexington, KY: Univ. of Kentucky Press, 2000); Brian McCallister Linn, *The Philippine War, 1899-1902* (Lawrence, KS: Univ. Press of Kansas, 2000).

to the Confederate strategic situation in April 1865. By April 1865, too few healthy Confederate soldiers remained to launch a successful War for Independence-inspired Fabian strategy like the regular armies of George Washington or Nathaniel Greene coupled with the more diffuse continuation of the irregular war strategy of Francis Marion or Charles Sumter. Simply put, a Confederate irregular strategy in 1865 would not have worked for securing an independent nation-state without a conventional army operating alongside highly proficient guerrilla leaders and commands. The enslaved population had grown considerably in the American South by 1865 from where it was in 1775-1783. Roughly 600,000 enslaved people lived in the American South during the War for Independence whereas that number was roughly 4 million in 1861-1865. The British recognized this weakness in 1775 with Lord Dunmore's Proclamation and the Abraham Lincoln government recognized in it 1862 with the preliminary Emancipation Proclamation. Both were fundamentally strategic military moves meant to weaken the respective rebellions.[19]

It is also worth briefly examining Gen. Robert E. Lee's historical experience with guerrilla warfare during his own life and military career. As commander of Lee's Legion, Robert E. Lee's father, Maj. Gen. Henry Lee III ,also known by his *nom de guerre* "Light-Horse" Harry, was a principal practitioner of partisan warfare during the War for Independence. Lee's father, a presence of absence in his life, may have provided yet another reason to avoid the use of these tactics of hit-and-run during the Civil War. Lee's father's example in life was a proud one from a purely military perspective but not from the standpoint of personal conduct, landing in debtors' prison in later life. So, it is possible that Lee sought the "West Point way" of conventional, regular warfare strategy and tactics in his own career, in some small way for this reason. He wanted to distance himself from his father's complicated legacy. Indeed, Virginia partisan ranger John Singleton Mosby seemed to think that Lee's own father was one reason he took an initial interest in meeting Mosby himself. Mosby speculated in his

---

19   John Oller, *The Swamp Fox: How Francis Marion Saved the American Revolution* (Boston, MA: Da Capo Press, 2016); Ryan Cole, *Light-Horse Harry Lee: The Rise and Fall of a Revolutionary Hero* (Washington, DC: Regnery History, 2019); Ricardo A. Herrera, "The Zealous Activity of Capt. Lee': Light-Horse Harry Lee and *Petite Guerre*," *The Journal of Military History*, vol. 79, no. 1, 9-36.

Lee's wartime experience with cavalry was more along the traditional lines of Jeb Stuart (left) than the guerilla style of John Singleton Mosby (right). What if Mosby had been able to advise Lee in those final hours of the Army of Northern Virginia's existence—what kind of counsel might he have offered? *Library of Congress/Library of Congress*

own memoir on this issue. Lee's direct interaction and role in protecting the Confederacy's most famous partisan ranger began in August of 1862. According to Mosby, he brought Lee the intelligence about Union Maj. Gen. Ambrose Burnside supporting the army of John Pope in Virginia. Mosby recounted in his *Memoirs* how Lee "took deep interest in my operations, for there was nothing of the Fabius in his character. Lee was the most aggressive man I met in the war, and was always ready for an enterprise. I believe that his interest in me was largely due to the fact that his father, "Light-Horse Harry," was a partisan officer in the Revolutionary War."[20]

20   John S. Mosby, *Mosby's Memoirs: The Memoirs of Colonel John Singleton Mosby* (New York: Barnes & Noble, 2006), 236-237; In his 1917 posthumously published *Memoirs*, Mosby referred in this passage to Quintus Fabius Maximus Verrucosus, a Roman statesman general known for his use of delaying tactics and guerrilla warfare. He deployed these tactics versus Hannibal's forces during the Second Punic War in the third century B.C.

Mosby encountered Lee three times during the Petersburg Campaign and was wounded just prior to two of those occasions. After introducing Mosby to Lt. Gen. James Longstreet, Lee said to Mosby: "Colonel, the only fault I have ever had to find with you is that you are always getting wounded." Mosby found the comments endearing and clearly admired the Old Grey Fox and his audacity. "Such a speech from General Lee," Mosby remembered "more than repaid me for my wound." It is clear that the admiration and respect was mutual between Lee and Mosby. The last official order Lee ever sent to Mosby during the Civil War reflected this trust. "Collect your command and watch the country from the front of Gordonsville to Blue Ridge, and also the Valley. Your command is all now in that section, and the general (Lee) will rely on you to watch and protect the country. If any of your command is in Northern Neck, call it to you. W.H. Taylor. Assistant Adjutant General." Mosby recalled that the last words Lee ever said to him, spoken by one of the most aggressive fighters in the old Confederate army, were "Colonel, I hope we shall have no more wars." These words, Lee spoke only about two months before his death in October of 1870, a time when Ku Klux Klan violence had taken hold at the county and regional level in many parts of the American South.[21]

During the American Civil War, Robert E. Lee's interest in irregular warfare and partisan corps remained restrained to the tactical deployment of these type of units by exceptional officers in the field. He even encouraged Mosby to use "Mosby's Regulars" as an official name for his unit. But, supply interdiction/capture and scouting/information reconnaissance was primarily how Lee used and wanted Mosby to use his time. Raiding was a by-product of that supply capture, interdiction, and disruption mission in 1863-64 in northern Virginia and the Shenandoah Valley. But he was not promoting a "people's war" as Virginia Governor John Letcher attempted to encourage in the Shenandoah Valley in 1864. There was a distinction between Lee and Letcher. A strategy of guerrilla warfare simply made no sense to Lee, who understood the severe manpower and resource issues under which the Confederate army operated. Lee was an excellent judge of superlative military officers. He frequently juggled men in the Army of Northern Virginia to ensure they would be more successful at a particular

21 *Mosby's Memoirs*, 236-240.

level of command. Lee recognized at the tactical level that Mosby ranked among the small group of officers who had the skills for independent command using the full range of *petite guerre*. Lee recognized, perhaps because of his own father and his experiences during the U.S. War with Mexico, that this was not a common set of characteristics for an officer. Yet, Lee also understood the manpower deficiencies of the Confederate army and guerrilla warfare as "people's war" threatened that mission by drawing off men needed for his own conventional army. The discipline of these units also made them difficult to control in the field. These were the primary reasons why Lee encouraged the Confederate Congress to repeal the Partisan Ranger Act, which it did in February 1864 after only twenty-two months in effect. The units spared conversion were retained at Lee's suggestion by the Confederate War Department.[22]

During Lee's service during the U.S. War with Mexico in the 1840s, Gen. Winfield Scott's American army experienced first-hand the impact of guerrillas on a war. The use of guerrilla warfare by both sides in this conflict included Texas and Arkansas volunteers who committed atrocities in response to Mexican *guerrillero* attacks. The U.S. Army experience in Mexico was just one additional deterrent in Lee's own personal military history pointing away from deploying a guerrilla strategy in 1865.[23] It was the consistent position for Lee to discourage a widespread guerrilla strategy as part of Confederate overall military strategy. Lee did not advocate the broader "people's war" approach of men like John Hunt Morgan in Kentucky. His strategy was focused on winning the war through a campaign of major battle engagements to destroy the regular, conventional U.S. Army in the eastern theater in the vicinity of Washington, D. C., and Richmond, Virginia. Furthermore, the options for protraction were limited for Confederates because of the absence of a geographically close, friendly enclave state to operate guerrilla bases out of and restore forces seasonally. The guerrilla conflicts did rage in a large number of counties in the South in 1865 and this was further evidence to Lee of the problems of under-directed and ungovernable irregulars. He saw them as a manpower drain but also as

---

22   Ryan Cole, *Light-Horse Harry: The Rise and Fall of a Revolutionary Hero* (Washington, DC: Regnery History, 2019).

23   Peter Guardino, *The Dead March: A History of the Mexican-American War* (Cambridge, MA: Harvard Univ. Press, 2017), 123-202.

Western cavalrymen Nathan Bedford Forrest and John Hunt Morgan were both highly adept at irregular warfare, but by 1865, Morgan was dead and Forrest would disband his men peaceably, urging them to "submit to the powers to be, and to aid in restoring peace and establishing law and order throughout the land." Later, as Grand Wizard of the Ku Klux Klan, Forrest seemed to defy that very admonition. What if Forrest had followed his own advice? *Library of Congress/Library of Congress*

a problem to the Confederacy's white population, leading to social chaos and the destruction of slavery and more generally the southern race-state.[24]

Since he had ample evidence of what type of irregular war strategy was dangerous and what type of irregular units tactically worked in conjunction with his large, conventional Army of Northern Virginia, it is not surprising that Lee made the strategic decision not to convert the limited number of his troops healthy in April 1865 into a "guerrilla army." Nonetheless, many men from that army and others of the Confederacy would continue to use terrorism and irregular tactics as part of white paramilitary organizations during Reconstruction. This continued the state of war at a lower but still significant level of violence through the ultimate military defeat of the Ku Klux Klan by the U.S. Grant administration, U.S. Justice Department, and the U.S. Army in the early 1870s. Lee was opposed to this continued violence,

24   James A. Ramage, *Rebel Raider: The Life of Gen. John Hunt Morgan* (Lexington, KY: Univ. Press of Kentucky, 1995).

and he was not involved in the military direction of this effort following his personal surrender in April 1865. He did not participate in this activity and eschewed further violence in favor of pursuing the administration of a small college in the final five years of his life. This is a profession he had executed capably as superintendent of the U.S. Military Academy at West Point in the 1850s.[25]

Union Army counter-irregular efforts were becoming more sophisticated and more aggressive by 1865. The Union cavalry, which shouldered this responsibility for most of the war, was a much-improved arm by that point, and it included many bright minds, e.g., Sheridan, Custer, etc. With many of the Confederacy's best cavalry commanders dead or captured by Appomattox, even if the access to horses would have been possible, it would have been difficult to wage an immediate, successful resistance. Lee also recognized this problem in his mentioning the need to live off the population and the potential violence that Union counter-irregular efforts would bring to the public.

In the months following Appomattox, Lee did sit for an interview with a *New York Herald* journalist where he discussed the ongoing military situation of the South and the political situation of Reconstruction. Within that he did suggest that there were still reserves of strength in the old Confederacy. He may have been suggesting the leadership like John Gordon who remained alive, but he does use the word "protracted" to describe the possibility of a resumed military effort. The conditional nature of Appomattox was essentially at the base of Lee's comments.[26]

In many ways the Confederacy lacked a great "guerrilla strategist" at the very top echelon of its high command structure at the beginning of the war. It had many skilled guerrilla practitioners at the tactical level (captains, colonels, and the occasional brigadier general) that aided its military effort through raids, incursions, ambushes, and supply interdictions. Confederates often pursued the opportunistic raid both successfully and unsuccessfully. Lieutenant General Nathan Bedford Forrest, who eventually became the first Grand Wizard of the Ku Klux Klan, was the highest-ranking officer among the adept practitioners of irregular tactics/mobile warfare by 1865. But, the

---

25   Ron Chernow, *Grant* (New York: Penguin Press, 2017), 701-712.

26   Elizabeth R. Varon, *Appomattox: Victory, Defeat, and Freedom at the End of the Civil War* (New York: Oxford Univ. Press, 2014).

overall Confederate military strategy of irregular war used by Confederates was pursued in a very haphazard manner with little overall direction from the top of the Confederate high command. The very nature of how irregulars were used (with occasional high-profile successes) has almost certainly led to the speculation that a wide use and better direction from Lee or someone else at the top of the command structure would have led to a different outcome for the war in 1865. Given the specific historical situation of the Confederacy which had the internal military weakness of slavery as an institution, it is unlikely that the use of "guerrillas" alone would have been a successful way to wage a war for Southern Confederate independence. For the Confederacy to have any real chance at permanently establishing the nation-state it sought, it was necessary to have at least one major regular army in the field as a symbol of nationalism, a rallying point, and which offered legitimacy on the international stage. A solely irregular warfare strategy would have in either 1861 or 1865 threatened the permanency of plantation-based slavery itself by causing enormous disruption internally. The use of these tactics during Reconstruction were often directed at the African American population as well as white Republicans and the U.S. Army and Freedmen's Bureau agents, but they were used primarily as a method of control and instilling fear and political terrorism. So, the direction of the Reconstruction violence was toward a different goal of home rule and control of locality as opposed to a U.S. army that was much larger and actively engaged in destroying Confederate forces of all types in the field to end an independence struggle. In other words, the use of the violence had a more modest military goal of local destabilization to reestablish a racial *status quo antebellum* over the possibility of winning a separate, independent nation-state, which required defeating the Union Army prior to its massive demobilization in 1865.[27]

For the sake of exploring contingency, however, if Lee had executed E.P. Alexander's strategic idea and 10,000 Confederates did manage to reconstitute themselves as small irregular bands loosely coordinated by Lee, it would have been difficult to centrally coordinate this plan for very long given the limitations of communications technology in the mid-

---

27 Brian Steel Wills, "Nathan Bedford Forrest and Guerrilla War" in McKnight and Myers eds. *The Guerrilla Hunters*, 52-76.

nineteenth century. It would have required civilian support for supply, food, intelligence, and communication between forces secretly. All of these issues would have drawn women and children directly into the violence of the war at a new level of suspicion and likely persecution. What scholars have already written about the impact of guerrilla conflict during the American Civil War upon the civilian population points to an even bleaker war of harsh survival, atrocity, and famine.

It is difficult to imagine a scenario within the realm of real possibility that a converted guerrilla army of 10,000 troops deployed at the late stage of the Civil War in April 1865 would have been successful at garnering an independent nation-state for Confederates. There were simply too many obstacles by April 1865 for this few irregulars to be successful at achieving the goal of Confederate independence. The fiction author and master of the so-called alternative-history literary genre, Harry Turtledove, posited at the base of his classic fantasy work *Guns of the South* that Confederates could have been victorious with the aid of AK-47s in 1865. With that few troops and resources, it truly would have been necessary for something that fantastical and science fiction oriented to occur in order for guerrilla warfare to have been a successful strategy by that late point in the war. The Union war effort had finally assembled a crack team of determined generals to execute an end game strategy backed by a logistical juggernaut. It would have also taken a completely different strategic mindset from its highest-ranking military officers who sought an end to the war through conventional military campaigns, even at that late date.[28]

But, for the sake of conjecture, if Lee's 10,000-man collection of guerrilla bands did actually deploy to harass Grant and Sheridan in the east, it may have taken some considerable time to round up all of the warriors tucked into rural counties in the Virginia southwest, which was ideal country for hiding. That small war could have gone on like the Hatfield and McCoy feud for years, but with little hope of securing Confederate independence. General Joe Johnston was also no great supporter of partisan warfare or guerrilla bands coming out of his experience in the Seminole War in Florida or the Mexican-American War. He also would have assuredly rejected this type of proposal.

---

28 Harry Turtledove, *Guns of the South* (New York: Random House, 1992).

If Lee's own health were better, his historical life experience had been different, his education at West Point had not happened, and his keen strategic mind were applied not to conventional regular armies but to a "guerrilla strategy"—and those are many, many "ifs" and counterfactuals—then as a younger man Lee might have had some timely success in the role that John Mosby and John McNeill served as a partisan company or regiment leader at the tactical level. But, this would have only been an augment to the Confederacy's regular army effort. The conversion of that regular army to a diffuse force led by many commanders would have meant a split-second assessment by Lee of his remaining company, regiment, and brigade leaders. During the course of the American Civil War, Lee had an excellent eye for officers and able commanders in their respective roles; he juggled them throughout commands despite the enormous difficulties of attrition in battle. Given time, he might have assessed the best for leadership of perhaps twenty groups of fifty soldiers that could have been sent toward the mountains of the Shenandoah Valley and toward North Carolina's Appalachian region to continue the conflict. This would have only increased the level of violence from the existing county-level guerrilla wars in those regions.[29] Increased bloodshed added to the estimated 750,000 already dead, an even more difficult reconciliation, and harsher punishment for those who were found guilty of treason would have followed a converted war to a broader guerrilla strategy with Lee's Army of Northern Virginia. We know this because it had happened during the war in many places. We have the scholarly evidence for it occurring over and over again at the county level. We also see what happened to men like Tennessee guerrilla Champion Ferguson, who participated in this activity and was tried for war crimes in 1865. This led to his execution.[30]

Even if Lee had given the order to wage a "bushwhacking" strategy at this contingent moment, it would not have been centrally directed for very long by Lee. Confederate President Jefferson Davis had also taken flight. Alexander and Lee did discuss southern governors Joseph Brown of

---

29   Barton A. Myers, *Rebels Against the Confederacy: North Carolina's Unionists* (New York: Cambridge Univ. Press, 2014), 121-161.

30   Brian D. McKnight, *Confederate Outlaw: Champ Ferguson and the Civil War in Appalachia* (Baton Rouge: Louisiana State Univ. Press, 2011), 156-178.

Champ Ferguson, who operated as a Confederate guerilla-style partisan in Unionist eastern Tennessee, ended the war at the hangman's noose. He was such a celebrity, though, that his guards posed for a photo with him. What if Lee had been handled in the same way after the war instead of given the clemency promised by Ulysses S. Grant? *Library of Congress*

Georgia and Zebulon Vance of North Carolina as possibly negotiating a separate peace. Yet, North Carolina was already immersed in a guerrilla conflict spread across the state. Georgia also had unionist pockets in the mountains fighting, neighborhood-based guerrilla conflict, and simply put, guerrilla wars were raging in every Confederate state by 1865. In the final analysis, Lee's age, health, training, and historical experience all worked against him promoting, leading, or encouraging this kind of strategy. Even Mosby, identified that there was "nothing of the Fabius in his character." Lee was correct in his assessment that guerrilla warfare is a young man's game. He was not a "guerrilla thinker" tactically. He recognized good ones like Mosby but he saw most of them as "bushwhackers" and criminals. It was extremely difficult to form a positive opinion of this optional strategy for that reason. His own notion of the West Point way and honorable conduct meant being able to see your enemy and defeat them on a traditional, conventional field of battle, even if that was part of a grand campaign that amounted to an opportunistic raid, like the one into Maryland in 1862 or Pennsylvania in 1863. A bushwhacking strategy launched in 1865 with what remained of Confederate forces never would have permitted that final, clear-cut victory that secured a Southern nation-state.[31]

In sum, the historical experience of the "guerrilla option" was really not a particularly good strategic option for the major Confederate forces by early 1865. A few brief reasons are enough to demonstrate why. It would have been difficult to escape Phillip Sheridan. Those who made it to the mountains or out of state would have been on their own. If there was a grand plan to reconvene, it still would have required leadership and been diffuse for much of the time. It would have easily led to some of the problems discovered during the war through the deployment of the Partisan Ranger Act. There were not enough good leaders conducting this type of warfare to be successful in establishing independence. This strategy could have caused more internecine violence even sooner in the American South and perhaps lower North/Border South, at least for a period of time. If specific core leaders were chosen and dispersed with company-sized detachments, it might have continued and made military occupation of the American South longer and harder, and deepened bitterness. In the end, however, Lee made an accurate assessment of his strategic situation in the early days of April 1865 and surrendered the Army of Northern Virginia.

31   David Williams, *Bitterly Divided: The South's Inner Civil War* (New York: The New Press, 2008); Jonathan Dean Sarris, *A Separate Civil War: Communities in Conflict in the Mountain South* (Charlottesville, VA: Univ. of Virginia Press, 2006); *Mosby's Memoirs*, 236-240.

CHAPTER TWELVE

What If Lincoln Lived?

The Civil War's Perennial Counterfactual

Brian Matthew Jordan and Evan C. Rothera

On April 14, 1865, in a flag-festooned presidential box at Ford's Theater, John Wilkes Booth fired the first pistol crack of a sustained southern counterrevolution that sought to reverse Union victory, undo emancipation, and preserve white supremacy. Electoral fraud, domestic terrorism, and historical amnesia eventually overwhelmed Reconstruction's radical promise. As with anything in the past, however, nothing about Reconstruction's demise was inevitable. Indeed, reversing the results of Appomattox—transmuting military defeat into cultural victory—was no small feat. Generations of historians have advised against narratives that slavery yielded inexorably to segregation. Such narratives not only efface Reconstruction's radical possibilities, but also the ever-so-brief moment in which they were actually realized. Nothing in the past had to turn out the way that it did. Perhaps nobody understood that so well as John Wilkes Booth.[1]

It did not take long for Lincoln's contemporaries to begin pondering how things might have turned out differently if Lincoln had lived. Barely a month after the assassination, *Trubner's American and Oriental Literary Record*

---

1 On Reconstruction as a counterrevolution, see George C. Rable, *But There Was No Peace: The Role of Violence in the Politics of Reconstruction* (Athens: University of Georgia Press, 2007). On the notion that the counterrevolution of Reconstruction and white supremacy was "work," see Stephen Kantrowitz, *Ben Tillman and the Reconstruction of White Supremacy* (Chapel Hill: University of North Carolina Press, 2000).

   For the most famous of the admonitions against narratives of declension leading from slavery to segregation, see C. Vann Woodward, *The Strange Career of Jim Crow* (New York: Oxford University Press, 1955).

insisted that it could not "speculate upon what might have been had Lincoln lived"— before engaging in that very project. "We know his heart yearned towards his brethren in the South," the periodical commented. "We cannot fathom the mystery of Providence in permitting the deed which deprived his country at such a time of the services of such a man." Henry Watterson, a journalist and editor from the president's native Kentucky, supposed that had Lincoln lived, "there would have been no era of reconstruction." The

President Lincoln's first choice for a theater guest for the evening of April 14, 1865, was Lt. Gen. Ulysses S. Grant and his wife, Julia. What if Grant had been in the president's booth at Ford's Theater when the assassin came to call? *Chris Mackowski*

president "knew all about the South," he contended.[2] Some of Lincoln's critics agreed with the idea that Old Abe would have been too gentle and merciful with the former rebels. U. S. Senator Benjamin F. Wade of Ohio, for example, proclaimed, when visiting President Andrew Johnson shortly after Lincoln's assassination, "Johnson, we have faith in you. By the gods, there will be no trouble in running the government." That statement came back to haunt Wade and other Radical Republicans, but the Ohioan's view

2 *Trubner's American and Oriental Literary Record*, May 16, 1865; Arthur Krock, comp., *The Editorials of Henry Watterson* (New York: George H. Doran Company, 1923), 199-200. For excellent analysis of these alternate histories see Matthew David Norman, "Had Mr. Lincoln Lived: Alternate Histories, Reconstruction, Race, and Memory," *Journal of the Abraham Lincoln Association* 38, no. 1 (Winter 2017): 43-69.

THE SURRENDER OF GEN⸴ JOE JOHNSTON NEAR GREENSBORO N. C. APRIL, 26ᵀᴴ 1865.

William T. Sherman learned of Lincoln's assassination just as he was about to depart to negotiate the surrender of Joseph E. Johnston's Army of Tennessee. When Sherman shared the news to his Confederate counterpart, Johnston called it "the greatest possible calamity to the South." That forecast soon came to bear on surrender negotiations. Sherman tried to work out an agreement in the spirit of Lincoln's philosophy of "Let 'em up easy"—which Sherman had personally discussed with Lincoln and Ulysses S. Grant—but Secretary of War Edwin Stanton rejected the terms out of hand and sent Grant south to take over negotiations. What if Sherman had been given a freer hand to strike a deal? *Library of Congress*

that Lincoln would have been too lenient became widely shared. "If Lincoln had lived," the *Emporia Gazette* sniffed, "his name would not be a cue for applause." "Crowds are fickle," the Kansas editor continued, "but they are afraid of dead men."[3]

Questions about what Lincoln would have done had he lived persist today.[4] With the possible exceptions of Stonewall Jackson's death and the Army of Northern Virginia's defeat at Gettysburg, no other wartime event has invited more sustained or impassioned counterfactual thinking. Many white

3   Benjamin Wade as quoted in George W. Julian, *Political Recollections: 1840 to 1872* (Chicago: James McClurg & Company, 1884), 257; *Emporia Gazette*, November 11, 1899.

4   Stephen L. Carter, *The Impeachment of Abraham Lincoln* (New York: Alfred A. Knopf, 2012).

southerners reached quick accord with northerners that Lincoln's death was a great calamity. This line of thought emerged in 1865 and solidified over the next half century. In "The Birth of a Nation," the silent, twelve-reel epic infamous for its racist depiction of the war and Reconstruction, director D. W. Griffith went to great lengths to recreate the Lincoln assassination. He interpreted Booth's dastardly act as a hinge moment for the defeated South. In Griffith's view, the loss of Lincoln—the South's "best friend"—supplied the entering wedge for supposedly "vengeful" radicals in Congress to wrest control of the South. This idea—that Lincoln would have followed a similar, if not identical course, to Johnson, possibly ending in his impeachment—has proven oddly resilient. It does not, of course, take into account ideological differences between the two men; nor, for that matter, do exponents of this view consider Lincoln's infinitely greater skills as a political operator.

Academic historians bristle at counterfactual questions. Because historians traffic in the past—in what actually happened—we cannot absolutely know what *might* have happened *if* Lincoln had lived. Yet "fictional questions" may "be heuristically useful," David Hackett Fischer suggests, "for the ideas and inferences which they help to suggest."[5] Historian LaWanda Cox concluded her landmark *Lincoln and Black Freedom* with an extended discussion of what might have happened if Lincoln had lived, entitled "Reflections on the Limits of the Possible."[6] This essay extends Cox's analysis by considering what might have happened if Lincoln had lived—with that caveat such speculations are, well, speculations. Beyond a certain point, speculation becomes difficult to sustain. There is no question that Lincoln would have behaved quite differently than his successor, Andrew Johnson. Lincoln and Johnson's attitudes about race provide an excellent way to differentiate the two men.

Questions concerning Lincoln and race, or Lincoln's attitudes towards abolition and his ideas about the place of African Americans in U.S. society, have similarly vexed scholars for generations—perhaps because the questions concerning Lincoln and race are more far-reaching than the sentiments of one man. If Lincoln was merely a closet racist and grudging liberator who

---

5 David Hackett Fischer, *Historians' Fallacies: Toward a Logic of Historical Thought* (New York: Harper Perennial, 1970), 16.

6 LaWanda Cox, *Lincoln and Black Freedom* (Columbia: University of South Carolina Press, 1981).

After the Lincoln-Douglas Debates, the Illinois legislature returned Stephen A. Douglas to the Senate, but Lincoln gained a national reputation. The two would square off against each other again in the presidential election of 1860. A split Democratic party delivered the victory to Lincoln, but what if the election had gone to Douglas as the more-experienced politician? Or to Douglas's party rival, John Breckenridge, the vice president? *Library of Congress*

believed in colonization and considered African Americans inferior to white folks, any triumphalist, celebratory version of U.S. history becomes little more than a series of comforting falsehoods.

Lincoln's arch political rival, Senator Stephen A. Douglas, delighted in hitting Lincoln on the race question. During the 1858 Lincoln-Douglas Debates, Douglas mocked Lincoln and his notion that all men were created equal. He savaged Lincoln for what he considered a flawed interpretation of the Declaration of Independence. Jefferson and the founders, Douglas insisted, "desired to express by that phrase [all men are created equal], white men, men of European birth and European descent and had no reference either to the negro, the savage Indians, the Fejee, the Malay, or any other inferior and degraded race."[7] Faced with Douglas's demagoguery, and Douglas's insistence on a "whites-only" version of the Declaration of Independence, Lincoln did not present a consistent front. His assertion at Charleston, Illinois, that "there is a physical difference between the white

---

7 *The Lincoln-Douglas Debates*, eds., Rodney O. Davis and Douglas L. Wilson (Urbana: Knox College Lincoln Studies Center and the University of Illinois Press, 2008), 96.

and black races which I believe will forever forbid the two races living together on terms of social and political equality," is well-known. Historian Don E. Fehrenbacher claimed several decades ago that these sentiments were becoming "the most quoted passage in all of Lincoln's writings."[8] Scholar Lerone Bennett concluded that in the Charleston debate, Lincoln demonstrated that he was "a racist, who believed, as much as any other White man, in White supremacy and the subordination of Blacks."[9] Lincoln biographer David Herbert Donald noted that it "was the politically expedient thing to say . . . perhaps it was a necessary thing to say" and also posited that this "represented Lincoln's deeply held personal views."[10] Historian Allen Guelzo regarded Lincoln's remarks "a disgraceful catalog of all the civil rights he, fully as much as Douglas, believed blacks could be routinely deprived of."[11]

That said, Lincoln's statements in the debates were far more expansive than his remarks at Charleston. Furthermore, Lincoln never repudiated his personal position that slavery was an evil: "I confess myself as belonging to that class in the country who contemplate slavery as a moral, social, and political evil."[12] In addition, Lincoln advocated the notion of an inclusive Declaration of Independence, a risky political maneuver in Illinois, which was among the most anti-Black states in the antebellum U. S.[13] Donald noted that Lincoln "was not personally hostile to blacks" and that Lincoln's attachment to colonization was rather vague.[14] Benjamin Quarles determined

---

8 Davis and Wilson, 131; Don E. Fehrenbacher, *Lincoln in Text and Context: Collected Essays* (Stanford: Stanford University Press, 1987), 101.

9 Lerone Bennett, *Forced Into Glory: Abraham Lincoln's White Dream* (Chicago: Johnson Publishing Company, 1999), 209.

10 David Donald, *Lincoln* (New York: Simon & Schuster Paperbacks, 1995), 221.

11 Allen C. Guelzo, *Lincoln and Douglas: The Debates that Defined America* (New York: Simon & Schuster Paperbacks, 2008), 192-193.

12 Davis and Wilson, 193.

13 George Fredrickson, *Big Enough to Be Inconsistent: Abraham Lincoln Confronts Slavery and Race* (Cambridge: Harvard University Press, 2008), 35. Illinois has competition for the title of "most Negrophobic state in antebellum America," see Robert R. Dykstra, *Bright Radical Star: Black Freedom and White Supremacy on the Hawkeye Frontier* (Cambridge: Harvard University Press, 1993). See also Matthew D. Norman, "The Other Lincoln Douglas Debate: The Race Issue in a Comparative Context," *Journal of the Abraham Lincoln Association* 31 (Winter 2010).

14 Donald, 221.

that Lincoln's relations with African Americans and his subsequent actions were more important than the statements he made at Charleston.[15] LaWanda Cox asserted that Lincoln's remarks at Charleston did not necessarily preclude civil rights for African Americans, but should be seen for what they were: denials that he had championed civil rights in the past and that he was not doing so in the present. "More prescient for his presidential record," Cox concluded, "than his concessions to racism was Lincoln's prewar resistance to embracing white supremacy wholeheartedly."[16] Don E. Fehrenbacher reminds historians of the problematic nature of the word "racist" when investigating Lincoln. "Terminological differences may also arise in the study of history, and such is the case with the word 'racist,' which serves us badly as a concept because of its denunciatory tone and indiscriminate use," he cautioned.[17] Fehrenbacher observed that use of the word "racist" substituted moral judgment for historical empathy. Thus, Lincoln's statements at Charleston were "essentially disclaimers rather than affirmations. They indicated, for political reasons, the *maximum* he was willing to deny the Negro and the *minimum* that he claimed for the Negro."[18] Finally, Matthew D. Norman offered an excellent recent discussion about the debates. While conceding that the remarks at Charleston were "regrettable and indefensible," Norman called for new analysis of the Lincoln-Douglas Debates and contended that, "if his rhetoric is placed within the larger context of the campaign, some mitigating factors emerge."[19] Norman juxtaposed Lincoln with Illinois Senator Lyman Trumbull and concluded that Trumbull's success in the 1858 canvass proved that Republicans could mount an effective campaign without discussing natural rights of African Americans or the morality of slavery. However, as Norman demonstrated, Lincoln refused to take the easy route: "Despite unrelenting attacks, Lincoln did not abandon his position that African Americans were entitled to natural rights."[20] Norman demonstrated that Lincoln's insistence on discussing

15 Benjamin Quarles, *Lincoln and the Negro* (New York: Oxford University Press, 1962).

16 Cox, *Lincoln and Black Freedom*, 22.

17 Fehrenbacher, *Lincoln in Text and Context*), 102.

18 Fehrenbacher, 105.

19 Norman, 20, 17.

natural rights and slavery were courageous political maneuvers. "Lincoln could have taken the path of least resistance and made matters much easier for himself and his supporters if he had followed a strategy similar to that of Trumbull," he said. "Instead he took a risk by claiming that African Americans were included in the Declaration."[21]

While Douglas defined Lincoln as a racial extremist who wanted to see African Americans and white people exist in a perfect state of equality, African American leaders like Frederick Douglass were decidedly less certain. The most frequently cited remark by Douglass concerning Lincoln and race emanates from an 1876 speech. When dedicating Thomas Ball's Freedman's Monument in Washington, D. C., Douglass displayed a decidedly ambivalent attitude. On the one hand, Lincoln "was preeminently the white man's President, entirely devoted to the welfare of white men"[22] On the other, when "viewed from the genuine abolition ground, Mr. Lincoln seemed tardy, cold, dull, and indifferent; but measuring him by the sentiment of his country, a sentiment he was bound as a statesman to consult, he was swift, zealous, radical, and determined."[23] Historian Michael Burlingame recently discovered a speech Douglass gave in June 1865 in which Douglass displayed a very different line of thought. "Lincoln made an impressive record which entitled him to be considered 'in a sense hitherto without example, emphatically the black man's president: the first to show any respect for their rights as men.'"[24]

Stephen Douglas's certainty and Frederick Douglass's indecision concerning Lincoln, not to mention disagreements among various scholars,

---

20 Norman, 17.

21 Norman, 18. Race baiting was popular in Illinois politics. "In the *Tribune*'s report of Trumbull's speech, his comments on "wooly heads" and the "various breeds of negroes" were met with laughter and cheers from the audience. Similarly, Lincoln's now-infamous opening at Charleston was interrupted several times by laughter, cheers, and applause." See Norman, 18.

22 Frederick Douglass, "Oration in Memory of Abraham Lincoln, Delivered at the Unveiling of the Freedman's Monument in Memory of Abraham Lincoln, in Lincoln Park, Washington, D.C., April 14, 1876," in *Frederick Douglass: Selected Speeches and Writings*, ed. Philip S. Foner (Chicago: Chicago Review Press, 1999), 618.

23 Douglass, "Oration in Memory of Abraham Lincoln," 621.

24 Michael Burlingame, "Abraham Lincoln: New Information, Fresh Perspectives," 48th Annual Robert Fortenbaugh Memorial Lecture (Gettysburg College: 2009), 11. See also Burlingame, *Lincoln*.

should not prove surprising. As Lincoln's political opponent, in a state marked by virulent racial prejudice, Douglas had a vested interest in portraying Lincoln as a closet abolitionist. Douglass, on the other hand, looking at Lincoln from a very different perspective and in wildly different contexts (soon after Lincoln's assassination, and again close to the end of Reconstruction) came to very different conclusions. Scholars who read (or sometimes ignored) evidence found proof of very different attitudes by Lincoln. Discussions about Lincoln and race always risk sounding like they should be reserved for graduate seminars, but Lincoln's attitudes about race, colonization, citizenship, and suffrage are key to understanding how he might have behaved if he had lived.

Despite the comments at Charleston, Lincoln's ideas about race did not remain static; rather, they changed over time. Like many of his contemporaries, Lincoln accepted the Crittenden-Johnson Resolution's narrow definition of the U. S. Civil War. In July 1861, during the special session of the 37th Congress, Representative John J. Crittenden of Kentucky offered a resolution which read, in part, "this war is not waged upon our part in any spirit of oppression, nor for any purpose of conquest or subjugation, nor purpose of overthrowing or interfering with the rights or established institutions of those States; but to defend and maintain the supremacy of the Constitution and to preserve the Union."[25] In other words, the war occurred for one reason, and one reason alone: the preservation of the Union. The war was not to be an abolition crusade resulting in citizenship and civil rights for African Americans. That said, U.S. war aims never remained static; they, too, evolved over the course of the conflict and in response to battlefield events. Despite the cautious framing of the Crittenden-Johnson Resolution, black and white people, from the very beginning, understood the possibilities war offered and challenged the notion that the conflict was a white man's fight. The actions of enslaved people had an enormous impact on the war.[26] Lincoln did not want to make the war about emancipation from

---

25   Edward McPherson, *The Political History of the United States of America, during the Great Rebellion* (Washington, DC: Philp & Solomons, 1865), 286. The House of Representatives passed Crittenden's resolution and the Senate passed a resolution offered by Senator Andrew Johnson of Tennessee with very similar wording.

26   See, for example, Ira Berlin, Barbara J. Fields, Steven F. Miller, Joseph P. Reidy, and Leslie S. Rowland, *Slaves No More: Three Essays on Emancipation and the Civil War* (Cambridge: Cambridge University Press, 1992); David Williams, *I Freed Myself: African*

the beginning because, as scholars have repeatedly demonstrated, he was concerned about the impact of such a decision on the slaveholding Border States. His reaction to General John C. Frémont's emancipation proclamation in Missouri spoke volumes. As Lincoln said on more than one occasion, he could not afford to drive Kentucky out of the Union. However, the federal government's policy toward African Americans during the early years of the war looked somewhat schizophrenic. On the one hand, some military commanders routinely returned fugitive slaves; on the other hand, others protected fugitive slaves and became, as one scholar has noted, "practical liberators."[27] Lincoln's attitudes about race during this period are often reduced to his espousal of colonization—transporting Africans Americans somewhere else (either in South America or Africa).

As 1861 gave way to 1862, so, too, did Lincoln's ideas about race start to evolve. Lincoln pushed for Congress to pass a resolution endorsing gradual, compensated, and "voluntary" emancipation. He flirted with using tiny Delaware to demonstrate how such a program might work. Lincoln met with the Border State Congressmen and urged them to accept compensated emancipation before the frictions and abrasions of war destroyed slavery. In the disappointing aftermath of the Peninsula Campaign, he moved closer and closer to issuing an emancipation proclamation of his own, forestalled from so doing on the advice of his Secretary of State, William H. Seward, who counselled that Lincoln needed to wait for a military victory lest his act appear as one of desperation. Lincoln, in a less-worthy meeting, urged African Americans to accept colonization. He also used an editorial by the mercurial Horace Greeley to issue his famous reply to the "Prayer of Twenty Millions":

> My paramount object in this struggle *is* to save the Union, and is *not* either to save or to destroy slavery. If I could save the Union without freeing *any* slave I would do it, and if I could save it by freeing *all* the slaves I would do it; and if I could save it by

---

American Self-Emancipation in the Civil War Era (Cambridge: Cambridge University Press, 2014); and Joseph P. Reidy, *Illusions of Emancipation: The Pursuit of Freedom and Equality in the Twilight of Slavery* (Chapel Hill: University of North Carolina Press, 2019).

27 Kristopher A. Teters, *Practical Liberators: Union Officers in the Western Theater during the Civil War* (Chapel Hill: University of North Carolina Press, 2018).

> freeing some and leaving others alone I would also do that. What
> I do about slavery, and the colored race, I do because I believe it
> helps to save the Union; and what I forbear, I forbear because I do
> *not* believe it would help to save the Union.[28]

In other words, Lincoln declared that he would free as many or as few slaves
as it took to save the Union. What he did about slavery, Lincoln contended,
he did to save the Union.

Five days after the Army of the Potomac flushed Lee from Maryland
at the battle of Antietam, Lincoln issued his Preliminary Emancipation
Proclamation. He gave the states then in rebellion several months to resume
their loyalty and, if not, declared that all slaves in areas in rebellion would
be forever free. Critics at the time derided Lincoln for seeming to encourage
slave insurrections, even though he did not. Critics in a later century derided
Lincoln for freeing enslaved persons in areas he did not control, and none in
the areas he did. Such complaints miss the critical point that Lincoln exercised
his war powers, which both empowered and limited what he could do.

As it turned out, the states in rebellion did not see fit to cease their
fratricidal bloodletting; consequently, the Emancipation Proclamation
took effect on January 1, 1863, to the cheers of abolitionists and the scorn
of Lincoln's political opponents. The president keenly understood that the
Emancipation Proclamation was a step toward ending slavery, but that it
would not achieve that end by itself. Thus, he pushed Congress for the next
two years to pass a constitutional amendment to destroy slavery in the United
States. The resulting Thirteenth Amendment—the work of many determined
hands—did so, though it was not ratified until after Lincoln's assassination.

Over the course of a bitter conflict, Lincoln, who stated repeatedly that
he always hated slavery, did much to undermine the institution, as did many
other people, both white and black. However, Lincoln could have been like
many of his contemporaries, who were supportive neither of slavery nor
of African Americans. Lincoln's actions, however, suggest that his ideas
about black people were also undergoing significant evolution. Lincoln's
remarks at Charleston, cited above, may have been an expression of deeply

28   Roy P. Basler, ed., *The Collected Works of Abraham* Lincoln (New Brunswick, New
Jersey: Rutgers University Press, 1953), 5:389.

held sentiment, or they may have been some red meat for the crowd. At any rate, they certainly stand at odds with his assertions that black and white people shared the same natural rights—and his growing conviction that black soldiers deserved suffrage rights and citizenship.

As time passed, Lincoln not only worked to end slavery and win the war, he also thought about how to put the Union back together. Lincoln's most famous statement to this effect came on December 8, 1863, in his Proclamation of Amnesty and Reconstruction, known more colloquially as the Ten-Percent Plan. Lincoln offered a pardon to anyone who took and kept a loyalty oath. Moreover, when ten percent of the people who cast ballots in the 1860 presidential election swore the loyalty oath, they could form a government, which would be recognized as the official government of the state.[29] Louisiana and Tennessee became Lincoln's primary laboratories to test reconstruction. Andrew Johnson cut his teeth as Lincoln's military governor of Tennessee and, in Louisiana, Unionists in New Orleans and its hinterlands held out the possibility of forming the nucleus of a new government. Lincoln encouraged these Unionists, who kept the process moving along.

Lincoln's March 13, 1864, letter to Michael Hahn, the newly elected Unionist governor of Louisiana, merits quotation at length:

> I congratulate you on having fixed your name in history as the first-free-state Governor of Louisiana. Now you are about to have a Convention which, among other things, will probably define the elective franchise. I barely suggest for your private consideration, whether some of the colored people may not be let in—as, for instance, the very intelligent, and especially those who have fought gallantly in our ranks. They would probably help, in some trying time to come, to keep the jewel of liberty within the family of freedom.[30]

Although the letter appears somewhat halting and lukewarm to modern eyes, Lincoln's endorsement of limited black suffrage was momentous.

29 Basler, ed., *Collected Works*, 7:54 – 56.

30 Basler, ed., *Collected Works*, 7:243.

Nor was this Lincoln's only statement on the matter. Three nights before Booth pointed his pistol at the back of Lincoln's head, he had listened to the president address a jubilant serenade at the Executive Mansion. People had expected Lincoln to focus on the fact that the end of the war appeared imminent, but he chose instead to defend the reconstructed government in Louisiana. Lincoln clearly anticipated an intraparty struggle with the radicals in his party when, in speaking of Louisiana's new state government on April 11, 1865, he argued that, "we shall sooner have the fowl by hatching the egg than by smashing it."[31] Lincoln had opted, in 1864, to "pocket veto" the Wade-Davis Bill, a radical reconstruction measure that insisted a majority of a rebel state's registered voters swear an "ironclad" oath prior to that state's readmission. But his repetition of his sentiments from his letter to Hahn about black suffrage came as a surprise to many in the crowd. Booth is reported to have said that "this means nigger citizenship." He would kill Lincoln lest the president's dream become a reality.[32]

As stated above, some Radical Republicans believed Andrew Johnson would be more draconian than Lincoln and would actually punish the southern states. Although this mistake looks egregious in hindsight, Radicals had good reason to initially think Johnson was one of them. For example, in a June 10, 1864, speech in Nashville, Johnson blasted the "exclusive aristocracy about Nashville," declared fire-eaters had killed slavery, proclaimed his belief in emancipation even as he urged African Americans to work rather than be idle, and asserted "treason must be made odious and traitors must be punished and impoverished."[33] As military governor of Tennessee, it made perfect sense for Johnson to discuss the death of slavery and punishment for traitors, and he repeated the line about treason on multiple occasions. Furthermore, many regarded Johnson as a folk hero because he was an

---

31   Basler, ed., *Collected Works*, 8: 399-405. For greater context, see Louis P. Masur, *Lincoln's Last Speech: Wartime Reconstruction and the Crisis of the Union* (New York: Oxford University Press, 2015).

32   Burlingame suggested that Lincoln was a "martyr to black civil rights, as much as Martin Luther King," Michael Burlingame, *Abraham Lincoln: A Life* (Baltimore: Johns Hopkins University Press, 2008), 2: 811.

33   *Biographical Sketch of Andrew Johnson, of Tennessee, Together with his Speech at Nashville, June 10, 1864, and his Letter Accepting the Nomination as Vice President of the United States, Tendered him by the National Union Convention* (Washington: Union Congressional Committee, 1864), 8 and 11.

ardent Unionist and the only United States senator from a seceded state to remain loyal. Hoosier Congressman George Julian, who accompanied Senator Wade to visit Johnson shortly after Lincoln's assassination, remembered that Johnson repeated his famous admonition that "treason must be made infamous, and traitors must be impoverished." Julian, writing nearly twenty years after the meeting, remembered, "we were all cheered and encouraged by this brave talk."[34]

Andrew Johnson made a mess of things as Lincoln's successor, stirring up such trouble with Congress that he became the first president ever impeached. He survived conviction by only one vote—and it was a close one. What if the Senate had convicted him? *Library of Congress*

Any analysis of what Johnson did and what Lincoln would have done has to consider several factors. For one, Fehrenbacher's cautions about the word "racist" aside, it is clear that while Lincoln held beliefs that would be considered racist by today's standards, Lincoln always regarded slavery as a moral abomination. Andrew Johnson, on the other hand, was, like the vast majority of his fellow white southerners, a virulent racist. Moreover, Johnson was born to a poor white family. By virtue of hard work and with significant help from his wife, he learned how to read and made himself into a force in Tennessee politics. He also enslaved several human beings. Johnson never forgot his humble roots, and he never outgrew

34 Julian, *Political Recollections*, 257.

his profound envy of the slaveholding class. As his remarks in Nashville betrayed, Johnson held the slaveholding class responsible for the war. Thus, whereas Lincoln saw the justice of enfranchising black men who were literate and who fought in the U.S. army, Johnson saw freeing the enslaved and confiscating plantations as a way to punish the slave aristocracy. Radicals mistook Johnson's language as a sign of ideological kinship when, in reality, even Johnson's desire to humiliate the old masters did not stop him from undercutting the attempts of the victors to reap the fruits of their victory.

Two examples of the differences between Lincoln and Johnson illustrate something about how they operated and their divergent courses of action. In March 1864, as we have seen, Lincoln had endorsed a limited black suffrage by emphasizing its essential justice: "they would probably help, in some trying time to come, to keep the jewel of liberty within the family of freedom." In August 1865, Andrew Johnson broached the subject of black suffrage with Mississippi Governor William Sharkey—but in dramatically different terms. "If you could extend the elective franchise to all persons of color who can read the constitution of the United States in English and write their times, and to all persons of color who own real estate valued at not less than two-hundred and fifty dollars," he wrote, "you would completely disarm the adversary and set an example the other States will follow."[35] For Johnson, black suffrage was not the war's charge, but rather a cheap bargaining chip with which he could defang his radical Republican opponents. Frederick Douglass recounted being received by Lincoln on Inauguration Day in 1865 at the White House and Lincoln's solicitousness toward Douglass. Lincoln wanted to know what Douglass thought of the speech, and he seemed pleased when Douglass deemed it a sacred effort. When Douglass met with Andrew Johnson, the tenor was quite different. Johnson talked *at* Douglass instead of talking with him. According to at least one recollection, Johnson insulted Douglass and called him a racial epithet after the meeting was over. These differences alone suggest one important point about the two men: although Johnson spent much longer than Lincoln as an officeholder, Lincoln was a far more skilled politician—one who knew how to work with diverse groups of people. To be sure, Lincoln irritated

---

35   Basler, ed., *Collected Works*, 7:243; Andrew Johnson, telegram to Mississippi Gov. William L. Sharkey, August 15, 1865, in *Impeachment Investigation: Testimony Taken Before the Judiciary Committee of the House of Representatives* (Washington: GPO, 1867), 1106.

both Radical and Conservative Republicans at times, but it is difficult to see Lincoln engaging in a scorched-earth conflict with the Radicals in the way Johnson did.

The situation in 1865–66 was critical. As the war ended, thousands of people were on the road: battle-scarred veterans returning home; formerly enslaved people exploring the limits of their newly found freedoms; wheedling speculators and northern capitalists looking to turn a quick profit; and active soldiers moving to new theaters of conflict. Johnson issued two proclamations: one outlining procedures for pardons, and the other regarding his plan for restoring the Union. Johnson made a pardon contingent on a loyalty oath and accepting the Thirteenth Amendment. He declared fourteen categories of high-ranking ex-rebels ineligible (most notably, those holding more than $20,000 worth of property), though they could make a personal application to him for pardon. Johnson also began appointing provisional governors for the ex-rebel states. Radical Republicans grew increasingly fretful, particularly because Congress would not convene until December, and Johnson refused to call a special session. Many people saw Johnson's haste as unseemly. Others were angry that the southern states would now receive more votes in the House of Representatives (one ironic consequence of slavery's demise was that the Three-Fifths Clause had been rendered moot). Who had won the war after all? Johnson claimed that he remained faithful to Lincoln's plans for Reconstruction, but Lincoln's plans were designed to end the war. In other words, Lincoln's plans for Reconstruction were created under one set of circumstances that had shifted once the war ended.

Was there a moment when the white South stood ready to accept the terms of the victors? Some contemporary commentators certainly thought so and, in their telling, the failure to exploit that opportunity rested squarely with Andrew Johnson. In truth, the "one moment" thesis is greatly overstated; it makes Johnson a ready, convenient scapegoat for the collapse of northern interest in Reconstruction. However, without a doubt, Johnson made many former rebels believe they had a good friend in Washington, D. C. White southerners defiantly belted the states of the former Confederacy with the Black Codes—laws that mocked notions of freedom by restricting black rights to assemble, bear arms, and even worship. The unapologetic obstinacy with which former Confederates challenged the war's results testified to the radical possibilities the conflict had unleashed. Within a year, ugly race riots tore through the streets of Memphis and New Orleans; a knot of Confederate veterans exchanged their gray uniforms for the garb of the Ku Klux Klan; and white supremacist terrorists intimated, tortured, and killed newly freed enslaved people and their white Republican allies alike. Johnson was not committed to the project of Reconstruction, preferring the less pugnacious term, "restoration." His official acts worked to undermine the newly won freedoms of African Americans everywhere. In September 1865, he rescinded Special Field Order No. 15, the directive that had divided abandoned lands along the coasts of South Carolina, Georgia, and Florida among newly freed enslaved persons in forty-acre plots.

Lincoln's Reconstruction almost certainly would have turned out much differently than the nightmare his successor presided over. For one, it is very difficult to see Lincoln taking the same course of action as Johnson when it came to the initial proclamations. Second, the man who wrote to James Cook Conkling praising black soldiers for their heroism, bravery, and manhood from the ramparts of Fort Wagner to the laurels of Olustee would not have rolled over as rebels attempted to revive slavery's ghost. Lincoln would not have issued so many pardons so quickly, and it is difficult to envision him rescinding Special Field Order No. 15. Nor, for that matter, would Lincoln have treated Congress so antagonistically. In fact, he might have called for a Special Session of the 39th Congress in the summer of 1865, not least of all because Congress had the ultimate authority over whether they were going to admit representatives and senators from the southern states. In other words, in the early and critical months of Reconstruction, Lincoln would have behaved very differently than his successor. In addition, because he likely would not have pressed forward nearly as quickly as Johnson did on trying to get the rebel states readmitted, Lincoln would not have created a situation in which Congress rejected the fruits of his effort (although Lincoln might have tried to get Tennessee and Louisiana readmitted, since his wartime efforts had some success in these states).

One of the important elements of the Reconstruction story is how Andrew Johnson alienated a key wartime constituency—the Moderate Republicans—and helped to place the Radical Republicans firmly behind the tiller. In February 1866, Johnson vetoed the measure extending the life of the Bureau of Refugees, Freedmen, and Abandoned Lands, the federal agency which, tasked with managing the transition from slavery to freedom on the ground in the South, not only negotiated labor contracts, but also supplied free public education and much-needed medical care to the formerly enslaved. Many Republicans had come to see extending the life of Bureau as critical because large portions of the South stood in ruins, and someone had to help people navigate the chaos of the early postwar period. Johnson had led many Moderate Republicans to believe that he supported the measure; his veto message came like thunderclap. Several days later, Johnson gave a most vulgar and intemperate speech to mark George Washington's birthday, during which he identified Radical Republicans—not rebel traitors—as the real enemies of the republic. Nineteenth century Americans did not want their president to behave like a vulgar stump demagogue. Johnson had excelled in the hardscrabble world of Tennessee politics, but such a performance by a sitting president seemed beneath the dignity of the office; it alienated many moderate Republicans who might have otherwise supported Johnson. As though this were not enough, Johnson wielded his veto pen once more in March 1866, rejecting the Civil Rights Act. Again, he had led Moderate Republicans to believe that he would support the measure. Johnson's veto messages addressed constitutional qualms. He believed that Congress, by refusing to admit the reconstructed southern states, did not have a quorum. However, the veto was also a product of Johnson's racial animus and his extreme strict-constructionist attitude. For Moderate Republicans, this was the Rubicon. On the first anniversary of Lee's surrender at Appomattox, Republican majorities in Congress enacted the Civil Rights Act over the president's veto. Not to be denied, they then overrode Johnson's veto of the Freedmen's Bureau measure. Unlike Johnson, Lincoln would never have alienated the Moderate Republicans in this way; he would have worked with them to shape appropriate legislation. Interestingly, that would have completely changed the dynamics of the 1866 midterm elections, which boiled down to a simple question for voters: Johnson's policy or Congress's policy. In an alternative scenario, Republicans would have been united, with the edges of the party no doubt dissatisfied with Lincoln's actions, but most of the party holding. Congress then may or may not have passed the Military Reconstruction Acts.

Although he did not win in his fight with Congress (which culminated in his impeachment and acquittal by one vote in the Senate), Johnson nevertheless continued to do harm. Cranking out thousands of pardons, vetoing legislation, and then looking the other way as former rebels effortlessly returned to political power (the "provisional" governments that Johnson propped up in the South returned scores of high-ranking former rebels, including ten brigadier generals, to Congress), Johnson privileged national healing over a real reckoning with the war's cost, charge, and consequences. Encouraged by Johnson and the many northerners who embraced a swift sectional reconciliation, white southerners continued their multi-pronged campaign to render moot the results of the war. By the late nineteenth century, with blacks disenfranchised, lynching a subject for postcards, and the myth of the Lost Cause thoroughly mainstream—the Confederacy declared victory at last.

If Lincoln had lived, he would not have made the mistakes Johnson made and would not have behaved in the ways Johnson did. How Lincoln's second term would have ended is an open question, but, as historians have argued, it is difficult to contend that things would have been worse. Given how things turned out, Frederick Douglass was undoubtedly correct when he declared that for "the colored people of the country," Lincoln's murder was "an unspeakable calamity."[36]

---

36 Frederick Douglass, "Abraham Lincoln: A Speech," Frederick Douglass Papers, Library of Congress.

Lincoln's Second Inaugural Address articulated a postwar vision that did not come to pass: "With charity for all, and with malice toward none. . . ." What if Americans had risen to meet the moment?
Chris Mackowski

Suggested Reading

Although subject to ongoing cycles of analysis, interpretation, and revision, "events" become stubbornly fixed in the historical record—shoehorned into eras, sorted into causes and effects, regarded as either momentous or insignificant. While counterfactual questions cannot retrieve real historical answers, they can amplify a profound yet underappreciated truth: nothing in the past had to turn out the way that it did. The landscape of the past is veined with roads not taken. History abounds with alternatives lost and opportunities found; it is peopled by characters who made seemingly illogical choices, working with the limited information available to them.

Taken together, the essays in this volume suggest that counterfactual questions can be useful implements in the historian's toolkit. To be sure, alternative endings and wishful thinking cannot reliably guide us in our travels to the past. But counterfactual questions can help us to realize just how tentative, uncertain, and indeterminate the past really was. When we reckon with the full range of choices available to historical actors in a given moment, we not only resist the temptations of hindsight, but arrive at a more complete, more nuanced, and ultimately more empathetic understanding of how the past was actually felt, intuited, and experienced.

If nothing else, we hope that these essays have encouraged you to think more deeply about a few, fabled moments in the war's history. We hope that moving forward, you engage "what if" questions not with reckless speculation, but with inventory of the historical context. We hope that you will reach beneath fictive false dichotomies and plumb the complex depths of the war's lived realities.

To that end, the volume's contributors have supplied below a few recommendations for further reading. While in no way exhaustive, these lists will nonetheless equip you to ask even better historical questions.

The Battle of Shiloh

After decades of relative neglect, the Battle of Shiloh has, in recent years, generated a significant body of scholarship. For a helpful introduction to the battle, see Gregory Mertz, *Attack at Daylight and Whip Them* (Savas Beatie, 2019). For narrative treatments, see Edward Cunningham, *Shiloh and the Western Campaign of 1862* (Savas Beatie, 2008); Larry J. Daniel, *Shiloh: The Battle That Changed the Civil War* (Simon and Schuster, 1997); Wiley Sword, *Shiloh: Bloody April* (Morningside, 2001); James L. McDonough, *Shiloh: In Hell Before Night* (University of Tennessee Press, 1977); and Timothy B. Smith, *Shiloh: Conquer or Perish* (University Press of Kansas, 2016). Also useful are Timothy B. Smith, *The Untold Story of Shiloh* (University of Tennessee Press, 2006); Timothy B. Smith, *Rethinking Shiloh: Myth and Memory* (University of Tennessee Press, 2013); and the essays collected in Steven E. Woodworth, ed., *The Shiloh*

What if Beauregard had managed to salvage something out of the fighting on the second day at Shiloh? Would we be singing a different tune? *Library of Congress*

Campaign (Southern Illinois University Press, 2009). Mark Grimsley and Steven E. Woodworth›s *Shiloh: A Battlefield Guide* (University of Nebraska Press, 2006), is an indispensable guide for battlefield stompers. For the rather unique experiences of the rank and file at Shiloh, see Joseph Allan Frank and George A. Reaves, *"Seeing the Elephant": Raw Recruits at the Battle of Shiloh* (University of Illinois Press, 1983). Finally, Gail Stephens›s *Shadow of Shiloh* (Indiana Historical Society Press, 2013), reconsiders the controversial role of Lew Wallace during the battle.

The Battle of Antietam

Any study of the Maryland Campaign and the Battle of Antietam must begin with two core sources: Volume 19, Parts 1 and 2 of the *Official Records of the War of the Rebellion* and Ezra Carman›s *Maryland Campaign of*

The 27th Indiana's monument at Antietam sits on the north side of Cornfield Avenue. What if members of a different regiment had found Lee's Lost Order? Would the 27th have still found themselves in the crucible of fire just a few days later? *Library of Congress*

September 1862. The trilogy edited by Thomas G. Clemens and published by Savas Beatie within the last decade is the best version of Carman's masterful work. In particular, Volume 2, which covers the Battle of Antietam, provides the most detailed account ever written about the bloodiest single day battle in American history. Regarding the Army of the Potomac's high command at the battle, there is plenty of recent scholarship about these generals. Ethan Rafuse's *McClellan's War: The Failure of Moderation in the Struggle for the Union* (Indiana University Press, 2005), William Marvel›s *Radical Sacrifice: The Rise and Fall of Fitz John Porter* (University of North Carolina Press, 2021), Mark A. Snell›s *From First to Last: The Life of Major General William B. Franklin* (Fordham University Press: 2002), and Marion V.

Armstrong Jr.›s *Unfurl Those Colors: McClellan, Sumner, & the Second Army Corps in the Antietam Campaign* (The University of Alabama Press: 2008) all provide in-depth examinations of the command decisions made during the Battle of Antietam.

International Intervention in the American Civil War

International and maritime theaters were as critical as any on land. In *One War at a Time: The International Dimensions of the American Civil War* (Potomac

Books, 1999), Dean B. Mahin describes the Lincoln administration's deep concern for European threats. Don H. Doyle's *The Cause of All Nations: An International History of the American Civil War* (Basic Books, 2015) presents the view from European capitals struggling with conflicts between liberalism and reaction. *Union in Peril: The Crisis over British Intervention in the Civil War* by Howard Jones (University of North Carolina Press, 1992) is a classic study of British neutrality while his *Blue & Gray Diplomacy, A History of Union and Confederate Foreign Relations* (University of North Carolina Press, 2010) takes a broader approach. A most cogent and concise window into British minds is *The Glittering Illusion: English Sympathy for the Southern Confederacy*, Sheldon Vanauken (Regnery Gateway, 1989). Amanda Foreman's *A World on Fire: Britain's Crucial Role in the American Civil War* (Random House, 2010) is a highly praised study of British volunteers on both sides. *No Need of Glory: The British Navy in American Waters 1860-1864*, Regis A. Courtemanche (Naval Institute Press,

LOOK OUT FOR SQUALLS.

Jack Bull. "YOU DO WHAT'S RIGHT, MY SON, OR I'LL BLOW YOU OUT OF THE WATER."

What if the United States had adopted a more defiant stand when Great Britain began to suggest possible support for the Confederacy? *Punch*

1977), covers British sea power. Gordon H. Warren's *Fountain of Discontent: The Trent Affair and Freedom of the Seas* (Northeastern University Press, 1981) addresses that crisis. *The Confederate Navy in Europe* by Warren F. Spencer (University of Alabama Press, 1983) describes programs to purchase or build a navy in Europe with the legal and political impacts. Frank J. Merli provides a similar study in *Great Britain and the Confederate Navy, 1861-1865* (Indiana University Press, 1970, reprint 2004). *Gray Raiders of the Sea: How Eight Confederate Warships Destroyed the Union's High Seas Commerce* by Chester G. Hearn (International Marine Publishing, 1992) is an excellent review of commerce raiders.

What If Someone Else Had Been Offered Command
of the Army of the Potomac?

Of the three generals examined in the chapter, Ethan Allen Hitchcock's papers are the most abundant. The majority of it is held at the Library of Congress and the Missouri Historical Society. Some material is published in length in

Ambrose Burnside turned down command of the Army of the Potomac twice before finally accepting it. What if he had accepted it on either of the first two occasions? Conversely, what if he had turned it down the third time it had been offered? *Frank Leslie's Illustrated Weekly*

another outstanding resource, Ethan Allen Hitchcock, *Fifty Years in Camp and Field: Diary of Major-General Ethan Allen Hitchcock*, U.S.A., ed. by William A. Croffut (New York, NY: Putnam, 1909). For an article-length investigation of Hitchcock's role as an advisor to Stanton and Lincoln, see Marshall True, "A Reluctant Warrior Advises the President: Ethan Allen Hitchcock, Abraham Lincoln and the Union Army, Spring, 1862," *Vermont History* 50 (1982): 129-50. The only biographical study on Israel B. Richardson is Jack C. Mason, *Until Antietam: The Life and Letters of Major General Israel B. Richardson, U.S. Army* (Carbondale: Southern Illinois University Press, 2009). Mason relied heavily on Richardson's journal and letters in Tom Lane's private collection. Despite repeated attempts, the author of this chapter was unable to contact Mr. Lane to gain access to this material. Hopefully one day this material will be available to historians. Though dated, Edward J. Nichols, *Toward Gettysburg: A Biography of General John F. Reynolds* (University Park: Pennsylvania State University Press, 1958) has stood the test of time. Nichols includes a succinct chapter at the end of the book on Reynolds' offer to command the Army of the Potomac. The general's correspondence is held at the Franklin & Marshall College Archives & Special Collections. For a detailed look at the political turmoil within the Army of the Potomac, refer to both Stephen R. Taaffe, *Commanding the*

Army of the Potomac (Lawrence: University Press of Kansas, 2006) and Zachery A. Fry, *A Republic in the Ranks: Loyalty and Dissent in the Army of the Potomac* (Chapel Hill: University of North Carolina Press, 2020).

What If Stonewall Jackson Had Not Been Shot?

A veritable hill (see what I did there) of Jackson content began flowing from writers' pens even before the war ended. When it comes to Jackson, the unquestioned "Bible" about the man is James Robertson's *Stonewall Jackson: The Man, They Soldier, the Legend* (Macmillan Publishing, 1997). The best dissection of Jackson's wounding at Chancellorsville is provided in Robert Krick's *The Smoothbore Volley That Doomed the Confederacy: The Death of Stonewall Jackson and Other Chapters on the Army of Northern Virginia* (Louisiana State University Press, 2002). To learn more about the last two weeks of Jackson's life see *The Last Days of Stonewall Jackson* (Savas Beatie, 2013), co-written by me and Chris Mackowski. If it's the Chancellorsville Campaign that you wish to dissect, cure your insomnia by reading John

What if Stonewall Jackson had been at Gettysburg on July 1? He certainly wouldn't have taken any back-talk or hemming and hawing from Jubal Early the way Richard Ewell did. *Library of Congress*

Bigelow's *The Campaign of Chancellorsville: A Strategic and Tactical Study* (Yale University Press, 1910). When it comes to Gettysburg, look no farther than Harry Pfanz's *Gettysburg: Culp's Hill & Cemetery Hill* (The University of North Carolina Press, 1993). If you wish to dive into the war of the Lost Cause—the Confederate v. Confederate version—then look no further than their treatment of Dick Ewell on July 1st at Gettysburg. It's account after account of postwar revisionist history at its finest. Perhaps the most balanced Lost Cause version of events is laid out in Douglas Southall Freeman's *Lee's Lieutenants: Gettysburg to Appomattox, Vol. 3* (Charles

Scribner's Sons, 1944). Possibly the most fanciful retelling of Jackson tales and the Ewell incident on July 1 is Henry Kyd Douglas's *I Rode With Stonewall: The War Experiences of the Youngest Member of Jackson's Staff* (The University of North Carolina Press, 1968). Chris Mackowski and I have also written about this in "The Most Second-Guessed Decision of the Civil War" as an appendix in our book *Fight Like the Devil: The First Day at Gettysburg* (Savas Beatie, 2015) and Chris has written about it in "If Stonewall Jackson Hadn't Gotten Shot" in *The Last Days of Stonewall Jackson* and "Stonewall Jackson at Gettysburg" in *The Summer of '63: Gettysburg* (Savas Beatie 2021). Being limited by word count I would add the blanket statement to see The *Southern Historical Society Papers* and *Confederate Veteran*. Scores of pages were devoted in both to the wounding of Jackson, his life, and the Confederate failures at Gettysburg. In particular, the *Southern Historical Society Papers, Vol. 4*, produced in 1877 has an astounding number of comments and editorial notes from Jubal Early; "Causes of the Defeat of Gen. Lee's Army at the battle of Gettysburg: Opinions of Leading Confederate Soldiers" is worth the price of admission and illustrates the vitriol hatred between onetime allies now turned historian enemies, a.k.a. Jubal Early vs. James Longstreet.

Lee, Longstreet, and Hood on the Second Day at Gettysburg

For a general historiography that discusses the frictions over strategy and tactics between Lee and Longstreet and Longstreet and Hood, start with Edwin B. Coddington's Gettysburg: A Study in Command (Simon & Schuster, 1968) followed by Harry Pfanz's Gettysburg: The Second Day (UNC Press, 1987). To then get into the weeds of Lee vs. Longstreet and Longstreet vs. Hood, try Glenn Tucker's *Lee and Longstreet at Gettysburg* (Bobbs-Merrill, 1968); Helen D. Longstreet, Lee and Longstreet at High Tide: Gettysburg in the Light of the Official Records (self-published, 1905); James Longstreet's *From Manassas to Appomattox* (Dallas Publishing Company, 1896); and John B. Hood's *Advance and Retreat* (G. T. Beauregard, 1880). For a more recent assessment, try Cory Pfarr's *Longstreet at Gettysburg: A Critical Reassessment* (McFarland, 2019). My favorite biography of Longstreet comes from Jeffry Wert, *General James Longstreet: The Confederacy's Most Controversial Soldier* (Simon & Schuster, 1993); my favorite biography

John Bell Hood was seriously injured during an attack he had argued against making. What might have happened to him if Confederates had gone around to the right as he had argued? *Library of Congress*

What if Joseph E. Johnston took command of the Confederate Army of Tennessee either time Jefferson Davis had asked him to? *Library of Congress*

of Hood comes from Richard McMurry, *John Bell Hood and the War for Southern Independence* (University of Nebraska Press, 1992).

Braxton Bragg, Jefferson Davis, and Confederate High Command in the Western Theater

The literature concerning Braxton Bragg and Jefferson Davis, and the high command in the Civil War's Western Theater breaks down into two parts – biographies of Bragg and assessments of Davis as a military commander. Bragg has been the subject of four significant biographies (a low number for a major Civil War commander). The first, Don C. Seitz, *Braxton Bragg, General of the Confederacy* (The State Company, 1924) is a standard early twentieth century treatment that focuses almost solely on Bragg's Civil War career and features significant extracts from the general's person correspondence. Grady McWhiney and his student Judith Lee Halleck collaborated on a set of two biographies of Bragg, with each author covering a portion of the general's life. WcWhiney, *Braxton Bragg and Confederate Defeat, Volume 1: Field Command* (Columbia University Press, 1969) takes Bragg's story through his relief from field command after the battles for Chattanooga. *Halleck, Braxton Bragg and Confederate Defeat: Volume 2* (University of Alabama Press, 1991) begins in 1863 and covers the remainder of Bragg's Civil War career and short postbellum life. Both authors have some contempt for Bragg, McWhiney especially. The most recent and balanced treatment of Bragg can be found in Earl Hess, *Braxton Bragg: The Most Hated Man of the Confederacy* (University of North Carolina Press, 2016). For Davis as commander two works stand out. First, Steven E. Woodworth, *Jefferson Davis and His Generals: The Failure of Confederate Command in the West* (University of Kansas Press, 1990) and Joseph T. Glatthaar, *Partners In Command: The Relationships Between Leaders in the Civil War* (Free Press, 1998), both of which treat Davis fairly as a commander in chief who meddled too extensively in the operations of his military commanders.

The North Anna Phase of the Overland Campaign

I often refer to North Anna as "the most overlooked phase of the Overland Campaign" because so little has been written about it. J. Michael Miller's *"Even To Hell Itself": The North Anna Campaign* (H. E. Howard, 1989) was the seminal work on the battle, but written in the pre-digitized world, Miller's book drew on a limited body of resources. Miller did an update for a 2015 issue of *Blue & Gray* magazine. Gordon Rhea's *To the North Anna River: Grant and Lee, May 13-25* (LSU Press, 2000), covers the North Anna phase of the Overland Campaign in much greater detail. It remains the most comprehensive microtactical study of North Anna. For more of an intro-level account, my own *Strike Them a Blow: Battle Along the North Anna* (Savas Beatie, 2015, 2021) offers a reader-friendly overview, amply illustrated with more than 200 photos and maps. *No Turning Back: A Guide to the 1864 Overland Campaign* (Savas Beatie, 2014) by Robert M. Dunkerly, Donald C. Pfanz, and David R. Ruth provides a driving tour from the Wilderness to the James River, including many stops along the marching routes from Spotsylvania to the North Anna River.

Sterling Price and the 1864 Missouri Expedition

While there is quite a limited historiography on Price's 1864 Missouri Expedition, there are several recommended books to learn more about this overlooked campaign. Perhaps the most well-researched and comprehensive modern volume on the campaign is *The Last Hurrah: Sterling Price's Missouri Expedition of 1864* (Rowman & Littlefield, 2015) written by historian Kyle Sinisi of The Citadel. For social and political histories, Mark Lause's *Price's Lost Campaign: The 1864 Invasion of Missouri* (University of Missouri Press, 2011) and *The Collapse of Price's Raid:*

The loss of much-needed supplies at the battle of Mine Creek undermined Sterling Price's ability to serve as a serious threat in the Trans-Mississippi. What if his wagon train had been able to successfully escape? *Wikipedia*

The Beginning of the End in Civil War Missouri (University of Missouri Press, 2016). The best biography of Major General Sterling Price is Albert Castel's *General Sterling Price and the Civil War in the West* (Louisiana State University Press, 1993). There are also several narratives of the major battles: Bryce Suderow and R. Scott House's *The Battle of Pilot Knob: Thunder in Arcadia Valley* (Southeast Missouri State University Press, 2014), Walter Busch's *Fort Davidson and the Battle of Pilot Knob: Missouri's Alamo* (History Press, 2010), Paul Kirkman's *The Battle of Westport: Missouri's Great Confederate Raid* (History Press, 2011), and Jeffrey D. Stalknaker's *The Battle of Mine Creek: The Crushing End of the Missouri Campaign* (History Press, 2011).

Sherman, Sheridan, and Lincoln's Reelection

While an astonishing number of books have been written about President Abraham Lincoln, Stephen Oates, *With Malice Toward None: The Life of Abraham Lincoln* (Harper and Row, 1977) remains a classic. David Donald's

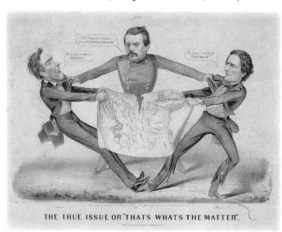

THE TRUE ISSUE OR "THATS WHATS THE MATTER".

As Lincoln and Davis try to tear the country apart, an editorial cartoon posits, what if McClellan took on the roll of peacemaker? *Library of Congress*

deeply-researched *Lincoln* (Simon & Schuster, 1994) and Michael Burlingame's exhaustive two-volume *Lincoln: A Life* (Johns Hopkins University Press, 2008) are also highly recommended. For deeper reflections about the 1864 election Charles Bracelen Flood, *1864: Lincoln at the Gates of History* (Simon & Schuster, 2009) and John C. Waugh, *Reelecting Lincoln: The Battle for the 1864 Presidency* (Da Capo Press, 2001) offer important insight. Arguably no book, however, is more important to understanding the election, particularly the circumstances surrounding the support of Union soldiers for Lincoln, than Jonathan W. White, *Emancipation in the Union Army, and the Reelection of Abraham Lincoln* (Louisiana State University Press, 2014). For examinations of General William T. Sherman's impact on the election Richard M. McMurry, *Atlanta 1864: Last Chance for the Confederacy* (University of Nebraska Press, 2000), Gary Ecelbarger, *The Day Dixie Died: The Battle of Atlanta* (St. Martin's Press, 2010), and John F. Marszalek, *Sherman: A Soldier's Passion for Order* (Free Press, 1993) all offer important insight. The value of Sheridan's victories in the Shenandoah Valley, including the manner in which Republicans used "Sheridan's Ride" to further bolster Lincoln's chances is analyzed in Jonathan A. Noyalas, *The Battle of Cedar Creek: Victory from the Jaws of Defeat* (History Press,

2009) and Jonathan A. Noyalas, *The Battle of Fisher's Hill: Breaking the Shenandoah's Valley's Gibraltar* (History Press, 2013). Important discussions about the obstacles George B. McClellan confronted can be found in Stephen W. Sears, *George B. McClellan: The Young Napoleon* (Ticknor and Fields, 1988) and Jennifer L. Weber, *Copperheads: The Rise and Fall of Lincoln's Opponents* (Oxford University Press, 2006).

Robert E. Lee, Guerrilla Warfare, and Confederate Surrender

Full-scale studies of General Robert Edward Lee include Emory M. Thomas's *Robert E. Lee: A Biography* (W.W. Norton and Co., 1997) and Elizabeth Brown Pryor's *Reading the Man: A Portrait of Robert E. Lee Through His Private Letters* (Viking, 2007). Other informative sources on Lee's military thought and its intersection with irregular warfare are Clifford Dowdey, ed., *The Wartime Papers of Robert E. Lee* (Da Capo Press, 1997) and *Mosby's Memoirs: The Memoirs of Colonel John Singleton Mosby* (Barnes

What if guerrilla warfare threatened the towns and cities of the east in the same way it devastated communities in the west? *Harper's Weekly*

and Noble, 2006), which are also excellent sources for exploring Lee's thoughts on partisan and guerrilla warfare during the 1860s. *Fighting for the Confederacy: The Personal Recollections of General Edward Porter Alexander* (University of North Carolina Press, 1998) is another important source on Lee's thinking in the final days of the Appomattox Campaign on the issue of guerrilla warfare. On guerrilla warfare during the Civil War, readers can refer to Daniel E. Sutherland, *A Savage Conflict: The Decisive Role of Guerrillas in Civil War America* (Univ. of North Carolina Press, 2009) and Brian D. McKnight and Barton A. Myers, eds., *The Guerrilla Hunters: Irregular Conflicts during the Civil War* (Louisiana State Univ.

Press, 2017), in particular, the "Readers' Bibliography of Civil War Guerrilla Studies" for a thorough introduction to the sources. On the surrender at Appomattox and the early Reconstruction-era military history, see Elizabeth Varon's *Appomattox: Victory, Defeat, and Freedom at the End of the Civil War* (Oxford Univ. Press, 2014) and Gregory Downs's *After Appomattox: Military Occupation and the Ends of War* (Harvard Univ. Press, 2019).

Lincoln's Assassination, Race, and Andrew Johnson's Reconstruction

Had Lincoln lived, would he have ascended to the American pantheon? *Chris Mackowski*

The best, single-volume treatment of Lincoln's assassination remains Edward Steers, *Blood on the Moon: The Assassination of Abraham Lincoln* (University of Kentucky Press, 2001). For an engrossing account that recovers the raw, immediate reaction to Booth's dastardly act, see Martha Hodes, *Mourning Lincoln* (Yale University Press, 2015). Louis P. Masur supplies a superb and accessible guide to Lincoln's plans for Reconstruction in *Lincoln's Last Speech* (Oxford University Press, 2015). On the sixteenth president's blueprints for Reconstruction, see also William C. Harris, *With Charity for All: Lincoln and the Restoration of the Union* (University of Kentucky Press, 1997), and John C. Rodrigue's slender but thoughtful *Lincoln and Reconstruction* (Southern Illinois University Press, 2013). Lincoln's ideas about slavery and race have generated a sizeable literature, including LaWanda Cox's now classic *Lincoln and Black Freedom* (University of South Carolina Press, 1981); George M. Fredrickson, *Big Enough to Be Inconsistent: Abraham Lincoln Confronts Slavery and Race* (Harvard University Press, 2008);

Richard Striner, *Lincoln and Race* (Southern Illinois University Press, 2012); and Brian R. Dirck, *Abraham Lincoln and White America* (University Press of Kansas, 2012). Andrew Johnson has not generated anything approaching the Lincoln bibliography, though his reputation has tracked the wild fluctuations in historical assessments of Reconstruction. For the best modern biography of the Tennessee tailor turned president, see Hans Trefousse, *Andrew Johnson* (W.W. Norton, 1989). Also useful is Brooks D. Simpson, *The Reconstruction Presidents* (University Press of Kansas, 1998), and Brooks D. Simpson, LeRoy P. Graf, and John Muldowny, eds., *Advice After Appomattox: Letters to Andrew Johnson, 1865-1866* (University of Tennessee Press, 1987). On the early years of Reconstruction, see also Mark Wahlgren Summers, *A Dangerous Stir* (University of North Carolina Press, 2009); Gregory P. Downs, *After Appomattox* (Harvard University Press, 2015); and Dan T. Carter, *When the War Was Over* (Louisiana State University Press, 1985).

Contributor Notes

Peter Tsouras is a retired senior analyst of military all-source intelligence for the U.S. Government (National Ground Intelligence Center and the Defense Intelligence Agency), specializing in the Soviet Union, Russia, and terrorism. He served as a senior analyst for the U.S.-Russian Joint Presidential Commission on POW/MIAs on the Korean War. He is also a retired lieutenant colonel in the U.S. Army Reserve and has written 33 books on military history and alternate military history.

Brian Matthew Jordan is Associate Professor of Civil War History and Chair of the History Department at Sam Houston State University. He is the author or editor of several books, including *Marching Home: Union Veterans and Their Unending Civil War*, which was a finalist for the Pulitzer Prize in History.

Chris Mackowski is the editor in chief and a co-founder of Emerging Civil War and managing editor of the Emerging Civil War Series published by Savas Beatie. Chris is a writing professor in the Jandoli School of Communication at St. Bonaventure University, where he also serves as the associate dean for undergraduate programs, and he is the historian-in-residence at Stevenson Ridge, a historic property on the Spotsylvania Court House battlefield.

Edward Alexander is a freelance cartographer at Make Me a Map, LLC. He is a regular contributor for Emerging Civil War and the author of *Dawn of Victory: Breakthrough at Petersburg* in the Emerging Civil War Series. Edward has previously worked at Pamplin Historical Park and Richmond National Battlefield Park. He has written for the Emerging Civil War blog since March 2013.

Dwight Hughes graduated from the U.S. Naval Academy in 1967 and served twenty years as a Navy surface warfare officer and Vietnam War veteran. He now serves as public historian speaking and writing on Civil War naval history. Dwight is author of two books and a contributing author at the Emerging Civil War blog (https://emergingcivilwar.com/). He has presented at numerous Civil War roundtables, historical conferences, and other venues. See https://civilwarnavyhistory.com.

A native of Cleveland, Ohio, **Frank Jastrzembski** studied history at John Carroll University (B.A.) and Cleveland State University (M.A.). He's written dozens of articles and two books on British officers. He's also a regular contributor to Emerging Civil War's blog. He runs "Shrouded Veterans," a nonprofit mission to identify or repair the graves of Mexican War and Civil War veterans.

Barton A. Myers is the Class of 1960 Professor of Ethics and History and Associate Professor of Civil War History at Washington and Lee University. He is the author of the awarding-winning *Executing Daniel Bright: Race, Loyalty, and Guerrilla Violence in a Coastal Carolina Community, 1861-1865* (LSU Press, 2009), *Rebels Against the Confederacy: North Carolina's Unionists* (Cambridge Univ. Press, 2014), and co-editor with Brian D. McKnight of *The Guerrilla Hunters: Irregular Conflicts during the Civil War* (LSU Press, 2017).

Jonathan A. Noyalas is director of Shenandoah University's McCormick Civil War Institute, founding editor of *Journal of the Shenandoah Valley during the Civil War Era*, and a professor in the history department at Shenandoah University. He is the author or editor of fourteen books including *Slavery and Freedom in the Shenandoah Valley during the Civil War Era* (University Press of Florida).

Kevin Pawlak is a historic site manager for Prince William County, Virignia's, Historic Preservation Division and serves as a Certified Battlefield Guide at Antietam National Battlefield and Harpers Ferry National Historical Park. He is the author or coauthor of three books and several articles, and he chairs the editorial board for the Emerging Civil War blog.

Evan C. Rothera is Assistant Professor of History at the University of Arkansas–Fort Smith. His current book manuscript, which is under advance contract with Louisiana State University Press, analyzes civil wars and reconstructions in the United States, Mexico, and Argentina. He has published articles in *Nebraska History, The Journal of Mississippi History,* and the *Journal of Supreme Court History*, several book chapters, and many book reviews and encyclopedia entries.

Timothy B. Smith teaches history at the University of Tennessee at Martin. He is the author or editor of more than twenty books, including *Shiloh: Conquer or Perish* and *The Real Horse Soldiers: Benjamin Grierson's Epic 1863 Raid through Civil War Mississippi*. He is currently writing a five-volume history of the Vicksburg Campaign and is under contract to produce a new examination of Albert Sidney Johnston's command in the Western Theater.

Kristen M. Trout is the Museum Director at the Missouri Civil War Museum in St. Louis. She received her BA in History and Civil War Era Studies at Gettysburg College, and her MA in Nonprofit Leadership from Webster University. Trout has worked with the American Battlefield Trust, the Civil War Institute, the Gettysburg Foundation, and the National Park Service. She has been a contributor with Emerging Civil War since July 2018. A native of Missouri, Trout's focus of research is the Civil War in Missouri.

Dan Welch is a public school teacher and seasonal Park Ranger at Gettysburg National Military Park. Dan received his B.A. in Instrumental Music Education from Youngstown State University and an M.A. in Military History with a Civil War Era concentration from American Military University. He is the co-author of *The Last Road North: A Guide to the Gettysburg Campaign, 1863*. He has been a contributing member at Emerging Civil War for over six years.

Kristopher D. White is the deputy director for education at the American Battlefield Trust and the co-founder of Emerging Civil War, the Emerging Civil War Series, and the Engaging the Civil War Series. White is a graduate of Norwich University with an M.A. in Military History, and a graduate of California University of Pennsylvania with a B.A. in History. For nearly five years, he served as a ranger-historian at Fredericksburg and Spotsylvania National Military Park.

Cecily N. Zander completed her Ph.D. in Civil War history at the Pennsylvania State University in 2021. A Colorado native, she is a 2015 graduate of the University of Virginia. In addition to being a regular contributor at Emerging Civil War, she has published her work in Civil War Times magazine, the journal *Civil War History*, and has written essays for several edited collections.

*   *   *

Emerging Civil War is the collaborative effort of more than thirty historians committed to sharing the story of the Civil War in an accessible way. Founded in 2011 by Chris Mackowski, Jake Struhelka, and Kristopher D. White, Emerging Civil War features public and academic historians of diverse backgrounds and interests, while also providing a platform for emerging voices in the field. Initiatives include the award-winning Emerging Civil War Series of books published by Savas Beatie, LLC; an annual symposium; a speakers bureau; and a daily blog: www.emergingcivilwar.com.

Emerging Civil War is recognized by the I.R.S. as a 501(c)3 not-for-profit corporation.

www.emergingcivilwar.com

What If George Meade

Had Been Captured at Spotsylvania?

Chris Mackowski with Daniel T. Davis

On May 14, 1864, Army of the Potomac commander Maj. Gen. George Gordon Meade nearly fell into enemy hands during the battle of Spotsylvania Court House.[1] Then into its second week, fighting had shifted toward Grant's left and the Fredericksburg Road, away from the Brock Road that first brought the army out of the Wilderness. Leading a special assault force, newly minted Brig. Gen. Emory Upton drove a small band of Confederates from the top of a nearby hill, denying it to the Southerners as an artillery position. The Confederates counterattacked, and as they swept down the hillside, they nearly nabbed Meade, who had come to that sector to inspect the newly acquired ground.

My friend Daniel T. Davis and I, longtime armchair veterans of Spotsylvania, knew the episode well.[2] One day as we sat at the bar at the Capital Ale House in downtown Fredericksburg, Virginia, we decided the story needed our fullest consideration as we enjoyed our beers.

"If Meade had been captured at Myers Hill, who would have taken over for him?" I asked.

"Not Warren," Dan said.

By that point in the campaign, Maj. Gen. Gouverneur K. Warren was already in Grant's doghouse. On May 10, Grant had even given permission to Meade to relieve Warren if the V Corps commander didn't obey orders fast

---

1 Adapted from a blog post published at Emerging Civil War on November 3, 2017.

2 Dan, ECW's former chief historian, works in the education department at the American Battlefield Trust.

enough—ironic, since Warren had once been the "golden child" of the army and had been bandied about as a replacement for Meade should anything happen to the Army of the Potomac commander. However, Warren's star had fallen considerably since the start of the campaign. By May 10, Grant had even given Meade permission to relieve Warren if Warren didn't act with more alacrity and vigor.[3]

"If it had happened *in the Wilderness*, maybe Warren," I suggested. "But no way by the 14th."

"Hancock," Dan decid-ed, referring to the II Corps commander, Maj. Gen. Winfield Scott Hancock. "He's Grant's go-to guy."

"Certainly by the end of the campaign. You think Grant sees him that way already?" (That is, by May 14?)

"I think so."

I took a sip, nodded. "So take Hancock's aggressive-ness and apply it on the army level . . . " I mused. "Then who takes over at corps command?"

"Gibbon," Dan replied.

"Is he senior? What about Birney?"

Dan thought about it for a moment. Hancock has three good choices: major generals John Gibbon, David Bell Birney, and Francis Barlow. Gibbon and Birney are both great division commanders, and Barlow's none too shabby, either, although we know *he*'s not senior enough. Neither of us knows the dates of commission for either Gibbon or Birney. The internet would know; so would Kris White. But we're two beers into this conversation already and we don't want to ruin the momentum. (Dan would check later and discover that Birney was senior to Gibbon by less than three months.)

Dan mulled it over more. Gibbon eventually gets a corps, although it's not until later in the war and not until Maj. Gen. Andrew Humphreys gets the II Corps after Hancock's departure in November, prompted by Hancock's old Gettysburg wound. By then, Hancock's other original division commanders were gone—Birney had transferred out (and then died) and Barlow left on sick leave—and a slighted Gibbon was appeased only by transfer out from under Humphreys to a new corps command in the Army of the James.

For now, it looks like Gibbon is our answer, but I pose one more question. "If Hancock takes over the Army of the Potomac," I ask, "you don't think that wastes his talents, taking him too far away from the action?"

3 Grant to Meade, 12 May 1864, O.R. XXXVI, pt. 2, 654.

Dan tilted his head in consideration. "You still have good fighting instincts at the corps level if Gibbon takes over the II Corps," he finally said.

We did a quick survey of the other corps commanders just to be sure Hancock's the answer. Major General John Sedgwick was most senior, so he'd have been next in line, seniority-wise, but he's dead by the 9th. His replacement, Maj. Gen. Horatio Wright, is too junior to step up to army command.

Alfred Waud sketched the "Narrow escape of Genl. Meade" at Spotsylvania Court House. But what if Meade had been captured? How might that have affected the prisoner exchange system, which Grant had by that point suspended? *Library of Congress*

"You know what," I suggested, "[Maj. Gen. Ambrose] Burnside was actually senior to Meade. He could've done it. And he'd have probably been the best choice, temperamentally."

Dan raises his eyebrows.

"If you think about the way Grant actually ran the army—so 'hands on.' Meade chafed under that. Burnside would've been much more apt to just suck it up and take it."

"There's no way he's coming back to the Army of the Potomac, though," Dan says. At that point in the campaign, Burnside was serving as an independent command [of the IX Corps]. He wouldn't get folded into the AoP's command structure for another week—a move Burnside sucked up and took. In fact, he went so far as to call his de facto demotion "a military necessity."

"Imagine what that would do to the Army of the Potomac," Dan continued. "What it would do for morale. After Fredericksburg, to have him come back? I think Lincoln's entire cabinet would've freaked out."

"And Burnside would have wanted no part of it, anyway," I added. "That whole experience with the Army of the Potomac left a bad taste in his mouth. So, it's got to be Hancock."

"But I wonder . . . " Dan said. "Considering that he eventually has to step down because of his Gettysburg wound, I wonder how much of that is bothering him on May 14. And how much of a problem that would be if he was army commander."

"But who else does Grant have, really?"

I took a drink. Dan did too.

I tossed out a question in answer to my own question: "Humphreys?"

"He does get a corps later."

"But maybe he has to stay on as chief of staff to help give someone like Hancock continuity when he takes over."

"I guess that would go back to the relationship between Hancock and Humphreys, but I don't really know what that was. I don't remember reading anything about that," Dan said. "I do think about the ill effects of a hostile chief of staff—I guess it's fair to characterize [Maj. Gen. Daniel] Butterfield that way when Meade first took over going into Gettysburg."

"Absolutely," I agreed. "Butterfield threw Meade under the bus."

"But Meade was close with Humphreys. And with Hancock."

"So Humphreys and Hancock had to have known each other."

"I have to imagine it was cordial between them."

He each inspect our suds to see if they might hold any other possible answers.

Maybe Sheridan? On May 14, the Federal cavalry commander was on a raid toward Richmond, not to return until May 24. He would miss out on army command just by virtue of not being there. Grant would give Sheridan independent command in the Shenandoah Valley in August, though, but it's not clear that Grant yet saw him ready for that step by mid May.

"He doesn't have anyone else," I said.

We both forget William "Baldy" Smith, who at that point is serving with the Army of the James—out of sight, out of mind for us. Formerly exiled from the Army of the Potomac for conspiring against Burnside, Smith ingratiated himself to Grant by leading the effort to raise the siege of Chattanooga in the fall of 1863. When Grant came east in the spring of '64, he brought Smith with him as a possible replacement for Meade. This might have posed problems, Grant well knew, and not just because of Smith's former contentious place within the army. "[M]ore or less dissatisfaction would necessarily be produced by importing a General to command an Army already well supplied with those who have grown up, and been promoted, with it," Grant had noted the previous August when he, himself, has been floated as a possible Army of the Potomac commander.[4]

4   *The Papers of Ulysses S. Grant*, vol. 9: July 7, December 31, 1863, John Y. Simon, ed. (Carbondale, IL: Southern Illinois University Press, 1982), 145-148. Available online at https://msstate.contentdm.oclc.org/digital/collection/USG_volume/id/2725/rec/1.

Grant ultimately kept Meade in command and assigned Smith to Benjamin Butler's army, but Smith was always there in Grant's back pocket if needed. Later, Smith would fall out of favor with Grant for much the same reason Smith alienated everyone he worked for: a perpetual malcontent, he complained and connived. But in mid May, Smith still held Grant's esteem.

Fortunately for Grant, for the Army of the Potomac, and for Meade himself, the old "Snapping Turtle" did not get captured on May 14, 1864. Instead, he and his staff forded the Ni River and rode through the brush, capturing in turn a Confederate officer who tried to capture them. "Quite an excitement was caused at headquarters by the incident," a correspondent reported.[5]

With his dander up, Meade retaliated by ordering Myers Hill retaken—mobilizing the V and VI Corps to do it. What began as a brigade-level dust-up escalated dramatically, and Federals recaptured—and kept—the hill for the remainder of their time at Spotsylvania.

Meade's near-capture and its possible implications are small questions in the grand scheme of the war, but talking out the scenarios has helped us re-evaluate the strengths and weaknesses of army leadership, the interpersonal relationships between commanders, and the changing attitudes and performances of officers over time. It has also given us new questions to research. These are not hypotheticals, even if our initial question was. Asking "What if" has given us a better understanding of "What was."

And we had a good time hashing it out, too. Cheers!

5   R. Roy, 15 May 1864 dispatch, New York Daily News, 19 May 1864, quoted in Gordon Rhea, *To the North Anna River: Grant and Lee, May 13-25, 1864* (LSU Press, 2000), 87.

Index

Adams, Charles Francis, 50, 62

Alexander, Edward Porter, 142, 157

Anaconda Plan, 47, 141

Anderson, Robert, 72

Antietam, Battle of, 21, 28, 29, 45, 66, 86, 88

    and emancipation, 60

    Army of the Potomac's strength in, 30-31

    McClellan's reserves and, 37

    performance of Israel Richardson during, 78

Antietam National Battlefield, 39

Barlow, Francis C., 101

Battles and Leaders of the Civil War, 4, 6, 11

Beauregard, P.G.T., 2, 6, 8, 17, 61, 84, 95, 139, 144, 145

    at First Bull Run, 10

    attack made by at Shiloh, 10-13

    blame for Shiloh heaped upon, 14-15, 16

    neutralizes the Hornet's Nest, 10

    takes medical leave after Corinth siege, 133

Blair, Austin, 74

blockade running, 49

Bloody Angle (Spotsylvania), 148

Bloss, Sgt. John, 19

Boteler's Ford, 39, 42-43

Bragg, Braxton, 15, 106, 110, 130, 135-136, 139, 142, 143

    and the question of Confederate defeat, 145-146

    assumes command of Army of the Tennessee, 133

    contemporary criticism of, 138

    failures of, 131

    historical assessments of, 134

    performance of during Kentucky campaign, 135

    subordinates' lack of faith in, 141

    retreat to Chattanooga, 142

Brandy Station, Virginia, 107

Bridges, Hal, 143

Buell, Don Carlos, 3, 13, 136

Bull Run, Second Battle of, 60, 85

Bulloch, James, 56

Burnside, Ambrose, 23, 31, 36, 81, 92, 158-159

Bushman Farm (Gettysburg), 124

Camp Jackson Affair, 175

Cemetery Hill (Antietam), 35

Cemetery Hill (Gettysburg), 107, 110

Chalmers, James, 15

Chambliss, John R., 158

Chancellorsville, Battle of, 93

Chandler, Zachariah, 81

Chattanooga, Tennessee, 144

Clausewitz, Carl von, 94

Colston, Raleigh, 102

Corinth, Mississippi, 13-14, 133

CSS *Alabama*, 58

CSS *Florida*, 58

CSS *Nashville*, 52, 55-56

Curtin, Andrew G., 86, 90

Curtin, John J., 158

Curtis, Samuel R., 69, 190

Daniel, Larry, 8

Davis, Jefferson, 5, 51, 130, 134

    accepts resignation of Bragg, 144

    compared to Abraham Lincoln, 132

    politicking of, 133

Early, Jubal Anderson, 106, 107

Emmitsburg Road, 120

Ewell, Richard S., 93, 107, 108, 153

    compared with Stonewall Jackson, 108

Ewing, Jr., Thomas, 186

Fisk, Clinton, 189

Forrest, Nathan Befrod, 142

Fort Donelson, Tennessee, 135

Fort Henry, Tennessee, 135

Fort Monroe, Virginia, 72

Franklin, William B., 31, 32, 34, 35, 41

Frederick, Maryland, 19, 23

Fredericksburg, Battle of, 95

Gaines's Mill, Battle of, 85

Gettysburg [1993], 113

Gordon, John Brown, 165

Grant, U.S., 3, 78, 132, 144-145, 147

    arrives in the East, 92

    reflects on Shiloh, 3, 9

Guinea Station, Virginia, 93

Hagerstown, Maryland, 23, 25

Haley, John West, 170

Halleck, Henry W., 21, 34, 69, 70

Hancock, Winfield S., 64, 109

    and defensive perch on Cemetery Hill, 110

    and Milford Station, Virginia, 160-162

Hanover Junction, Virginia, 152

Hardee, William J., 136, 140

Harpers Ferry, Virginia, 23, 42

Haywood, Abel, 62

Hazel Grove (Chancellorsville), 101, 102

Hill, Ambrose Powell, 44, 98, 104, 105, 106

    evaluation of performance as leader, 106

    performance at North Anna, 167-168

    tensions with Stonewall Jackson, 105

Hill, Daniel Harvey, 23, 26

Hitchcock, Ethan Allen, 65, 67, 70-72

    biographical sketch of, 67-68

    as commissioner for prisoner exchange, 74

HMS *Warrio*r, 57

Hood, John Bell, 113

Hooker, Joseph, 31, 79, 81-82, 92

    prepares for Chancellorsville campaign, 96-97

Hornet's Nest, 3-4, 10

Howard, Oliver Otis, 77, 89, 109

Jackson, Mississippi, 106

Jackson, Thomas Jonathan "Stonewall", 43, 93, 103, 104

   flank march at Chancellorsville, 97-98

   wounding of, 96, 98

Jefferson City, Missouri, 183, 184

Jericho Mill, Virginia, 166

Johnston, Albert Sydney, 2, 133

   historiographical debate over, 8-9

   impact of his death evaluated, 4-6

Johnston, Joseph E., 72, 106, 133, 139, 141

Johnston, Samuel, 114

   reconnaissance conducted by, 125

Kearny, Philip, 64

Kentucky Campaign of 1862, 135

Laird rams, 58, 62

Law, Evander, 116

   prepares troops to make assault on July 2, 123

   voices opposition to Hood at Gettysburg, 122

Lee, Robert E., 21, 101, 102, 103, 133, 169, 170

   divides his army in Maryland, 23

   illness during fight along North Anna, 169-171

   withdrawal after Antietam, 39

   scouts perch along Seminary Ridge, 124

Letterman, Jonathan, 79

Lexington, Missouri, Battle of, 175, 177

Lincoln, Abraham, 24, 77, 87, 92, 135

   assessment of Kentucky's importance, 135

   concept of Union, 59

   imposes blockade, 49

   visits Israel Richardson, 80-81

Little Round Top, 120

Livermore, Thomas L., 78, 79

London Times, 52, 128

Long, Armistead, 129

Longstreet, James, 79, 113, 116

   deployment of corps at Gettysburg, 116

   objection to Lee's strategy at Gettysburg, 117-118

   reflects on Gettysburg in 1893, 125

   writes to McLaws in 1877, 126

Lost Cause mythology, 1-2, 12, 17

Lyon, Nathaniel, 175

Lyons, Lord, 47, 50, 55

   estimate of William Seward, 50

Magruder, John Bankhead, 178

Mahan, Dennis Hart, 114

Maine regiments

   17th, 170

Mallory, Stephen R., 52, 56, 57

Marcy, Randolph B., 26

Marmaduke, John S., 185

Mason, Jack, 80

McClellan, George B., 19, 65, 69, 92

   crippled by typhoid fever, 73

   grouses about accuracy of intelligence, 22

   informs Lincoln of his position in Md., 24

   observes battle of Antietam, 31-32

   plans attack on September 14, 27

   pursuit of Lee after Antietam, 38-39, 42

   speculates about Lee's movements in Md., 23

   strategy for reserves at Antietam, 33-34, 38

McDonough, James Lee, 9

McLaws, Lafayette, 121

McPherson, James M., 20

Meade, George Gordon, 88, 101, 107, 115

plans to fall back to Pipe Creek, 109-110

weighs in on Longstreet's advice to Lee [1870], 126

Mine Run Campaign, 90

Missionary Ridge, Tennessee, 142

Missouri State Guard, 175

Mitchell, Pvt. Barton, 19

Napoleon III, 60

Nashville, Tennessee, 142

New Hampshire regiments

5th, 78

North Anna River, 147

North Carolina regiments

18th, 96, 104

Norvell, John M., 79

Orange Turnpike (Chancellorsville), 99

Outhwaite, Joseph H., 16

Overland Campaign, 148-149, 165

comparative strengths of armies in, 149

Ox Ford (North Anna), 168

Palmerston, Lord, 53, 62

Pea Ridge, Arkansas, Battle of, 177

Pegram, Robert B., 52-53

Pemberton, John C., 139

Pendleton, William Nelson, 39

Peninsula Campaign, 66, 77

Pennsylvania regiments

118th, 44

Perryville, Kentucky, Battle of, 136

significance of, 137

Pfanz, Donald C., 169

Pilot Knob, 185, 186, 187

Pipe Creek, Maryland, 109-110

Pleasonton, Alfred H., 25, 29, 33, 40-41, 64

Poison Spring, Arkansas, 181

Pomeroy, John N., 69

Pope, John, 69

Porter, Fitz John, 35, 36, 37, 40

Porter, Horace, 147

Prentiss, Benjamin, 3, 69

Price, Sterling, 173, 179

Prize Cases, 51

Pry House (McClellan's Headquarters), 29, 31

Quasi War (1798-1800), 49

Randolph, George W., 90

Reed, David W., 3

Reynolds, John F., 31, 65, 87-89, 91, 107

biographical sketch of, 83

political ideology of, 90

Reynolds, Thomas C., 178

Richardson, Israel B., 65, 74, 75

death of, 80

performance at Antietam by, 78

physical description of, 76

service in the U.S. War with Mexico, 75

Richmond, Kentucky, 136

Robertson, Jr., James I., 167

Rodes, Robert E., 102

Roland, Charles, 8

Rosecrans, William S., 64, 140, 186

relieved of command, 144

RMS *Trent*, 53

Russell, Lord John, 55

Salem Church, Battle of, 167

Scott, Winfield, 47, 84

Second Winchester, Battle of, 107

Seddon, James A., 178

Sedgwick, John, 32, 64, 99

Sellers, W.H., 123

Seven Pines, Battle of, 72

Seward, William H., 47

Shelby, Jo, 181-182

Shenandoah Valley, 23, 73

Shepherdstown, Virginia, 44-45

Sheridan, Phil, 137, 149, 152

Shiloh National Military Park, 1, 16

Sickles, Daniel, 101

Sigel, Franz, 69

Slaughter, Montgomery, 90

Smith, Andrew Jackson, 186

Smith, Edmund Kirby, 136, 139

Smith, Robert A., 15

Snead, Thomas, 177

South Mountain, Battle of, 28

Special Orders No. 191, 19, 23

    discovery of, 22, 25

    evaluation of, 28

    historiography of, 21n4

    significance to McClellan, 26

St. Louis, Missouri, 174-175

Steele, Frederick, 179

Stone's River, Battle of, 140

Strother, David Hunter, 28

Stuart, James Ewell Brown, 41, 102, 105, 157

Sumner, Charles, 55

Sumner, Edwin V., 32, 39, 64

Supreme Court, U.S., 51

Sword, Wiley, 8

Sykes, George, 29, 33, 38, 44

Texas infantry regiments,

    1st, 116

Tullahoma Campaign, 141

United Daughters of the Confederacy, 1, 3

United States Ford (Chancellorsville), 99

USS *Tuscarora*, 53, 56

Wainwright, Charles S., 79

Wallace, Lew, 3, 16

Wallace, W.H.L., 3

War of 1812, 49, 55

Warren, Gouverneur K., 37, 152, 162, 163

Watson, Peter H., 70

Webster, Joseph D., 13

Welles, Gideon, 53

    proposes ironclad program, 57

West Woods (Antietam), 32

Wilkes, Charles, 52-53

Willard's Hotel (Washington, D.C.), 70

Willcox, Orlando B, 74

Williams, Alpheus S., 110

Williamsport, Maryland, 24, 39, 43

Work, P.A., 116

Wright, Horatio G., 155, 164

Yandell, D.W., 5

What If...

there was a second "What If" volume?

Stay tuned at www.savasbeatie.com. . . .